THE SMIT

THE VISUAL DOCUMENTARY

JOHNNY ROGAN

OMNIBUS PRESS
LONDON · NEW YORK · SYDNEY

Edited by **Chris Charlesworth**
Cover & Book designed by **Four Corners**, London
Picture research by **Johnny Rogan** and **David Brolan**
ISBN: 0.7119.3337.5
Order No: OP 47284

Exclusive Distributors
Book Sales Limited,
8/9 Frith Street,
London W1V 5TZ, UK.

Music Sales Corporation,
257 Park Avenue South,
New York, NY 10010, USA.

Music Sales Pty Limited,
Lisgar House, 30-32 Carrington Street,
Sydney, NSW 2000, Australia.

To the Music Trade only:
Music Sales Limited,
8/9, Frith Street,
London W1V 5TZ, UK.

Photo credits:
Allman Archives: 16, 31; Peter Anderson/SIN: 165b, 166tr&br, 167; Richard Bellia: Pat Bellis: 6, 132, 136, 140, 142tr&b, 143, 147b, 148l&r, 149, 152b, 154b, 162, 165, 168, 176 (background); 154t; George Bodnar: 39; Harry Borden: 95b; Douglas Cape/Retna: 100, 104t; Andy Catlin: 141b – /Retna: 63b, 114 – /SIN: 64; Hettie Church: 1, 2/3, 46tl,r&c; Chris Clunn: 128b, 144l&r, 151t&b, 153t, 155; Jöelle Dépont: 34, 42, 45t&b, 48, 63t, 76, 77b, 84, 85, 111; Steve Double: 129b – / SIN 129c; Bob Gruen/Star File: 20, 23, 28; Jayne Houghton:/SIN: 152t; Mitsue Kakuta: 169t; Rob Kerford: 86x4, 101b, 112l; Jim Kutler: 142tl; London Features International: 14/15 (background), 22, 24, 26, 29, 30, 32, 41r, 46t, 54, 55tl, 71t, 86, 87, 88, 89, 91t, 93r, 101t, 102, 104b, 115, 117t&b, 120, 121, 123t, 137t&b, 141b, 150, 164, 170; Marr Family Collection: 118b; Messenger Family Archives: 17t; Courtney/Corrigan Family Archives: 10t&b, 11, 12t&b, 13t&b, 14, 15, 17b; Peter Noble/SIN: 5, 53t; Cindy Palmano/Retna: 154b; Pictorial Press: 47, 163; Barry Plummer: 8, 21, 55b, 66, 80t, 91bx3, 92b, 106x3, 107b, 127t&b, 153b, 171; Patrick Quigley/Retna: 159, 160; Steve Rapport/Retna: 90; Vini Reilly: 10/11, 12/13 (background), 169b; Zbysiu Rodak/SIN: 55tr, 174; Eugene Shaw/Star File: 107t, 112r; Tom Sheehan: 27, 33, 43, 60, 69, 70, 71b, 82, 93tl&b, 95br, 124, 125, 129t; Grant Showbiz Collection: 40b, 92tx6, 98b, 145, 147tr; Paul Slattery: 35x3, 36/37, 38, 40t&b, 45, 49, 51, 52, 56, 57, 58x3, 59t&b, 61t&b, 62, 65, 72t, 73, 74, 75l&r, 77r&tl, 78, 79, 80b, 97, 98t, 99b, 116t; Ian Tilton/SIN 138t&b, 139; Laurence Watson: 94, 118t, 119, 123b, 135, 156, 158t, 166l; Jane Whyle: 25; Stephen Wright: 7x2, 35b, 53b, 95tl, 108, 109, 110, 113, 122, 126, 128t, 130/131, 133, 147tl, 157t, 158b; Russell Young/Retna: 83.

Every effort has been made to trace the copyright holders of the photographs in this book but one or two were unreachable. We would be grateful if the photographers concerned would contact us.

Printed and bound in Singapore.

A catalogue record for this book is available from the British Library.

DEDICATION

For **TERESA WALSH**

By The Same Author:

Timeless Flight: The Definitive Biography Of The Byrds
Neil Young: Here We Are In The Years
Roxy Music: Style With Substance
Van Morrison: A Portrait Of The Artist
The Kinks: The Sound And The Fury
Wham! (Confidential) The Death Of A Supergroup
Starmakers & Svengalis: The History Of British Pop Management
The Football Managers
Timeless Flight Revisited
Morrissey & Marr: The Severed Alliance

Contents

TITLE PAGE & CONTENTS: The Smiths in the white heat of performance, 1983.

Acknowledgements

FIRST AND FOREMOST, I would like to thank Morrissey for his engaging sense of humour, good sportsmanship, witty responses and pithy conversation. From The Smiths' camp, Johnny Marr, Mike Joyce, Andy Rourke and Craig Gannon provided detailed stories of high drama and comic trivia, all of which I greatly appreciated.

The supporting cast is crucial in any serious book and I am especially grateful to the following for their cooperation and willingness to speak: Rob Allman, John Barratt, Richard Boon, Peter Cassan, Steve Cassan, Gary Curley, Jimmy Curley, Noel Devaney, Howard Devoto, Bobby Durkin, Mike Ellis, Andy Farley, Gary Farrell, Phil Fletcher, Rita Flynn, Mike Foley, John Fox, Ken Friedman, Seamus Gilsenan, Dave Haslam, Fred Hood, Paddy Jacobs, Stuart James, Bob Johnson, Matt Johnson, Danny Kelly, Kevin Kennedy, Nick Kent, Chris Lukes, Steve Mardy, Dennis Matthews, Oz McCormick, Annette Messenger, Eddie Messenger, Mick Middles, Quiblah Montsho, Mike Moore, Ann Morrissey, Carmel Morrissey, Ellen Morrissey, Patricia Morrissey, Peter Morrissey, Joe Moss, Ian Moss, John Muir, Nora Nolan, Patrick Nolan, John O'Brien, Ivor Perry, Scott Piering, Graham Pink, Stephen Pomfret, John Porter, Chris Power, Patrick Quinn, Vini Reilly, Beryl Roche, Margaret Roe, Michael Roe, Mike Roe, Gary Rostock, Grant Showbiz, Richard Smith, Steve Smythe, Stephen Street, Matthew Sztumph, Geoff Travis, James Verrechia, Michele Weaver, Tony Wilson and Simon Wolstencroft.

Additional thanks to Hilary Donlon for her enthusiasm, hard work, exquisite good humour and indefatigable PR skills. For welcome support, information, feedback, notes and queries: Hannah Bayman, Peter Doggett, Tony Edwards, Robert Fairclough, Pete Frame, Mike Haldenby, Mark Johnson, Andrew King, Jeff Pelletier, Mark Taylor, Howard Tinker and Teresa Walsh.

ON THE BRINK of greatness in 1983: Johnny Marr, Mike Joyce, Morrissey and Andy Rourke on the set of 'The Tube.'

The Smiths have been well documented in newspapers and magazines over the years and I must express grateful thanks to the following, which were invaluable for contemporaneous information, rumours, concert/record reviews or choice quotes: *City Life, Debris, Début, Face, Him, Hit, Hot Press, i-D, Irish Times, Jamming!, Kids' Stuff, Les Inrockuptibles, Melody Maker, Munster Express, New Musical Express, No 1, Observer, Record Collector, Record Mirror, Rolling Stone, Smash Hits, Smiths Indeed, Sounds, Sun* and *Time Out*.

Since *The Severed Alliance* I have received many letters, predominantly from new followers of Morrissey. I would like to thank them for their interest, and promise to deal with the various issues when I finally address Steven's solo career. Anyone wishing to write regarding any future volumes may contact me at the publisher's address. At present there are, not surprisingly, no fanzines dedicated solely to The Smiths, but there are numerous titles world-wide chronicling Morrissey's solo adventures abroad. These include such items as *Celibate Cries, Get Off The Stage, Lucky Lisp, Oscillate Wildly, Sing Your Life, The Darkened Underpass, Glamorous Glue, Morrissey Drive Me Home,* and *Wilde About Morrissey*. Write to *The Morri'zine* at PO Box 255733, Sacramento, Ca. 95865, USA, for further information. In the UK, there are three 'zines known to me at the time of writing: *A Chance To Shine, Frankly Charming* and *Miserable Lies*. For more details of the latter, including complete fanzine addresses, send IRC/SAE to Hannah, 18 Parolles Road, London, N19 3RD.

MORRISSEY, 1984.

Now that this volume is over I can relax for awhile but, looking back, this has at times been a strange, slightly jinxed undertaking. Occasionally, the Morrissey *fatwah* looked like becoming a reality. Midway through the book I ventured out one afternoon and found myself on a collision course with a double decker bus. I returned to Teresa Walsh's flat bleeding profusely and was subsequently taken to casualty with a damaged arm and laceration of the hands, which meant no more writing for several weeks. This accident did not seriously delay the book, but what happened several months later threatened to undo the entire project. My publisher had lent me a word processor on which to compose the book but, just as I was reaching the penultimate chapter, disaster struck. The complete book was erased and, worse and weirder still, all but one of the back-up disks failed to function. I was in a state of shock and found myself obsessively walking miles, wandering the streets till 5.30 in the morning. Losing material in this way is every author's worst nightmare. Fortunately, sizeable chunks of material were retrieved from the inners of the faulty machine thanks to the intervention of computer expert Michael Walsh. With a skeleton text and reams of cut-up material interspersed with computer symbols, I was able to soldier on and reconstruct the edifice that had all but ceased to exist. Barring further setbacks, the complete text should at last be in your hands, which is a great relief. For all that, this was an immensely enjoyable book on which to work, and I thank you all.

Johnny Rogan

THE SMITHS in Rough Trade publicity pose, 1986.

Preface

AFTER COMPLETING *Morrissey & Marr: The Severed Alliance* in 1992, I vowed to continue The Smiths' story, despite their vocalist's insistence that I should die in an M3 pile-up or perish slowly and painfully in a hotel fire. Fortunately I don't drive and the only time I stay in a hotel is when I'm promoting a book for my publishers, about once every four years. When Morrissey later proclaimed, "If God exists, then Johnny "The Rat" will be devoured by his German Shepherd dogs", it struck me that, while I did not own any German Shepherds, Johnny Marr did house a soulful canine couple named Rufus and Curtis. So, perhaps Steven was making a Freudian slip. Who knows?

One of the few advantages of being a full-time author, as opposed to a working journalist, is that you can literally pursue a project to its ultimate conclusion, unfettered by other career concerns or anything else for that matter. When Morrissey wearily said to me: "But you go on, and I go on", he was not merely stating a fact but laying down a challenge. Since the manuscript of *The Severed Alliance* was delivered I have continued researching this project, and pointedly refused offers of any other work. However, those who have attempted to rush me into writing about Morrissey's solo career will have to wait. Why should I rush? I need the time to think and to plot. Meanwhile, I have found myself grappling with the minutiae of The Smiths' tale once more, overseeing the entire chronology, making sense of it and getting it out of my system. I felt the need for what can best be described as an "interim work" in which all that additional research from the past could be deposited for those who wish to see more. I suppose this visual documentary is my equivalent of a *Hatful Of Hollow* and, never forget, there were some people who actually preferred that rough and ready compilation to The Smiths' major releases.

MORRISSEY AND MARR in partnership at the Free Trade Hall, Manchester, 1984.

The challenge in compiling a work of this nature was to avoid the pitfalls of similar scholarly books, which have often degenerated into laundry lists or served merely as bland coffee table material. I trust that this extensive diary of events may be read as a continuous document and not merely as a quick reference book for researchers seeking concert performances and record release dates. There are two parallel stories running through the text: the public and the private. Looking back over The Smiths' career I was fascinated to see how they were perceived in their time, both by their detractors and champions. The hopes, predictions, poll results, angry letters, eulogistic reviews and contemporaneous interviews remind us of what The Smiths meant in their heyday. They were the darlings of the music press most of the time but, as with Morrissey today, there were periods when they fell out of favour, tottered on the brink of self-parody or found themselves accused of becoming part of the rock establishment. As with all great pop stories, myth was a dominant feature in their biography. The music press and the fans tended to see them as a partnership, a view fostered and reinforced by Morrissey and Marr's utopian talk of a gang mentality. The Smiths were a gang, but the membership was never equal, as their undisclosed contracts and business dealings brutally revealed. With hindsight, and the freedom of the participants to discuss their past without the fear of derailing their PR machine or losing vested interests, we have a more piercing and provocative account of events. Using the wealth of interviews and documentation amassed from ex-Smiths and their myriad associates, I have attempted to juxtapose the old public story of events as they happened with the revised reality. At times, this produces a strange mixture of comedy and pathos as we witness an engaging innocence seen through the sadder and wiser eyes of experience. As the narrator, I have taken the opportunity to pen a lengthy introduction to each crucial year in The Smiths' calendar in order to provide a personal overview. Anyone wishing a swift career perspective on The Smiths is advised to read the chapter openings successively.

'Melody Maker', 3 November 1984

THE GROUP'S gang myth was once real, 1984.

Some people, including Morrissey, maintain that The Smiths broke up tragically prematurely, while others insist that they romanticized their existence by leaving the stage while they were still great. There is an argument for both viewpoints, yet it should always be remembered that pop groups are not abstract institutions but volatile human beings. The oft-touted "musical differences" is usually a euphemism for more serious career pressures, financial disagreements, personality clashes or petty jealousies festering towards antipathy. Fans and starry-eyed critics who perceive the unit as a mythical music making machine, all too often ignore how easy it is for any ideal partnership to lose its self-love. For my part, I wish The Smiths had continued for at least one more album as I always felt they were in the process of undergoing some radical musical changes. What might have followed we will now never know... but that too is part of the appeal. On reflection, I now see that the sad and slightly tawdry aspect of The Smiths' demise is one reason why their story continues to fascinate. Like suicides or the young dead, they secured their myth in a cruel but most effective way.

Johnny Rogan

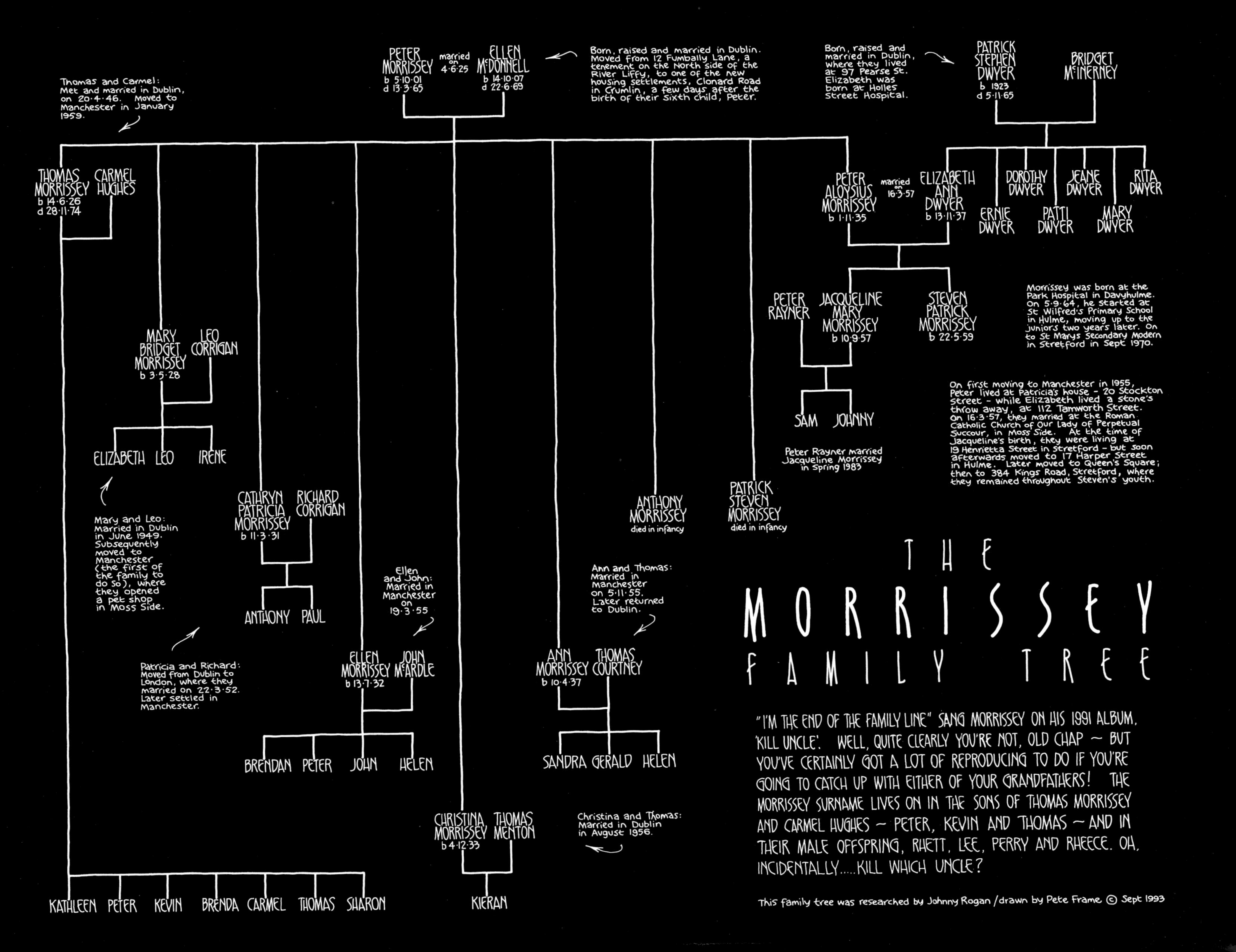

THE MORRISSEY FAMILY TREE
PETER MORRISSEY b 5·10·01 d 13·3·65
married on 4·6·25
ELLEN McDONNELL b 14·10·07 d 22·6·69
Born, raised and married in Dublin. Moved from 12 Fumbally Lane, a tenement on the North side of the River Liffy, to one of the new housing settlements, Clonard Road in Crumlin, a few days after the birth of their sixth child, Peter.
Born, raised and married in Dublin, where they lived at 97 Pearse St. Elizabeth was born at Holles Street Hospital.
PATRICK STEPHEN DWYER b 1923 d 5·11·65
BRIDGET McINERNEY
Thomas and Carmel: Met and married in Dublin, on 20·4·46. Moved to Manchester in January 1959.
THOMAS MORRISSEY b 14·6·26 d 28·11·74
CARMEL HUGHES
PETER ALOYSIUS MORRISSEY b 1·11·35
married on 16·3·57
ELIZABETH ANN DWYER b 13·11·37
DOROTHY DWYER
JEANE DWYER
RITA DWYER
ERNIE DWYER
PATTI DWYER
MARY DWYER
PETER RAYNER
JACQUELINE MARY MORRISSEY b 10·9·57
STEVEN PATRICK MORRISSEY b 22·5·59
Morrissey was born at the Park Hospital in Davyhulme. On 5·9·64, he started at St Wilfred's Primary School in Hulme, moving up to the juniors two years later. On to St Marys Secondary Modern in Stretford in Sept 1970.
MARY BRIDGET MORRISSEY b 3·5·28
LEO CORRIGAN
SAM
JOHNNY
Peter Rayner married Jacqueline Morrissey in Spring 1983
On first moving to Manchester in 1955, Peter lived at Patricia's house - 20 Stockton Street - while Elizabeth lived a stone's throw away, at 112 Tamworth Street. On 16·3·57, they married at the Roman Catholic Church of Our Lady of Perpetual Succour, in Moss Side. At the time of Jacqueline's birth, they were living at 19 Henrietta Street in Stretford - but soon afterwards moved to 17 Harper Street in Hulme. Later moved to Queen's Square; then to 384 Kings Road, Stretford, where they remained throughout Steven's youth.
ELIZABETH
LEO
IRENE
CATHRYN PATRICIA MORRISSEY b 11·3·31
RICHARD CORRIGAN
ANTHONY MORRISSEY died in infancy
PATRICK STEVEN MORRISSEY died in infancy
Mary and Leo: Married in Dublin in June 1949. Subsequently moved to Manchester (the first of the family to do so), where they opened a pet shop in Moss Side.
Ellen and John: Married in Manchester on 19·3·55
Ann and Thomas: Married in Manchester on 5·11·55. Later returned to Dublin.
ANTHONY
PAUL
Patricia and Richard: Moved from Dublin to London, where they married on 22·3·52. Later settled in Manchester.
ELLEN MORRISSEY b 13·7·32
JOHN McARDLE
ANN MORRISSEY b 10·4·37
THOMAS COURTNEY
BRENDAN
PETER
JOHN
HELEN
SANDRA
GERALD
HELEN
CHRISTINA MORRISSEY b 4·12·33
THOMAS MENTON
Christina and Thomas: Married in Dublin in August 1956.
KATHLEEN
PETER
KEVIN
BRENDA
CARMEL
THOMAS
SHARON
KIERAN
"I'M THE END OF THE FAMILY LINE" SANG MORRISSEY ON HIS 1991 ALBUM, 'KILL UNCLE'. WELL, QUITE CLEARLY YOU'RE NOT, OLD CHAP ~ BUT YOU'VE CERTAINLY GOT A LOT OF REPRODUCING TO DO IF YOU'RE GOING TO CATCH UP WITH EITHER OF YOUR GRANDFATHERS! THE MORRISSEY SURNAME LIVES ON IN THE SONS OF THOMAS MORRISSEY AND CARMEL HUGHES ~ PETER, KEVIN AND THOMAS ~ AND IN THEIR MALE OFFSPRING, RHETT, LEE, PERRY AND RHEECE. OH, INCIDENTALLY.....KILL WHICH UNCLE?
This family tree was researched by Johnny Rogan / drawn by Pete Frame © Sept 1993

INTRODUCTION

Beginnings: The Irish Connection

THE STORY OF THE SMITHS IS, in one sense, a tale of Irish emigration. Morrissey, Johnny Marr and Mike Joyce were the offspring of parents born and educated in Eire. Andy Rourke's father was also of Irish ancestry, as were the families of several subsidiary figures in the group's story. Tracing The Smiths' genealogy means traversing the waters from Manchester to Dublin, and beyond the Pale. It requires a shift in attitude and sensibility away from their familiar Northern environs to a twilight world of half-remembered sayings, musical influences and Catholic dogma, which characterized their upbringing. The Irish link in The Smiths' story was always underplayed, for Morrissey chose the language and imagery of Northern England as his theme. Musically, the group owed more to traditional American rock influences than to any discernible Irish tradition. Yet, for all that, there was something ineffably Irish about the group. It was there in their humour, their melody lines, their gang mentality, and a peculiar sense of longing in their music, which betrayed the ambivalence of first generation immigrant sons caught between present and past. As critic John Waters noted with characteristic precision:

> ***The Smiths needed no translation in Ireland. Their dark introspection, tragic narcissism, ironic world-view and swirling tunefulness fashioned a profound, existential connection with those of us born into the era of the First Programme for Economic Expansion, a connection which it is impossible to explain in other than mystical terms.***
>
> ***The Smiths, more than most of the native-grown rock bands, can claim citizenship of that elusive territory so beloved of the President, Mrs Robinson and Richard Kearney – The Fifth Province.***

The history of Ireland weighs heavily on The Smiths, and can even be seen working on Morrissey's paradoxical character. His obsession with all things English, and tasteless immersion in the lost ideals of a mythical Great Britain, reached its apogee in the title track of The Queen Is Dead, *and its sad nadir in the introduction of a Union Jack into his stage act. Morrissey's fascination with a lost verdant England betrays the confusion of a dislocated personality, seeking refuge in a national tradition from which he has been excluded through education, religion and family background. His assimilation of English cultural values is an uneasy compromise which becomes more visible whenever he returns to his ancestral home. Morrissey still visits Eire, albeit with the air of a culturally refined modern day Oscar Wilde. The hold that Eire has over his sensibility can be gauged from a glimpse at the following series of events. Reinventing your past is one thing, escaping from it is quite another.*

LEFT: Morrissey at his first communuion in 1966 at seven years old.
BELOW: Steven's grandparents Peter and Ellen on their wedding day in 1925.

Tales of Irish emigration often include some element of tragedy or premature death and Steven's youth had its small share. Any account of Morrissey's childhood inevitably includes references to the Moors Murders, an event that looms large in any psychological understanding of his morbidity. Morrissey's icons and dark nightmares appear to have their origins in that eventful year of 1965. It was then that he bought his first record, saw James Dean on the screen, became entranced by Sandie Shaw and felt the cold horror of the Moors Murders. The whispers that he heard about the frightening abduction and murder of children were events on the periphery of his life but, that same year, he experienced loss in his own extended family. Within a matter of months his two grandfathers passed away and, less than three weeks after the Moors Murder convictions, his uncle Ernie died at the age of 24, the victim of alcohol abuse. This represented nothing less than the extinction of the male family line on the Dwyer side, with Bridget Dwyer left a widow and her only son dead. For Steven, an age of innocence was already receding. His world was increasingly dominated by strong women who, after mourning their dead, simply had to carry on with their lives. The men in Steven's life either appeared fallible or died young, while the women stood together as a strong family network. Those deaths of 1965, matters that Steven has never discussed in print, arguably had more effect on his psychology than the macabre Moors Murders which he has frequently alluded to as the well of his oldest fears. In his mind, the private grief experienced in the home received a chillingly public manifestation through the fascinating evil of child slaughter. What is inescapable is Steven's early realization that death in the family and in the streets was a reality as gruesome as the blackest fairy tale.

MARY Bridget Morrissey, 1945, aged 17.

CATHRYN Patricia Morrissey, 1948, aged 17.

CHRISTINA Morrissey, 1950, aged 17.

EARLY YEARS

1901 - 5 OCTOBER
Peter Morrissey, Steven's grandfather, born in Dublin.

1907 - 14 OCTOBER
Ellen (McDonnell) Morrissey, Steven's grandmother born in Dublin.

1925 - 4 JUNE
Peter Morrissey (Steven's grandfather) marries Ellen McDonnell in Dublin. They move from Poddle Park to the North City, just above the River Liffey.

1926 - 14 JUNE
Thomas Morrissey, Steven's uncle, born in Dublin.

1928 - 3 MAY
Mary Bridget Morrissey, Steven's aunt, born in Dublin.

1931 - 11 MARCH
Cathryn Patricia Morrissey, Steven's aunt, born in Dublin.

1932 - 13 JULY
Ellen Morrissey, Steven's aunt, born in Dublin.

1933 - 4 DECEMBER
Christina Morrissey, Steven's aunt, born in Dublin.

1935 - 1 NOVEMBER
Peter Aloysius Morrissey, Steven's father, born at 12 Fumbally Lane, North City, Dublin.

9 NOVEMBER
The Morrissey family move to the new housing estates in Crumlin.

1937 - 10 APRIL
Ann Morrissey, Steven's aunt, born in Dublin. Her parents have two further children, Patrick Steven and Anthony, but both die in infancy. "They died around a year old," Peter Morrissey remembers. "I was only a kid myself. I didn't know what was going on. I do remember being in the house when my mother started screaming. Patrick was in the pram and he was turning a different colour. There were two boys who died around a year old. They weren't twins. They were both younger than me. Although I was only six or seven I can vividly remember those incidents."

13 NOVEMBER
Elizabeth Ann Dwyer, Steven's mother, born at Holles Street Hospital, Dublin before returning home to 97 Pearse Street.

1946 - 20 APRIL
Thomas Morrissey marries Carmel Hughes in Dublin.

1949 - JUNE
Mary Bridget Morrissey marries Leo Corrigan. They subsequently settle in Moss Side, Manchester where they open a pet shop.

1952 - 22 MARCH
Patricia Morrissey marries Richard Corrigan in London. "My sister Mary then became my aunt by marriage," Patricia laughs. Before long the newly-weds move to Manchester, which will become the second family home.

1955 - 19 MARCH
Ellen Morrissey marries John McArdle in Manchester. Meanwhile, Peter Morrissey has moved to Patricia's house at 20 Stockton Street. His girlfriend, Elizabeth Dwyer also emigrates from Eire and finds digs a few streets away at 112 Tamworth Street.

5 NOVEMBER
Ann Morrissey marries Thomas Courtney in Manchester, but they decide to return to Dublin.

1956 - AUGUST
Christina Morrissey marries Thomas Menton in Dublin. The Morrissey family set up a marquee in their back garden for the reception, complete with a live band.

1957 - 16 MARCH
Peter Morrissey marries Elizabeth Dwyer at the Roman Catholic Church of Our Lady of Perpetual Succour. Peter's friend Thomas Ronan is the best man, and Elizabeth's sister Dorothy serves as the bridesmaid. Appropriately, Tab Hunter's 'Young Love' is at the top of the charts. An all-night celebration follows at Patricia Morrissey's house in Stockton Street. "It was the day before St Patrick's Day," Patricia remembers. "Betty's sisters came over for the wedding and decided to stay then. It was a big house and the wedding was great. I'd go through it all again. I did it all myself. We bought the wedding cake and I did the food. All the Dwyers were over and there was another crowd of Morrisseys. It went on all night. We stayed in the house – there was plenty of food and drink, so we didn't have to go anywhere else. We had some music, and it was beautiful. Peter gave me money towards it – he saw to it."

"We had the reception at Patricia's place," Peter Morrissey remarks. "It's funny. I got married there and I didn't even know what was happening. I was a very quiet person. I was at this wedding and there were periods when I didn't realize it was my wedding I was at. Everything was happening. Patti was trying to take care of things, getting in on the act."

10 SEPTEMBER
Less than six months after the marriage, Jacqueline Mary Morrissey is born at Crossley Hospital in Ancoats. At the time of the birth, the Morrisseys are living at 19 Henrietta Street in Stretford. "That was just rooms; digs," recalls Peter Morrissey. "An old couple lived there and they gave us the top floor. They told us, 'No children' and we said, 'Oh, no!' But they liked us so much that when Jackie did come along they didn't want us to leave."

CARMEL Hughes, who later married Thomas Morrissey.

ELIZABETH Dwyer's birth certificate, 1937.

THOMAS and Peter Morrissey in O'Connell Street, Dublin, 1952.

5 NOVEMBER
Betty Dwyer provides details of her daughter's birth to the Registrar in Manchester. Before long, the family move to a new home at 17 Harper Street, Hulme.

1959 - 6 JANUARY
Thomas and Carmel Morrissey move to Manchester from Dublin.

22 MAY
Steven Patrick Morrissey born at Park Hospital, Davyhulme, Manchester. The baby is greeted by the chart topping strains of Elvis Presley's 'A Fool Such As I'/'I Need Your Love Tonight'. As the Fifties close, both sides of Steven's extended family have made the crossing from Eire, ensuring that the child has a wealth of aunts, uncles and cousins in his vicinity. "All my family came from Dublin," Morrissey recalls, "and suddenly they all moved to Manchester... I've been round this huge Irish family since I was created."

STEVEN'S mother and grandmother.

16 JULY
Steven's parents register his birth in Barton. His parents have named their child in honour of Peter's dead brother Patrick Steven and Betty's father Patrick Stephen Dwyer.

1962
John Joseph Maher and Frances Patricia Doyle leave their home in Kildare, Eire, marry, and settle in Manchester. They secure a terraced house at 12 Hayfield Road in Ardwick. Meanwhile, the Morrissey family move again, this time to Queen's Square.

1963 - 1 JUNE
Michael Joyce, born in Chorlton-on-Medlock, Manchester.

21 OCTOBER
John Martin Maher born at 122 Everton Road, Chorlton-on-Medlock, Manchester.

20 NOVEMBER
John Maher's birth is registered at Manchester Central.

1964 - 17 JANUARY
Andrew Rourke born in Manchester.

5 SEPTEMBER
Steven Morrissey enrols at St Wilfred's Primary School in Hulme. Although well liked and reasonably bright, Steven is not among the high flyers academically. "He never made much of a mark," class mate Steve Smythe reveals. "We used to have exams every year and if you didn't finish in the top six, there wasn't much of a chance afterwards. And I can never remember Steven Morrissey doing well."

PETER and Ellen Morrissey in the early 1950s.

21 OCTOBER
John Maher's first birthday coincides with Sandie Shaw's first number 1 hit, 'There's Always Something There To Remind Me'. Twenty years later, Shaw and Marr will record together and appear on *Top Of The Pops.*

LATE 1964
By this point, the Morrissey family have moved from Queen's Square to 384 King's Road, Stretford, where they will remain settled for the duration of Steven's youth. For a time, Betty's sister Mary Dwyer joins the household, and Steven is captivated by her Dusty Springfield beehive image and maternal solicitude. She will later emigrate to America, eventually settling in Colorado, where Steven visits her on several occasions.

1965 - 13 MARCH
Peter Morrissey Snr, Steven's grandfather, dies in Dublin. This is the first of three deaths in the family this year. "He worked at CIE in Dublin and was on nights," recalls Peter Morrissey. "I remember as a kid they used to call him at 10 o'clock. That night someone went up to call him. He sat up in the bed all right, then just fell back on it. He died then. It was thrombosis. He was just being called for work."

MARCH
Steven Morrissey purchases his first record, Marianne Faithfull's 'Come And Stay With Me', at Paul Marsh Records in Alexander Road. "I began to buy records in 1965," Morrissey notes, "very obvious pop things of the time, which were the most important things in life to me, and it always remained so. All the records I bought were friends. These people knew me and I knew them, and they were in my life. Things like Dusty Springfield, Marianne Faithfull and Cilla Black and the very obvious big Sixties names. I still have them all and like them even more now."

5 NOVEMBER
Patrick Stephen Dwyer, Steven's grandfather, dies from a heart attack at the age of 52. His eldest daughter Dorothy deals with the paperwork confirming his death at the family home in Rye Street, Chorlton-on-Medlock.

6 DECEMBER
Committal proceedings are opened against the Moors Murderers, Ian Brady and Myra Hindley. "I did have a fixation on the Moors Murderers as a potential victim, if you like," Morrissey later observed. "It was a very strong subject in Manchester throughout the late 1960s, very strong, almost an unspoken thing. It was too horrific for people to think about and to discuss." Morrissey will later break this taboo by documenting the pair's grisly exploits in The Smiths' 'Suffer Little Children'. Although Steven claims that he was acutely aware of the Moors Murders at the innocent age of six, it seems more likely that his morbid memories were stirred by tragic events at home later this month.

21 DECEMBER
Betty's mother Bridget Dwyer is admitted to hospital after falling down in the kitchen and breaking her leg. Meanwhile, even worse news is about to descend on the family.

22 DECEMBER
Three days before Christmas, the Dwyers are shocked by another sudden death in the family when Steven's uncle Ernie passes away at the tragically young age of 24. Dwyer is pronounced dead on arrival at Ancoats Hospital. A post mortem without inquest reveals that the cause of death is heart failure brought on by "acute yellow atrophy of the liver". The report testifies to chronic alcohol abuse, a fact well known to Dwyer's drinking companions who recall his heavy consumption of whisky. Bridget Dwyer receives the shock news in hospital where she has been confined to a wheelchair. Back at home, Steven witnesses the tears of his mother and sisters as the security of the adult world is suddenly exposed as unreal.

29 DECEMBER
Betty Dwyer registers the death of her brother Ernest at the General Registry Office in East Central Manchester. The funeral, meanwhile, is a sad and pathetic spectacle, which causes more grief for the family when the coffin proves too large to be placed in the grave. The mourners leave the rain-swept cemetery as the priest apologises for this unfortunate turn of events. So ends a tragic year in the history of both the Morrissey and Dwyer families.

1966 - 9 MARCH
Ronald Kray, later diagnosed a chronic paranoid schizophrenic, shoots George Cornell dead at the Blind Beggar pub in Whitechapel Road. The homosexual hood takes particular exception at fellow criminal Cornell calling him "a big fat poof".

EASTER
Steven Morrissey takes his first communion at St Wilfred's Church in Hulme.

30 JULY
England win the World Cup, beating West Germany at Wembley. Earlier that day the evil empire of gangster Charles Richardson crumbles about his feet when he is arrested at his home in Camberwell, South London.

31 JULY
Craig Gannon born in Salford, Manchester.

SEPTEMBER
Steven is promoted to the Juniors at school. "Primary school was just a pleasant time," recalls class mate Noel Devaney. "Morrissey was quiet. He was interested in music then and we used to

ELLEN Morrissey on her wedding day, 1955.

PETER, Christina, Patricia and Peter Morrissey Snr at Clonard Road in 1954.

say to each other, 'Did you hear a certain record in the charts?' He was into music, like The Beatles and The Stones – mainly the pop side and the charts."

1967 - 4 APRIL

The trial of Charles Richardson begins at the Old Bailey. The media dub the case "The Torture Trial" following allegations of scarcely believable cruelty by the Richardson gang, most notably involving an electric box whose live wires are used to inflict excrutiating agony on the firm's victims. In a grotesque parody of the homosexual act, the torture concludes with the wires being thrust up the backsides of those falsely imprisoned. After hearing the evidence, Justice Lawton concludes: "This case is not about dishonesty or fraud, it is about violence... vicious and brutal violence systematically inflicted deliberately and cold bloodedly and with utter and callous ruthlessness". The trial ends with a 25-year sentence for the former gang boss. It later transpires that Richardson is also a supporter of the South African régime and is involved in robbing anti-apartheid groups in London. This then is the man that the pacific, non-racist Morrissey later glorifies on album sleeve and concert backdrops. " I model my life on his", quips the singer. While glorifying "glamorous" gangsters, Morrissey has yet to comment on Richardson's racial views or gut retching violence.

8 MAY

Steven watches his heroine Sandie Shaw win the Eurovision Song Contest with the catchy 'Puppet On A String'.

1968 - 29 MAY

Steven's favourite football team Manchester United make history by winning the European Cup at Wembley Stadium.

DECEMBER

While in Miss Redmond's class, Morrissey adapts the hymn 'We Three Kings', which is retitled 'We Four Stevens' in deference to several class mates of the same name.

1969 - 16 MAY

One week before Steven's 10th birthday, London's most notorious gangsters Ronald and Reggie Kray are sentenced to 30 years' imprisonment. Morrissey later immortalizes them in the lyrics to 'The Last Of The Famous International Playboys' and even features the Krays' home street Vallance Road on the sleeve of *Bona Drag*. It is another intriguing contradiction of Morrissey's character that, while abhorring cruelty to animals and consistently condemning the Moors Murderers, he chooses to glorify the grisly exploits of the Krays and Richardsons.

22 JUNE

Ellen Morrissey, Steven's grandmother, dies during a holiday south of Dublin. "She died in a pub," Peter Morrissey explains. "She wasn't even ill. My sisters Ann and Chrissie and their husbands were on holiday. They had the kids with them and they were getting cranky and wanted something to eat. So they stopped at this little pub. Now my mother never went in pubs and didn't drink and my father was never a drinker either. Anyway, they stopped at this pub and the woman there said 'Bring the children in' and made them sandwiches. My mother was sitting between the brothers-in-law and they were having a heated discussion...Then she had a brain haemorrhage and died there. That was it. She wasn't even in hospital. It was all very quick."

DECEMBER

Steven appears as Joseph in the St Wilfred's School Nativity Play. His first "girlfriend" Kathleen Geoghan is cast as Mary. The audience is impressed by the unselfconscious humour of the normally shy Morrissey. "It sounded very grown up," recalls head boy Chris Lukes. "He was saying lines like, 'Sit down and put your feet up'. It was very funny and people immediately clicked because it was just like your mother talked. There was an actor in him, even then."

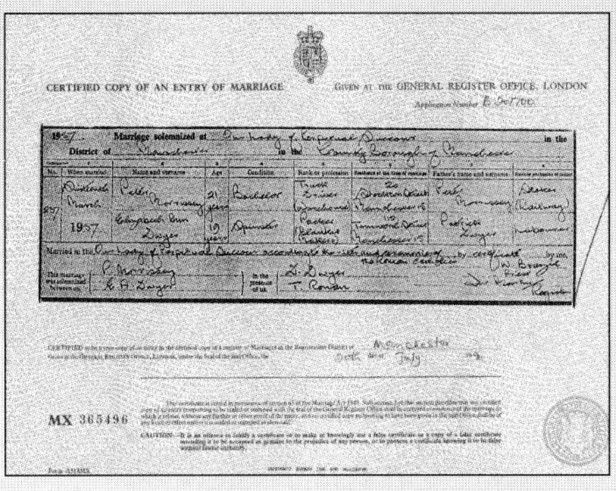
CERTIFIED COPY OF AN ENTRY OF MARRIAGE
GIVEN AT THE GENERAL REGISTER OFFICE, LONDON
MX 365496

PETER and Elizabeth Morrissey's marriage certificate, 1957.

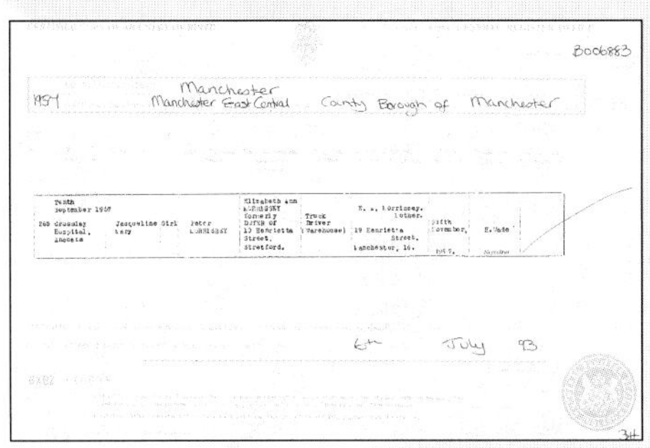
1957 Manchester Manchester East Central County Borough of Manchester

JACQUELINE Mary Morrissey's birth certificate, 1957.

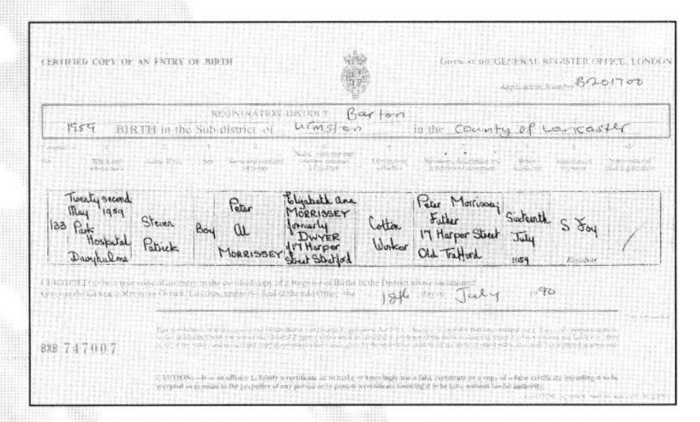
CERTIFIED COPY OF AN ENTRY OF BIRTH
1959 BIRTH in the Sub-district of Urmston in the County of Lancaster

STEVEN Patrick Morrissey's birth certificate, 1959.

FOURTH from left middle row, Morrissey celebrates his first Holy Communion, 1966.

'Johnny was one of those guys that had natural ability. When he played music he'd just excel.'

PETE CASSAN, A CONTEMPORARY

CHAPTER ONE

Children Of The Revolution

THE SMITHS MAY HAVE BEEN the group of the Eighties, but they were also the children of the Seventies. This was the period when Marr first learned to play the guitar and began fraternizing with older Wythenshawe lads, assimilating their formidable record collections along the way. Johnny was the classic eager young learner, a hungry music fan, who enjoyed the rock 'n' roll myths long before he had a chance to experience them first hand. Rourke was part of the gang and joined his colleague in nascent groups such as The Paris Valentinos and White Dice. Along with cider drinking and bass practice, Rourke also inherited a drug habit that would later result in his brief dismissal from The Smiths. The Marr/Rourke friendship saw them pass through a range of musical experiments, embracing Crosby, Stills, Nash & Young harmonies, Stones riffs and funk interludes. It was this fascinating musical menu that would later provide a key to The Smiths' musical power. Beneath the eclecticism was the belief that you should find a particular style and hone it to perfection. Allied to that was Marr's appreciation of the importance of fashion and playful use of pop imagery, manifested in a series of subtle image changes over the years. By the early Eighties, Johnny had already transformed himself into the perfect right hand man – a guitarist with no pretensions about writing lyrics or singing lead vocal, who knew precisely his worth and exactly where he was going.

The apprenticeship of Mike Joyce was, like his personality, positive and happy-go-lucky. Adolescence in the Seventies meant the wild liberation of punk and a chance to show off his spiked hair and love of Buzzcocks. Playing under age with The Hoax was a fascinating adventure which prepared him for his later stint with Victim and that all-important audition for The Smiths. Musically, Joyce shared little in common with his colleagues beyond the unifying punk ideals. What he could offer them was a juxtaposition in style – the hard drumming of a former punk allied to Marr's lustrous melodies and Morrissey's impassioned vocals.

For Morrissey, older and more troubled than his future fellow Smiths, the Seventies was a formative period spent searching for an identity. His schooldays passed in a Dante-like nightmare which was still resonant enough a decade on to inspire the cathartic 'The Headmaster Ritual'. Steven left school on a gloomy note and, for a time, attempted to find his way in the world. A year at a further education college brought him three O-levels, a scale of achievement that was a testament to his enduring laziness, as much as his academic ability. After a short term on the dole, Morrissey found a job and, more surprisingly, stuck it for a full year before leaving in disillusionment. The trouble with work was that it stifled his dreams and merely underlined the rut in which he was stuck. The years of unemployment that followed should have done the same, but Morrissey found gratification locked away in his bedroom, fantasizing about fame, listening to records and bombarding the world with letters. His limitless capacity for self-absorption inevitably brought depression and moroseness, but the youth's often inflammatory railings against the world suggested that beneath the misanthropy there was a fighting spirit.

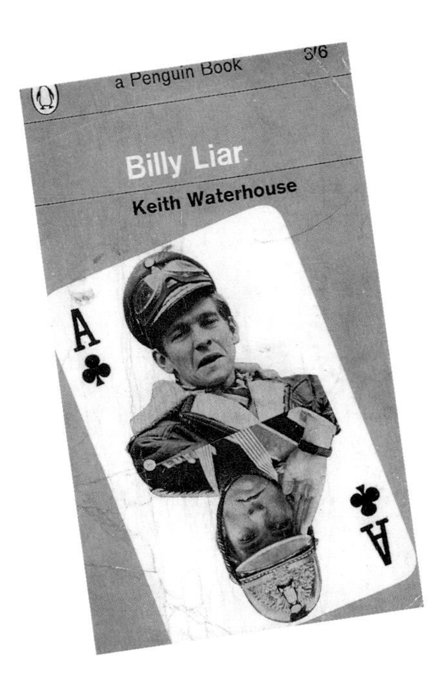

THE film/book 'Billy Liar' appealed to Morrissey's imagination.

STEVEN (FAR RIGHT) at King's Road in the early Seventies.

The most extraordinary aspect of Morrissey's legendary isolated adolescence and youth was that his post-fame accounts of the period are frighteningly true. This was no poor boy pop star façade – Morrissey was genuinely a troubled youth. He rightly saw himself as a misfit, whose dreams could not be accommodated in the real world of academic qualifications and tax returns. "Many people go through what he went through at a certain age," his father confides. "You don't know what you're going to do with your life. That's what happened to him around the age of 15. Most lads go through that, but he took it more seriously than anyone we knew."

Steven's feelings of isolation were compounded by insecurities about his sexuality and some brief and embarrassingly unerotic fumblings which temporarily convinced him that he was probably physically incapable of producing children. Morrissey's answer to confused sexuality and emotional impoverishment was the old stand-by of bedroom retreat. Self-imposed solitary confinement fuelled fantasies and this proved a great source of strength. Alone in his bedroom, pen in hand, Morrissey found the same imperious arrogance that he revealed as a performer many years later. The most fascinating aspect of Morrissey's teenage life is the way its very mundanity serves as creative fuel for his later pop star creation. His youth is a vast panorama of empty hopes, failed groups, fantasies without foundation and a wilful solitariness that cannot fully disguise a genuine loneliness and sad emotional insecurity.

STEVEN MORRISSEY joins The Nosebleeds, 1978.

Although Morrissey does not lie about his past, it is characteristic that he should ignore the fleeting good times and severely underestimate what was available. His weakness as a chronicler of his youth, then and now, is that he is so self-obsessed that he neglects to consider how much worse his life might have been. It is true that his parents split up, but they never had rows in the house or indulged in screaming matches or violent outbursts. They remained surprisingly close after the separation and continued to offer Steven support in various ways. Even after his pop star fame, his parents stayed in frequent contact and the family was far less fragmented than music press readers might assume. The solitariness which characterized his youth was largely self-inflicted.

Steven's reclusiveness, while true, has to be balanced by the staggering number of concerts he attended throughout the late 70s. When he wasn't alone in his bedroom he appears to have been greedily assimilating every promising musical act that passed through town. Moreover, while his interviews and songs glorify a gloomy claustrophobic Manchester, with Steven cast as the city's Billy Liar, this tale of urban imprisonment is only half true. If Steven could not escape, he was certainly capable of taking a holiday to relieve his morbidity. He travelled to London frequently and visited America on, not one, but several occasions. For a refugee from the dole queue, this was a luxury which few, if any, of his contemporaries could even dream about, let alone enjoy. The final qualification that has to be made about Steven is his supposed lack of friends. It's true that he was a loner, yet he always appeared to find a spiritual companion or soul mate, even in his most bleak moments. Steven... remember Richard, Marcia, Anna and Johnny D – all four of whom were great intimates and can tell so many sexy stories! Then there was Linder and James Maker, who kept him entranced long before Johnny Maher arrived at his door.

TALES OF working class life helped shape the Morrissey world view.

In spite of the above considerations, there is no doubting the severity of Morrissey's self-imposed isolation. How much longer could he have maintained his illusions before the realities of the adult world finally undid his lazy resolve? This was a question that was becoming increasingly pointed by the closing months of 1981. In his worst fantasies Morrissey saw himself ending it all, but the end could just as easily have been a capitulation to the adult world as a bottle of sleeping pills or a car crash on the M3. The darker questions remained unanswered thanks to the exuberance, self-confidence and ambition of Johnny Maher.

1970 - SUMMER TERM
Morrissey's mediocre academic record is compounded when he fails the 11 plus, though only three of his class mates pass the notorious examination.

SUMMER
Johnny Maher enjoys regular visits to Ireland, where his uncle plays guitar and sings traditional ballads. Maher's father is also a music lover, plays the accordion and teaches his son the harmonica. "My father, his sister and my grandmother and a couple of in-laws all sang," Johnny recalls. "We had parties pretty much two to three times a week."

SEPTEMBER
Morrissey enrols at the all boys St Mary's Secondary School in Renton Road. "I remember the first day at St Mary's," class mate Noel Devaney reflects. "I got to school early before the bell went and some of the other lads who went to St Wilfred's said, 'Who's coming from Wilfred's?' I said, 'Steven Morrissey' and one of the lads said, 'You ought to hear the voice!' It was a very girlish, very effeminate voice and his mannerisms were very effeminate." Morrissey's stay at St Mary's will later be immortalized in The Smiths' 'The Headmaster Ritual'.

'One of the lads said, "You ought to hear the voice!" It was a very girlish, effeminate voice and his mannerisms were very effeminate.'

NOEL DEVANEY on Morrissey's first school day

NOVEMBER
Morrissey carefully collates his small collection of monster magazines, which include such titles as *Movie Monsters* and *Quasimodo's Monster Magazine*. Copies exist to this day, each boasting his name and age inscribed on the covers in that distinctive wiry hand.

1971 - EARLY.
Andy Rourke's family move from their home in Truro Drive, Ashton-Upon-Mersey to Hawthorn Drive.

20 MARCH
Marc Bolan's group T. Rex tops the charts with 'Hot Love'. Morrissey is infatuated with the elfin pop star and spends hours drawing his picture instead of concentrating on his lessons. "He used to spend the whole day doing it," recalls class mate Mike Moore. "And it was the same picture. It was good, but the same picture, over and over again. Just his face... I kept looking at him and thinking, 'What's he doing the same picture for?'" Years later, Morrissey would cover T. Rex's 'Cosmic Dancer', write an introduction to a Bolan biography and use Bolan's musical influences on such songs as 'Metal Guru' and 'Certain People I Know'. Indeed, a limited edition of the latter featured a pastiche sleeve of 'Ride A White Swan', with Steven in the Bolan pose pictured underneath the word "Moz" instead of "T. Rex".

1972 - 22 JANUARY
In a *Melody Maker* interview, David Bowie confesses to journalist Michael Watts that he is "bisexual". Shortly afterwards, Morrissey turns up at school with his hair streaked blond. "That was also the first time I ever saw him wear glasses", recalls Mike Ellis, who sat next to Steven in class. "Whether he had the flash to offset the glasses I don't know... He was quite self-conscious about wearing glasses. I don't think he had the flash for very long. I think he had it taken out." Although Morrissey occasionally joked about and exaggerated the incident in interviews, his most memorable recollection of the day can be found in the lyrics of 'I Know Very Well How I Got My Name'.

FEBRUARY
Morrissey becomes involved in a heated and petty argument with his class mate Mike Moore over Wings' 'Give Ireland Back To The Irish'.

EARLY
Morrissey attends his first concert, T. Rex at Belle Vue, Manchester. His father drives him to the gig. "I used to do the running around," Peter Morrissey laughs. "I'd drop them off at the Seymour Hotel and then come back and pick them up." School friend Mike Foley remembers Steven's determination to see concerts, even at an early age. "In the first and second year, if he wanted to go to a concert, he'd take a half-day off and his dad would drive him. His parents were 20 years ahead of their time... They let their kids get on with life and do what they wanted. Even at 14, if you went out with his mum and dad you'd have a good time. It was like going out with a mate and his girlfriend."

AUGUST
Mott The Hoople's career is magically resurrected by Bowie who produces their memorable hit, 'All The Young Dudes'. Morrissey takes them on board as his latest heroes and signs up to the Mott The Hoople Fan Club. Kris Needs, the fan club president, remembers Morrissey as one of the group's most dedicated enthusiasts. "He was the most faithful member," Needs claims.
"I used to write back and got Ian Hunter to write little messages to keep him happy. I spoke to him twice on the phone. He was Mr Weird."

OCTOBER
Mike Joyce purchases his first single, Alice Cooper's Top 5 hit 'Elected'.

1973 - 7 JUNE
Morrissey and his friend Mike Foley dress up in glam gear and attend Bowie's concert at Manchester Free Trade Hall. Mike Ellis is also in attendance. Such outings are often accompanied by a hint of danger, most notably from glam-hating gangs intent on spoiling Steven's fun. Fortunately, the persuasively intimidating Foley has the charm to maintain the peace.

JUNE
Morrissey finishes first in the finals of the long jump at his school's Sports Day, and is also commended for his running. "The 100 metres was my *raison d'être*", he later explained. Although he is strong at athletics, his motivation rapidly declines with each successive school term.

AUTUMN
The Maher family move from Ardwick to a council estate in Baguley, Wythenshawe.

NOVEMBER
Morrissey is smitten by the sight of The New York Dolls on *The Old Grey Whistle Test*, and dubs them "the official end of the Sixties". He later noted apocryphally: "I was 13 and it was my first real emotional experience. The next day I was 29. Being devoted to the Dolls ruined my education. The teachers were very worried and expected me to turn up for Maths in drag."

1974 - 14 JUNE
Morrissey stuns several class mates by actually getting a letter printed in the *New Musical Express*. The missive is a fulsome tribute to Sparks, whose début album *Kimono My House* was a best seller at the time. Morrissey concluded: "Today I bought the album of the year. I feel I can say this without expecting several letters saying I'm talking rubbish... I

THE NEW YORK DOLLS, early Seventies symbols of rock 'n' roll decadence.

bought it on the strength of the single. Every track is brilliant – although I must name 'Equator', 'Complaints', 'Amateur Hour' and 'Here In Heaven' as the best tracks, and in that order." Morrissey's naïve enthusiasm certainly caught the attention of letters editor Charles Shaar Murray, who gently mocked the youth with the reply: "The eyes of Mr Morrisey [sic] gleam with a missionary zeal that shames into submission the cringing doubts of those not yet convinced."

SEPTEMBER
Both Johnny Maher and Andy Rourke are allocated places at St Augustine's Grammar School. Although they are initially placed in separate classes, they are well aware of each other. "We were in rival gangs," Rourke recalls. "There was me, Phil Powell and Jimmy Sales. We were the bad lads. Johnny had his little gang in his class. Everybody looked up to Johnny in his class. He always used to have a trendy haircut and trendy pants on. He wasn't particularly hard, but thought he was, and used to act it."

SEPTEMBER
Mike Joyce secures a place at St Gregory's Grammar School. His first instrument is the flute, but his mother subsequently purchases him a drumkit.

1 OCTOBER
McDonald's food chain opens its first hamburger joint in the UK. Morrissey is already well on the way to becoming a vegetarian. "I believe that everything went downhill from the moment the McDonald's chain was given licence to invade England," Morrissey complained. "To me, it was like the outbreak of war and I couldn't understand why English troops weren't retaliating."

28 NOVEMBER
Thomas Morrissey, Steven's uncle, dies in Manchester.

1975 - JANUARY
Morrissey visits White Coppice on a field trip with Geography teacher Mr Twist. "It was just outside Chorley," recalls Steven's friend Mike Ellis, "a very small backwater where the youngest in the village was about 65 and the oldest about 105. There were old mines there... We went and talked to a lot of different people in the village. You had to cross a weir to get to it. I remember the whole class was walking along this ledge about three foot wide, with a stream running down, but at one point there was an outcrop of rocks which you had to shuffle sideways around. The only person that wouldn't do it was Steve!"

APRIL
As the final term of Morrissey's school days begins, he is still no nearer to mastering a musical instrument, having played around with a guitar, purchased a saxophone and tinkered with a piano. "He was always the person who would impress by *talking* about music," recalls class mate Jim Verrechia, who had the unenviable task of attempting to teach Steven the guitar. "He was enthusiastic about music. He always liked to learn something, but he didn't have patience. He wouldn't stick at it." Steven's lazy streak would consistently hamper his musical progress for many years after school.

SPRING
Morrissey attends Hunter/Ronson's performance in Manchester with his school friends Mike Ellis and Chris Power. Morrissey would, of course, later employ the services of Mick Ronson as producer on his 1992 album, *Your Arsenal*.

JUNE
Morrissey leaves St Mary's School at the same time as the headmaster Vincent "Jet" Morgan. "I learned that if I ever wanted to be educated I'd have to leave school," Morrissey concluded. "So anything I learned was from outside of the education system. I came from a working-class background and very brutal schooling, which is no use to anyone who wants to learn. So, education, quite naturally, had no effect on me whatsoever." Class mate Mike Ellis was sympathetic towards this viewpoint. "The standard was very very bad," he confirms. "It was a bog standard curriculum. No languages. No music. In fact, there was no music teacher at all, not even a recorder, so he didn't get anything from school. The headmaster was on the verge of retirement and wasn't particularly fussed."

SEPTEMBER
Morrissey enrols at Stretford Technical School, signing up for four O-levels: English Literature, Sociology, History and the General Paper. Fellow students still remember him as the shyest member of the class.

AUTUMN
Rourke falls in with some drug dealers in Wythenshawe and starts experimenting with pills and barbiturates. "I used to turn up at school and fall asleep on my desk," he remembers. Eventually, the matter is brought to the attention of the headmaster, Monsignor Guinness. A kindly teacher, Mr Thorpe, encourages Maher to keep an eye on the troubled Rourke.

1976 - EARLY
Morrissey writes to Tony Wilson at Granada Television suggesting that the presenter should feature The New York Dolls on his forthcoming music programme *So It Goes*. "The music industry hated them and that was good enough for me," Morrissey explained in defence of his enduring passion. "I think they were the single most important group to me as an adolescent."

20 JULY
Morrissey attends The Sex Pistols' second gig at Manchester's Free Trade Hall during which they play 'Anarchy In The UK' for the first time. Although he is unaware of the reaction he is causing, Morrissey's presence is noticed by at least three people in the audience: Phil Fletcher, Stephen Pomfret and Jimmy Walsh (Bobby Durkin's cousin). They accurately identify him as the person who has been sending missives to the music press from Stretford. "It has to be him!" Fletcher exclaims, spotting the boy's New York Dolls T-shirt and the copy of their first album tucked ostentatiously under his arm. Although Morrissey is not approached by this Wythenshawe clique, the incident is the first link in a chain of events that will eventually lead him to his future songwriting partner Johnny Marr.

SUMMER
Morrissey completes his O-levels. He passes English Literature, Sociology and the General Paper, but fails History. Meanwhile, he travels to New York and New Jersey, where he visits his Aunt Patti and Aunt Mary. He enjoys the trip so much that he returns home with plans to emigrate.

SEPTEMBER
Maher and Rourke's school, St Augustine's, is reorganized along comprehensive lines as St John Pleasington. By this point, the pair are regularly playing guitars in their spare time. "Johnny and Andy always hung round together," recalls their school contemporary Pete Cassan. "Probably out of all of us, Johnny was going to make it musically, which he proved. He was one of those guys that had natural ability when he played the guitar. When he played music he'd just excel... while we'd be twanging away, he'd come around and say, 'Listen to this', and play something in five minutes that you'd been trying to play for the last two years."

During the first week of September, Morrissey signs on the dole. He is required to appear at the Civic Centre every Wednesday at 10.15 am. "I thought it would be a bit degrading at first," he tells friends, "but now I couldn't give a damn."

14 SEPTEMBER
Morrissey writes to Ann-Marie McVeigh, whom he secretly idolizes, asking for the return of his History notes. She doesn't reply. He consoles himself with tea and French toast.

24 OCTOBER
Morrissey travels to Birmingham to see Patti Smith. There, he meets a woman named June Durkin whose husband is a journalist and manages to sneak Steven backstage. In spite of his feminist readings, the youth still enjoys a few misogynistic aphorisms. "Never trust a woman," he jokes, "except with a bank account." Over the next few years Morrissey writes regularly to his new penfriend, spilling forth his ambitions, frustrations and darkest desires.

OCTOBER
Morrissey sees Deaf School and Split Enz in concert.

6 NOVEMBER
Morrissey witnesses music press hopefuls Roogalator at Manchester University. Back home in his bedroom, he ponders his sex life. "I have spent the night with girls and not had sex," he observes, "and, believe me, it doesn't boost your reputation. I don't have sex much, in fact I can count the number of times. I have an inferiority complex that way. I feel as though nobody would be bothered with me." Steven's shyness at the time, a trait noticed by many of his contemporaries, merely exacerbates his feelings of isolation.

11 NOVEMBER
Melody Maker prints one of several letters from Morrissey to the music press on the state of punk. It is clear that his attitude towards The Sex Pistols is at best ambivalent. He concludes: "The likes of The Sex Pistols have yet to prove that they are only worthy of a mention in a publication dealing solely with fashion, and if the music they deliver live is anything to go by, I think that their audacious lyrics and discordant music will not hold their heads above water when their followers tire of jumpers and safety pins." In a second missive on the same page, he declares: "British Punk Rock is second to the New York equivalent, in that it does not possess the musical innovation. The New York Dolls, Patti Smith, The Ramones and Jobriath can withstand accusations of novelty value because, although a great deal of their act was based on image, they also had the musical professionalism and variation to suitably recompense for their image-conscious inclinations. However, although British punk bands are emerging by the truckload, even

IAN HUNTER of Mott the Hoople.

the most prominent are hardly worthy of serious musical acceptance."

NOVEMBER
The bedroom bound Morrissey still bemoans his lack of success with the opposite sex, but decides to find solace via a temporary job. Although he has no musical experience, he does seem to harbour vague desires of becoming successful, even though there are no obvious outlets available."I find it hard to believe that there are people out there who *don't* want to be stars," he complains.

20 NOVEMBER
Morrissey secures a job with the Civil Service but quits within a fortnight. "I never really felt that I could work," Morrissey explains. "I blatantly refused to work and just do somebody else's chores, because that's the way I saw it... I couldn't really come to terms with that. So I did live in a semi-poverty state. But it seemed the only way that I could survive".

MORRISSEY RETURNS TO THE LETTERS PAGES OF the *NME*, this time extolling The New York Dolls. "Methinks that The Dolls weren't the damp squid that Nick Kent would have us believe," he argues, "because if you look closely at the increasing number of British punk bands emerging by the shipload you will see in each one, a little bit of The Dolls. You know it makes sense."

5 DECEMBER
One of Morrissey's handful of friends, Angie, has been stricken with leukaemia. He visits her in hospital and is severely shaken up by the experience. "Seeing her today was worse than if I heard of her instant death," he wrote. "It's so sad you wouldn't realize. It opened my eyes to a lot of things..." Despite the eye-opener, Steven's morbidity soon resurfaces although for a time he seems thankful that he is healthy and alive.

7 DECEMBER
Morrissey's dole is cut to a paltry £5.00 a week as a result of leaving his job. "Now nobody wants to know me," he complains. "I have no money, yet those from overseas amongst us are rolling in cash. Oh, isn't England a wonderful place." His peculiar feelings, ranging from xenophobia to nationalism, will be restated in his subsequent songwriting career.

9 DECEMBER
The Sex Pistols return to Manchester, appearing at the Electric Circus as part of their ill-fated Anarchy Tour. They are supported by The Heartbreakers, whom Morrissey idolizes, due to their New York Dolls' pedigree.

23 DECEMBER
The marriage of Steven's parents effectively ends when Peter Morrissey leaves 384 Kings Road, the family home. "My parents got divorced when I was 17," Steven later recalled, "though they were working towards it for many years. Realizing that your parents aren't compatible gives you a premature sense of wisdom that life isn't easy and it isn't simple to be happy... but my parents weren't the basis of my neuroses." By the time of the separation, Steven appears capable of accepting the rift and merely refers to it matter of factly. "He was 17," Peter Morrissey reiterates. "He was a man. I didn't walk out on a little boy. I was nearly married by his age... Even today, I've never done anything against Steven. I've never even raised my voice to him. I let him do what he wanted... I was always very good to them, but something happened to Steven and I can't explain it." Despite Steven's comments about his parents' relationship, they did not divorce until long after their initial estrangement and , unlike many separated couples, they remain in close and frequent contact to this day.

31 DECEMBER
Morrissey decides to become an Au Pair Boy, and applies for a job. "They're gonna have to change the rules," he asserts, more in hope than earnest. "If women get equality, so can men." Alas, his application is turned down soon after. Many years later, on the promotional disc of 'Interesting Drug', Morrissey is credited as the "Au Pair Motorcycle Boy", a clear indication that he had not forgotten the incident.

JOHNNY'S guitar god Rory Gallagher.

1977 - EARLY
Morrissey "auditions" as bassist for the CJs, a semi-professional group formed by school friends Jim Verrechia and Chris Power. "He turned up," recalls Power, "and we said, 'What can you sing?' He didn't know any of our songs and we didn't know any of his, so it wasn't much good." Not surprisingly, Steven fails the audition. "We couldn't really see him fitting in playing Working Men's Clubs," Verrechia wryly adds.

MAHER AND ROURKE TEAM UP WITH BOBBY Durkin and Kevin Williams (later Kevin Kennedy aka Curly Watts of *Coronation Street* fame) in a local group, The Paris Valentinos. "It was a very young band, " Kennedy recalls. "We used to play Tom Petty covers and Rory Gallagher numbers. Johnny was well into Rory Gallagher and he got me into him. In fact, I've still got Johnny's first guitar – it was an old Rory Gallagher copy, battered beyond recognition."

JANUARY
Morrissey completes an interesting short story titled *Sic Transit Gloria Mundi*. Already there is evidence of an ability to pen smart aphorisms and witty rejoinders which some friends interpret as literary skill.

4 FEBRUARY
"It sounds like a wonderful idea to be rich and famous," Steven muses. "A swift trip to stardom has occupied my mind for as long as I can remember." Beneath such fantasies, however, are the chilling thoughts that he will not find an outlet for his dreams. "I am totally disillusioned with life," he concludes in a maudlin relapse. "Time passes and things get progressively worse."

MARCH
Morrissey accepts a clerical post at the Inland Revenue, where he receives a wage of £22.50 per week. "Seems like I'm going bourgeois in my old age," he quips.

9 MARCH
Steven awakes with a pounding headache, made worse by listening to Tony Blackburn's cheery morning show on Radio 1. "When he goes into that 'Tiny Tots' spot escapade, I almost foam at the mouth," he protests. After finishing his breakfast, Steven boards the bus, then heads for the dole office to sign on one last time.

14 MARCH
The Monday morning blues overwhelm Morrissey, even at this early stage of his working career. His time at the Tax Office will not be particularly happy and causes him

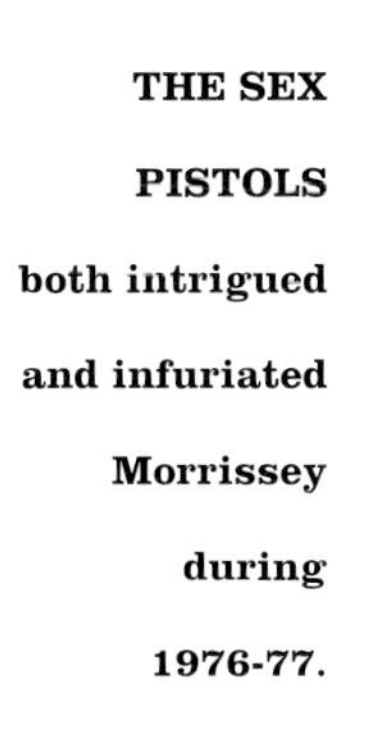

THE SEX PISTOLS both intrigued and infuriated Morrissey during 1976-77.

to reflect, "When I had no job I could pinpoint my depression, but later when I did get a job I was still depressed." These unhappy sentiments will later inspire the song 'Heaven Knows I'm Miserable Now'.

APRIL

During the first week of this month, Morrissey boasts of having completed two more short stories, *I Want To See The Bright Lights Again* and *Diddy Wah Diddy*. Both titles are taken from songs.

4 APRIL

Morrissey purchases six books: *The Facts Of Rape* (Barbara Toner), *Women And Madness* (Phyliss Chesler), *Dialogue With Mothers* (Bruno Bettelheim), *Diary Of A Harlem Schoolteacher* (Jim Haskins) *Sex And Racism* (Calvin C. Hernton) and *Against Our Will* (Susan Brownmiller). Books are clearly a panacea for the workday blues. "They give you a new lease of life," Morrissey enthuses, before devouring the tomes in question.

30 APRIL

Isolation is not always splendid, as Steven realizes on this bleak evening. "Oh, a lone wolf am I, endless nights alone, oh growing up is hard," he complains forlornly. Anticipating a move to the States before long, he satirizes punk torn England by cataloguing some trifling dislikes: "I loathe the Queen. I hate Angela Rippon. I despise the M1. I detest BBC. I'm in favour of Anglophobia."

19 MAY

Three days before his 18th birthday, Morrissey watches the sands of time slip through his fingers. "I'm sick of being the undiscovered genius," he moans. "I want fame now, not when I'm dead. I'm getting old. Time isn't on my side and I'm busy doing nothing."

EARLY SUMMER

Morrissey sees a spree of gigs from such New Wave American invaders as Talking Heads, The Ramones, Blondie and Television. Maher is also attending similar gigs during this period.

JUNE

The Paris Valentinos secure their first gig at a Jubilee Party in Greenwood Road, Benchill. "Everyone put in a tenner for booze except us," recalls bassist Kevin Kennedy. Their repertoire consists mainly of Thin Lizzy and Rolling Stones' covers, with some Tom Petty And The Heartbreakers and Rod Stewart's 'Maggie May' thrown in for good measure. The set is followed by a cider drinking binge, after which the lads stagger home in triumph.

MORRISSEY MARCHES IN A BAN THE JUBILEE protest, while The Sex Pistols' 'God Save The Queen' climbs to the summit of the *NME* charts. "The establishment, the monarchy and the government don't care as far as I can see," Morrissey notes in one of his less acerbic outbursts.

3 JUNE

Morrissey announces that he has just begun work on his first book, to be titled *When Will Ms Muffett Fight Back?* Several witty chapter titles are completed, but like so many Morrissey ideas from this period, the work is never written.

PUNK progenitor Patti Smith.

JULY
Obviously in search of a new image, Morrissey humorously considers changing his name to Byron De Niro, a monicker which he regards as "nice 'n' elegant".

LATE JULY
While perusing some new releases at Virgin Records, Morrissey is accosted by a fellow enthusiast who enquires, "Are you Steven Morrissey?" The mystery youth is Phil Fletcher, the observant Wythenshawe concert goer who had first noticed Steven at a Sex Pistols' gig three months before. "He was quite taken aback," Fletcher recalls. "I said, 'I've read letters by you in the press and seen you at the Free Trade Hall'. I even described what he was wearing at the Free Trade Hall and he found it hilarious that somebody would notice him. I think he was quite honoured." Morrissey is surprised to discover that there is a Wythenshawe clique of New York Dolls' fans and seems pleased when Fletcher invites him to join them at a Wayne County gig. On the night, however, Morrissey fails to show up.

EARLY AUGUST
"I've been spitting blood constantly," Morrissey informs his doctor. He is duly despatched to hospital, but after a series of tests medical specialists fail to find a Morrissey cure.

SUMMER
The Paris Valentinos can occasionally be heard playing at folk masses at the Sacred Heart Church. "The folk masses weren't a gig, just a couple of guitars and a couple of tambourines at 5.30 pm Sunday mass," explains drummer Bobby Durkin with due modesty.

AUGUST
Phil Fletcher finally introduces Morrissey to his Wythenshawe friends and fellow New York Dolls fans, whose numbers include Stephen Pomfret and Billy Duffy.

5 AUGUST
Having recently purchased the book *Sex And Racism*, it is not too surprising to see Morrissey commenting on both subjects. His feminist reading has obviously helped him make some sense of his confused sexuality and provided a term with which he feels comfortable: "asexual". "I've always thought that I was asexual because I'm not really stimulated by either male or female," he admits. "There was a period when I thought I could be gay, but then it suddenly dawned on me that I didn't like boys either."

If Morrissey is confused about sex, his attitudes to racism are only marginally clearer. He is reflective and full of egalitarian thoughts when pondering on the role of black people in society. "My best friend is black," he notes, "she's more thoughtful than most people." In detailing his feelings about racial prejudice, Morrissey reveals a liberal conscience, befitting a person whose reading list has included such titles as *Diary Of A Harlem Schoolteacher*. While it is pleasing to see the youth denouncing prejudice, it is also disappointing to observe his irreverent attitude in referring to the "aroma" of Pakistanis and the uncharacteristically lazy thinking behind the 18-year-old's flippant contention, "I don't hate Pakistanis, but I dislike them immensely". Such inconsistencies of thought may partly explain the ambiguous point of view in such songs as 'Bengali In Platforms' and 'Asian Rut', but it is perhaps salutary to remember Morrissey's later words in the media spotlight: "I am incapable of racism". It is also worth noting that two of Morrissey's female friends during this period were black. His inconsistency on this issue is revealing.

> **'There was a period when I thought I might be gay, but then it suddenly dawned on me that I didn't like boys either.'**
>
> MORRISSEY

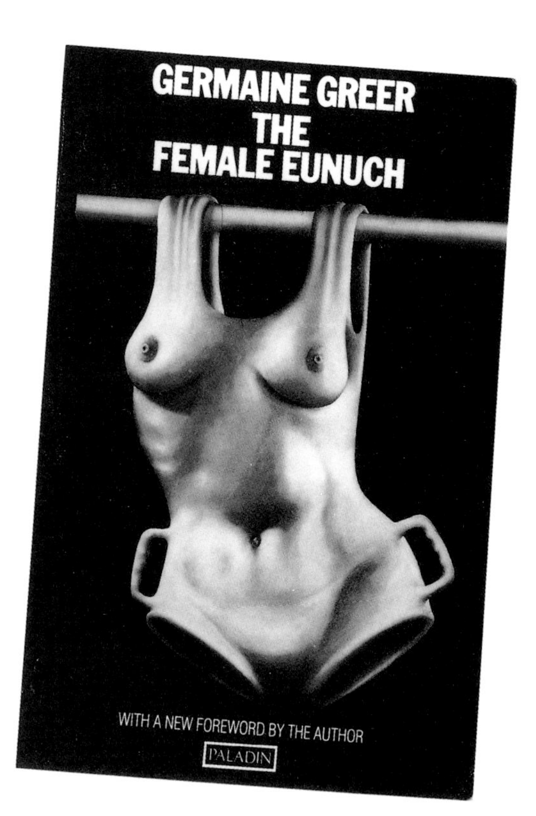

MORRISSEY greatly admired Greer's work.

SEPTEMBER
Morrissey appears in the fanzine *Kids' Stuff*, which includes a fulsome retrospection on the career of The New York Dolls.

OCTOBER
Morrissey rehearses with Billy Duffy and Stephen Pomfret in a new group. Steven decides to christen the venture Sulky Young and persuades Pomfret to write a song of that title. "They were supposed to be New York kids looking a bit upset like The Voidoids," Phil Fletcher explains with a smile.

NOVEMBER
Morrissey has a change of heart and retitles the group The Tee-Shirts. He is appointed singer in the group and can be heard practising in Pomfret's front room on a primitive PA. At one point Morrissey invites Pomfret to 384 King's Road where he is introduced to a 16-year-old black girl whom Steven wishes to include in the group. According to Pomfret she was even more nervous than Morrissey and less musically accomplished. The quiet girl with the punk-styled dyed hair is Quibilah Montsho who, like Phil Fletcher, met Morrissey one afternoon in Virgin Records. "I wanted to start a band and put an

ad in the *NME*," she recalls. "Morrissey answered it. We arranged to meet at Virgin. I just said a little bit about myself because I wasn't really sure about what music I wanted to get involved with." Despite the meeting with Pomfret and Morrissey, Montsho's musical ambitions are not realized, although Steven zealously attempts to convert her to the sound of The New York Dolls. "We'd talked briefly about forming a band together," Quibilah confirms, "but nothing ever came of it. Instead we used to write to one another and one day I told him that I was gay. He was patronising and sarcastic about what I felt had been a huge revelation on my part, and all he wanted to know was why I hadn't considered his sexuality!" Quibilah saw no reason why she should have been expected to unravel Steven's confused sexuality or guess that he was possibly gay. "I had just assumed he was straight as I would with any other man or woman that I'd met," she noted. "I thought he'd be supportive and understanding, but I remember the feeling when I read his letter. I wished I hadn't said anything at all, which is a shame." Morrissey subsequently sent her a humorous postcard with a lesbian joke that she appreciated.

Meanwhile, Morrissey's involvement with the Tee Shirts proves peripheral. He has a habit of unnerving Pomfret by taking him aside and asking bizarre questions in a hushed voice, such as "Do you like chocolate?" Realizing that the group require proper equipment, Pomfret suggests that they should consider saving some money. Morrissey's solution to the problem is to turn up one evening clutching a microphone which boasts a price tag in the £8 region. "It's not exactly what I had in mind, Steven," Pomfret patiently retorts. Soon after, The Tee Shirts play two gigs at the Lindow, Sale, but neither Morrissey nor Billy Duffy are in the line-up. Morrissey attends the first of these with his good friend Richard, but leaves immediately after the set has ended without saying a word.

ABOVE: Mike Joyce during his time with The Hoax.

THE HOAX. Left to right: Mike Joyce, Steve Mardy and Andy Farley.

1978 - JANUARY

In issue 7 of *Kids' Stuff*, Steve Morrissey pens a rambling piece on the impact of punk titled: "A Fabulous Adventure... A True Story." The article opens excitedly: "So you think you're cool cos you're on the dole and you think you're hip because you've got a swastika splashed across your torn tee shirt and you think you're tough because The Clash are Your band, well big deal! If you live in Manchester then I'm running with you, but if you're an out of towner: wipe the mascara out of your eyes 'cos London burned down with boredom and sparks fly in downtown Manchester! And if you're not around to feel the beat, well that's just too bad babbeee!"

His tribute to his home city prompts some comparisons with the early Sixties beat boom and he predicts a healthy turnover of fresh, young talent. "Sure you've heard of Buzzcocks," he teases, "and you might have a Slaughter And The Dogs single, but ever since The Sex Pistols first venture into Mancunian territory in June '76, a new generation of home grown bands has emerged. Yeah, the story's the same and one band's good until you've seen the next. And suddenly The Hollies and Herman's Hermits won't fare too well the next time someone does a feature on Manchester Rock and Roll."

6 JANUARY

Steven starts the year on a sour note, when he becomes embroiled in an argument with the tax inspector at work. "God, it was awful," he notes. "I argued, stood my ground and spat as much feathers as he did, but I still felt awful afterwards. Nobody understands me!"

7 JANUARY

Still deflated by the row at work, Steven spends Saturday morning mulling over his inept social skills. "The world hates me!" he concludes. "Looks like I've got a personality crisis!"

21 JANUARY

Morrissey takes a sideswipe at *Sounds* journalist Jon Savage. In the letters column, under the title "Ooo, Bitch!", Steven purrs: "The age of romance is upon us again. Jon Savage tips Manchester as *the* place to be in '78. You remember Manchester – the kids don't think you're tough if you pronounce your T's, and a gig at the Circus was always like guerrilla warfare. Too late, too late, Mr Savage. Save your enthusiasm for the intense drama at the Vortex, but watch you don't smudge your lipstick."

FEBRUARY

Morrissey switches his allegiance from Stephen Pomfret's Tee-Shirts and throws in his lot with Billy Duffy in a revamped line-up of The Nosebleeds. "I can't stand it anymore," he explodes."So many people messing me about with this dumb group. Morrissey has already been sending Duffy lyrics, featuring such titles as '(I Think) I'm Ready For The Electric Chair' and 'Peppermint Heaven', which are soon added to The Nosebleeds' repertoire.

27 FEBRUARY

"I'm listening to nothing but 'Hard Nipples', and I've got no money", Steven claims. However, his professed penury does not prevent him from wandering into the Mac Market later that afternoon and spending 95 pence on a slice of cream cheesecake.

28 FEBRUARY

Morrissey sets out for a Patti Smith press conference in London. His reading material for the trip is Germaine Greer's *The Female Eunuch*. "I idolized Patti Smith," Morrissey recalls. "I certainly wanted to meet her. I did meet her too and it was hugely disappointing... It was at a fanzine conference... and the room was crowded with young, impressionable people. There was one boy at the front who was no more than 17 and she walked up to him in this crowded, quiet room and

POST-Punk bands on the late Seventies Manchester scene: Howard Devoto's Magazine (LEFT) and the inspirational Ludus featuring Linder (RIGHT).

loudly asked him an extremely vulgar question about how sexually endowed he was... The lesson here is that it's sometimes better to cherish your illusions."

MARCH
Morrissey leaves his Inland Revenue job after exactly one year's employment.

7 APRIL
Morrissey suffers a severe case of indigestion, only a week before his performing début with The Nosebleeds. "I couldn't leave the house due to these constant burps," he complained, "and on the few occasions when I did I'm sure people must have thought me the most ill-mannered person ever." Fortunately, his doctor comes to the rescue with a prescription for some burp-conquering milk pills.

8 APRIL
Patti Smith's Rainbow concert receives a scathing review in *Sounds* by Jane Suck, much to Morrissey's consternation.

15 APRIL
The Nosebleeds appear at Manchester University at the foot of a bill hosted by Rabid Records which includes Slaughter And The Dogs, Gyro and Jilted John.

20 APRIL
Morrissey re-signs on the dole.

21 APRIL
In a most uncharacteristic diatribe, Morrissey turns against the written word itself. "I hate poetry," he explodes. "Most poetry is essentially useless. Books really bore me these days."

22 APRIL
Morrissey's Wythenshawe friend Phil Fletcher has a letter published in *Sounds* supporting the much debated Smith review: "Jane Suck's review of Patti at the Rainbow was the most honest piece of journalism ever printed. She summed up everything that was wrong at the concert. If Patti can say, 'I have no guilt' after playing such a sad excuse for a rock 'n' roll gig, she's an even bigger rip-off than I thought. And the London audience were such a pretentious sycophantic bunch of weekend hippies. Fancy pretending to understand the poor bitch when she doesn't even understand herself."

24 APRIL
Fletcher receives a stinging missive from Morrissey criticizing his pedestrian prose and severely castigating him for having the audacity to criticize the great Patti Smith. Their friendship crumbles in an instant.

APRIL
The Hoax form in Manchester with a line-up comprising Steve Mardy (bass), Ian Chambers (guitar) and Andy Farley (guitar/vocals). After rehearsing with a series of stand-in drummers over the next few months they recruit future Smith Mike Joyce.

8 MAY
The Nosebleeds play their second and final gig, appearing at the Ritz, supporting Magazine. Phil Fletcher is in the audience: " I saw him perform as The Nosebleeds at the Ritz, and that's the first time I saw him sing 'Teenage News' by Sylvain Sylvain. At that time he hadn't learned to sing and had a very high-pitched scream."

3 JUNE
NME journalist Paul Morley does a round-up of up-and-coming Manchester groups: The Nosebleeds, Snyde and Joy Division. Amazingly, The Nosebleeds are billed above Joy Division, while Morley enthuses: "The Nosebleeds have also noticeably metamorphosed, though probably due more to personal changes than anything else. Last year they were the entirely forgettable Ed Banger And The Nosebleeds... now Banger has gone his own so-called eccentric way. The Nosebleeds resurface boasting A Front Man With Charisma, always an advantage. Lead singer is now minor local legend Steve Morrison [sic], who, is at least aware that rock 'n' roll is about magic and inspiration. So The Nosebleeds are now a more obvious rock 'n' roll group than they've ever been. Only their name can prevent them being this year's surprise."

SOUNDS SMALL ADS REVEAL THAT SISTER RAY urgently require a bassist. The group will later boast Johnny Maher among its ranks. "They were a bunch of vagrant, biker nasties," Johnny recalls with a grin. "The guys were a lot older than me and had a bit of a history. They'd had a couple of records out and a few gigs that had got them a bit of notoriety because the singer was crazy."

JUNE
Despite the *NME*'s favourable predictions, The Nosebleeds ignominiously split; leaving Morrissey as an unemployed lyricist. "Billy Duffy was quite pleased with the lyrics," Rob Allman reminds us. "A lot of them were quite formulaic, like an update of The New York Dolls."

12 AUGUST
Morrissey gives notice to the world of a new love in his life when he places an advertisement in the Special Notices column of *Sounds* imploring: "Linder! Call Steven Morrissey! Spare ribs". The reference to *Spare Rib* reflects their common interest in feminist literature. "I think they were into it independently," opines Linder's label manager Richard Boon. "In terms of influence, I think he drew some of the way he repeats lines and phrases in songs. That was something she was very deliberately doing that he may have absorbed from her."

THE CRAMPS in action, and the fan-club badge for The Legion Of The Cramped.

31 AUGUST
Morrissey's heroine Patti Smith appears at his local Manchester Apollo. Earlier that day, Steven and his friend Steve Pomfret spend a lonely vigil outside the venue and are amazed when Smith suddenly emerges and jumps into a car. Caught up in the drama, Morrissey and Pomfret hail a taxi and chase their heroine across town. She disembarks at A1 Music, fully aware of the two disciples now standing outside. Finally, she opens the door of the shop and offers her pursuers two plectrums on which are inscribed "Rock 'n' Roll Nigger". Although the parties do not exchange a single word, Stephen and Steven depart in triumphant mood.

22 OCTOBER
Morrissey accompanies Slaughter And The Dogs to London for a record company audition which is unsuccessful. Steven's chances of becoming their permanent lead vocalist thereby fade. Billy Duffy remains with the group, who move to London early the following year and secure a contract with DJM Records as The Studio Sweethearts. "The Nosebleeds (then Slaughter) decided to become The Studio Sweethearts and Morrissey got lost on the way," Rob Allman contends. "I think Morrissey was still on the lookout to get another band."

28 OCTOBER
A touch of irony here. While Morrissey has been ducking down to London, Linder's group Ludus have made their début in Manchester, supporting The Pop Group. They receive a reverential review in *Sounds* from Mick Middles, who will later pen a short biography of The Smiths. Middles is obviously taken with Linder: "She glided across the stage like a disturbed spirit and the vision was only flawed by first night nerves."

29 OCTOBER
In rhapsodic mood, Morrissey casts himself as a frustrated Romeo, with former college friend Ann Marie McVeigh as the unlikely object of his secret affection. "Another case of unrequited love in which I, as ever, take the leading role," he muses. "I only wish there was something I could do to make her adore me, but there isn't. The trials of the meek continue, my heart weakens by the hour."

1 NOVEMBER
Morrissey journeys to Arvada, Colorado, where he stays with his Aunt Mary. His sister Jackie secures a job there, and it is originally intended that the family will emigrate. Steven, however, is not taken with the place. "Arvada is so isolated," he complains. "This place will kill me in a month. All the kids walk like John Wayne and eat oatmeal eight ways. I wore a pink tie and everyone thought I was a transvestite... People are so masculinist." His most memorable comment on the sojourn, however, is summed up in the resigned quip: "There is no sex in Colorado."

1979 - JANUARY
Steven gets homesick for Manchester and persuades his mother to bring him back. Magnanimously, she sells her car to assist his passage. His sister remains in Colorado for a spell, but the family's emigration plans all but end here.

EARLY
Following the break-up of The Paris Valentinos, Maher teams up with a tough local group, Sister Ray. The Velvet Underground-inspired unit are booked to play a local festival, but the gig is cancelled. Shortly afterwards, Maher plays live with them for the one and only time at the Wythenshawe Forum.

FEBRUARY
Morrissey briefly secures a job at Yanks Records in Chepstow Street. Although it seems the ideal employment for the record-obsessed youth, he takes exception to the low wages and long hours and soon moves on.

3 FEBRUARY
Proving that Morrissey is not the only Ludus champion, Middles returns to the pages of *Sounds* with another rave review in which he compares Linder to "a cross between Cleo Laine and Annie Haslam". He then outdoes Morrissey in effusiveness by concluding: "The potential of this band is immense, almost frightening".

3 MARCH
Outflanked by Middles, Morrissey is reduced to advertising in the music press Small Ads, demanding: "New York Dolls, David Johansen, anything, everything wanted".

MARCH
Mike Joyce is now playing regularly in punk group The Hoax, who had initially expressed concern about his age. "He was still at St Gregory's," recalls bassist Steve Mardy. "We'd had a string of inconsistent drummers and when he turned up and we realized he was still at school, we thought we couldn't play anywhere because he was under-age." Fortunately, Joyce has no problems with promoters and before long The Hoax graduate from playing youth clubs in Ashton and Denton to more prestigious bookings at the Mayflower, Cyprus Tavern, Band On The Wall and Manchester Polytechnic.

APRIL
Morrissey is invited by friends to stay in Bermondsey, London. He later pays tribute to this period in the video of 'The Last Of The Famous International Playboys'.

5 MAY
Ludus seek a replacement guitarist via *Sounds* while Morrissey watches their progress with increasing fascination. "He was very excited about Ludus," Steve Pomfret stresses. "He thought they were going to be the future of rock 'n' roll... But I don't think he and Linder were that close then. I really don't. I always thought they were just of like minds, somebody to go out with, somebody to talk to. I don't think he saw that much of her."

5-14 MAY
Morrissey returns to Manchester and contents himself watching the movies *Invasion Of The Bodysnatchers, California Suite, Double Indemnity, The Hills Have Eyes, Hallowe'en, Some Like It Hot* and *West Side Story*. In later years he will play down the trashier side of his movie viewing, preferring to stress his love of English monochrome classics. "I became very interested in film history," he stresses, "quite specifically films from the early Sixties such as A *Taste Of Honey, Saturday Night And Sunday Morning*, films with a common thread... *A Kind Of Loving, The Family Way*, were about people in the North specifically with their tail trapped in the door almost, trying to get out, trying to get on, trying to be somebody, trying to be seen. I found that very appealing ."

10 MAY
"There are no lengths I would not go to in order to live in Paris," Morrissey fantasizes, as several of his local friends head off for France.

MAY
Morrissey's time-wasting doodlings reveal that he is now reduced to conjuring imaginary names for groups that will never form. Among his self-aggrandizing favourites are: Stevie And The Stepladders, Stevie And The Socialites, The Silly Sluts and The Stupid Sluts.

30 JUNE
Morrissey bombards the music press with epistles in favour of The Cramps. A letter in *Sounds* enthuses: "I've just seen The Cramps and they're at that funny stage. This is the kind of group that start revolutionary outrages and all that."

7 JULY
Morrissey continues his appeal on behalf of The Cramps with an enthusiastic letter to the *NME*. "Paradoxically, The Cramps are worth their weight in gold for making The Police seem like a great big sloppy bowl of mush... The Cramps were enough to restore faith in the most spiritless. They have it all, and their drummer is the most compelling in rock history. Back To The Cramps, or perish. It is written."

WHITE DICE found inspiration in the work of Crosby, Stills, Nash and Young.

SEPTEMBER
On the advice of bassist Steve Mardy, The Hoax cut demos at Cargo Studios in Rochdale and subsequently release 'Only The Blind Can See In The Dark' on their record label, Hologram Music. "We set up a little business because we weren't getting any help from anyone else," Steve Mardy explains. "We called it the Hologram label. Rough Trade did our first deal in taking some records off our hands." In spite of the recording, Ian Chambers decides to leave and the group elect to continue as a trio.

AUTUMN
Steven takes a passing interest in Manchester-based group Sacred Alien, whose brand of glam/heavy metal is scorned by virtually everybody else. "They were like bricklayers in drag," recalls Mick Middles, who had the dubious honour of interviewing what he termed "a barrage of lipstick, rouge and stubble".

27 OCTOBER
No prizes for guessing the identity of the "Jobriath Fan from Manchester" who writes to *Sounds* recalling that disc jockey David Hamilton had made Jobriath single of the week on Radio 1 back in 1974. The fan demands that Elektra re-release the Jobriath catalogue forthwith, adding coyly, "Can we have a big pic in *Sounds* of Jobriath (who is better looking than Sonja Kristina)".

WINTER
Ex-Paris Valentinos, Maher, Rourke and Durkin are recruited to Robin Allman's group, White Dice, which also features keyboardist Paul Whittall. "That came about

BILLY DUFFY, latterly of The Cult.

because I had a wealth of songs and knew Johnny," Allman recalled. "He used to come round to our house a lot and was at a loose end at the time. He'd just finished with The Paris Valentinos. What I liked about him was that he could pitch a harmony. Me and Paul, who was a good keyboard player, had been doing this close harmony work and used to practise a lot of stuff. Johnny would sometimes come round and jam with us... Paul was in The Freshies. He was the only one with musical training. I played folk music as well as rock music and used to jam with people like Billy Duffy... I asked Johnny one evening, 'How do you fancy joining me and Paul and getting a band together and seeing how it goes?' He then got in touch with Andy."

DECEMBER

White Dice enter a competition in the *NME* sponsored by Jake Riviera's F-Beat Records. Remarkably, Riviera spots some potential in their crudely recorded cassette tape, which features the Crosby, Stills, Nash & Young-influenced 'Somebody Waved Goodbye'. As a result of this, the group will be invited to London the following spring for a recording session.

CHRISTMAS

A forlorn Steven watches television over Christmas, but can find little festive cheer. "'Twas the season to be miserable," he laments, before joking, "If not for *Christmas In Connecticut* I would have hounded Stretford precinct committing acts of gross indecency."

NEW YEAR'S EVE

As the Seventies close, Morrissey can be found alone in his bedroom reading Jane Austen's *Pride And Prejudice*. The youth's views on money, marriage and women are all challenged by Austen as early as that famous opening sentence: "It is a truth universally acknowledged that a single man in possession of a good fortune must be in want of a wife."

1980 - 5 JANUARY

Peter Morrissey secures his son a job at a hospital. The vegetarian Morrissey takes exception to the more gruesome aspects of the job and leaves two weeks later. "I removed blood, bits of flesh, bits of veins and uh, bits of things from surgeons' coats," he grimaced. "Not being particularly fond of the torrid stench of dried blood – after two weeks slaving over a cold corpse I decided to throw in the towel."

> **'I told him that I was gay. He was patronising and sarcastic... and all he wanted to know was why I hadn't considered his sexuality.'**
>
> **QUIBILAH MONTSHO** comes out to Morrissey

3 FEBRUARY

Morrissey attends an anti-Abortion Act march. There are no comments on the tragic plight of the unborn child from the sensitive one, who lamely notes, "I love a good demonstration." Phil Fletcher spots him in the crowd and offers a conciliatory wave. Alas, they will never speak to each other again.

5 FEBRUARY

Robin Allman moves into the Rourke residence in Hawthorn Lane and White Dice rehearse a number of Allman originals. With their CSN&Y harmonies, use of keyboards and distinctive guitar style, the group show some promise. "A lot of people said we were a lot like Squeeze and XTC," Allman explained. "I wrote most of the songs, but Johnny used to get frustrated because he'd come up with quite a few riffs during that period and I'd often take him up on a riff and he'd want a co-credit on the song. So it would be Allman/ Maher. He was definitely keen on that. That was something that did stick in his mind for a long time. Johnny was into a lot of AOR albums then, like Heart before they became popular. He had spent hours learning The Cars' 'My Best Friend's Girl' and was very keen on learning The Beatles' 'I Feel Fine'. He always had Rory Gallagher riffs knocking around and we'd do Thin Lizzy or Steely Dan twin lead. We'd have Paul with his Supertramp keyboards and a really big harmony. There was a lot of potential there which never came to much."

4 MARCH

Morrissey and a friend witness a fleet of flying saucers, which is enough to convince Steven that aliens and UFOs are real, and they are *here*! "It was a very eerie feeling..." he explained. "The whole thing had an astounding effect on me, and every time I think about it, I get the strangest sensations."

29 MARCH

Steven Morrissey makes an inauspicious entry to the pages of *Record Mirror* with a lacklustre review of The Photos.

APRIL

White Dice travel to London, where they undertake an audition for Jake Riviera's F-Beat Records. Six songs are completed from the pen of Allman/Maher: 'Someone Waved Goodbye', 'Makes No Sense', 'The Hold', 'On The Beach', 'It's Over' and 'You Made Me Cry'. Alas, their recording adventure does not end in superstardom, and Riviera declines to sign them.

APRIL

Morrissey enthuses over his latest heroes The Cramps and leaves *Record Mirror* readers in no doubt about their alleged brilliance. "They are the most beautiful, yes, Beautiful group I have ever seen," he sighs.

18 APRIL

At precisely 2.30 pm, Morrissey claims to have seen a ghost in the kitchen of 384 King's Road. The spiritual presence returns at tea-time, where it lodges in the bathroom. There is a school of thought that blames this elusive spirit for the release of 'Ouija Board, Ouija Board'.

LATE APRIL

Morrissey's beloved Ludus appear at the Beach Club, Manchester, a venue run by Tony Wilson and Richard Boon. Morrissey ensures that they appear in *Record Mirror*'s reviews column where he praises Linder for providing "a wild mélange of ill-disciplined

WHITE DICE. Far left: Rob Allman, Johnny Maher and Paul Whittall at Andy Rourke's house, 5 February 1980.
LEFT: The second line-up of White Dice: Rob Allman, Paul Whittall, Craig Mitchell, Johnny Maher and Andy Rourke.

and extraneous vocal movements apparently without effort".

MAY
Maher attempts to emulate Allman by writing lyrics of his own. 'Don't Cry', a Nashville style lament, is subsequently recorded on cassette with Allman in Bristol, but Maher decides not to continue the experiment and concentrates on guitar.

13 MAY
Still on the dole, Steven sits alone in his room reading *Hollywood Babylon* and perusing *The Murderers' Who's Who*. "Oh, I thought life would be so interesting, but it isn't," he cries.

22 MAY
Steven has a quiet 21st birthday, which is tinged with some regret at the prospect of growing up. "I'm 21, but I don't look a day over 20", the vain one muses. "I can feel myself slowing down."

EARLY SUMMER
Having released another single, 'So What?', The Hoax make their one-and-only appearance on national radio when John Peel plays their raucous 'World War III', from the Manchester compilation, *Unzipping The Abstract*.

AUGUST
In an attempt to further White Dice's chances of success, Robin Allman purchases a Telecaster guitar and an amplifier on hire purchase. "There might have been a chance to gig if people had tried hard enough," he reflected. "We didn't have enough gear for quite a long time. Johnny didn't have an amplifier for ages."

OCTOBER
Maher enrols at Wythenshawe College Of Further Education and keeps up with the music of the day by purchasing The Comsat Angels' *Waiting For A Miracle*, The Cure's *17 Seconds* and U2's *Boy*. Before long, he is appointed president of the Students' Union.

1 OCTOBER
Following a reply to an advertisement in *Sounds*, Morrissey finds a new pen pal, Robert Mackie, who sometimes bears the brunt of the Mancunian's witty sarcasm. "I don't believe you're 16," Steven cattily remarks, "you sound much younger – at least 14 years younger!" They nevertheless find some common musical ground in a mutual liking for David Bowie. When they eventually meet many months later, Steven provides an evening's entertainment at a pub featuring a transvestite performer.

13 OCTOBER
Morrissey is still uttering occasional Wildean aphorisms, telling the world, "I don't work, except at my genius." Detailing his musical favourites of the moment, he champions The New York Dolls, Jobriath, Nico and Magazine. Despite his appreciation of girl singers, he shows no mercy to the talented Kate Bush. "The nicest thing I could say about her is that she's unbearable," he notes. "That voice! Such trash!"

22 OCTOBER
Steven explodes in a frenzy of anger about the trivialization of great pop by the electronic music brigade, and goes in particularly hard on Orchestral Manoeuvres In The Dark and Gary Numan. "I hate, loathe, detest, abhor, abominate, cannot stand or abide Miss Numan," he froths. "To me all electronic music is just a sad accident." It should be stressed that Morrissey, as ever, has considerable time on his hands, as the prospect of work seems further away than ever. "I'd much rather lounge around the house all day looking fascinating," he admits. In such an accommodating household, the work shy youth is allowed his fantasies without rebuke.

WINTER
White Dice appear at the Squat, an annexe of the University Theatre, supporting Scorched Earth and Foreign Press. Maher sings lead vocal on the group's version of 'Take Me To The River', but there are few people listening.

"That gig was a disaster from start to finish", Allman confirmed. "Drink was flowing freely, and there was a lot of inebriation generally. I was centre stage and I was fed up with it. We'd had no chance to rehearse and everybody was nervous anyway. I thought, 'This is terrible'. The group knew I had glandular fever, which may have contributed to it. It was downhill from there. It was a disaster." In fact, the gig is such a disaster that Maher decides to quit the group and try something new. "I think Johnny wanted a way out anyway," Allman concluded. "Any excuse would have been adequate. He wasn't bound."

13 NOVEMBER
Morrissey champions The Monochrome Set's 'Love Zombies', wryly observing: "It's a lovely record, but I feel I would enjoy it much more if I had a long mac." When he is not waltzing around Manchester looking "sultry and over-educated", Steven is predictably locked away in his bedroom, cataloguing his state of mind and musical tastes. His turntable favourites for mid-November consist of 'Today I Died Again' (Simple Minds), 'How I Wrote Elastic Man' (Fall), 'The End' (Nico), 'Frankenstein' (New York Dolls), 'Sweetheart Contract' (Magazine), 'Fantastic Voyage' (David Bowie), '6060-842' (B-52s) and 'My Cherry Is In Sherry' (Ludus).

2 DECEMBER
Steven sees new wave hopefuls The Motels, but is unimpressed by Martha Davis, despite her classy rendition of 'Total Control'.

4 DECEMBER
Steven discovers a new favourite tipple to while away the hours – Cinzano and vodka. While speculating on CND, he unwittingly pre-empts the lyrics of 'Everyday Is Like Sunday' when suggesting, "People have been panicking about the Bomb since the early Fifties. Things haven't changed. But if it *does* drop, well, meet me on the desert shore." In an allusion to his sexuality, Steven uncharacteristically uses the word 'bisexual' rather than his usual 'asexual' but closes with the familiar litany "I hate sex". He also emphasizes a particular aversion to the female form, a viewpoint he will return to in more parodic mode on 'Some Girls Are Bigger Than Others'.

6 DECEMBER
Morrissey settles in front of the television at 4.30 pm for a repeat of *Murder She Said*, starring one of his favourite thespians, Margaret Rutherford. He waits impatiently for a repeat of her appearance in *The Happiest Days Of Your Life*. Later, he catches Loudon Wainwright in concert on the box. Although Morrissey is not particularly enamoured of the American school of singer/songwriters, he frequently cites Wainwright as a favourite.

9 DECEMBER
The world awakes to the news of John Lennon's assassination. Although Morrissey appears to have been largely immune to the genius of The Beatles, the epoch of Lennon's death has a strong, numbing resonance that disturbs the bedroom misanthrope. "So sad about John," Steven notes reflectively. "I almost cried. I have none of his records and I don't care about The Beatles, but when people who devote a part of their lives to 'peace' are shot five times for it, well, THAT disturbs me. It's always the wrong people. Nobody would assassinate our dear prime minister. Is all life sad?" With his thoughts still locked on the past, Morrissey spends a depressive evening watching Gen X attempt to recapture former punk glories. "The group were appalling and I'll know better next time," he laments.

MATT JOHNSON, Johnny Marr's early confidante and future The The collaborator.

14 DECEMBER
BBC 2 runs *The Last Picture Show*, one of Morrissey's favourite films of the period. "That film!" he enthuses. "It was my first real sexual relationship. To me, seeing and loving a great film is like having a sexual relationship."

31 DECEMBER
Steven ends the year on a characteristically low note. "My New Year's Eve was really Thrillsville," he deadpans. "I almost smirked. Is everybody's life as boring as mine?" The rhetorical question remains unanswered.

1981 - 10 JANUARY
Morrissey flies to America again, taking the familiar route from his Aunt Patti in New York to his Aunt Mary in Arvada, Colorado. It is worth considering how different his life might have been if he had taken the chance to emigrate. As it is, his sojourn in New York is partly spoiled by the cold weather. "I caught terminal pneumonia," he remarks ungraciously.

13 JANUARY
White Dice struggle through their final rehearsal and shortly afterwards Allman leaves the troubled Rourke household. "We still rehearsed together, but White Dice had really finished as a unit," Allman confirmed. "Johnny was working on his own stuff with Andy parallel to White Dice. He was busy forming his own idea of a new band. He wanted to do something different that was Johnny Maher."

19 JANUARY
"Even Beethoven had problems," exclaims Morrissey, in innocent anticipation of his live solo album 12 years later. His advice to those who share his sense of boredom is to take up embroidery or start a religion.

FEBRUARY
Immediately after his return from America, Morrissey forms another short-lived group with the intriguing name, Angels Are Genderless.

EARLY
Having already decided to move into a funk direction, Maher and Rourke record a tape at Decibel Studios titled 'Crak Therapy'. Shortly afterwards, they recruit a drummer Simon Wolstencroft and name themselves The Freak Party. Their music has a hard funk edge, as Wolstencroft confirms. "When I think back

now, what we were doing was way ahead of its time," he enthuses. "It was dance stuff really... it was like the feel you've got today, wah-wah guitars and funk-style drumming, which is what I really wanted to do and what Andy was into at the time. It was the tail-end of the Brit funk movement. We were all, especially me and Andy, into British funk."

14 MARCH
Roxy Music finally achieve their one and only number 1 single, a cover of John Lennon's 'Jealous Guy'. It all comes a bit too late for Morrissey who complains, "Roxy Music don't surprise me any more. They're still looking for something that they've always wanted but was never theirs."

MARCH
Morrissey returns to London in search of further UFOs. In an offhand note, he condemns rockabilly revivalists The Polecats, who have just reached the lower regions of the chart with a cover of David Bowie's 'John, I'm Only Dancing'. "If they really had any imagination they'd shoot themselves," Morrissey sneers. Fortunately, Boz Boorer fails to take such advice and will still be around a decade later to help Morrissey revitalize his solo career with *Your Arsenal*.

MAY
The Hoax release another 12-inch titled "Quiet In The Sixpennies" That same month they embark on an exciting, but ill-fated tour of Belgium. "There were problems there with the authorities in Antwerp", Steve Mardy recalls. "They were like pro neo-Nazi. Anybody who had a leather jacket on or had alternative clothes or hairstyles would be given a hard time. Gigs would be closed down and they'd say, 'Go home or we'll confiscate your passport'."

SPRING/SUMMER
Maher and Rourke continue the funk experiments but despite several auditions fail to find a suitable singer. At one session, Maher is actually arrested by the police on suspicion of receiving stolen goods and the rest of the group are interrogated. When not involved in such drama, Maher bides his time working at a clothes boutique during the day and guesting as a disc jockey by night with his friend Andrew Berry. For a brief period he even becomes a bassist and attends some rehearsals with Robin Allman and Paul Whittall in their short-lived group Thirty Years.

JUNE
The Hoax guest on another compilation *Ten From The Madhouse*. "It was set up by a bloke in Bury," Steve Mardy explains. "It featured 10 bands from the North West, mainly Manchester. We did a track and that was the last thing we ever recorded." That same month, the group appear at Manchester's UMIST after which they split up.

JAMES MAKER, "who lives it".

4 JULY
Morrissey witnesses Iggy Pop playing an Independence Day gig at the Manchester Apollo. Steven is not impressed and, two weeks later, uses the *Record Mirror* forum to express his distaste with the stinging: "This year Iggy models the jaded gigolo look, a style for which the voice must always be out of tune, it seems. The new Iggy is really into crowd participation and insists that every song ends with a running 'la-la-la'. One would imagine that the next step for him would be the Golden Garter or, better still, retirement."

11 JULY
Morrissey's small pamphlet on The New York Dolls, published by Babylon Books, receives a short belated review in *Record Mirror*. In an effusive acknowledgement, Morrissey praises his gay friend and clubbing compatriot James Maker, "who lives it".

SUMMER
Maher's record shop managing friend Pete Hope introduces him to Matt Johnson, who has recently put together the group The The. Johnny brings his guitar over to Hope's house and a jamming session ensues. "I took an instant liking to him," Matt recalls. "He seemed a genuine person. We had very similar influences and hit it off straightaway. There was a chemistry there. We were thinking about him joining the band – that's what the intention was, that's what we were going to do. He would have joined The The, but at that time it was a bit awkward because I was based in London and he was in Manchester and neither of us had a lot of money." It would be over seven years before Maher fulfilled Johnson's original plan and finally teamed up with The The.

AUGUST
Morrissey gets another chance to lionize Ludus in the pages of *Record Mirror* when the group support Depeche Mode at Rafters. The bard concludes jovially: "Linder was born singing and has more imagination than Depeche Mode could ever hope for."

WINTER
Mike Joyce teams up with Manchester based Northern Ireland group, Victim. The group have already recorded a couple of singles, and this is a streamlined, second generation outfit, featuring Joe Moody (vocals/guitar) and Wes Graham (bass). The group secure a brief residency at the Portland Bar in Piccadilly, Manchester.

MAHER MOVES INTO THE HOUSE OF TELEVISION presenter and author Shelley Rohde. As a result of this connection, Maher appears on a couple of television programmes, including *The Devil's Advocate* on which he proclaims his right to receive dole money.

DECEMBER
Steven settles down to a feast of television movies, including *Whatever Happened To Baby Jane*, *Autumn Leaves*, *Tiger Bay* and *Passport To Pimlico*. Manchester suddenly seems bereft of excitement, but he finds some consolation in a fleeting glimpse of the singer Nico, looking splendid in her black cape. His appreciation of the singer is later emphasized when he nominates *Chelsea Girl*, *Desertshore* and *The End* as his three favourite albums.

10 DECEMBER
Morrissey remains in a state of listlessness, listening to Noël Coward, George Formby, Sandie Shaw and Cilla Black. Even the elements are conspiring against him. "I hate snow; snow hates me," he complains. "I've spent the last hour shovelling the path. And I thought I'd be in Hollywood by now."

24 DECEMBER
A Christmas Eve of mixed blessings for Morrissey. His sister Jackie returns home from her sojourn in the USA, but Steven is recovering from a day in hospital, where he has suffered three painful injections during the removal of his "gangloin" (Steven no doubt meant ganglion – an abnormal collection of nerve fibres forming a cyst on a tendon). Although Jackie had secured a job in Colorado and enjoyed the adventure, she too elects to settle in Manchester.

'It was an event I'd always been looking forward to and been waiting for since my childhood.'

MORRISSEY

CHAPTER TWO

The Secret Origins Of The Smiths

THE FORMATION OF THE SMITHS is one of the enduring myths of Eighties pop music. Morrissey and Marr have each described their meeting in grandiloquent terms, carefully avoiding the intrusion of any prosaic details. For Marr, the quest for Morrissey is not a calculated campaign, but a wild moment of spontaneity, prompted by a viewing a documentary on the career of songwriters Leiber and Stoller. "Joe Moss gave me a video of a Leiber and Stoller interview where one of them said it had got to the point where he knew where the other guy was and they hadn't met and he thought, ... I'll just go over there, knock on his door and say, 'Let's get together and write songs'. It sounded very idealistic but it caught my imagination... so that's what I did."

Morrissey has reinforced the myth by speaking of their meeting in almost mystical terms. "It was an event I'd always been looking forward to and unconsciously been waiting for since my childhood," he explained. "Time was passing. I was 22 and Johnny was much younger, but it seemed I'd hung around for a very long time waiting for this magical, mystical event, which definitely occurred. I had a slight tremulous feeling a long time before then, that something very unusual would happen to me, and I interpreted it as fame of some magnitude." In his more melodramatic moments, Morrissey has even suggested that he might have ended his life if Marr had not appeared at his door. Caught in more modest mood, he confesses that the dream of performing was something that he had despaired of by early 1982. "It's very strange for me," Morrissey muses, "because I tried to do it for a very long time and during this period that he came I decided that I would no longer try. Then everything happened. It was very weird."

While the above accounts are essentially true, it's what each party chooses to omit that is interesting. The spontaneous Marr, for example, underplays the extent to which he investigated Morrissey's background in discussion with such Wythenshawe acolytes as Robin Allman and Stephen Pomfret. Morrissey also likes to embellish the tale of the meeting by picturing Johnny peering through his window and leaving a chocolate coated stain on the glass. Conveniently, both parties have consciously written Pomfret out of the script, for fear of spoiling the myth.

"The mythical meeting was a fable," Pomfret reveals, "and the chocolate stain on the window is bollocks". In an interview with me, Johnny admitted that he had to get Morrissey's address from Pommy, but neglected to add that, when he caught the 263 bus to 384 King's Road, he was not alone. Pomfret, in fact, accompanied him to Morrissey's house and provided a formal introduction. "Morrissey took an age to come down the stairs," Pomfret recalls. "I said, 'Hi! Steven. I'd like you to meet a friend of mine, Johnny'." After being invited upstairs to Morrissey's bedroom, Marr predictably took over the spiel. "I really expected Morrissey to say he wasn't interested at all," Pomfret explains. "But he said, 'Oh yes, Oh yes'." Not for the first time, Marr's enthusiasm and ability to sell himself proved a crucial asset. "Morrissey was as excited as he can get," Pomfret says.

JOYCE AND ROURKE hamming it up.

FLOWERS in pocket.

"I put him over to Johnny and they started to just talk. Leiber and Stoller, huh! They talked and talked and I just sat and looked through Steve's record collection. At that moment I knew I was out of it already. Absolutely, instantly, out of it."

Although Maher had been excitedly gabbling like a speed freak on the way over to Morrissey's house, Pomfret was struck by his near silence on the journey back. All he kept saying were the words, "This is the future". In the weeks that followed Pomfret noticed that his new friend was appearing less and less at his door. Maher already knew that Pomfret was not a strong enough musician to fulfil his new ambitions. "Johnny was right," Pomfret admits. "I didn't have it. There were some awfully talented musicians around and I was very ordinary. But Johnny never wanted another guitarist. If I'd been the greatest guitarist in the world, I wouldn't have been in the band."

What Morrissey and Marr actually wanted remained relatively open. "Morrissey and Johnny had a plan," Richard Boon reckons. "They had drive and ambition and knew where they wanted to be, even if they weren't clear on the details of how to get there. For a time, the duo considered working primarily as songwriters in the classic Leiber and Stoller tradition. Fortunately, their love of live performance and the realization that they could make a greater impact with a group set-up encouraged them to seek suitable backing musicians. The search was undertaken with fastidious care, although they carefully restricted themselves to word of mouth recommendations and sounded out friends rather than advertising.

Looking back over the first year of The Smiths, it is intriguing to see how dominant and influential Marr was in putting the pieces together. Cataloguing Marr's movements during this period you begin to realize the full extent of his contribution. First, he tracked down Pomfret, then saved Morrissey from bedroom oblivion, then secured studio time and even persuaded his friend Joe Moss to manage the group. The recruitment of Wolstencroft, Dale, Joyce and Rourke all came through Marr, while Morrissey's sole discovery was James Maker. Marr also nurtured the contacts by which The Smiths secured their first gig and did the initial hustling which won them a record deal with Rough Trade. In many of the early interviews, the voice of the newly-christened Marr took equal billing alongside his more loquacious counterpart. In almost every area then, Marr could claim to have created and developed the concept of The Smiths. Inevitably, as the months passed, the spotlight on Morrissey would intensify, but for the best part of a full year after their first gig, Marr could claim to be the real understated force in the group.

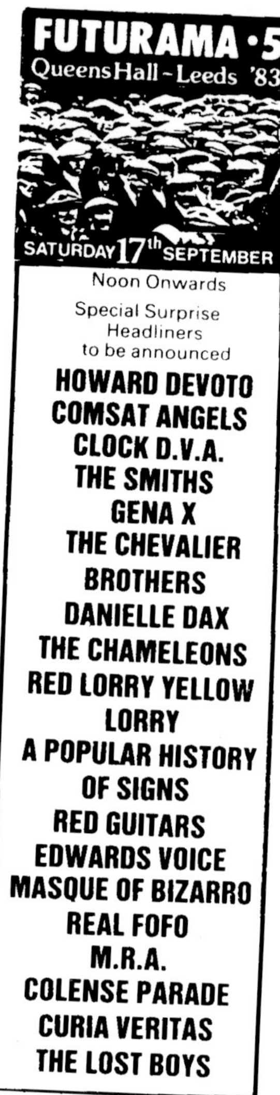

LEFT: An advertisement for the unreleased single 'Reel Around The Fountain'.

1982 - EARLY

The Freak Party have still not found a singer, even after rehearsing for over a year. "At that stage the singer had to look the part," their drummer stresses. "There wasn't a particular role model, but we didn't just want somebody with a good voice who didn't fit in with the clothes we wore." For Maher, the project has clearly gone stale and he decides it is time to move on from funk into other musical areas. Rourke disagrees and elects to remain with Wolstencroft for the present. Maher, meanwhile, falls in with Crazy Face boutique owner Joe Moss, who becomes his musical mentor. "For a young lad, he had a good knowledge of roots music and the blues, which I was into," Moss recalls. "From there we got talking and he came over and started playing. Before long, he was firing his problems at me!"

APRIL

Maher speaks with Rob Allman about his desire to form a new group. The White Dice founder mentions Morrissey, whom he had once seen rehearsing with The Tee-Shirts. Before leaving for London, Billy Duffy had told Allman that he ought to collaborate with Morrissey, so Rob now passes the same advice on to his younger colleague. Realizing Morrissey's legendary shyness from past experience, Allman advises Maher to find a sympathetic mediator. The perfect candidate appears to be Tee-Shirts founder Stephen Pomfret, who is one of the few people from Wythenshawe still in touch with the Stretford bard.

Employing a touch of cynical intrigue, Allman tells Maher that he should "use Pommy as a means of getting to Morrissey". Shortly afterwards, Pomfret is approached by Maher one evening outside a newsagent's. Initially, Maher suggests that both of them should approach Morrissey and consider forming a group. Johnny then strikes up a friendship of sorts with Pomfret, and they socialize and attend several gigs together. The subject of Morrissey is temporarily dropped from conversation, but Maher still harbours ideas of forming a new group.

MAY

The mythological meeting of Morrissey and Maher takes place at 384 King's Road. Although Pomfret is involved, his place in the scheme of things will soon be eroded as the songwriting duo take flight. Maher is entranced by the originality of Morrissey's lyrics and regularly appears at his house armed with lustrous melodies and unquenchable enthusiasm. "He gave me a whole series of songs," Maher explained, "batches of words, and just to see them on paper – I'd literally never seen anything like it." The sparkling effusion of Maher is enough to rouse Morrissey from his recent creative stupor and revitalize his moribund spirit. "He seemed terribly sure of what he wanted to do, which I liked," Morrissey explained. "He said, 'Let's do it and do it *now*'. So we did it."

JUNE

Morrissey, Maher and Pomfret undertake their first rehearsal. Three songs are attempted, 'The Hand That Rocks The Cradle', 'Don't Blow Your Own Horn' and a cover of The Cookies' 'I Want A Boy For My Birthday' (aka 'I Want A Boy'). The set list, written in Maher's hand, indicates that the chord sequence of 'The Hand That Rocks The Cradle' is based on

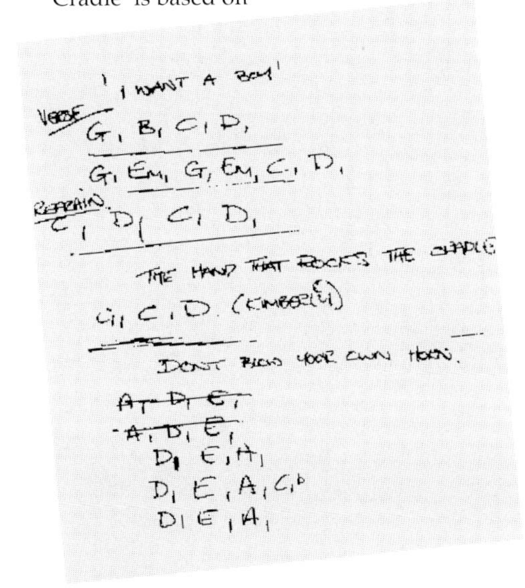

'I WANT A BOY'
VERSE
G, B, C, D,
G, EM, G, EM, C, D,
REFRAIN
C, D, C, D,
THE HAND THAT ROCKS THE CRADLE
G, C, D. (KIMBERLY)
DONT BLOW YOUR OWN HORN.
~~A, D, E,~~
~~A, D, E,~~
D, E, A,
D, E, A, C,
D, E, A,

Patti Smith's 'Kimberly'. Given the songwriting duo's mutual appreciation of *Horses*, the borrowing is apt. Although the initial rehearsal proves reasonably successful, it soon becomes clear that the songwriters are likely to be looking for stronger musicianship if their plans for a group are to be realized. Pomfret attends a handful of rehearsals, but soon realizes that his services are not required, so leaves the duo to their own devices. Johnny attempts to mollify his recent friend by suggesting the possibility of forming an offshoot R&B group but, not surprisingly, this unlikely idea is soon forgotten.

SUMMER

In the wake of Pomfret's departure, the duo briefly considers the possibility of adding a keyboardist and invite Maher's former White Dice colleague Paul Whittall to a rehearsal. The whim soon passes, however, and Morrissey/Maher return to their songwriting. "Our immediate goal was for there to be a single with a great song on the A-side," Johnny explains. "Whether it had our names on the label as the group was secondary. It was our names being in the brackets that was much more important. We were very much into the songwriting ethic."

Before long, Morrissey and Maher record some 8-track demos at Decibel Studios, employing the services of an engineer named Dale, who is invited to play bass. The rhythm section is completed by drummer Simon Wolstencroft and two tracks are cut: 'The Hand That Rocks The Cradle' and 'Suffer Little Children'. Maher attempts to persuade Wolstencroft to join the group on a permanent basis, but the drummer refuses to be drawn. Morrissey and Maher convince themselves that even if they find difficulty forming a group, they can work successfully as songwriters, using Joe Moss's workplace as a base.

SEPTEMBER

Local boy Gary Farrell is approached to fill the vacant drummer's stool. He recalls a meeting in which Morrissey produces some cardboard on which are inscribed the names Smithdom, Smiths Family and Smiths. Steven seems pleased that Farrell prefers the title Smiths. After taking away the Morrissey/Maher tape Farrell declines the opportunity to join the new venture. "I couldn't get anything out of it," Gary innocently pleads. The rejection seems sufficient to ensure that Morrissey never speaks to the lad again. "I think he felt I'd insulted him," Farrell concludes.

Soon after, Morrissey settles on The Smiths as the name for his new enterprise. "When

MIKE JOYCE, 1983.

we started, inflated and elongated names were the order of the day," he pointed out. "I wanted to explain to people that it wasn't necessary to have long names, dress in black and be pofaced. Our task was to choose the most ordinary of names and yet produce something of artistic merit." Although the title Smiths has certain connotations of Englishness and non-élitism, Morrissey stresses its vagueness. "It occurred to me that nobody could put any possible connotations on the name," he recalled, "and I really liked that because it came at a time when group names were monstrous and had a great deal to say. They were very long and were in themselves a lifestyle. I wanted to get rid of all that kind of rhetorical drivel and just say something incredibly basic. The Smiths sounded quite down to earth."

THROUGH VARIOUS CONTACTS, MAHER ATTEMPTS to put The Smiths on the map. A prestigious fashion gig is booked for the following month and publishing deals seem in the offing. In a strange twist of pop history, Wham! secure a recording deal with Innervision Records and Morrison/Leahy publishers, while the same parties decide to pass on The Smiths.

THE SEARCH FOR A DRUMMER ENDS WITH THE recruitment of Mike Joyce, who abandons his current venture, Victim, after being enthralled by the silver tongue of Maher. "The next day I saw Victim's equipment for sale down in A1 Music in Manchester, which was a bit of a blow," Joyce reflects. "The transition stage was difficult to start with, but I knew I was going to leave Victim and join The Smiths. I thought I'd be stupid not to... I didn't hear an audition tape of The Smiths. I just went down for the audition. At the time, I was having a bit of fun with the old experimentals. It was all a bit hazy. As far as I was concerned, I was meeting people. What I do remember is that I had some mushrooms before I went in for the audition, and I started playing. I was playing away and it started to come on. I was looking around at Morrissey and I saw this dark figure in a long overcoat, walking stealthily across the room. By the time we finished I was pretty out of it."

Maher is impressed as much by Joyce's brashness as his playing and has no doubts about confirming his recruitment. "He was tripping out of his head, which was quite weird," Johnny remembers. "I thought, 'Right, you're in. You've got balls'."

> **'He was tripping out of his head which was quite weird. I thought, "Right, you're in. You've got balls".'**
>
> **JOHNNY MARR** recalls Mike Joyce's audition

4 OCTOBER

The Smiths make their début at the Ritz, supporting Blue Rondo A La Turk. Realizing that The Smiths have only a handful of songs ready, Marr is determined to make an impression. "A lot of people had turned up just to see if we'd fall through the stage," he recalled. "I knew the Blue Rondo audience wouldn't give us much of a chance, so we went out there to be aggressive... I really had this attitude of 'I know you people just want to stand around the bar posing, but listen to this, you're not going to hear anything like it again'. We were really threatening. I think we had to be at that particular time."

Mike Joyce recalls a feeling of exhilaration and trepidation, reinforced by pop star rivalry and the lack of a proper soundcheck. "Blue Rondo were bastards to us," he remarks. "They were the 'in' group and we were the local support. We couldn't use any of their equipment."

The group's problems are not made any easier by the height of the microphone, which forces Morrissey to crouch unflatteringly. The audience's attention is further distracted by the surprise recruitment of James Maker as master of ceremonies and go-go dancer. Among the audience is New Hormones label boss and Buzzcocks manager Richard Boon, who remembers: "James was in stilettos, go-go dancing and banging a tambourine. He was dispensable. I thought it was spare parts, a nice joke, but it didn't add anything and they didn't need it." The involvement of Maker, however, ensures that The Smiths have another strong link with the gay community and enhances their all round appeal. As Joe Moss remembers: "Initially, Johnny thought it was something that could be really good, but wouldn't be totally commercial. It was something that would really get him going... he thought it would appeal to the gay crowd... he just knew it would get him known."

Set List: 'The Hand That Rocks The Cradle'; 'Suffer Little Children'; 'Handsome Devil'; 'I Want A Boy'.

DECEMBER

The Smiths assemble at Drone Studios for a recording session, financed by EMI. Despite the evident potential of the group, EMI is not impressed enough with the tapes to offer a deal. Ironically, the company will later sign both Steven and Johnny for post-Smiths recordings.

The Drone sessions also represent Andy Rourke's first involvement with the group. After he arrives at the studio, The Smiths' erstwhile bassist Dale is politely given his marching orders. Amazingly, Rourke admits he had no prior knowledge of The Smiths and had not even been invited to their first gig. "I hadn't heard anything, or seen the Ritz gig," he confirms. "I didn't have a clue what it would be like." Fortunately, the old musical rapport between Maher and Rourke is successfully resurrected and he is immediately inducted. The line-up of the group is now settled, although the terms under which Joyce and Rourke have been recruited will later create considerable acrimony.

1983 - 6 JANUARY

The Smiths perform their first headlining show at Manhattan Sound, Manchester. Manager Joe Moss secures the gig, which again features gay, go-go dancer James Maker. "James was there with a dinner suit, stilettos and maracas," Rourke recalls. "I was a bit embarrassed by it all. I think everyone was. But Morrissey wanted him in, so we said, 'OK'. The gig went well. It was weird. There wasn't a stage as such. We were on the dance floor and the audience were there in

ANDY ROURKE, 1983.

front of us... We did about eight songs. There were about 300 people there, which wasn't bad for my first gig."

Joyce voices similar enthusiasm. "The guys that worked there were hip for the trip," he recalls. "The thing I remember most was that we'd only done one gig, but we'd really tightened up so much. The idea of performing became such a natural thing... I was totally taken aback by it."

The appearance of Tony Wilson and Richard Boon in the audience provides renewed anticipation of a record contract. As the gig closes, in a shower of confetti, observers agree that there is something ineffably special about The Smiths, and Maher's ambition is duly noted.

FEBRUARY

Having paraded before the fashion élite at The Ritz in October, it is perhaps not surprising that the first national magazine to interview The Smiths should be the style-orientated *i-D*.

4 FEBRUARY

A much touted appearance at the Haçienda, Manchester, alongside funk group 52nd Street and disc jockey Marc Berry (Andrew Berry), proves The Smiths' most important gig to date. The club is festooned with flowers, a gesture which Morrissey denies was a mere gimmick. "The flowers actually have a significance," he later told *Melody Maker*. "When we first began there was a horrendous sterile cloud over the whole music scene in Manchester. Everybody was anti-human and it was so very cold. The flowers were a very human gesture. They integrated harmony with nature – something people seemed so terribly afraid of. It had got to the point in music where people were really afraid to show how they felt – to show their emotions. I thought that was a shame and very boring. The flowers offered hope".

Set list: 'These Things Take Time'; 'What Difference Does It Make?'; 'The Hand That Rocks The Cradle'; 'Handsome Devil'; 'Jeane'; 'What Do You See In Him?' (a blueprint for 'Wonderful Woman'); 'Hand In Glove'; 'Miserable Lie'.

21 FEBRUARY

Rafters, Manchester. A memorable gig for Morrissey and Marr, who are excited at the prospect of supporting that progenitor of punk, Richard Hell. Rourke seems more lackadaisical after the event. "Rafters with Richard Hell was quite good, but nothing spectacular," he remembers. At the end of the gig, Morrissey is approached by Babylon Books' supremo John Muir, who is clutching a bound copy of Steven's second booklet, *James Dean Is Not Dead*. By this stage, Morrissey is having second thoughts about the prospect of becoming a published author, particularly in view of the superficial work he has compiled. "We must loosely call it a book, it's nothing more than a rather thick pamphlet," he later admits. "It was done at a time when I was incredibly desperate. I was just lucky enough to be able to write about something I loved quite dearly – a person, at any rate – but it was really thrown together... It was a long time ago. Most other things from the past don't seem to embarrass me, I don't know why, but that does." Muir is still hopeful about publishing a third Morrissey tome in his possession. *Exit Smiling*, a potted directory of minor film stars, is a more interesting project that will never see print.

Having played Tony Wilson's club, the Haçienda and appeared at Rafters, where Joy Division had made their début appearance, it is widely assumed in Manchester that The Smiths will sign to Factory Records. Wilson, however, plays Pontius Pilate and passes the group's demo tape to New Order manager Rob Gretton. "The tape's shit," Gretton retorts, despite his belief in The Smiths. While Factory spurn The Smiths, Morrissey will soon retaliate with some mild castigation of his own. "Factory aren't really interested in new groups," he points out. "Factory have been good, but they now belong to a time that is past. Look, we had a great social life, Factory has been great, but let's leave all that behind us now."

LATE FEBRUARY

Craig Gannon joins Aztec Camera as rhythm guitarist, having written a letter to Roddy Frame asking for an audition. "He was only 16," recalls the group's manager Bob Johnson. "The first album was finished and out and if we were to tour we needed another guitarist, so we took him on...." Following the audition, along with nearly 60 other hopefuls, Craig's father is amazed to learn that his son has routed the competition and been given the job. "Is he really that good?", he asks Roddy Frame. "Yes", replies the Aztec Camera creator, emphatically. Although Craig insists that the post offered was permanent as far as he was concerned, his time in the group will prove very brief.

MARCH

Manager Joe Moss finances the recording of The Smiths' début single, 'Hand In Glove'. Morrissey vividly recalls the night he wrote the song. "I was in my room, alone with a cassette recorder with a guitar tune on it and I was surrounded by lots of words, and I just sat there for two hours and threw the whole thing together... It was to be our first record and it was important to me that there was something searingly poetic in it, in a lyrical sense, and yet jubilant at the same time." The projected flip side of the single is a live version of 'Handsome Devil', taken from their recent Haçienda gig.

23 MARCH

The Smiths' London début takes place at Covent Garden's Rock Garden. The Smiths are advertised as a "five-piece", but James

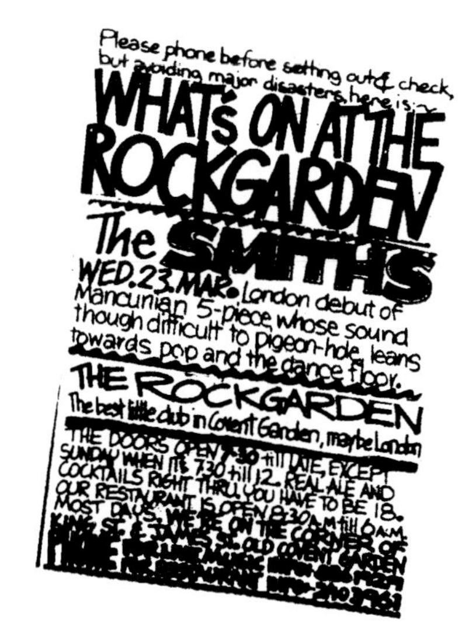

Maker is by now a part of their hidden history. "I didn't have any designs on being involved in the music business then," Maker insists. "It was just helping out a friend." With a strong contingent of friends and supporters making the trip from Manchester, the gig goes well but is undocumented in the music press. It will be several months more before the capital sees its first outbreak of Smiths gig hysteria.

APRIL

Rough Trade Records supremo Geoff Travis is accosted by the persuasive Johnny Maher and encouraged to listen to the tape of 'Hand In Glove'. After playing the cassette over the weekend, Travis agrees to release the single: "I didn't think this was going to be one of the

GEOFF TRAVIS, Rough Trade supremo.

IN THE Smiths' office on the eve of the release of 'Hand In Glove.'

most important groups there's ever been," he recalls, "but I thought it was a great record."

MAY

'Hand In Glove' is released, but fails to reach the Top 40. Morrissey, nevertheless, modestly calls it "the most important song in the world". The sleeve of the single features the work of Seventies gay porn photographer Jim French. Several months later, Morrissey enthuses to the gay publication *Him*: "I adore the picture, it blends with the record and it evokes both sorrow and passion. It could be taken as a blunt, underhand statement against sexism, yet in using that picture I am being sexist. It's time the male body was exploited. Men need a better sense of their own bodies. Naked males should be splashed around the Co-op. I'm sure this would go a long way to alleviate a great many problems, even that of rape."

6 MAY

University of London Union. This support gig to The Sisters Of Mercy serves as a gathering of the tribes for several key personnel in The Smiths' story. It is here that caretaker manager and record plugger Scott Piering first meets the group. Also in the audience is sound engineer Grant Showbiz. "It was amazing," he recalls. "There were 20 people in the room who were all going berserk. I don't think there were many people there who weren't in the business." The enthusiastic Grant is

GRANT SHOWBIZ, sound engineer.

recruited to the camp after proclaiming The Smiths, "the punk Hollies". The BBC is also present in the form of producer John Walters, who immediately books the group for a John Peel session. Early acolyte Dave McCullough is on hand to describe the music, and it is interesting to see the unusual and wide-ranging frame of reference he uses in seeking to place the group. "The singer is totally mad," he opines. "On the first number, he hits students over the crust with dead daffodils and goes on to wave the things around in some mystical respect for the cover of *Power, Corruption And Lies* (New Order)... The music? Smiths are kind of Feelgood meets Second Daylight Magazine: their stage arrogance is clearly Fall related, their whiplashing guitar moments Nightingales endowed. But their songs meander and climax as only Smiths Crisps songs could. The guitar man is obviously Costello obsessed, and this adds a polish to the arranging that sets Smiths up as something special and possibly very singular indeed. Their usual last song, 'Miserable Lie', is in the classic mould of 'Freebird' or 'Whole Lotta Love'. It starts slowly, the singer telling how he's just murdered another female then all hell breaks loose, his voice suddenly rising from Devoto deadpan to unheard of heights of Robert Plant squealing... 'Miserable Lie' will one day wow them in the Hammersmith Odeon."

14 MAY

The Smiths enjoy their first *NME* interview, which is undertaken by Cath Carroll, an old friend of Morrissey's, who would later record as a solo artiste for Factory. While discussing the importance of independent record labels, Morrissey unintentionally predicts his own future with the ironic line: "Being on EMI doesn't constitute any degree of power over the public."

During the same week as the *NME* interview, rival music paper *Sounds* publishes a review of the University of London Union gig in which reviewer Dave McCullough praises Morrissey's lyrics, but in doing so makes some unfortunate errors in transcription. "Most of his word-packed lyrics are about child molesting, and more mature sexual experimentation," he argues. "He hates women with a vengeance, but is still the intellectual... The refrain 'Climb Upon My Knee, Sonny Boy' in another song is used as a child-molesting come on to a seven-year-old in a park. This kind of ultra-violent, ultra-funny grime is just what is needed to pull rock 'n' roll out of its current sloth."

18 MAY

The Smiths enter the BBC Studios to cut four tracks ('What Difference Does It Make?'; 'Miserable Lie'; 'Reel Around The Fountain'; 'Handsome Devil') with producer Roger Pusey.

21 MAY

The Smiths join forces with The Fall for the first time at the Electric Ballroom, London. Mark E. Smith's group effortlessly headline, but the billing positions will soon be reversed as Morrissey and Marr's group draw the attention of the London music media. "When The Smiths were successful that immediately alienated Mark E Smith," remarks Rough Trade's founder Geoff Travis. "I don't think Mark was thrilled to see these upstarts pass him by and I can understand why he felt like that. But it's not that straightforward either. At the same time that there was jealousy, there was also a great deal of pride that Manchester was doing something."

Set List: 'You've Got Everything Now'; 'Accept Yourself'; 'What Difference Does It Make?'; 'Reel Around The Fountain'; 'These Things Take Time'; 'I Don't Owe You Anything'; 'Hand In Glove'; 'The Hand That Rocks The Cradle'; 'Handsome Devil'; 'Miserable Lie'.

31 MAY

The BBC recordings are broadcast on the John Peel Show and receive a rapturous response, prompting various repeats. The tracks are subsequently collated on the compilations *Hatful Of Hollow* and *The Peel Sessions*.

MAY

Despite evident progress, the line-up of the group is momentarily placed in jeopardy. Mike Joyce's playing comes under scrutiny and there is talk of appointing a new member. Simon Wolstencroft receives a phone call from Rourke and is told: "We'd like you back in the group." Joyce's problems are compounded following an ill-advised attempt to improve his style through traditional drum tuition. Wolstencroft, meanwhile, moves his drumkit into the Crazy Face rehearsal rooms. "When Mike found out that Si's drumkit was in there he really started panicking," Rourke recalls. "There was some pressure put on him to get his act together, which he did. I was asked to make that phone call. But it was never a definite thing." Marr only vaguely remembers the incident, which he maintains was never that serious: "Mike was in and that was it. Then he got to be good... I didn't get Mike into the group lightly. I've never got anyone in any group lightly. He really had to cut it."

2 JUNE

The Smiths set out for one of their least memorable and most frightening gigs, playing at a miners' gala in Cannock Chase. "We arrived there with an entourage and when we stepped into pubs the jukeboxes stopped," recalls Mike Joyce. "They thought we were a bunch of weirdos." Morrissey's fey persona inflames macho passions to such a degree that the performance ends with a small shower of thrown bottles and a police escort.

3 JUNE

The Fighting Cocks, Birmingham, achieves a small note in pop history by being the first venue to woo The Smiths to the city. "That was upstairs at a pub," Rourke recalls, "a terrible gig."

Set List: 'You've Got Everything Now'; 'Handsome Devil'; 'Accept Yourself'; 'What Difference Does It Make?'; 'Reel Around The Fountain'; 'Wonderful Woman'; 'These Things Take Time'; 'I Don't Owe You Anything'; 'Hand In Glove'; 'Miserable Lie'.

4 JUNE

The Smiths return to London for a show at the Brixton Ace, where they are sandwiched between Assaulto Decento and The Decorators. For Grant Showbiz, the Brixton date was his first experience of seeing The Smiths backstage and he fondly remembers the exceptional camaraderie and banter that characterized their happy-go-lucky approach. "They were such a close-knit bunch," he reflects. "Ollie May was the best mate and seemed fraught because he had to be the 'responsible' person before I came along. There was no demarcation between them... they were all in the same room chatting away. They had these in-words and phrases and I wasn't entirely sure what they were talking about. I was very impressed by this. I'd known Mancunian slang before, but this was different. There were little things about them that were different. Johnny had this little rip on the bottom of his jeans, which was something I hadn't seen before. He was like a stick insect, and had shades on. It was like watching The Monkees or The Beatles at a press conference. They were witty and all bounced off each other." The image of "four lads against the world" is fostered here.

MARK E. SMITH had mixed feelings about his rivals.

THE GROUP pictured on their office security camera, May 1983.

Set List: 'You've Got Everything Now'; 'Handsome Devil'; 'Accept Yourself'; 'Reel Around The Fountain'; 'These Things Take Time'; 'Miserable Lie'.

SOUNDS SCRIBE DAVE MCCULLOUGH RETURNS TO the paedophilia theme during an interview in which he notes: "The subject of child molesting crops up more than a few times in Smiths' songs. They are hilarious lyrics, more so because they will suddenly touch on the personal." Although Morrissey bristles at this suggestion during the interview ("We do not condone child molesting. We have never molested a child"), this is assumed to be cautious public relations. "Child molestation claims they will reject out of hand," McCullough casually notes. "This is all part of The Smiths' plan. Gonna be huge."

MORRISSEY at the Brixton Ace, 29 June 1983.

26 JUNE

A second Smiths BBC session is produced by Dale Griffin for the David Jensen Show. Four tracks are recorded: 'Hand In Glove', 'These Things Take Time', 'You've Got Everything Now' and 'Wonderful Woman'.

LATE SPRING

After some prevarication, The Smiths decide to sign to Rough Trade Records. The independent label offers the biggest advance in its short history, but the figure is a mere fraction of what the group could have commanded from a major label. Label founder Geoff Travis is clearly overjoyed by their decision. He informs the press: "The confidence that The Smiths have shown by signing with us will help to reverse the trend of bands defecting to majors for money at the expense of their long term career and artistic development." The distinct advantages for Morrissey and Marr are greater artistic control and a profit-sharing agreement by which the record company agree to pay half of all recording expenses. Morrissey expresses his philosophy in a nutshell: "It's curious, but once you get your foot in the door, you realize that there is a tremendous amount of money there to be had, and you realize that it's more likely to be picked up by someone who certainly doesn't deserve it." Two such undeserving cases are apparently Joyce and Rourke, whose signatures are conspicuously absent from the Rough Trade contract. "I felt we were all signed to Rough Trade," Joyce innocently remarks. "It didn't bother me until later when I realized what that entailed. Then, it frightened the life out of me." Rourke also voices disillusionment with the set-up. "We were all led to believe it was a group," he laments. "If they'd said, 'You're the backing or session players', then maybe we'd have thought twice about it." By now, however, it seems too late. In case there was any doubt about the matter, the contracts confirm that Morrissey and Marr *are* The Smiths.

> **'It's time the male body was exploited. Men need a better sense of their own bodies. Naked males should be splashed around the Co-op.'**
>
> MORRISSEY

29 JUNE

The Smiths return to the Brixton Ace for the second occasion in a month, this time supporting The Sisters Of Mercy. It is at this gig that manager Joe Moss finds himself considering his future with the group. Although his relationship with Morrissey is still cordial, there will be a growing rift between the two due to Moss's close friendship with Johnny Marr.

Set List: 'You've Got Everything Now'; 'Handsome Devil'; 'Reel Around The Fountain'; 'What Difference Does It Make?'; 'Wonderful Woman'; 'These Things Take Time'; 'Hand In Glove'; 'I Don't Owe You Anything'.

30 JUNE

Pre-empting their elevation to the college circuit, The Smiths play an end of term bash at Warwick University, Coventry, in a multimedia event that also features Aztec Camera. Muff Winwood, CBS Records' A&R head and former Spencer Davis Group bassist, appears backstage on a scouting mission, only to learn that The Smiths have already signed to Rough Trade. "I trusted Morrissey's instincts on that one," Marr stresses. "I knew that he'd thought about it long and hard. It was almost like he was just waiting for the group to form... Signing to Rough Trade was part of an overall philosophy Morrissey had: especially financially. The 50:50 deal was important. It was. But what was more important was the Rough Trade aesthetic."

SUMMER

Morrissey and Marr consider a publishing deal with the Zomba group, but eventually sign to Warner Brothers Music. Warners also acquire a distribution deal for the group's product in the American market which, by the end of the year, sees The Smiths signed to Sire Records. "It sounds a bit brutal to say that it's just a distribution deal," Morrissey notes, "but I suppose, at the end of the day, that's what it amounts to. They seemed quite fairly agreeable, the people at Sire. We haven't had enormous contact but everything seems quite suitable and the money they offer is high... It seems quite agreeable on most levels, so I'm pleased."

1 JULY

The Midnight Express Club in the seaside resort of Bournemouth plays host to The Smiths. Despite its remoteness from the Manchester/London axis, the gig is reasonably well attended and the performance is well received. With manager Joe Moss accompanying the small road crew, the mood backstage is very friendly and relaxed, and there are few signs of any pressure or bossiness. "When Morrissey and Johnny decided to do something like go and eat and do the gig, that's when it happened," recalls Grant Showbiz. "I'm an organizer and felt there was a real vacuum that I could step into. Like telling Ollie May to tune the guitars and pack up the amp. Joe didn't have that – he was very much a personal manager, not walking around like a stormtrooper, standing on your right shoulder all the time. It was amazing to be given that much freedom in some respects."

Set List: 'You've Got Everything Now'; 'Handsome Devil'; 'Reel Around The Fountain'; 'What Difference Does It Make?'; 'Wonderful Woman'; 'These Things Take Time'; 'Hand In Glove'; 'I Don't Owe You Anything'; 'Miserable Lie'; 'Accept Yourself'.

4 JULY

Craig Gannon journeys to America with Aztec Camera for an Independence Day show at the New Music Seminar. The group stay on for a number of shows and return later that summer, supporting Elvis Costello.

THE DAVID JENSEN SESSIONS ARE BROADCAST ON Radio 1 and Morrissey gives his first interview on national radio. "Normally they don't usually give the same band sessions on the two shows," Scott Piering points out. "But Smiths fever was on. It wasn't just smouldering, it was aflame...Within weeks of finishing the Peel show, we were given another." Prior to the Jensen appearance, Morrissey despatches several postcards to friends alerting them to his radio début.

6 JULY

The Smiths return to the Haçienda, Manchester, as bill toppers. Tony Wilson is already stoical about having failed to sign the group to Factory, while Morrissey offers an olive branch in interviews. "We've had a great deal of personal support from the people at the Haçienda," he observes diplomatically. "They could easily have ignored us for signing with Rough Trade in London rather than Factory in Manchester, and that's good because that means attitudes are at last changing."

Set List: 'You've Got Everything Now'; 'Handsome Devil'; 'Reel Around The Fountain'; 'What Difference Does It Make?'; 'Wonderful Woman'; 'These Things Take Time'; 'Hand In Glove'; 'I Don't Owe You Anything'; 'Miserable Lie'; 'Accept Yourself'.

7 JULY

"Pass out if you want to," Morrissey purrs as The Smiths complete a triumphant return to London with a sell-out gig at the Rock Garden. Their recent BBC sessions encourage an enthusiastic response, which is rewarded by two encores. Rourke reflects on this sudden upsurge of fame: "Afterwards, a Japanese and an American journalist came back to interview us. That was the first time people really started showing an interest in us from a journalistic point of view. It was really an exciting time around then, and we were getting really good." Morrissey, meanwhile, retires to his hotel room to catch up on his correspondence. He confirms that the recent Rough Trade signing will cover four albums, expiring in 1986.

Set List: 'You've Got Everything Now'; 'Handsome Devil'; 'Reel Around The Fountain'; 'What Difference Does It Make?'; 'Wonderful Woman'; 'These Things Take Time'; 'Hand In Glove'; 'I Don't Owe You Anything'; 'Miserable Lie'; 'Accept Yourself'; 'Hand In Glove'.

24 JULY

The Smiths are billed to appear at the Hammersmith Palais supporting Roman Holliday and Altered Images. At the last moment, however, they are dropped from the bill, allegedly at the request of Altered Images. This was Morrissey's first exposure to power group politics, at which he later proved himself to be a master.

JULY/AUGUST

While London is engulfed by a heat wave, The Smiths are busily at work in an underground studio in Wapping recording material for their début album with Troy Tate. Despite weeks of work, however, the sessions will be terminated as fears mount that the product is not good enough. "Basically, we weren't enjoying it, and that came out in the final recording," Rourke recalls. "We just sounded like we were going through the motions. It just sounded like a demo. It didn't sound good enough for a début LP. We weren't happy with it and the record company weren't. But Troy was a really nice guy and it was a difficult decision to make. Troy was devastated. I think it was his first go at producing. He really did take it badly, and we felt badly about it but, obviously, we had to look out for ourselves. We couldn't bring out a substandard first LP. It had to be good." Despite Tate's obvious disenchantment with the decision to scrap his work, Marr is quick to stress that there was no personality clash. "We didn't fall out with Troy," he insists. "We were just really sorry to hurt his feelings. It was a professional decision and he obviously took it badly. He'd got himself wrapped up in it, and understandably so."

TROY TATE, ill-fated first producer.

Troy Tate Demo Tape: 'The Hand That Rocks The Cradle'; 'You've Got Everything Now'; 'These Things Take Time'; 'What Difference Does It Make?'; 'Hand In Glove'; 'Handsome Devil'; 'Accept Yourself'; 'I Don't Owe You Anything'; 'Reel Around The Fountain'; 'Miserable Lie'; 'Wonderful Woman'; 'Suffer Little Children'; ' Pretty Girls Make Graves'.

7 AUGUST

The Smiths are greeted by a more mute response at the Lyceum, London, despite providing a strong set. "If you bought this record, why don't you buy it again?" Morrissey suggests as he launches into 'Hand In Glove'. The optimistic promotion seems likely to fall on deaf ears as audience response is muted. The Smiths placing on a bill beneath Howard Devoto and industrial ensemble SPK indicates that they still need to prove their worth to concert promoters. The music press also has some Doubting Thomases. *Melody Maker*'s Adam Sweeting gives a cool reception to all three acts and admits that the lure of the bar outweighed Morrissey's appeal. "The Smiths were in flight when I arrived," he observed, "warbling into the gloom as though the indifferent crowd somehow *owed* them something. Thrumming and strumming like The Farmers Boys, with cow dung spilling into their waders. The Smiths remained obstinately and depressingly earthbound. I headed for the sorum [sic] of the bar."

Set List: 'You've Got Everything Now'; 'Handsome Devil'; 'What Difference Does It Make?'; 'Reel Around The Fountain'; 'These Things Take Time'; 'I Don't Owe You Anything'; 'Hand In Glove'; 'Miserable Lie'.

9 AUGUST
Two days after the Lyceum, The Smiths are headlining again at Dingwalls in Camden. "Dingwalls was a good one," Rourke recalls. "That was when we first realized we had a strong following of Smithsmaniacs. It was boiling hot and we were flying high. There was a lot of press at the gig. It sold out and there were queues outside. After we came offstage Mike started hyperventilating because it was so hot and the dressing room was just like a little toilet. He couldn't breathe for half-an-hour. That's one thing that still sticks in my mind."

Set List: 'You've Got Everything Now'; 'What Difference Does It Make?'; 'Handsome Devil'; 'Wonderful Woman'; 'Reel Around The Fountain'; 'These Things Take Time'; 'I Don't Owe You Anything'; 'Hand In Glove'; 'Miserable Lie'; 'Accept Yourself'; 'Hand In Glove'; 'Handsome Devil'.

11 AUGUST
The Smiths discover a more wary and discriminating audience awaiting them at the Warehouse, Leeds, where the patrons are allowed to drink until two in the morning. There is time to reflect on the offer of a tour supporting The Police, a group that Morrissey lambasted during his reviewing days in the late Seventies. Not surprisingly, the singer takes perverse pleasure in rejecting the support slot and later looks back with pride on that decision. "We just didn't want to be associated with them," he confirmed, "which sounds quite brutal but we'd come a long way, nobody had helped, and we didn't want anyone like The Police to feel they had a helping hand in helping us."

Set List: 'You've Got Everything Now'; 'What Difference Does It Make?'; 'Handsome Devil'; 'Wonderful Woman'; 'Reel Around The Fountain'; 'These Things Take Time'; 'I Don't Owe You Anything'; 'Hand In Glove'; 'Miserable Lie'; 'Accept Yourself'; 'Hand In Glove'.

12/13 AUGUST
The Smiths play Dingwalls venues in Hull and Newcastle, eager to spread their reputation through touring. "A lot of the time we used to travel back in the Reno van," Rourke remembers. "We had a mattress in the back and we all used to get our heads down and drive back after the gig. The money we were getting didn't really justify staying in hotels."

19 AUGUST
After nearly a week off, The Smiths are back on the road, this time travelling to East Anglia for a stint at the Gala Ballroom, Norwich. Morrissey, as promotion conscious as ever, continues to sing 'Hand In Glove' twice. Although The Smiths' version of the single will never be a hit, Morrissey calls it "the most special song we've ever done". Not entirely resigned to its failure, he adds: "I still hope it will go further and become somewhat of an anthem, at least in this country. Everywhere, in fact."

Set List: 'You've Got Everything Now'; 'What Difference Does It Make?'; 'Handsome Devil'; 'Wonderful Woman'; 'Reel Around The Fountain'; 'These Things Take Time'; 'I Don't Owe You Anything'; 'Hand In Glove'; 'Miserable Lie'; 'Accept Yourself'; 'Hand In Glove'; 'Handsome Devil'.

25 AUGUST
John Porter, newly appointed producer of The Smiths, works with them at another BBC session for The David Jensen Show. Four songs are recorded: 'Accept Yourself', 'I Don't Owe You Anything', 'Pretty Girls Make Graves' and 'Reel Around The Fountain'.

THE SUN, VIA *SOUNDS'* GARY BUSHELL, REVIVES McCullough's "child molestation" observations for its own sensationalist purposes. In an article headed: "Child Sex Song Puts The Beeb In A Spin", the newspaper alleges: "The Manchester band's controversial song is titled 'Handsome Devil'. It contains clear references to picking up kids for sexual kicks." The strange allegation about "picking up a seven year old in a park" is also thrown in for good measure, despite its evident inaccuracy. Overnight, The Smiths find themselves thrust into the spotlight for all the wrong reasons and Morrissey tastes his first slice of national notoriety. The BBC do indeed ban a song, although contrary to the tabloid newspaper reports, it is 'Reel Around The Fountain' which causes offence. In the wake of the controversy Rough Trade threatens legal action against *The Sun*, even though they have no intention of pursuing the matter to court. The unfortunate matter ultimately ends to The Smiths' advantage when they are offered another BBC John Peel session by the crusading John Walters.

30 AUGUST
Dingwalls, London beckons once more for a memorable performance that ends with a stage invasion during which Morrissey is relieved of his microphone. Among the stage revellers is Gordon Charlton, an A&R scout who had once hoped to persuade CBS to sign the group. Mike Joyce also has fond memories of this gig. "I remember when we were doing 'I Don't Owe You Anything' at Dingwalls. I was nearly reduced to tears. It was so powerful."

Set List: 'You've Got Everything Now'; 'What Difference Does It Make?'; 'Wonderful Woman'; 'Pretty Girls Make Graves'; 'Handsome Devil'; 'Reel Around The Fountain'; 'Miserable Lie'; 'These Things Take Time'; 'I Don't Owe You Anything'; 'Hand In Glove'; 'Accept Yourself'; 'Hand In Glove'; 'Handsome Devil'.

3 SEPTEMBER
The Smiths commence their autumn college tour with a low key gig at Woods Centre, Colchester, Essex. That same day *Melody Maker* run an interview with Morrissey, fresh from completing the Troy Tate sessions. With wine glass in hand and quips at the ready, the singer clearly makes a strong impression on interviewer Frank Worrall. The introduction describes Morrissey in amusingly melodramatic fashion: "He displays the sort of impassioned conviction you expect from a man out to avenge the murder of a close relative. His eyes glint dangerously at the merest hint of a put-down of his music, his voice or his band. He stresses that he knows what he wants, how he's going to get it and that nothing is going to stand in his way. Morrissey, the public face of The Smiths, is, as you might have guessed, a shock to the system."

Morrissey lives up to the powerful prologue by providing some characteristically intense answers, most notably when quizzed on the importance of pop music. "It's a matter of life and death to me," he announces. "Music affects everybody and I really think it does change the world!"

14 SEPTEMBER
Roger Pusey takes the controls for the second BBC Radio 1 John Peel Session. Four tracks are recorded: 'This Charming Man', 'Back To The Old House', 'This Night Has Opened My Eyes' and 'Still Ill'. Marr is enthusiastic about the session and predictably flattering about his colleague's songwriting. "His lyrics are really sad and emotional," he recalls. "I think so many of the songs reflect his personality. I mean, you listen to a song like 'Still Ill' and the title alone sums up Morrissey."

Ironically, thanks partly to BBC politics and *Sounds'* misreading of lyrics, The Smiths are more visible than ever on evening national radio. "The Smiths were so hot at this time that they were really on a roll and they even repeated the sessions a lot earlier than they should have done," Scott Piering explained. "So we had Peel repeating the first session, David Jensen repeating their sessions; we had Peel's new sessions and, not long afterwards, Mike Hawkes gave us another session. This all happened in the space of a few months, so there was lots of air time on the prime evening shows with The Smiths' fan base."

15 SEPTEMBER
After an overnight stay in London, the group play a Rough Trade showcase at the Venue in Victoria. The Go-Betweens and Felt (or Fault as they're referred to in the Venue's trade advertisement!) complete the bill. Tequila Sunrises are liberally downed but the *NME*'s ever perceptive Barney Hoskyns is on hand with a fulsome account, marred only by an

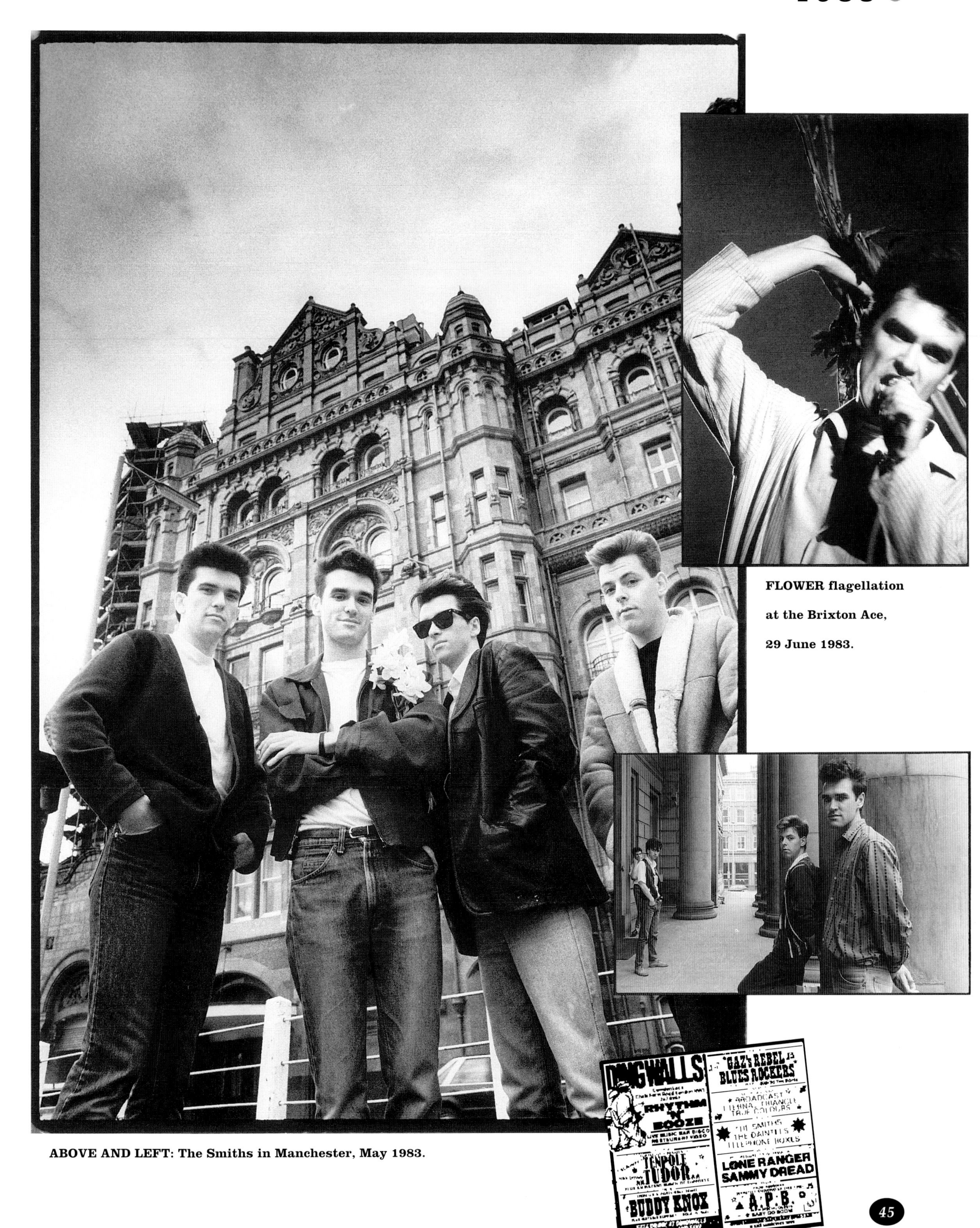

FLOWER flagellation at the Brixton Ace, 29 June 1983.

ABOVE AND LEFT: The Smiths in Manchester, May 1983.

over fondness for 'Hand In Glove'. "The Smiths are saucy," he announces. "Morrissey may just be another fruitcake in the line of Harley, Cope, Rowland, but 'Hand In Glove' is one of the year's few masterpieces, a thing of beauty and a joy forever. To say that all other Smiths' songs are grafted from this splendid stalk only testifies to its perfection. Jeans hanging off his ass, beads round his neck, Morrissey brandishes his flowers like a new sign of Gabba Gabba Hey... He's compulsively watchable, compulsively listenable too. If first impressions are ones of provincial punk-folk, there's a wavering sadness in this monkish maverick's larynx which calls to mind a Tim Buckley or the great folk purists. Every song is put to an idealized 'you', a genderless receptacle of love... These loose, crisp songs, fired by the alternately churning and sparkling Rickenbacker of Johnny Marr, are injected with the ascetic lust of Genet."

Set List: 'Handsome Devil'; 'You've Got Everything Now'; 'These Things Take Time'; 'This Charming Man'; 'Reel Around The Fountain'; 'Miserable Lie'; 'Still Ill'; 'I Don't Owe You Anything'; 'What Difference Does It Make?'; 'Accept Yourself'; 'Hand In Glove'; 'Handsome Devil'.

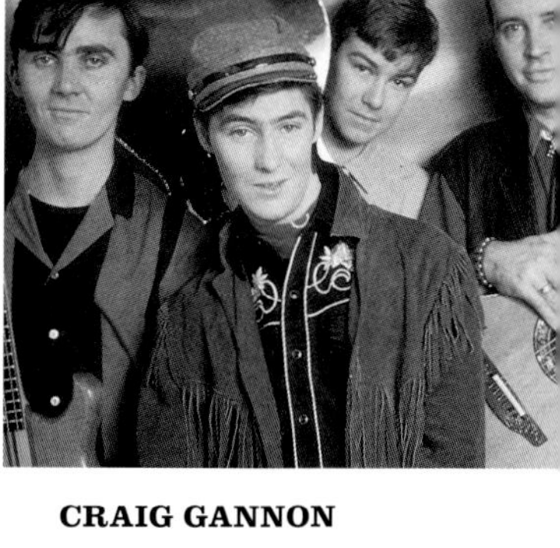

CRAIG GANNON

in Aztec Camera, 1983.

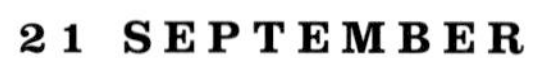

ABOVE AND LEFT: In full flow, September 1983.

16 SEPTEMBER

Bathos beckons at the Moles Club, Bath, but after their busy time in London, The Smiths needed a break from all the intensity. Although they are scheduled to appear at Manchester's September In The Pink Festival, Morrissey is already beginning to distance himself from the gay movement in the wake of the *Sun* child sex scandal. "Yes, the gay connotations could well be harmful when it comes to dealing with the press," he admits. "I simply can't get down to gender. I don't mind who listens. I wouldn't want to be thought of as a gay spokesman though, because it's just not true."

17 SEPTEMBER

Morrissey is featured in a phone interview on London's LBC Radio.

21 SEPTEMBER

The Peel Sessions, recorded on 14 September, are broadcast on Radio 1.

24 SEPTEMBER

Gigs pencilled in for Leeds and Bristol are jettisoned, but The Smiths prepare for another London gig with an appearance at Brighton's Escape Club. Meanwhile, one month after the child molesting controversy, Morrissey is still in the news pages of the music press defending his lyrics. "I can't understand why anybody should write such a thing about us," he announces, seemingly oblivious to the evident ambiguity in his lyrics. "We must stress that 'Handsome Devil' is aimed entirely towards adults and has nothing to do with children and certainly nothing to do with child molesting. It's an adult understanding of quite intimate matters." The controversy underlines the power of the press and teaches Morrissey a valuable lesson. "It really proves that you don't have as much control over your destiny in this business as you think you do."

25 SEPTEMBER

Still awaiting a headlining gig at the London Lyceum Ballroom, The Smiths are this time placed beneath the politically-minded Gang Of Four. Although Morrissey has yet to make any major inflammatory political statements, it is

clearly only a matter of time before he warms to the task. "You have to be interested in politics these days, if you're not a completely lost individual," he notes. "Whereas years ago, politics seemed to be this thing that was secluded for a minority of intellectuals, these days you can't get away with that argument..."

Set List: 'Pretty Girls Make Graves'; 'Wonderful Woman'; 'Miserable Lie'; 'Reel Around The Fountain'; 'I Don't Owe You Anything'; 'Hand In Glove'; 'What Difference Does It Make?'; 'These Things Take Time'; 'Hand In Glove'.

29/30 SEPTEMBER

A Thursday evening appearance at the Gum Club in Blackburn is followed by a Friday night Fresher's Ball at the University of Birmingham. Meanwhile, plans are afoot to release 'Reel Around The Fountain' as The Smiths' next single. "We were going to release the session version, because we thought it was pretty good," Scott Piering recalls. "In retrospect, it doesn't sound so good, but I still have white labels of the seven-inch." Although the single is briefly advertised in the music press, there is still some doubt whether its controversial nature might again backfire on the group. Eventually, the release is scrapped when a more commercial song emerges from the group's recording sessions with their new producer John Porter. Audiences are given a preview of the next single, which will be 'This Charming Man'.

Set List: 'You've Got Everything Now'; 'This Charming Man'; 'Handsome Devil'; 'Still Ill'; 'Reel Around The Fountain'; 'Pretty Girls Make Graves'; 'Miserable Lie'; 'I Don't Owe You Anything'; 'Hand In Glove'; 'What Difference Does It Make?'; 'These Things Take Time'; 'Hand In Glove'; 'Accept Yourself'.

5 OCTOBER

One day after the anniversary of their first gig, The Smiths appear on the bill for the ICA's Rock Week in London. Appropriately, their old champion and paedophilia hunter Dave McCullough is there to pen a review, which is a partisan mixture of passion and hyperbole. "By the way, The Smiths are becoming massive," he announces. "I can tell you that The Smiths at the abysmal ICA made me, for the first time in about five years of rock writing, think in terms of phrases like 'the new Beatles' and 'bigger than the Stones'... They would make the perfect last ever 'great' 'mega' rock band. Even at the present, they seem to contain the elements necessary for such a feat – a bloated, overblown feeling, together with a knack for manipulation." The review concludes with a few fashion pointers for those eager to emulate The Smiths' look. "Johnny Marr has had a drastic remodelling job done on his head," McCullough enthuses. "Gone is the Costello clone look, overtaken now by what I can only describe as a mop top look. He looks like a butcher's boy, but even then he makes that seem the height of fashion. Morrissey now sports an arty smock: it's that Oscar Wilde, just-come-down-from-the-garret-to-answer-the-door look. Playing live is a trial, dears. He says it with flowers. The bassist looks as though he's just recovering from ETC treatment. The drummer slobbers and is still handsome. The sight of them makes me tingle"... And for good measure, The Smiths débuted 'This Charming Man'.

Set List: 'You've Got Everything Now'; 'This Charming Man'; 'Handsome Devil'; 'Still Ill'; 'Reel Around The Fountain'; 'Pretty Girls Make Graves'; 'Miserable Lie'; 'I Don't Owe You Anything'; 'Hand In Glove'; 'What Difference Does It Make?'; 'These Things Take Time'; 'Hand In Glove'.

THE SMITHS on the bill at the ICA Rock Week, 5 October 1983.

7-14 OCTOBER

A spree of college gigs sees The Smiths traverse the country, stopping off at the University of Durham (7th), Liverpool Polytechnic (8th), Polytechnic of Wales, Pontypridd (12th) and Bangor University (14th).

21 OCTOBER

Johnny Marr celebrates his 20th birthday with a gig at the North East London Polytechnic. Morrissey is characteristically full of praise for his partner, reminding the world that "Johnny can take the most basic threadbare tune and you'll just cry for hours and swim in tears."

The guitarist is still broadening his musical horizons, ever eager to embrace the influences of Morrissey and Joe Moss. "He was really good for me, Joe," Marr reminisces. "He got me into a load of stuff. He encouraged me. Aside from that, he gave me jobs and let me stay at his house... He was so good to us. When I wasn't working with or for him, I'd be round his place watching Stones' videos and listening to blues records. He taught me a lot. He developed that."

The Morrissey influence, already manifest in Marr's passing comments on Sandie Shaw, speaks louder when he adopts the singer's portentous tone in speaking of the apparent inevitability of fame. "I feel I was destined for this," he says of stardom. "I worked for it because it was what I'd always wanted. People used to say it was a 'one in a million chance' that we'd make it, but I believed we would."

Set List: 'Still Ill'; 'These Things Take Time'; 'This Charming Man'; 'What Difference Does It Make?'; 'This Night Has Opened My Eyes'; 'Pretty Girls Make Graves'; 'Miserable Lie'; 'Reel Around The Fountain'; 'Hand In Glove'; 'Handsome Devil'; 'You've Got Everything Now'; 'Hand In Glove'.

MORRISSEY and manager Joe Moss confer backstage.

> **'Joe was really good for me... I'd be round his place watching Stones videos and listening to Blues records. He taught me a lot.'**
>
> JOHNNY MARR

22 OCTOBER

Like rival football teams, Manchester's Smiths find themselves compared in the press to Liverpool's Echo And The Bunnymen. The Smiths' reception at the Liverpool Polytechnic, however, is bereft of any partisanship. Morrissey reinforces his traditional links with Manchester with the recent addition to the group's set of 'This Night Has Opened My Eyes'. The more diligent among his following detect the influence of playwright Shelagh Delaney, as Morrissey borrows several lines from *A Taste Of Honey*. Morrissey is engagingly open about his influences, announcing, "The songs are personal, they're there to be discovered. The words are basic because I don't want anyone to miss what I'm saying."

Set List: 'Handsome Devil'; 'Still Ill'; 'This Charming Man'; 'What Difference Does It Make?'; 'Pretty Girls Make Graves'; 'This Night Has Opened My Eyes'; 'Hand In Glove'; 'Reel Around The Fountain'; 'Miserable Lie'; 'You've Got Everything Now'; 'Hand In Glove'.

27 OCTOBER

Kingston Polytechnic offers The Smiths supported by Shark Taboo. Anticipation is high for The Smiths' forthcoming single, 'This Charming Man', a title which is pure Morrisseyspeak. "People aren't used to thinking in a very charming or handsome way," the singer explains. "I think words like that can sweep away a lot of the grime because people are becoming so mentally depressed and inverted that they can't think of a positive language any more. The language that people use totally erodes the heart, but modern life doesn't give much opportunity for really inflated language. The art of conversation has definitely been destroyed".

28 OCTOBER

The Smiths' new single, 'This Charming Man' is officially released. According to Morrissey, the song was recorded within two weeks of its composition. "We had just written the song and we really felt, 'This has to be released at once'," he explains. "We all felt a particular energy about the song. There was a strange urgency to have it released straightaway." That same day, Kings College, London, opens its doors to the group. "Our reception hasn't surprised me at all," Morrissey explains. "In fact I think it will snowball even more dramatically over the immediate months. It really has to... I really think we merit a great deal of attention."

Set List: 'Handsome Devil'; 'Still Ill'; 'This Charming Man'; 'Pretty Girls Make Graves'; 'Miserable Lie'; 'This Night Has Opened My Eyes'; 'What Difference Does It Make?'; 'Reel Around The Fountain'; 'Hand In Glove'.

THE RHYTHM SECTION back to back, Manchester, 1983.

OCTOBER
Craig Gannon ends his association with Aztec Camera. "I expected to stay with them indefinitely and was really surprised when they kicked me out," he reflects. "Roddy wanted to get Malcolm Ross in from Orange Juice, who was his mate". Gannon soon finds new employment when he teams up with Terry Hall's new group Colourfield. He will later appear with them on *The Tube*. promoting their eponymous début single.

NOVEMBER
'This Charming Man' receives an additional release on 12-inch, enabling listeners to sample the Manchester and London versions of the song, along with the powerful 'Accept Yourself' and rare 'Wonderful Woman'. Producer John Porter credits Geoff Travis, not only for choosing the hit single, but also insisting that it be re-recorded. "He was good like that," Porter points out. "He had good ears and a good knowledge of the market he was trying to sell to... He was right to tell us to do it again because, although the first version was good, it was better for doing it again. It was good for them having just played it and done the whole thing three days before. It made the song more focused... I remember when we did 'This Charming Man' again, we did the drums last. I got them to work with a click track because, although Mike was a good drummer live, it's a very different thing in the studio and you're so conscious of what you're doing. So I took a Linn drum up to Manchester, programmed the drums on the Linn drum, put that down on tape, did the whole song (vocals and everything), and then put the drums on last and rubbed the Linn drum out." Although The Smiths used the Linn drum merely as a guide, it was still amusing to hear Marr telling the press a year later: "We would never use a Linn drum or a drum machine."

4 NOVEMBER
The Smiths appear on *The Tube*, where Morrissey flails feet deep in flowers during 'This Charming Man'. Rourke appears deathly pale, Joyce looks deadly serious and Marr's face is hidden from view for virtually the entire song.

8 NOVEMBER
Morrissey and Marr make a surprise appearance on Radio Sheffield in a light-hearted interview.

10 NOVEMBER
While The Smiths journey to Portsmouth Polytechnic, the ever quotable Morrissey is back in the music press discussing his controversial lyrics. "It's not a profession for me," he says of composing. "It's something I have to do. I write persistently. It started when I was about two and leapt upon a typewriter... the rest is history. I feel people are just waiting for someone to say something and I've got a great deal to say."

16 NOVEMBER
Leicester Polytechnic. The college tour continues while 'This Charming Man' ascends the charts. An exuberant performance is appreciated by the students, one of whom grabs the microphone from Morrissey and proclaims: "You're brilliant. I love you." Mike Joyce remembers this gig as something of a turning point in the group's performing career.

"At Leicester it just seemed to be 2,000 Mozzer fans, and that was a weird one for me," he recalls. "That's when I felt, 'Is it becoming more of a Morrissey thing? What do people really want from The Smiths?' That was the first time I noticed a chasm."

Set List: 'Handsome Devil'; 'Still Ill'; 'This Charming Man'; 'What Difference Does It Make?'; 'This Night Has Opened My Eyes'; 'Pretty Girls Make Graves'; 'Hand In Glove'; 'Reel Around The Fountain'; 'These Things Take Time'; 'Miserable Lie'; 'Accept Yourself'; 'This Charming Man'; 'You've Got Everything Now'; 'Hand In Glove'.

17 NOVEMBER

Westfield College, London. The success of 'This Charming Man' ensures that the group's live performances are in even greater demand. Morrissey is quick to flatter his followers with pleasing asides in the press. "I want people who hear us to feel charming and handsome," he notes. "The disciples we've accumulated are incredibly charming people. They don't spit or gob, they just bring flowers."

Set List: 'Handsome Devil'; 'Still Ill'; 'This Charming Man'; 'Pretty Girls Make Graves'; 'This Night Has Opened My Eyes'; 'What Difference Does It Make?'; 'Hand In Glove'; 'Reel Around The Fountain'; 'Miserable Lie'; 'Accept Yourself'; 'This Charming Man'; 'You've Got Everything Now'.

18 NOVEMBER

Edge Hill College, Liverpool, plays host to The Smiths as their latest interview in *Sounds* hits the stands. Interviewer Bill Black carefully skirts around the recent furore over their lyrics and is informed by manager Joe Moss that the incident is history. Morrissey, meanwhile, offers an olive branch, while stressing The Smiths' populist ambitions: "We want to make friends. We want to have people around us... All we really care about is being popular and that's why we try hard to please". Interestingly, the interview is dominated by Marr, who takes pains to explain the group's philosophy and their positive attitude to the music press. In responding to the question of The Smiths' Sixties influences, Marr provides an impressively detailed response. "We try and be adventurous but not to be overbearing, but then again we'd hate to be trapped by some revivalist tag, whatever it might be, because that's not what we're about... if you dig into either of our collections you will find music of quality from every period of popular music. For instance, in the Sixties, records were actually worth something. People went out and bought a seven-inch piece of plastic and they treasured it, which they don't do any more. We're trying to bring back the precious element which is, I suppose, reminiscent of an earlier time, but then, so what? It's good to take a part of pop culture and bring it back alive again and bring the human spirit back into it. It's exactly the same with the songwriting partnership Morrissey and I have. The whole idea of two people getting together with lots of common ground but with separate influences to bring out something we believe to be the best we've ever heard is something we feel has been missing since the Sixties. The Seventies was the decade of the solo artiste and the solo writer and that really doesn't appeal to me at all. I really get a buzz from the unpredictability of the way a Smiths' song turns out. It's joyous the way we work together and if that's reminiscent of the Sixties, that's fine."

Set List: 'Handsome Devil'; 'Still Ill'; 'This Charming Man'; 'Pretty Girls Make Graves'; 'This Night Has Opened My Eyes'; 'What Difference Does It Make?'; 'Wonderful Woman'; 'Hand In Glove'; 'Reel Around The Fountain'; 'Miserable Lie'; 'You've Got Everything Now'; 'This Charming Man'.

> **'Johnny was like a stick insect, and had shades on. It was like watching The Monkees or The Beatles at a press conference.'**
>
> GRANT SHOWBIZ

23 NOVEMBER

After a few days' break during which they'd promoted their new single and prepared for their first BBC television broadcast, The Smiths appear at Huddersfield Polytechnic. It is clear from their busy schedule and fondness for publicity that The Smiths are not content to remain some quaint indie group. Talking to Graham Smith of *Record Mirror*, Morrissey looks forward to greater fame and plugs the group's forthcoming album: "Being on a major label doesn't guarantee a thing. I think our record is almost perfect and it is going to happen – I can see no reason at all why The Smiths shouldn't be unbelievably massive. The most fulfilling thing must be to reach a lot of people, but nowadays the very idea of filling an auditorium has been spat upon by modern groups but that's just like criticizing *Top Of The Pops* by people who'll never be on there. *TOTP* is there to be used – we want to reach people."

24 NOVEMBER

The Smiths make their début appearance on *Top Of The Pops* playing 'This Charming Man'. It proves one of the highlights of Morrissey's life. That same evening, The Smiths appear at the Haçienda where they are besieged by screaming fans, several of whom are carted away after fainting amid the crush. A stupendous four encores ends the show on a high note. After the gig, a proud Joe Moss can be seen running down the streets of Manchester shouting "It's too late to stop now". At that point, he realizes that, with or without his further assistance, The Smiths have reached the big-time.

Set List:. 'Handsome Devil'; 'Still Ill'; 'This Charming Man'; 'Pretty Girls Make Graves'; 'Reel Around The Fountain'; 'Miserable Lie'; 'This Night Has Opened My Eyes'; 'What Difference Does It Make?'; 'Hand In Glove'; 'You've Got Everything Now'; 'These Things Take Time'; 'This Charming Man'; 'Accept Yourself'; 'Hand In Glove'.

26 NOVEMBER

Melody Maker publish a two page interview with Morrissey which, despite some evasion about his childhood and formative years, presents some revealing comments on Factory Records, the concept of Smithdom and the plight of modern music. Interviewer Ian Pye presents a suitably intense portrayal of the singer as an overwrought aesthete: "He frequently creases his brow and looks worried, yet rarely have I met a man so confident, so convinced by the worth of his own demanding mission. Looking out across a cruel landscape, he sees himself ushering in a new form of beauty." While Morrissey has previously been content to talk about sexual politics, he ends the interview with a radical flourish, anticipating the more proselytizing tone of 1984.

3 DECEMBER

The music press confirm the rush release of a François Kervorkian dance floor mix of 'This Charming Man'. The track, remixed at the Right Track in New York, has been available on import and Rough Trade intended to issue the 12-inch as a limited edition for clubs and disc jockeys. However, public response encourages the company to sanction a full release, retailing at £1.49. Although Morrissey and Marr have agreed to this decision, the former swiftly realizes that it does not fit The Smiths' image and can soon be heard raging against the offending item. Geoff Travis immediately orders the single's deletion but in spite of agreeing to Morrissey's dictates has to suffer some backhanded criticisms in the music press. "I'm still very upset about that," Morrissey continues to protest. "It was totally against our principles, the whole thing."

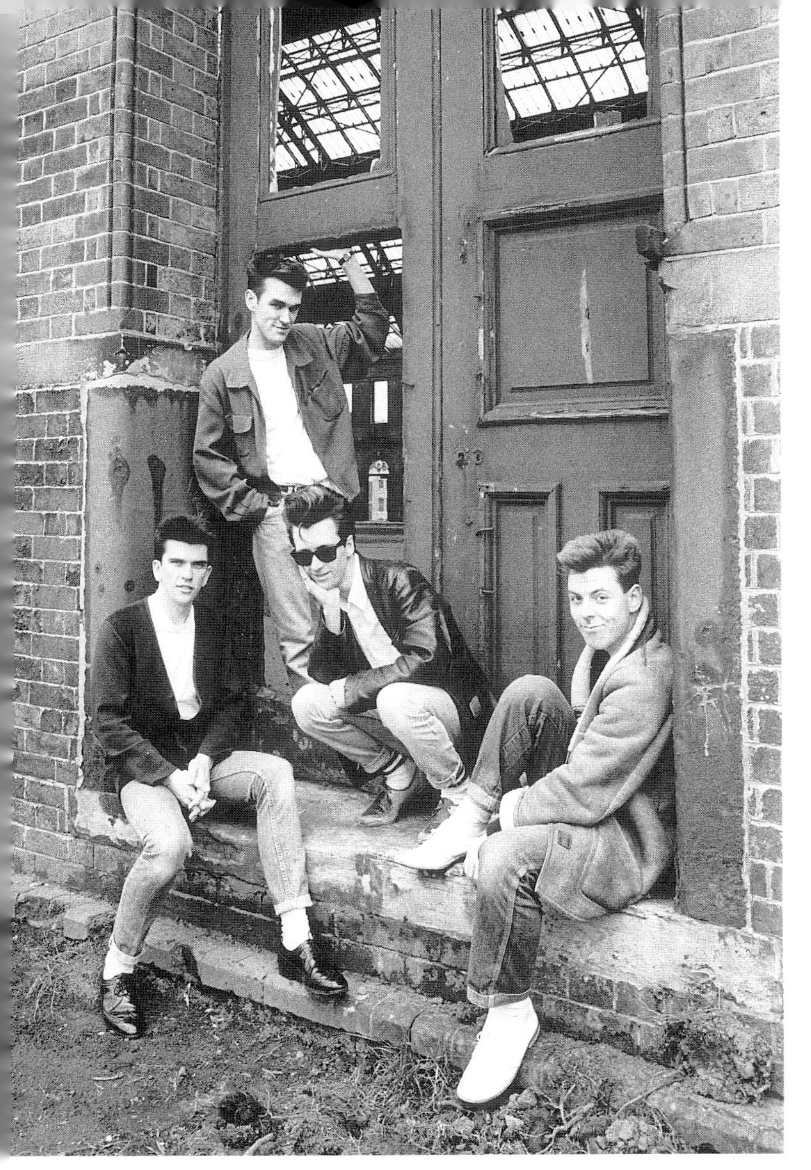

SLUMMING it in a derelict building, Manchester, 1983.

7 DECEMBER

The Smiths' performance at the Assembly Rooms, Derby is filmed by BBC's *The Old Grey Whistle Test*. Highlights include a sparkling version of 'This Charming Man', Morrissey insisting 'I think I can rely on me' during 'What Difference Does It Make?', a near instrumental 'Miserable Lie' and some strangled vocals on 'You've Got Everything Now'. A stage invasion ends the set prematurely, forcing the programmers to run part of the song sequence in reverse. For many, this was the first proper viewing of The Smiths on the small screen and several of Morrissey's school friends are astonished to see their shy contemporary flailing across their television screens. Despite the impact that this show had, Marr was very critical of the gig and embarrassed by the group's appearance.

Set List: 'Handsome Devil'; 'Still Ill'; 'This Charming Man'; 'Pretty Girls Make Graves'; 'Reel Around The Fountain'; 'What Difference Does It Make?'; 'Miserable Lie'; 'This Night Has Opened My Eyes'; 'You've Got Everything Now'; 'These Things Take Time'; 'Hand In Glove'.

9 DECEMBER

An eventful day for The Smiths, during which a pre-recorded Morrissey appearance is broadcast on Radio 1's *Roundtable* and the Derby gig is shown on *The Whistle Test*. In the meantime, the group have left the country to play their first gig on Irish soil at the SFX, Dublin. Morrissey's emergence as either a sex symbol or a sexless icon is still a matter of debate. Even the singer seems uncertain of the outcome. "I think a sex symbol is possibly the best thing to be." he enthuses. "I think if you're strong and determined no amount of triviality will crush you." Soon after, he qualifies that view, adding, "I don't think I am a sex symbol, actually, which is a great worry when one's picture appears in the music press. People generally bring me their problems as opposed to wanting to molest me, which is, of course, terribly distressing. People tend to see me as someone with a great deal of answers rather than as a sex symbol, so I'll have to work on that a bit longer."

18 DECEMBER

Morrissey appears on *The Great Rock 'n' Roll Trivia Quiz* in the unlikely company of Johnny Marr's future musical collaborator Matt Johnson.

19 DECEMBER

The Smiths play their biggest London gig to date, headlining at the Electric Ballroom. One of the surprises of the set is the introduction of 'Barbarism Begins At Home', a full 14 months before its vinyl release. This early version is most noticeable for its faster pace and additional lyrics, with Morrissey crooning, "I've always been such a decent lad," adding, "I am the man to keep you in place".

Set List: 'Hand In Glove'; 'Still Ill'; 'Barbarism Begins At Home'; 'This Night Has Opened My Eyes'; 'Pretty Girls Make Graves'; 'You've Got Everything Now'; 'What Difference Does It Make?'; 'Miserable Lie'; 'This Charming Man'; 'Back To The Old House'; 'Reel Around The Fountain'; 'Handsome Devil'; 'Accept Yourself'; 'This Charming Man'.

24 DECEMBER

Morrissey pens a lengthy appreciation of Sandie Shaw in the pages of *Sounds*. Amid the chart statistics, Morrissey throws in a sociological observation or two, including a few sentences which eclipse all his other prose pieces. It reads: "Without natural beauty, Sandie Shaw cut an unusual figure, and would herald a new abandoned casualness for female singers. The grande dame gestures of the late Fifties had gone, the overblown icky sentiment had gone, and in its place came a brashness and fortitude, girls with extreme youth and high spirits who were to boldly claim their patch in a business which was obviously a male domain."

31 DECEMBER

The year ends with The Smiths in New York. Although this should be the pinnacle of their achievement so far, the mood in the camp is decidedly low. The recent departure of Joe Moss and a temporary rift between Johnny and his girlfriend add a touch of melancholy to the festivities. "It was an incredible time," Grant Showbiz recalls. "We were really miserable, and it was supposed to be exciting... It was a weird vibe." In the early hours of New Year's Day, The Smiths step on to the stage of the Danceteria in what sound engineer Grant Showbiz describes as "more of a hip-hop scene than a Smiths' gig". Although Morrissey falls off the stage at one point, the gig, organized by Ruth Polsky, proves successful and the garrulous Grant enjoys his first experience of "cocaine huffing".

'I have no interest in solo success or individual spotlights. To me things are absolutely perfect.'

MORRISSEY, 1984

CHAPTER THREE

Steven Hero... Steven Villain

1984 SAW THE SMITHS undertake their most extensive tour to date in an attempt to extend their following. It was a period of intense activity, punctuated by a series of internal problems and management squabbles. With their first album scaling the charts and three more successful singles over the next nine months, the group seemed poised for international fame. Already, however, Morrissey's public pronouncements were causing a stir in the national press. There was also an element of perennial bad publicity that followed the group, some of it warranted, but much of it scaremongering. Morrissey's interest in the Moors Murderers temporarily backfired when the sensitive 'Suffer Little Children' was deemed tasteless and exploitative, much to the singer's chagrin. This did nothing to curb his tongue, however, and as the year passed his targets became more acute; bitter comments on Margaret Thatcher, the IRA Bombing and Band Aid all provoked uproar. By now, it was clear that Morrissey and controversy were synonymous and would remain so for the duration of The Smiths' career.

'Record Mirror', 11 February 1984

Morrissey's party political broadcasts were accompanied by familiar paragraphs on the state of his spiritual, emotional and sexual life. "I thought I couldn't be anything but completely honest," he pleaded in defence of such public soul searching. "When we began, I thought there was a need to find somebody who was honest to a fault. Nobody had been like that before, because all the popular figures had become like early Seventies rock stars. There was nobody out there putting their heart on the line. There was no-one singing as though they would die if they didn't. I had to be boringly personal. I'm beyond embarrassment now."

MANCHESTER Free Trade Hall, 1984.

In discussing his private life, Morrissey painted a picture of a completely isolated individual surrounded by books and a telephone that was all too often disconnected. Although he had long lost his faith in organized religion, Morrissey opened the year with an intriguing note. "I'm simply inches away from a monastery," he observed. "I feel that perhaps if I wasn't doing this then I'd probably be in one which, of course, is a frightening thing to dwell on." His comments were no doubt partly inspired by the fact that Johnny Daly, his most faithful male friend from the doleful late Seventies, had recently entered a friary. The two had shared a similarly lonely existence and now their respective fates could hardly have been more contrasting.

Although The Smiths enjoyed substantial success during 1984, they were not top of the indie heap in the way that their music press supporters had anticipated. In the increasingly frenzied arenas of pop, politics and sex, they were completely outflanked by Liverpool rivals Frankie Goes To Hollywood. While Morrissey played with homoerotic imagery and moaned about lack of radio airplay, the Frankies boasted the "outed" Holly Johnson and Paul Rutherford, and turned a complete BBC radio ban to spectacular advantage by taking their début single to number 1. 'Relax' took explicit sex to the top of the charts in a way that could not have been possible for the more urbane and minimalist 'This Charming Man'. Similarly, while Morrissey oozed vitriol in discussing Thatcher and CND, it was the Frankies who made the definitive musical statement with the extraordinary 'Two Tribes', a bitter attack on East/West relations, which topped the charts for an incredible nine weeks. The softer edged 'The Power Of Love', featuring another "controversial" video, completed a remarkable trio of number ones. In the space of a year, the Frankies effortlessly achieved what The Smiths could only dream of, but never realize: chart topping singles that sparkled with verve, intelligence and controversy. Even the Frankies' début album, Welcome To The Pleasure Dome, *a ragbag of covers, old singles and average originals spread thinly over four sides, proved a triumph of packaging – a snap, crackle and pop production that made* The Smiths *sound cheap and tinny by comparison.*

FRANKIE Goes To Hollywood dominated UK Pop in 1984.

If pop meant capturing the moment, then that moment has seldom been grasped more effectively than the Frankies' stranglehold of 1984. Everyone correctly predicted that they'd burn out, for it was already evident that they would struggle to convert their recorded material into live performance. What they did was make a mark rather than a career and, in doing so, highlighted The Smiths' inadequacies. The supreme pop achievement of capturing your time with a work that simultaneously boasted quality yet translated to the masses was something that proved frustratingly beyond The Smiths. For a group who prided themselves on singles and knew their pop history and heritage like no other of the period, it was ironic that they should ultimately remain locked to a fan base which could offer a lowly Top 10 record as the zenith of their commercial achievement. The great number one single that should have defined The Smiths' moment in the pop history books for all time had already passed them by and was lost forever. Unlike Frankie, their career would be measured in subtle stages rather than incandescent bursts.

MORRISSEY preaching the gospel of Smithdom, 1984.

1984 ultimately became a year of great progress in The Smiths' calendar, a glittering scale of the ladder, but there was no explosive breakthrough in the breathtaking fashion of Elvis, The Beatles, The Rolling Stones or even The Sex Pistols. Smithdom remained an insular and still small world, full of unrealized expectations but content in the knowledge that the best was still to come.

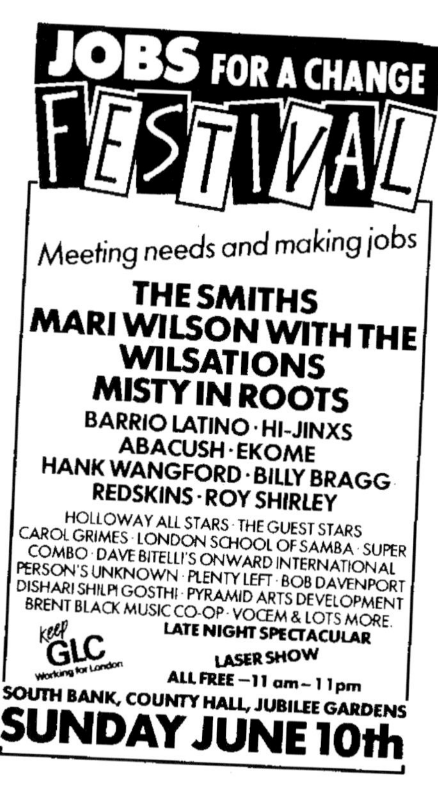

THE SMITHS began playing the festival circuit this year.

2 JANUARY

Mike Joyce awakes in a dreadfully weak state and soon discovers that he has been stricken with chicken pox. "His face was three times the size it was the day before," recalls Grant Showbiz. With their East Coast dates in jeopardy, Rough Trade's Geoff Travis suggests they recruit Clem Burke from Blondie. Instead, The Smiths decide to return home, leaving label mates The Go Betweens to fill several dates.

JANUARY

Joe Moss offers his house as a surrogate drug rehabilitation clinic for Andy Rourke who is wrestling with heroin addiction. "It started in a small way just before I joined The Smiths," Rourke recalls. "As I started getting some decent money in, it became easier for me to buy it in larger amounts." Although no longer manager, Moss is still helping out Johnny with his romantic problems and encouraging Rourke to go straight. "He was a really friendly bloke and sorted me out," Rourke recalls. "I used to live in the basement flat in his house, and Johnny lived upstairs." Remarkably, Morrissey appears blithely unaware of the secret drama in his midst, although Moss feels it is an open secret. As Rourke notes: "I think Morrissey always had his suspicions!"

JANUARY

Having moved from Manchester to London, Morrissey introduces the press to his new home in Cadogan Square. Among his pastimes is watching old films. "At the moment I'm completely handcuffed to *Saturday Night And Sunday Morning*," he notes. " I can't describe the poetry that film has for me, especially that of Albert Finney in the Arthur Seaton role." Morrissey's favourite icons are given prominence. Several volumes of Oscar Wilde's works are strategically placed on the mantelpiece as Morrissey gushes, "I've read everything he wrote and everything written about him and I still find him totally awe-inspiring." Above the books is a framed photograph of James Dean, which is subsequently employed for several photo sessions. Despite his obvious enthusiasm for Dean, Morrissey is keen not to overestimate the icon's thespian abilities. "It's not his acting, actually," he stresses. "I think he was a bit of a ham. I get quite embarrassed when I see those films. But I'm fascinated by the way he seemed to represent his time and his generation. " Visitors to Morrissey's flat also observe that the bathroom contains a mirror surrounded by lightbulbs, in dressing room fashion. Other indicators of his vanity include three framed self portraits which compete with the Dean visage for prominence.

MORRISSEY icons: Oscar Wilde and James Dean.

20 JANUARY

The Smiths' third single 'What Difference Does It Make?' is issued. "It's a very old song," Morrissey half apologizes. "Johnny

THE SMITHS, January 1984.

and I wrote it something like 18 months ago." Explaining the genesis of the song, Morrissey is quick to debunk any over-elaborate interpretations. "People seem to really look for quite staunchly philosophical edges in what I write," he observes, "and certainly they're there! But, 'What Difference Does It Make?' just struck me as a very necessary little term. I don't know. What difference does it make? I just wanted to have a very easy attitude and that's what the lyrics imply. People get so really neurotic about themselves – their lives, their hair, their teeth – but what difference can anything make really?"

Reviews of the single are mixed, with the most amusing suggesting, " What we have here is our man Morrissey harking back to look forward and coming up with something not a million leg-pulls away from an earlyish Jethro Tull B-side. The difference between 'What Difference...' and 'This Charming Man' is, in fact, charm. It lacks it, spectacularly substituting a rocking pace for its predecessor's lilting melody... Is 'What Difference...' any good? I'm undecided – I just wish it was great and it isn't."

Surprisingly, Morrissey's own views were roughly in accordance. Shortly after the disc's release he betrayed his reservations about the song which, it transpired, was largely championed by Marr and producer John Porter. "I remember 'What Difference Does It Make?' being a breakthrough, " Porter recalls. "I liked that because it had a bit of an R&B groove. That was where we explored the territory of overdubbing guitars." Marr, who borrowed the inspiration for the song from Jo Jo Gunne's hit 'Run Run Run', feels reasonably positive about its merits. "It was all right," he cautions. "A lot of people liked it. It followed 'This Charming Man' and was part of that peak. It went down great live, and that's when I really liked it."

> **'I'd hate to get sick of playing gigs, but I'm worried that by this time next year we'll have played so many we won't want to play again.'**
>
> JOHNNY MARR

23 JANUARY

Morrissey is introduced to his new tour manager Phil Cowie by All Trade Booking's Mike Hinck. Although the meeting at Morrissey's Kensington flat proves cordial and constructive, relations between the two will deteriorate as the forthcoming college tour gets underway.

"I'm glad they have a personal assistant, Ollie May," notes Cowie, "as I do not wish to always become involved on a personal level." If only he knew what he was letting himself in for.

26 JANUARY

The Smiths perform 'What Difference Does It Make?' on *Top Of The Pops*. In the wake of this appearance Morrissey adds a new accoutrement to his image and will soon be seen wearing a hearing aid, like a latter day Johnnie Ray. "Some people think it's a kind of sick joke," Morrissey explains, "but the truth is, a fan wrote to me telling me that she was deaf and felt very depressed about her handicap. At that time, we'd released 'What Difference Does It Make?', which is all about appearance making no difference to you. I thought it would be a nice gesture to wear the hearing aid on *Top Of The Pops* to show the fan that deafness shouldn't be some sort of stigma that you try to hide. Basically, I was trying to give her a bit of confidence in herself." The single rapidly climbs to number 12 in the UK charts, their most successful chart position to date. Meanwhile, there is a minor problem over the sleeve of the single, which features a shot of actor Terence Stamp, another camp icon who, amongst many roles, had

MORRISSEY and Marr, the University of East Anglia, 14 February 1984.

played the lead part in the movie adaptation of Melville's *Billy Budd*. When Stamp objects to The Smiths' use of his body as cover artwork, Rough Trade sanction a new set of sleeves with Morrissey substituted for his celluloid hero.

27 JANUARY
Morrissey makes a fleeting appearance on the television show *The Tube*. Interviewed at the Haçienda by Tony Fletcher, he immodestly plugs the group's new album. "I really do expect the highest critical praise for it," he insists. "It's a very, very good album. I think it's a signal post in music."

31 JANUARY
The UK tour commences at Sheffield University. In order to maintain a sense of camaraderie, Morrissey, the group and the crew share a dressing room. Cowie, meanwhile, observes the show with a degree of appreciation and quiet criticism. "I am very impressed by the band onstage and how powerful and accurate the sound is," he notes. "The stage, the backlines seem well under control, but not such a success from the front of the house, sadly. The sound is jagged and rough with a strange mix, and the lights seem to be operated without imagination or flair. I make a note to pay close attention to these vital aspects of the tour, but regard the fact that as this is the beginning of the tour, things should improve." The new Smiths' set introduces the striking 'Girl Afraid' and 'Heaven Knows I'm Miserable Now'.
Set List: 'Hand In Glove'; 'Heaven Knows I'm Miserable Now'; 'Girl Afraid'; 'This Charming Man'; 'Pretty Girls Make Graves'; 'Still Ill'; 'I Don't Owe You Anything'; 'Miserable Lie'; 'This Night Has Opened My Eyes'; 'Barbarism Begins At Home'; 'Back To The Old House'; 'What Difference Does It Make?'; 'Reel Around The Fountain'; 'You've Got Everything Now'.

LATE JANUARY
Craig Gannon joins The Bluebells and will stay with them for the next two years.

FEBRUARY
The Face runs a short interview in which Morrissey promises his fans, "We're not going to be unassailable or unapproachable." Marr concurs with this sentiment, and insists that élitism will be the death of The Smiths: "When we don't feel a kinship with the people who come to see us then we'll know it's time to jack it in." In keeping with the group's arrogant image, he concludes: "For a lot of people we're the event of the decade. We feel it would be a tragic waste not to buy our records."

1 FEBRUARY
A visit to the North Staffordshire Polytechnic in Stoke prompts Simon Scott to despatch a fawning review to *Melody Maker*. "Of course, The Smiths can do no wrong," he announces. "Given their status as the world's most wonderful band, mere lip service of a performance would have been slavered over for days to come. But that's not their way." Observing their performance, the reviewer laughs at the stage lights, but praises the sound: "The *raison d'être* is the sound, and the sentiment, and on those fronts, The Smiths score full marks. As Morrissey's voice weaved its powerful spell with 'Heaven Knows I'm Miserable Now', guitar, bass and drums provided backing that bristled with punch and sparkle, but never looked in danger of disturbing the delicate atmosphere. Perhaps the most interesting segment of a fascinating show was 'Barbarism Begins At Home', with Morrissey's lyrics going for the emotional jugular." With similarly effusive comments on 'Back To The Old House' and 'What Difference Does It Make?', the lather of praise concludes with the contention that The Smiths "make the most perfect observations of the human condition and then wrap them up in the most memorable melodies since Lennon and McCartney..."

ROURKE backstage at the UEA.

2 FEBRUARY
Trouble is already brewing as the group travel to their next gig at the University of Warwick, Coventry. "As I made clear," Cowie notes, "I was travelling with the crew and acting as driver to ease their considerable workload and, though not spelt out, to prevent a greater than necessary amount of involvement with the band. This situation seems to be working. We are arriving early and I can attend to all the necessary dealings well in advance." Unfortunately, there are some grumbles from the crew about their rider, which is swiftly amended by All Trade Booking. More seriously, Morrissey has to curtail the set without an encore and complains of a throat problem. The drama worsens when Cowie is confronted by The Smiths' personal assistant Ollie May, who is clearly at the end of his tether. Cowie is shocked to learn that he is quitting. "He has, he says, become very disillusioned and disappointed with both the band and the direction that their career has been and is going," Cowie notes. "This does not bode well. We decide in order neither to increase costs nor destabilize the situation, not to engage another person." Sound engineer, Grant Showbiz provides a suitable requiem for the idealistic May: "Ollie had been used to setting up the gear, having a spliff and watching the band... I don't think he knew the importance of a soundcheck. There was less time to have a chat with Morrissey or a laugh with the lads. I'm a big mouth and can take up a lot of space and I just felt Ollie was being squeezed out... But he was very pure. As soon as it stopped being a crack, he left."

3 FEBRUARY
Loughborough University: late afternoon. "The truck is unloaded when we arrive," Cowie notes, "and we are greeted by an irate driver who informs us that the band are not coming and demands to know why no-one from Manchester informed them." So begins the latest drama in the touring life of The Smiths, as cancellations follow. Scheduled gigs at Hull University (7th), Liverpool University (8th) and Birmingham Tower Ballroom (9th) are immediately axed as Morrissey retires to his sick bed.That same evening, an interview with the wan one appears on Radio Sheffield.

MORRISSEY in contemplative mood...

...and signing autographs.

4 FEBRUARY

The first major *NME* interview of the year sees The Smiths championed as possible all-time greats: "This decade's group looks like The Smiths, who are busy making some very powerful but delicate pop music – about love. That is probably why you, as readers, have selected them as the Best New Act in our poll for 1983." Morrissey provides some eminently quotable material, including the portentous, "I constantly speculate upon people who are entwined and frankly I'm looking upon souls in agony. I can't think of one relationship in the world which has been harmonious. It just doesn't happen."

Although the interview is dominated by Morrissey, Marr joins in towards the end and provides some interesting insights into his relationship with the singer: "Morrissey and I are total extremes. He's completely the opposite from me. Onstage Morrissey's completely different to the way he is offstage, he's extrovert and he's loud, whereas offstage I'm too loud and onstage I'm quite quiet. Everything – he's a non-smoker, he doesn't drink coffee, and I live off coffee and cigarettes. He's not a great believer in going out, because he doesn't have fun when he goes out, whereas I go out every night, so we're completely opposite cases." Although Marr might be said to have unconsciously catalogued some reasons behind the inevitable dissolution of the partnership, he also pinpoints one of the reasons why it worked so well. "It was important to me to be working with a frontman," he notes "and obviously someone who could write lyrics prolifically and somebody who could handle himself with journalists because if I was the main spokesman for The Smiths I'm not sure it would have been so spontaneous. So I'm in the ideal position so far as my relation to Morrissey goes." These words confirm Joe Moss's argument that The Smiths was a very calculated affair in which the use of Morrissey as a spokesperson was something that he and Marr had agreed upon at the outset.

4 FEBRUARY

On a lighter note, Morrissey is unleashed to savage a series of singles releases as the guest reviewer in *Record Mirror*. Among the offending discs under scrutiny are new releases from Sade, Style Council, Ultravox, Carmel, Genesis, Marilyn and Blue Rondo A La Turk.

5 FEBRUARY

The fate of the UK tour is still unresolved. "Many frantic phone calls to All Trade Booking and Rough Trade and no-one can give me an accurate assessment of this difficult, catastrophic situation," Cowie complains. "Morrissey's doctor in Manchester has advised many days' rest and I feel that, at this time, a second or third opinion is in order. I stress the seriousness of the predicament to the band at a meeting in the hotel but they can offer no practical advice. I decide that the only course is a direct intrusion into Morrissey's domestic environment."

6 FEBRUARY

The Smiths appear on the BBC North West show *YES* performing 'What Difference Does It Make?' and 'This Night Has Opened My Eyes'.

8 FEBRUARY

Morrissey is taken to the studios of *Top Of The Pops*, where he manages to complete another rendition of 'What Difference Does It Make?' "All Trade Booking have found a specialist to re-examine Morrissey," Cowie notes. "Suspicions confirmed! Previous diagnosis incorrect and specialist opines that we can proceed but does issue the warning that health must not be ignored and suggests rest between concerts. Morrissey is not up to par, but *Top Of The Pops* goes well." An eventful day ends with plugger Scott Piering celebrating his appointment as "caretaker manager" of The Smiths.

GROUP and crew relax backstage at the UEA.

AFTER THE UEA gig, Marr and Rourke are keen to oblige the grateful hordes with autographs.

ONE MAN and his guitar, pre-gig.

9 FEBRUARY
'What Difference Does It Make?' is broadcast for the second time on *Top Of The Pops*. The bespectacled Morrissey appears fresh-faced and noticeably thin as he dances on the spot like a drunk desperately trying not to fall over.

10 FEBRUARY
The Smiths appear on the *Oxford Road Show* performing 'What Difference Does It Make?'. "Morrissey is much better," Cowie observes. "Morale is high."

11 FEBRUARY
Ruth Polsky, who booked The Smiths at New York's Danceteria, announces that she is now the group's manager. Piering is not amused. That same day, *Record Mirror* print an interview with Morrissey in which he speculates on the ultimate break-up of The Smiths. "When people see us as simply grinding out sausages as it were, we'll have the sense to take a swift exit," he promises. "I don't want to bore people, so if I thought The Smiths were an absolute hindrance to the human race then we'd break up. There's a lot I want to do... There's a lot I want to achieve, most of which is illegal."

12 FEBRUARY
A still below par Morrissey struggles through a short set at London's Lyceum Ballroom, London. Even the reviews testify to his illness, with one noting: "Morrissey extracted a measure of gratuitous sympathy when he spluttered about being 'ill'. You could feel the unheard of cries of Affected Youth as they collectively squealed, 'I know Morrissey, I've been ill too. I know what it's like. I share your pain'. And that was a pain." After the show, managerial rivalry is apparently in the air. "Scott evidently unnerved by the presence of Ruth and her monopolization of Morrissey's attention publicly and in front of the band members," Cowie observes, Polonius-like. "He berates me about the organization of the event. Equally unprofessionally, I react to his suggestion and point out his part in the disruption of the concert." There will be no love lost between the various parties as the show rolls on.

Set List: 'Hand In Glove'; 'Heaven Knows I'm Miserable Now'; 'Girl Afraid'; 'This Charming Man'; 'Pretty Girls Make Graves'; 'Still Ill'; 'This Night Has Opened My Eyes'; 'Barbarism Begins At Home'; 'Back To The Old House'; 'What Difference Does It Make?'; 'You've Got Everything Now'.

JOYCE backstage, UEA.

14 FEBRUARY
Onward to the University of East Anglia, Norwich. The Smiths are "chronically late" and a patient crowd is kept waiting outside the venue in freezing conditions for over an hour. "Despite lateness and the crowd's situation, the band seem considerably aggrieved about their soundcheck," Cowie complains. "A large amount of reasoning about the consequences of lateness has to be delivered to them." Although it is already 8pm, Morrissey still manages to squeeze in an interview with the affable Hugh Fielder from *Sounds*. As they drive to the hotel in the fog, Morrissey discusses a book he is preparing on female singers which, like so many of his literary projects, will remain unpublished. After arriving at the gig, Morrissey collects several boxes of flowers and heads slowly towards the stage. The sympathetic Fielder is on hand to provide an instant review.

THE FAMOUS Smiths rider requirements, including beer, wine and flowers.

"The set is scarcely 40 minutes long," he notes, "and misses out a couple of Smiths' classics such as 'Reel Around The Fountain' which might cause permanent damage to Morrissey's throat if he were to attempt it. But such is the compelling emotional appeal of the band that the 11 songs are quite sufficient for one Smiths' session, leaving your senses sated even if your body could do with another couple of numbers to bop to. The sound is relatively quiet by rock'n'roll standards but with a clarity that enables every

HAMMERSMITH PALAIS, 12 March 1984.

I have to drive the van," Cowie complains. Grant Showbiz clearly isn't too keen on Cowie's driving. "He makes a passing insult, passed off as humour," the tour manager notes. "I dismiss it." The Smiths are also in complaining mood and start moaning about Rough Trade and All Trade Booking. The crew reassure them that with the help of legal and financial advisors their problems can be resolved without having to sacrifice a precious percentage of record and publishing income. Hanging on to their money is still uppermost in the thoughts of both Morrissey and Marr.

Set List: 'Hand In Glove'; 'Heaven Knows I'm Miserable Now'; 'Girl Afraid'; 'This Charming Man'; 'Pretty Girls Make Graves'; 'Still Ill'; 'This Night Has Opened My Eyes'; 'Barbarism Begins At Home'; 'Back To The Old House'; 'What Difference Does It Make?'; 'You've Got Everything Now'.

18 FEBRUARY

An interview with Morrissey is broadcast on Janice Long's evening show on BBC Radio 1. The group, meanwhile, are playing at the University of Essex, Colchester. "It's a good show," Cowie enthuses. "The atmosphere is slightly strained by the somewhat over-wrought Ruth Polsky." After being spat at by some nostalgic punks in the audience, the group complain about All Trade Booking's security arrangements. Part of the problem, of course, is The Smiths' insistence that there be no security barriers erected to protect them, though this is conveniently forgotten as tempers fray.

Set List: 'Hand In Glove'; 'Heaven Knows I'm Miserable Now'; 'Girl Afraid'; 'This Charming Man'; 'Pretty Girls Make Graves'; 'Still Ill'; 'This Night Has Opened My Eyes'; 'Barbarism Begins At Home'; 'Back To The Old House'; 'What Difference Does It Make?'; 'You've Got Everything Now'; 'Reel Around The Fountain'; 'Hand In Glove'.

nuance of guitarist Johnny Marr and the subtlety of the rhythm section to show through... The audience is stirred if not exactly ecstatic. But you get the feeling as they leave that they'll be thinking about The Smiths regularly over the next couple of days." In common with the audience, it is a cold Valentine's night for support group The Red Guitars who have travelled from Hull only to discover that they have no accommodation arranged. Several students come to the rescue and allow the group to sleep on their floors. Fielder, meanwhile, returns to the group's hotel only to discover that his interview with Morrissey has been jettisoned, as the wan one has retired to his bed. Fortunately, Johnny Marr proves an adequate replacement. The guitarist voices his feelings over the Troy Tate affair, John Porter's production, relationships with Rough Trade, and his love of the blues. He also provides some on the road insights into the rigours of touring: "We'd like to play two dates a week or something," he suggests hopefully, "but we're not that keen on doing traditional tours because it can become a bland circus. I'd hate to get sick of playing gigs, but I'm worried that by this time next year we'll have played so many that we won't want to play again."

Set List: 'Hand In Glove'; 'Heaven Knows I'm Miserable Now'; 'Girl Afraid'; 'This Charming Man'; 'Pretty Girls Make Graves'; 'Still Ill'; 'This Night Has Opened My Eyes'; 'Barbarism Begins At Home'; 'Back To The Old House'; 'What Difference Does It Make?'; 'You've Got Everything Now'.

> **'When The Smiths break-up I feel sure that the other three group members could walk on to something else, but I don't think I could...'**
>
> MORRISSEY

15 FEBRUARY

Having booked a gig at Nottingham University, The Smiths switch to the city's larger venue, Rock City. Piering is on the phone to Cowie insisting that Morrissey should be given a separate dressing room. While these instructions are carried out, Grant Showbiz and lighting engineer John Featherstone have a minor contretemps. Cowie feels that Grant is being unfairly critical and privately notes that "the lighting, following discussion with John, has improved, while the sound is erratic". Later that evening Morrissey appears on Radio Trent.

Set List: 'Hand In Glove'; 'Heaven Knows I'm Miserable Now'; 'Girl Afraid'; 'This Charming Man'; 'Pretty Girls Make Graves'; 'Still Ill'; 'This Night Has Opened My Eyes'; 'Barbarism Begins At Home'; 'Back To The Old House'; 'What Difference Does It Make?'; 'You've Got Everything Now'; 'Reel Around The Fountain'; 'Hand In Glove'.

16 FEBRUARY

Grumbles continue in the van as the entourage drive to the University of Leicester. "For all parties, it appears against my wishes

20 FEBRUARY

The Smiths' eponymous début album is issued. The work testifies to the power of the Morrissey/Marr songwriting team, but there is some disappointment about the quality of the recording. Even producer John Porter bemoans the fact that more money was not available to do justice to the work. "People make a lot of the production, but we weren't as good as we could have been," concedes Marr. "We got better." Rourke is equally modest about the album's quality. "It had its moments," he notes. "But some of the songs were a bit weak. 'Pretty Girls Make Graves' I never really got into... 'Reel Around The Fountain' was good. Paul Carrack turned up and played some piano and that brought the song up. 'Miserable Lie' – I could never get my head round. It was too rocky for me. I suppose overall it was a good first LP. It's very varied." That eclecticism also appealed to Joyce. "What really hit home to me was the light and shade," he remembers. "The difference between 'Miserable Lie' and 'I Don't Owe You Anything' and 'Suffer Little Children' and 'Still Ill'. When you play one of The Smiths' songs it doesn't sound like one of the fast ones slowed down. It's a totally different entity. That's what impressed me when I played the roughs at home. Everything to me sounds like a single."

Morrissey, not surprisingly, proved unashamedly immodest in proclaiming the album's greatness. "I'm really ready to be burned at the stake in total defence of that record," he announced soon after its release. "It means so much to me that I could never explain, however long you gave me. It becomes almost difficult and one is just simply swamped in emotion about the whole thing. It's getting to the point where I almost can't even talk about it, which many people will see as an absolute blessing. It just seems absolutely perfect to me." The singer's assurance is buoyed by the initial sales returns as the album rapidly climbs to number two in the charts.

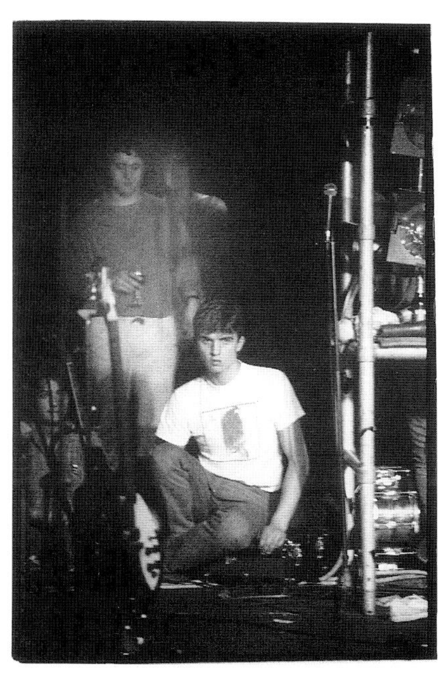

GUITAR Roadie Phil Powell.

21 FEBRUARY

Bournemouth Town Hall comes to the rescue with a reception which puts everybody back in good spirits. Smiths devotee and fanzine premier Mark Taylor recalls the view from the front: "The town hall was packed. The Smiths played their usual 30 minute set which stunned the crowd into silence. Cries of 'Is that all we're getting?' were heard. Then, after the disc jockey had put the music back on, The Smiths took the stage again – Morrissey asking, 'Listen, we're very confused. Do you actually like us, or not?' Then the band played 'What Difference Does It Make?' and left the stage with Morrissey shouting, 'Remind me, I must move to Bournemouth'. He returns within seconds to get the audience to shout, 'Smiths, Smiths, Smiths', but shouts them down by saying, 'Don't be trained'. Someone shouts 'Handsome Devil', Morrissey says 'No!', and they play 'Reel Around The Fountain', 'You've Got Everything Now' and 'Handsome Devil'... 'since you asked'. "

Set List: 'Hand In Glove'; 'Heaven Knows I'm Miserable Now'; 'Girl Afraid'; 'This Charming Man'; 'Pretty Girls Make Graves'; 'Still Ill'; 'This Night Has Opened My Eyes'; 'Barbarism Begins At Home'; 'Back To The Old House'; 'What Difference Does It Make?'; 'Reel Around The Fountain'; 'You've Got Everything Now'; 'Handsome Devil'.

22 FEBRUARY

The Bournemouth honeymoon turns sour within 24 hours as The Smiths face a hostile and ugly crowd at the University of Reading. As the abuse worsens, Cowie and the crew are forced into a physical confrontation with several members of the audience. After the show, there is premature talk about a possible European tour. "The crew wish to plan ahead," Cowie notes, "but no plans are made as everything is subject to the band's approval." These pie in the sky ideas will continue to be voiced throughout the tour. Morrissey ends the evening back at the hotel where he is interviewed by *Melody Maker*'s Allan Jones. The singer's tone throughout is one of complete confidence and acceptance of The Smiths' current fame. "I had absolute faith and absolute belief in everything we did and I really did expect what has happened to us to happen," he asserts. "I was quite frighteningly confident... since I absolutely believe in what I say, I want to say it as loud as possible."

Set List: 'Hand In Glove'; 'Heaven Knows I'm Miserable Now'; 'Girl Afraid'; 'This Charming Man'; 'Pretty Girls Make Graves'; 'Still Ill'; 'This Night Has Opened My Eyes'; 'Barbarism Begins At Home'; 'Back To The Old House'; 'What Difference Does It Make?'; 'You've Got Everything Now'.

23 FEBRUARY

Before setting off for the University of Swansea, the group and various members of the crew have a business meeting. Money is clearly uppermost in everyone's mind as the tour looks like producing a substantial profit. Cowie pushes for a profit sharing agreement with the crew. "This has to be a share of the net profit," he notes, "and only related to live work, thereby ensuring loyalty, efficiency and cost effectiveness as the crew would naturally grow and share with the band as it grew." Cowie is convinced that he has won the day but is already underestimating Morrissey and Marr's canniness in deflecting such discussions and appointing separate negotiators at a later date. As ever their acquiescence is illusory.

A further problem confronting the crew is the increasing division of power in the group. "It was aired publicly by members of the

MARR in repose, early 1984.

band to the crew that Morrissey had once again been separated from the band, fostering the already prevalent feeling that this was detrimental to the tour and morale of us all," Cowie reveals. Sorting this one out requires entering into Morrissey's troubled psyche and Cowie sadly falls prey to the singer's familiar mind games. "Each time this happens, he assures me that it is against his wishes," the tour manager observes with frustration. Having confronted Morrissey, Cowie then receives a verbal battering from Grant Showbiz. "I do not wish a confrontation as any such affair can seriously disrupt everything," Cowie notes dramatically. "Also it has been pointed out to me how much Morrissey would be upset if he thought we weren't getting on." It is now embarrassingly evident that the tour manager is caught up in Morrissey's own privately inflicted

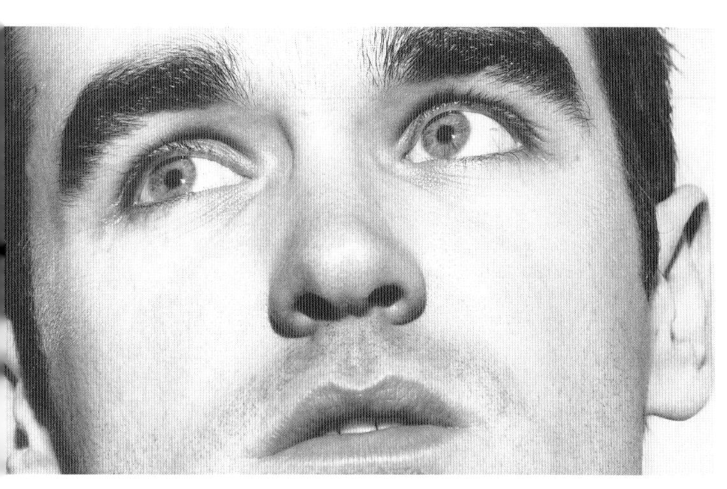

MORRISSEY awaits reviews of the first Smiths LP.

melodrama. "My special relationship with The Smiths notwithstanding, I must confront Morrissey on this matter," Cowie writes with an increasing air of desperation. At least the evening's gig proves successful, although there is further grief after the show due to the substandard catering.

Set List: 'Hand In Glove'; 'Heaven Knows I'm Miserable Now'; 'Girl Afraid'; 'This Charming Man'; 'Pretty Girls Make Graves'; 'Still Ill'; 'This Night Has Opened My Eyes'; 'Barbarism Begins At Home'; 'Back To The Old House'; 'What Difference Does It Make?'; 'Reel Around The Fountain'; 'You've Got Everything Now'; 'Handsome Devil'.

24 FEBRUARY

The mind games with Morrissey continue. Cowie plays the headmaster, berating that rebellious pupil Showbiz for his "wilful behaviour". Morrissey sits and listens. "I have to point out as the highest paid person pro rata on the tour Grant should be less concerned about others' responsibilities and more concerned about his own," Cowie complains. Of course, Cowie has no power to fire the sound engineer who refuses to take him seriously. "Phil was out of his depth and a rock'n'roller, totally mad," Grant laughs. "It was madness to have got him involved. Because we had Oz, Di, Phil and myself, we were getting on almost separate to Phil Cowie. But it was a great tour, that spring of '84." Fortunately, that night's show at the University of Bristol is one of the most successful on the tour and leaves everybody feeling calmer. Morrissey even enjoys some friendly banter with a small group of Alarm fans. Back at the hotel, Cowie and Grant surprise themselves by having a constructive conversation in which they successfully air their minor differences. For the moment, all is well. Meanwhile, plans are afoot to rid the group of their hired driver, whose quips are getting on their nerves.

Set List: 'Hand In Glove'; 'Heaven Knows I'm Miserable Now'; 'Girl Afraid'; 'This Charming Man'; 'Pretty Girls Make Graves'; 'Still Ill'; 'This Night Has Opened My Eyes'; 'Barbarism Begins At Home'; 'Back To The Old House'; 'What Difference Does It Make?'; 'Reel Around The Fountain'; 'You've Got Everything Now'.

25 FEBRUARY

Morrissey appears on BBC Radio 1's *Saturday Live* to promote the group's début album. An appearance at Brighton Polytechnic is surrounded by further mini-drama when the driver's boss arrives at the show to discuss grievances. He explains that due to an imminent spell in hospital he cannot possibly replace the recalcitrant driver. Fearful of losing the truck company, Cowie reluctantly agrees to compromise by persuading the driver not to impose upon the group in the future. "But they encouraged me in the first place," the driver retorts. After two encores the group have a small post-gig celebration. Rourke and Joyce remain in Brighton for a break while Morrissey and Marr journey to London to sort out some business matters.

Set List: 'Hand In Glove'; 'Heaven Knows I'm Miserable Now'; 'Girl Afraid'; 'This Charming Man'; 'Pretty Girls Make Graves'; 'Still Ill'; 'This Night Has Opened My Eyes'; 'Barbarism Begins At Home'; 'Back To The Old House'; 'What Difference Does It Make?'; 'Reel Around The Fountain'; 'You've Got Everything Now'; 'Handsome Devil'.

THE *NME* REVIEWS *THE SMITHS* IN A CRITIQUE that focuses full attention on Morrissey. "Consideration of The Smiths always ends up as attempted penetration of Morrissey's singular charms," Don Watson argues, "primarily because The Smiths in plural are as average as their uncharismatic name suggests. Where Morrissey is a wielder of the archaic art of the word, his cohorts are merely competent workers in the grimy craft of pop. Musically, The Smiths are little more than mildly regressive. What saves them is Morrissey's rare grasp of the myriad distortions of the pastel worlds of nostalgia. Much of the intrigue behind The Smiths is not what they have to offer but the seductive manner in which Morrissey offers it ..." The question of "Morrissey's credibility" dominates the review, impinging frequently on the aesthetic worth of the album. "It's a problem of plausibility," Watson muses, "and Morrissey is very believable; how convincing his aura of deceptive simplicity, how credible his imitation of the wide-eyed village boy adrift in the big city. When he claims to be 'a country mile behind the world', you believe him, largely because his view of the city is one visibly strained through early Sixties films of late Fifties novels – a notion of reality three times removed." These perceptive asides prove the highlight of a long review which, for all its merits, studiously avoids any firm judgmental conclusion. At a time before the *NME* took to grading its reviews, those readers demanding "Yes, but is it any good?" are left with an equivocal summation. "What Morrissey captures above all is a notion of despair reflected perfectly in the lacklustre sound of his cohorts, a death of the punk ideals that Morrissey is quite old enough to have been closely involved in... What does the suitor offer? A calculated plan, perhaps, but enough to haunt the imagination. For the moment that's enough."

MELODY MAKER OFFERS ITS OWN APPRECIATION of *The Smiths* in a tone as effusive as that of the rival *NME*. "These songs, this music," Allan Jones enthuses, "The Smiths themselves seem to owe nothing very much to anyone; they appear to exist without convenient contemporary comparisons. For music as lean and urgent, as passionately articulate and eerily beautiful as the most haunting episodes on this record, you have to refer back to the stark emotional lyricism of the Velvet Underground's third album... " In a final flurry, *MM* pleads a convincing case for the arrival of a powerful début. "They convey meaning through atmosphere; through the brush of voices, the twist of strings, the punctuation of rhythm," Jones uneasily explains. "To paraphrase 'I Don't Owe You Anything': life is never kind, but The Smiths know what will make you smile tonight, even if that distant chuckle is your own laughter chasing itself hollow down the hall. If most of your faculties are intact and you still feel like you can be moved by the power of music, this is the album for you."

27 FEBRUARY

A low-key gig at the University of Kent at Canterbury passes without incident. Morrissey, meanwhile, announces the group's plans to work with another girl singer, following their recent collaboration with Sandie Shaw. "We're also intending to record some songs with a woman called Amanda," he announces. "We met her in America, though she's from Brighton. She's going to be the next 'singing sensation'. She's got an English accent like Lady Penelope and she won't wear a stitch of clothing unless it's pre-1962. She seems to have sprung straight out of Liverpool's Cavern."

Set List: 'Hand In Glove'; 'Heaven Knows I'm Miserable Now'; 'Girl Afraid'; 'This Charming Man'; 'Pretty Girls Make Graves'; 'Still Ill'; 'This Night Has Opened My Eyes'; 'Barbarism Begins At Home'; 'Back To The Old House'; 'What Difference Does It Make?'; 'Reel Around The Fountain'; 'You've Got Everything Now'; 'Handsome Devil'.

28 FEBRUARY

Due to the late arrival of their truck, the group miss their soundcheck at the Hanley Victoria Hall, Stoke-on-Trent. Spirits are revitalized during the evening and the show is a triumph. "The band is happy, the sound is good," Cowie notes with contentment.

Set List: 'Hand In Glove'; 'Heaven Knows I'm Miserable Now'; 'Girl Afraid'; 'This Charming Man'; 'Pretty Girls Make Graves'; 'Still Ill'; 'This Night Has Opened My Eyes'; 'Barbarism Begins At Home'; 'Back To The Old House'; 'What Difference Does It Make?'; 'Reel Around The Fountain'; 'You've Got Everything Now'; 'Handsome Devil'.

29 FEBRUARY

The Smiths are troubled by sound problems and hecklers at the University of Leeds. As early as the first number, Cowie has to dive into the crowd to rescue a youth from a beating by over zealous bouncers. It is not a pleasant evening and typifies the contrasting responses that The Smiths receive from gig to gig.

Set List: 'Hand In Glove'; 'Heaven Knows I'm Miserable Now'; 'Girl Afraid'; 'This Charming Man'; 'Still Ill'; 'This Night Has Opened My Eyes'; 'Barbarism Begins At Home'; 'Back To The Old House'; 'What Difference Does It Make?'; 'Reel Around The Fountain'; 'You've Got Everything Now'; 'Handsome Devil'.

2 MARCH

The Smiths appear live on radio in Glasgow and later that evening perform at the university's Queen Margaret Hall. Marr, who overslept and missed the train, arrives prior to the gig, which is jam packed. The evening ends on a wildly exuberant note with the students in fine voice and full of appreciation.

Set List: 'Hand In Glove'; 'Heaven Knows I'm Miserable Now'; 'Girl Afraid'; 'This Charming Man'; 'Pretty Girls Make Graves'; 'Still Ill'; 'This Night Has Opened My Eyes'; 'Barbarism Begins At Home'; 'Back To The Old House'; 'What Difference Does It Make?'; 'Reel Around The Fountain'; 'You've Got Everything Now'; 'Handsome Devil'.

3 MARCH

Beer swilling hordes at the University of Dundee threaten the safety of the group and almost disrupt the gig after the first number. Morrissey twice retires from the stage, while Johnny Marr plays a nifty instrumental version of 'This Charming Man'. Morrissey assumes his headmaster role, admonishing the crowd with a firm directive: "If anybody throws beer or spits or cans, we will leave." After returning to the stage, the bard proclaims: "Remember the world is watching you Dundee. Do you really *care*?" Thereafter, the set continues without incident and the performance is exemplary. That same day, Morrissey appears in *No 1*, where he leaves readers in little doubt about his views on disco music: "It doesn't exist as far as I'm concerned. Not even to a minuscule degree. I can't fathom Michael Jackson at all."

Set List: 'Hand In Glove'; 'Heaven Knows I'm Miserable Now'; 'Girl Afraid'; 'This Charming Man' (instrumental); 'This Charming Man'; 'Pretty Girls Make Graves'; 'Still Ill'; 'This Night Has Opened My Eyes'; 'Barbarism Begins At Home'; 'Back To The Old House'; 'What Difference Does It Make?'; 'Reel Around The Fountain'; 'You've Got Everything Now'; 'Handsome Devil'.

4 MARCH

The performance at the Fusion Club, Aberdeen, serves as a backdrop to more business melodrama. Geoff Travis and Scott Piering have arrived to view proceedings and the latter is "promoted" from "caretaker manager" to "official representative". The euphemisms merely betray Morrissey's continued unwillingness to allow anybody to manage the group. Cowie, meanwhile, insists that Morrissey has agreed to allow the crew 20 per cent of the net profits from the tour.

Set List: 'Hand In Glove'; 'Heaven Knows I'm Miserable Now'; 'Girl Afraid'; 'This Charming Man'; 'Pretty Girls Make Graves'; 'Still Ill'; 'This Night Has Opened My Eyes'; 'Barbarism Begins At Home'; 'Back To The Old House'; 'What Difference Does It Make?'; 'Reel Around The Fountain'; 'You've Got Everything Now'; 'Handsome Devil'.

5 MARCH

The crew's van breaks down and the equipment truck fails to arrive in time for the evening gig at Edinburgh's Coasters. Fortunately, Regular Music provide the PA

THE FIRST 'NME' Smiths LP review, before albums were graded out of ten.

GLADIOLI ALL OVER

THE SMITHS

The Smiths (*Rough Trade*)

"And if you must go to work tomorrow
Well, if I were you I wouldn't bother" ('Still Ill')

WITHOUT BEING perjorative, there is something soporific about the sound of The Smiths. It's so easy to lapse into their languid dreams without stopping to question where precisely this man Morrissey should be placed in the infinite space between heaven and pillow.

Just how clinical and how innocent is this seducer of our imaginations? How genuine his successive (and often mutually exclusive) stances as corrupted and corruptor, reformed literary libertine and celibate gay bachelor? After contemplation of his flamboyant advances I've arrived at no conclusion as to what *precisely* he bears before him or what *exactly* he is after. What remains at the core of Morrissey's art is a mystique that has so far proved impenetrable – he affords the odd insight, but there is never enough glimpsed to dispel his fascination.

Consideration of The Smiths always ends up as attempted penetration of Morrissey's singular charms, primarily because The Smiths in plural are as average as their uncharismatic name suggests. Where Morrissey is a wielder of the archaic art of the word, his cohorts are merely competent workers in the grimy craft of pop. Musically The Smiths are little more than mildly regressive. What saves them is Morrissey's rare grasp of the myriad distortions of the pastel worlds of nostalgia. Much of the intrigue behind The Smiths is not what they have to offer but the seductive manner in which Morrissey offers it – his beguiling invitation to forget art and dance in a notion of animated camp. At this point we come to his enigma – of the uncalculated versus the contrived.

This has its opening in the cold quivering reflections of the aintive epic of 'Reel Around The Fountain' – a picture of virtual assical proportions, with Morrisey's world weary tones washing a ey tale of innocence lost. *"It's time the tales were told,"* he opens, *f how you took a child/And you made him old"* — you have to rouse rself from the pleasant malaise that the lazy pace induces to all that, at the end of the song, *nothing* of 'the tale' has actually n revealed.

Throughout the LP he captures a set of fascinations that appeal to the current mood – the only question is how many of them are indeed his own and how many the result of long years' research in a rented room in Whalley Range. Too frequently his philosophy of pop seems all too neatly prepared to appeal – the quaint campaign against the synthesiser for example. The mass appeal lies (unfortunately) in a form of traditionalism — so Morrissey offers the

Morrisey mullin' it over *Pic: Anton Corbijn*

fictional tradition of 'great pop' – complete this sequence in six letters: The Buzzcocks, Orange Juice, The . . . . . .

Calculation, though, can offer an aesthetic of its own and The Smiths, like Culture Club, weave an intricate web of insignia, delightful in its diversity, intriguing in its attention to detail, but finally impenetrable.

From the sexy male cover to 'Hand in Glove' Morrissey has proved himself adept at the gender identity game – another tradition of longstanding appeal. Throughout the LP he plucks at the same strings of homoeroticism. *"I'm not the man you think I am,"* he intimates coyly on 'Pretty Girls Make Graves' concluding *"I've lost my faith in Womanhood"* – both of which are in fact snippets open to entirely opposite interpretations.

When he breaks his genderless rule, it is with a slyness we might expect: *"into the depths of the criminal world I followed her . . ."* calling up a reference to Cocteau's *Orpheus* films (a comparison not so obscure when you consider that their star, and Cocteau's lover, Jean Marais was featured on the cover of 'This Charming Man'). Where Cocteau's Orpheus is left unable to look at his wife (perhaps he too had lost his faith in Womanhood), Morrissey ends with *"I need advice, because nobody ever looks at me twice."*

For every tendency in Morrissey's scheme of things, though, there is the necessary balance, for the heaving tragedy of *"And 'love' is just a miserable lie"* there's the flippancy of *"I know that wind-swept mystical air It means I'd like to see your underwear"*.

It's more than just a question of balance, though, it's a problem of plausibility, and Morrissey is very believable; how convincing his aura of deceptive simplicity, how credible his imitation of the wide-eyed village boy adrift in the big city. When he claims to be *"a country mile behind the world"* you believe him, largely because his view of the city is one visibly strained through early '60s films of late '50s novels – a notion of reality three times removed.

'Still Ill', for example, is a drama of flawed perfection, flickering fading values in dusty monochrome – Morrissey kissing beneath the iron bridge finds the fictional Britishness of his obsession slipping through his fingers. *"But we cannot cling to the old dreams any more."*

What Morrissey captures above all is a notion of despair reflected perfectly in the lacklustre sound of his cohorts, a death of the punk ideals that Morrissey is quite old enough to have been closely involved in. In turn what distinguishes him from a Weller is firstly his wit, and secondly the sensitivity to deal in despair without resorting to preaching in desperation.

What does this suitor offer? A calculated plan, perhaps, but enough to haunt the imagination. For the moment that's enough.

Don Watson

'Melody Maker', 3 March 1983

ABOVE: Sixties star Sandie Shaw joins The Smiths at the Hammersmith Palais, 12 March 1984.

and lights at short notice. The group is understandably out of sorts due to these setbacks, but a warm reception from the Edinburgh audience lightens the gloom.

Set List: 'Hand In Glove'; 'Heaven Knows I'm Miserable Now'; 'Girl Afraid'; 'This Charming Man'; 'Pretty Girls Make Graves'; 'Still Ill'; 'This Night Has Opened My Eyes'; 'Barbarism Begins At Home'; 'Back To The Old House'; 'What Difference Does It Make?'; 'Reel Around The Fountain'; 'You've Got Everything Now'.

7 MARCH

At last a new driver is appointed as The Smiths drive southwards to Newcastle-upon-Tyne. Their appearance at the Mayfair proves reasonably successful, although there is a solid contingent of hard rock fans with a tendency to display their burly manhood.

Set List: 'Hand In Glove'; 'Heaven Knows I'm Miserable Now'; 'Girl Afraid'; 'This Charming Man'; 'Pretty Girls Make Graves'; 'Still Ill'; 'This Night Has Opened My Eyes'; 'Barbarism Begins At Home'; 'Back To The Old House'; 'What Difference Does It Make?'; 'Reel Around The Fountain'; 'You've Got Everything Now'; 'Handsome Devil'.

8 MARCH

Drama on the road to Middlesbrough Town

Hall. The group are involved in a minor road accident, which causes a delay and further friction. "Morrissey takes me aside at the scene of the accident and expresses he is not confident," Cowie notes euphemistically. In an attempt to suppress rebellious influences, Cowie appoints Oz McCormick as the crew boss. "It was just someone who could be spokesperson for the group," McCormick recalls. "If the tour manager wanted to let the crew know something, rather than tell 10 different people, they'd have a chargehand." Meanwhile, Cowie continues his ego clash with Grant Showbiz, as an argument over the quality of the group's sound rages on in sarcastic fashion. "There's friction in any crew to a certain degree," Oz notes. "If you've got three to four departments – back line, PA, lights – there's always two people who'll want to use the space for different things... There were little arguments between people who were on the road and in each other's faces for four to five weeks. There was bickering over little points, blown out of all proportion because you're in such close proximity." While backstage friction ferments, volatile audiences have to be kept in check. Outside the town hall, 40 fans climb on top of the group's van in an attempt to gain access to the dressing room. When The Smiths appear onstage they are again greeted by a hail of spit, but Morrissey expertly calms matters in his authoritative manner.

Set List: 'Hand In Glove'; 'Heaven Knows I'm Miserable Now'; 'Girl Afraid'; 'This Charming Man'; 'Pretty Girls Make Graves'; 'Still Ill'; 'This Night Has Opened My Eyes'; 'Barbarism Begins At Home'; 'Back To The Old House'; 'What Difference Does It Make?'; 'Reel Around The Fountain'; 'You've Got Everything Now'; 'Handsome Devil'.

9 MARCH

The group arrive late for their appointment at the University of Lancaster. "Morrissey is most annoyed," Cowie notes, "but short of camping in people's houses or literally dragging them out of bed, I do not see what can be done." Fortunately, the music makes it all worthwhile, even for the beleaguered tour manager. "On a musical level, one of the high points of the tour," he enthuses, "and I feel very proud of the band." The audience is even more appreciative and joins Morrissey in a singalong version of 'Reel Around The Fountain'.

10 MARCH

From the sublime to the dreadful as The Smiths stumble towards a poorly organized gig at the Coventry Polytechnic. "Dreadful place, shabby treatment," Cowie notes, after which he strongly complains to All Trade Booking. The evening ends on a sour note when the tour manager has to be restrained from attacking the Polytechnic's social secretary. One can only imagine Morrissey's reaction to all this.

Set List: 'Hand In Glove'; 'Heaven Knows I'm Miserable Now'; 'Girl Afraid'; 'This Charming Man'; 'Pretty Girls Make Graves'; 'Still Ill'; 'This Night Has Opened My Eyes'; 'Barbarism Begins At Home'; 'Back To The Old House'; 'What Difference Does It Make?'; 'Reel Around The Fountain'; 'You've Got Everything Now'; 'Handsome Devil'.

12 MARCH

A grand return to London, where The Smiths are booked to play the Hammersmith Palais. The afternoon is a cauldron of chaos as management, record company personnel, journalists, crew and support acts all vie for Morrissey's attention. Most of the afternoon is wasted searching for drum parts and the group arrive late

for their soundcheck. Official representative Scott Piering is doing his best to placate an important representative from Warner Brothers, while *Rolling Stone* journalist James Henke waits for a crack at Morrissey. He, at least, is not disappointed. With characteristically insouciant spite, Morrissey suggests a solution to the problem of Margaret Thatcher: "She's only one person and she can be destroyed. I just pray there is a Sirhan Sirhan somewhere. It's the only remedy for this country at the moment."

While Morrissey issues his *bon mots*, all is not well backstage. Cowie is needling Showbiz about showing favouritism to The Frank Chickens and depriving The Red Guitars of a crucial soundcheck on their big night. "I've always had a problem with authority figures," Grant smiles, "and I felt 'Why have they imposed this guy on us?'... Phil wasn't a nasty person, just nothing to do with what The Smiths were about."

When Morrissey finally appears, he also seems on edge. "Morrissey is very cross when Sandie Shaw fails to be at the appointed place when she should be on," Cowie observes. Shaw, in fact, has fallen victim to last minute stage nerves, but recovers to perform a pleasing rendition of 'I Don't Owe You Anything'. "I was so nervous," Shaw recalls. "I'd been sitting at the side of the stage watching and they went marching off to the dressing room to look for me. When I wasn't there they thought I'd pissed off because I didn't like the show! So they're panicking up there and I'm sitting down on the stage thinking, 'They don't want me to go on, they've changed their minds'. Eventually, they found me and were begging me to go on... Afterwards, Morrissey rang me up at about three in the morning and said, 'Well?' I just told him I could have done an hour, one song just wasn't enough."

Set List: 'Miserable Lie'; 'Heaven Knows I'm Miserable Now'; 'This Charming Man'; 'Girl Afraid'; 'Pretty Girls Make Graves'; 'Still Ill'; 'This Night Has Opened My Eyes'; 'Barbarism Begins At Home'; 'Back To The Old House'; 'What Difference Does It Make?'; 'I Don't Owe You Anything' (featuring Sandie Shaw); 'Reel Around The Fountain'; 'Hand In Glove'; 'You've Got Everything Now'; 'Handsome Devil'; 'These Things Take Time'.

13 MARCH

In order to get the show back on the road, crew member John Marr stays up all night working on the equipment truck. The group arrive late in Manchester, but make up for lost time and end the evening with a stunning performance at the Free Trade Hall, in which scores of fans have to be rescued from their own self-destructive enthusiasm. Two people narrowly avoid being crushed and are offered tickets for another show as consolation.

Set List: 'Hand In Glove'; 'Heaven Knows I'm Miserable Now'; 'Girl Afraid'; 'This Charming Man'; 'Pretty Girls Make Graves'; 'Still Ill'; 'This Night Has Opened My Eyes'; 'Barbarism Begins At Home'; 'Back To The Old House'; 'What Difference Does It Make?'; 'Reel Around The Fountain'; 'You've Got Everything Now'; 'Handsome Devil'; 'These Things Take Time'.

14 MARCH

The revelries of the previous night clearly take their toll on the late rising Marr who cannot be contacted by phone. By lunch time, Cowie drives over to his house to rouse him. That evening, the group play the University of Liverpool and Morrissey receives some unexpected barracking from the more acerbic elements in the audience.

Set List: 'Hand In Glove'; 'Still Ill'; 'Heaven Knows I'm Miserable Now'; 'This Charming Man'; 'Girl Afraid'; 'Pretty Girls Make Graves'; 'This Night Has Opened My Eyes'; 'Barbarism Begins At Home'; 'Back To The Old House'; 'What Difference Does It Make?'; 'Reel Around The Fountain'; 'You've Got Everything Now'; 'Handsome Devil'.

15 MARCH

"Not a very happy experience," Cowie notes forlornly while recalling the evening's gig at the University of Hull. Grant and Cowie are embroiled in an argument about the hire of a monitor system for an appearance on the television show *The Tube*. The tour manager is appalled at the cost, a hefty £300, while the soundman merely shrugs his shoulders. "Grant is both unconcerned and unrepentant," his adversary notes. "Oh, Phil was so small time," Showbiz retorts with resigned amusement. The group are spared these backstage comic melodramas and at a private meeting reveal that they are now reasonably happy with the tour.

Set List: 'Hand In Glove'; 'Still Ill'; 'Heaven Knows I'm Miserable Now'; 'This Charming Man'; 'Girl Afraid'; 'Pretty Girls Make Graves'; 'This Night Has Opened My Eyes'; 'Barbarism Begins At Home'; 'Back To The Old House'; 'What Difference Does It Make?'; 'Reel Around The Fountain'; 'You've Got Everything Now'; 'Handsome Devil'.

16 MARCH

A tiring day concludes with an appearance on *The Tube* alongside Howard Jones and Madness. The Smiths perform 'Hand In Glove', 'Still Ill' and 'Barbarism Begins At Home'.

17 MARCH

Prior to The Smiths' appearance at Loughborough University, the nagging issue of tour bonuses drags on. Scott Piering listens sympathetically to the financial proposals and wisely says little before returning to hear Morrissey's version of events. The group, meanwhile, enjoy the St Patrick's Day activities.

18 MARCH

Morrissey insists via Piering that he never actually agreed to any tour bonuses. Cowie reluctantly lets the matter rest. Weariness appears to be setting in as the group return to the De Montfort Hall, Leicester. Although the tour has had its fun moments and the group are getting on well, the administrative hassles and sense of unreality produced by non-stop travelling along British motorways has obviously taken its toll. The Smiths' main strength appears to be their remarkable ability to insulate themselves from the encroaching problems that persistently threaten their good humour.

Set List: 'Hand In Glove'; 'Still Ill'; 'Heaven Knows I'm Miserable Now'; 'This Charming Man'; 'Girl Afraid'; 'Pretty Girls Make Graves'; 'This Night Has Opened My Eyes'; 'Barbarism Begins At Home'; 'Back To The Old House'; 'What Difference Does It Make?'; 'Reel Around The Fountain'; 'You've Got Everything Now'; 'Handsome Devil'; 'These Things Take Time'.

19 MARCH

A new PA system is used for the evening's gig at Sheffield City Hall, which is enough to cause niggles within the band. Cowie is severely critical of the sound: "The snare sounds like a pee in a tin and as per usual there is not enough bass guitar." The crowd clearly do not subscribe to this view and provide The Smiths with a rapturous welcome, accompanied by gratifying scenes of fan mania. When the crowd is on their side, it seems The Smiths can do no wrong.

20 MARCH

They say that if you hang around Morrissey long enough you're in danger of falling victim to his own little neuroses. On the last night of the tour at the Birmingham Town Hall, Cowie proves the point. "I am feeling very ill," he notes, "and the venue is profoundly depressing. The tour has gone on for too long." Morrissey, at least, concludes matters on a humorous note. As the audience bays for an encore, he politely asks them which song they would like to hear. The phrase 'Reel Around The Fountain' reverberates round the hall. Morrissey takes it all in, then launches into 'These Things Take Time' as a final comment on audience democracy.

30 MARCH

Sandie Shaw's version of 'Hand In Glove' is released. "From a recording point of view it was a tremendous success," Morrissey enthuses. "From a sales point of view, it wasn't. It reached number 27, but it should have done much more. I feel slightly angered because of that."

31 MARCH

Channel 4's *Earsay* features The Smiths (minus Morrissey) backing Sandie Shaw on 'Hand In Glove'. "At that time, I had not completed my reincarnation from Sixties Dolly Bird to Eighties Pop Icon," Shaw recalled in her autobiography. "I had turned up at the studio straight from the kitchen, still in my work clothes, having left a wash on... Frothing at the mike, I swirled around the highly amused Johnny, Mike and Andy... On transmission my embarrassment was intense. I thought I looked like a demented housewife in a washing powder commercial." Shaw's embarrassment is compounded by an old clip from *Ready Steady Go* which shows her singing 'Girl Don't Come' and being interviewed by Keith Fordyce. Morrissey, by contrast, thinks the excerpts are adorable and effuses about Shaw and their newsworthy collaboration.

MARCH/APRIL

The tour accounts are presented and some wide ranging plans, including a European tour, are mooted by the tour manager. Alas, he has now completely fallen out of favour. Cowie leaves The Smiths with a chilling Cassandra-like memorandum, which betrays a strangely idealistic resignation: "The band are in serious danger of exposure, of alienating their fans and becoming the next pop tarts. Their whole management seems to be an excuse for media manipulation. My wishes are falling on deliberately uncaring ears... the doctor's prophecy may come true... It is at this time too distressing to chronologically outline and discard the destruction of so much effort by so many people, even if we do not wish to exploit the band for every penny possible. But we do wish to see something that they've helped to nurture and grow into international success. Next week: *The Des O'Connor Show* or *Cheggers Goes Pop*".

Morrissey, at least, ought to have appreciated the melodramatic mind games that The Smiths provoked, unwittingly or otherwise. It was not just the fans that took them seriously, but virtually everybody in their orbit... and Morrissey still felt they weren't taken seriously enough! Ironically, while Cowie bemoans the dangers of The Smiths becoming "pop tarts" and appearing alongside the derided Cheggars, Morrissey seems quite willing to pursue this direction. "We will appear on *The Russell Harty Show* and *Cheggars Plays Pop*", he notes. "We think we can do these things and walk away with enormous credibility because we are very strong-willed characters and our belief is very deep-rooted. We just have immense strength... There is a great deal of depth that just hasn't seen the light of day, yet. It's self-evident... It's all in those songs."

> **'When Steven spoke about Thatcher and the Brighton bombing I was shocked... I couldn't believe it...'**
>
> PETER MORRISSEY

6 APRIL

Morrissey joins Sandie Shaw on the panel of Radio 1's weekly 'Juke Box Jury', *Roundtable.*

7 APRIL

Morrissey and Marr appear on ITV's *Datarun* performing a singalong acoustic version of 'This Charming Man' before an audience of children at St Wilfred's. Steven revisits old haunts when he is taken on a tour of his primary school.

MID-1984: The Smiths on the tour which saw the addition of NHS specs and hearing aid to Morrissey's stage persona.

12 APRIL

Melody Maker publish a rare but welcome interview with Johnny Marr, in which the guitarist spells out his own manifesto for The Smiths. "I think we're really getting back to the original inspiration for making music," he claims. "Right back at the birth of this phenomenon called pop music, music was a way of bringing young people together and inspiring them. That's exactly what we're trying to do: we're trying to get back to old values that have been lost... Too many people, even these days, like seven years after punk is supposed to have destroyed all this, too many people still want to be stars. All they can think about is hit records and money and being famous. They've just forgotten all the real reasons for making music in the first place. They're just wrecking the beauty of music, which is what The Smiths want to get back."

14 APRIL

Shaw, Marr and Rourke perform 'I Don't Owe You Anything' and 'Jeane' on Radio 1's *Saturday Live*.

19 APRIL

The Smiths fly to Brussels for a mini-tour of Europe.

21 APRIL

The Smiths appear at De Meervaart, Amsterdam for a party sponsored by the magazine *Vinyl*. Nick Cave plays as support. Part of the concert is subsequently broadcast on Holland's KRO Radio.

Set List: 'Hand In Glove'; 'Heaven Knows I'm Miserable Now'; 'Girl Afraid'; 'This Charming Man'; 'Barbarism Begins At Home'; 'This Night Has Opened My Eyes'; 'Miserable Lie'; 'Still Ill'; 'I Don't Owe You Anything'; 'What Difference Does It Make?'; 'Handsome Devil'; 'You've Got Everything Now'; 'These Things Take Time'.

22 APRIL

The short European sojourn continues with an appearance at the Brecon Festival in Bree, Belgium. "It was just mudsville," recalls Grant Showbiz. "We were between Snowy White and The Bollocks Brothers. A real wind-up. No soundcheck, just straight in there and do it. And we were supporting The Bollocks Brothers! We couldn't believe it!" Morrissey's jaundice is reflected in some amusing opening exchanges with the audience. "Does anybody have anything to say?" he deadpans. "Anything sensible? Anything English? Anything? Any messages? Anybody like this microphone?"

Set List: 'Hand In Glove'; 'Heaven Knows I'm Miserable Now'; 'Girl Afraid'; 'This Charming Man'; 'Barbarism Begins At Home'; 'This Night Has Opened My Eyes'; 'Still Ill'; 'Handsome Devil'; 'What Difference Does It Make?'; 'You've Got Everything Now'; 'These Things Take Time'.

24 APRIL

The Smiths travel to Zurich where Ollie May's brother Marcus is promoting a gig at the Rote Fabrik. Morrissey and Marr are showing signs of poor health, having lived off a diet of chocolate and chips. "Nobody was asking for proper food that didn't have meat in the soup," Grant sympathized.

Set List: 'Hand In Glove'; 'Heaven Knows I'm Miserable Now'; 'Girl Afraid'; 'This Charming Man'; 'Barbarism Begins At Home'; 'This Night Has Opened My Eyes'; 'Still Ill'; 'Handsome Devil'; 'What Difference Does It Make?'; 'You've Got Everything Now'; 'These ThingsTake Time'; 'Miserable Lie'; 'Pretty Girls Make Graves'; 'Hand In Glove'.

25 APRIL

The group fly back to the UK for an appearance on *Top Of The Pops*. They will not be returning to the Continent in the immediate future. Scheduled gigs in Vienna, Frankfurt, Cologne and Bremen are duly cancelled.

26 APRIL

A stiletto-heeled Sandie Shaw sings 'Hand In Glove' on *Top Of The Pops* backed by the shoeless Marr, Rourke and Joyce.

Morrissey stresses, "and I am thrust forward and other group members very rarely give their comments, and when they do they're much less serious than mine anyway. They don't really share my lyrical viewpoint. Most of the time they quite like it, but they certainly don't share it. But I don't mind... I suppose my input is more serious. And much more crucially personal. I think that at the end of this experience, if or when The Smiths break up, I feel sure that the other three group members could walk on to something else, but I don't think I could because I fear this is absolutely *it* for me, and my neck is in the noose, almost. The other three can step back and they *can* claim disinvolvement. But I never could. I'll risk anything."

Heaven Knows I'm Miserable Now

27 APRIL

' Heaven Knows I'm Miserable Now' is released and goes on to reach number 10 in the UK charts. More than any other song in The Smiths' repertoire, this single led to the caricature of Morrissey as Mr Miserable. In interviews of the period, he fully reveals the extent of his morbidity, thereby reinforcing the media's image of his darker side. "I'm very interested in being alone and people feeling isolated," he stresses, "which is the way I think most people feel at the end of the day. I think it's a general condition under which people live, and I often feel that it has something to do with death, because one is ultimately alone when one dies."

Later in his career, he agreed that he was a depressive character ("Almost every aspect of human life really quite seriously depresses me"), but still felt his "miserabilism" required qualification. "My self-view is that I'm more cynical than romantic," he stressed. "I'm not a jolly character, a life and soul of the party type, and I suppose I asked for the misery tag. I just didn't expect such a generous response! However, I dispute that I'm the Ambassador of Misery."

27 APRIL

The 12-inch version of 'Heaven Knows I'm Miserable Now' features an extra track, 'Girl Afraid', an excellent example of The Smiths' tendency to use quality tracks on flip sides. According to Marr, the song was originally conceived as a piano part, and ended up as one of the group's most distinctive intros. Morrissey's lyrics betray his anti-romantic leanings and age-old hatred of marriage. "'Girl Afraid' simply implied that within relationships, there's no real certainty and nobody knows how anybody feels," he explained. "People feel that simply because they're having this cemented communion with another person that the two of them will become whole, which is something I detested... Ultimately, you're on your own, whatever happens in life."

MAY

Morrissey achieves an adolescent ambition by actually interviewing one of his favourite stars: Pat Phoenix of *Coronation Street* fame. The piece is run in the May issue of the style magazine *Blitz*. "Pat Phoenix was simply a blizzard of professionalism – of goodwill, of warmth," Morrissey recalls. "At the end of the day when the interview had happened and we sat and talked about certain things and I was getting ready to leave, she took me aside and said, 'You're a very unhappy person'. I was momentarily frozen and she went on to explain why I was unhappy – and why I was ambitious and did the things I did. It seems that throughout the day she had been analysing the way I am. It was a very solemn half hour for me to listen to because she was so accurate. It seemed at that instance that there was even more to her than I had ever imagined – her skill and her ability as an observant person was quite awesome."

4 MAY

Not for the first time, the Irish magazine *Hot Press* publishes a brief but incisive interview with Morrissey. covering his childhood, religious attitudes and, inevitably, celibacy. The piece closes with some insightful comments on Morrissey's role in The Smiths and once again obliquely anticipates their break-up. "I am the spokesperson for the group," Morrissey stresses...

4 MAY

Rough Trade persuade The Smiths to return to Europe for some televised promotional work. The group appear at the Markthalle, Hamburg in a concert filmed for the series *Rockpalast*. "The gig was weird," Grant recalls. "A seated audience; television. It wasn't what we expected."

Set List: 'Hand In Glove'; 'Heaven Knows I'm Miserable Now'; 'Girl Afraid'; 'This Charming Man'; 'Pretty Girls Make Graves'; 'Still Ill'; 'Barbarism Begins At Home'; 'This Night Has Opened My Eyes'; 'Miserable Lie'; 'You've Got Everything Now'; 'Handsome Devil'; 'What Difference Does It Make?'; 'These Things Take Time'; 'This Charming Man'; 'Hand In Glove'; 'Barbarism Begins At Home'.

6 MAY

Sandie Shaw joins The Smiths in Germany to promote 'Hand In Glove' on the programme *Formel Eins*. Morrissey, speaking in the magazine *Jamming!* reminds the world of the importance of The Smiths' sole flop single. "The only tragedy for The Smiths," he overstates, "has been that 'Hand In Glove' didn't gain the attention it deserved. I won't rest until that song is in the heart of everything... It should have been a massive hit. It was so urgent – to me, it was a complete cry in every direction. It really was a landmark.... It was as if these four people had to play that song – it was so essential. Those words had to be sung."

9 MAY

The Smiths perform at the Theatre, El Dorado, Paris. "We're The Smiths," Morrissey announces authoritatively before launching into a suprisingly well enunciated version of 'Hand In Glove'. The set switches in mood from the lightness of 'Girl Afraid'

ROURKE, Marr and Joyce in playful and relaxed mood.

and 'This Charming Man' to a bombastic version of 'Barbarism Begins At Home', complete with some magnificent barking. Other highlights include a striking reading of 'Pretty Girls Make Graves' in which the song's misogynistic overtones are strongly voiced, and a poignant rendition of 'This Night Has Opened My Eyes'. A frantic 'Miserable Lie' ends the show, after which The Smiths are called back for several encores. "Listen," Morrissey announces, "Johnny wants to do 'Barbarism'. Do you mind? Yes? No? Do you mind?" With no one shouting articulately enough to disagree, The Smiths return to their favourite song of the moment, with Rourke in particularly fine form. Morrissey wavers off-key in several places but compensates by yelping even louder. Marr, meanwhile, adds some impromptu breaks as the song meanders towards a close. The evening ends, as it had begun, with 'Hand In Glove'. With cameras present, part of the show is later broadcast on *Les Enfants Du Rock*. "It was a great gig," Grant Showbiz concludes. "There were 2,000 people, and the Parisians loved it. I think by then the press had been strong enough in England, and the French knew the *NME*".

Set List: 'Hand In Glove'; 'Heaven Knows I'm Miserable Now'; 'Girl Afraid'; 'This Charming Man'; 'Barbarism Begins At Home'; 'Pretty Girls Make Graves'; 'This Night Has Opened My Eyes'; 'Still Ill'; 'You've Got Everything Now'; 'Handsome Devil'; 'Miserable Lie'; 'These Things Take Time'; 'What Difference Does It Make?'; 'Barbarism Begins At Home'; 'Hand In Glove'.

EARLY MAY

Morrissey appears on *Pop Quiz*. He looks back on this episode with severe embarrassment. "That was so depressing," he admitted. "It's easy to say that now, but as I sat in that chair next to Alvin Stardust, I thought, 'My God! I've really lost control'. Before the cameras rolled, Alvin told the audience a joke which was incredibly depressing and everybody laughed. I just thought, 'Oh no! I shouldn't be here'. I had nothing else to do, that's the only reason I did it."

17 MAY

The Smiths appear in Northern Ireland for the first time, performing at Belfast's Ulster Hall. A stinging review in *Melody Maker* focuses on Morrissey's foppishness. The reviewer maintains that "the only noteworthy aspect of this evening's show was that everybody's favourite shirt, Morrissey, is still managing to prance about with a well-tended window-box up his arse! Still playing at being a neo-hippy Byron in baggy trousers, flopping (and fopping) about like a bloodhound's jowl, it's about time Morrissey started acting his age on stage and not his bloody shoe size. Three songs into the set and the keen edge keels completely. There's no *brunt* behind anything". The criticisms culminate in a final shot at the apparent "collapse of the band into the annoying, silly blubbering, infantile mess on display tonight". Although Morrissey refrains from making any inflammatory statements about the political situation north of the border, he is quick to question the veracity of this review. "We played Belfast," he announces, "two-and-a-half thousand people in a sell-out concert. It was really quite hysterical and quite wonderful. We did four encores and everybody was enormously receptive, and then I read this review which implies that the whole thing was entirely damp, entirely forgettable and nobody cared!"

18 MAY

The group drive south to Dublin for a welcome appearance at the SFX Centre. The venue is covered in flowers as Morrissey thanks the "doomed delicates" in the audience.

Set List: 'Hand In Glove'; 'Still Ill'; 'This Charming Man'; 'This Night Has Opened My Eyes'; 'Heaven Knows I'm Miserable Now'; 'Miserable Lie'; 'I Don't Owe You Anything'; 'Barbarism Begins At Home'; 'Reel Around The Fountain'; 'What Difference Does It Make?'; 'These Things Take Time'; 'Hand In Glove'; 'You've Got Everything Now'; 'Handsome Devil'.

19 MAY

A second appearance at Dublin's SFX Centre is again well attended. Although the group are establishing themselves in the music business, Morrissey remains firmly on the outside. "Most of the people that I come across in the whole industry I have no real desire to form any friendships with," he confesses. "I still feel quite angry about most things and I still feel on the outside. Though we've had some degree of national success it doesn't really change to me. For some naïve reason, I thought that it would. The music industry is just like anything else in life."

Set List: 'Still Ill'; 'Hand In Glove'; 'Pretty Girls Make Graves'; 'This Charming Man'; 'This Night Has Opened My Eyes'; 'Heaven Knows I'm Miserable Now'; 'Miserable Lie'; 'I Don't Owe You Anything'; 'Barbarism Begins At Home'; 'Reel Around The Fountain'; 'What Difference Does It Make?'; 'Jeane'; 'These Things Take Time'; 'Hand In Glove'; 'You've Got Everything Now'; 'Handsome Devil'.

20 MAY

Forty-eight hours before Morrissey's 25th birthday, The Smiths complete their short Irish tour with a memorable gig at the Savoy in Cork.

Set List: 'Still Ill'; 'Hand In Glove'; 'Pretty Girls Make Graves'; 'This Charming Man'; 'This Night Has Opened My Eyes'; 'Heaven Knows I'm Miserable Now'; 'Miserable Lie'; 'I Don't Owe You Anything'; 'Barbarism Begins At Home'; 'Reel Around The

Fountain'; 'What Difference Does It Make?'; 'Jeane'; 'These Things Take Time'; 'Hand In Glove'; 'You've Got Everything Now'; 'What Difference Does It Make?'

25 MAY

Morrissey appears as guest reviewer on *Eight Days In A Week* in the unlikely company of George Michael and Tony Blackburn.

31 MAY

The group perform 'Heaven Knows I'm Miserable Now' on *Top Of The Pops*. Morrissey looks resplendent, this time appearing sans specs, but boasting an ambitious quiff, brooch and the controversial hearing aid featured earlier in the year. Marr is also looking fashionable in his round mirror shades and leather jacket. By now, Morrissey is well known for his eccentricities such as the bush that protrudes from the backside of his jeans as he flails across the studio floor. "It was the end of a stage for us and in a way it was a parody," he explains. "But, also, to me, it was high art. People laughed at the Pre-Raphaelites. Remember that I did think it was quite artistic. For one thing, it had never been done before, and to me it's quite serious."

1 JUNE

The Smiths fly to Finland, but prior to their arrival they encounter turbulent weather. One passenger recalls that Morrissey was in tears, and the singer later confirms this account. "It was a very horrendous plane journey," he remembers, "and for some reason the floodgates just opened, as they say, and didn't stop for the rest of the day. On the plane, in the airport, in the hotel, at the soundcheck. I just couldn't stop."

2 JUNE

Despite Morrissey's emotional state, The Smiths appear at the Provinssi Rock Festival, Seinajoki. "Finland was the first time I worked with them," remembers tour manager Stuart James. "I was a bit wary of the group because of what had been built up before. The picture that had been impressed upon me was that everyone had to look after their whims." As they travel across Finland, James is struck by their complete lack of interest in the country. "It was almost xenophobia," he notes. "Finland was somewhere I'd never been to before, and I knew they hadn't travelled widely... It almost didn't make any difference what country they were in. They were so insular as a unit."

7 JUNE

Rolling Stone publishes an interview with Morrissey headlined: "Oscar! Oscar! Great Britain Goes Wilde For The Fourth-Gender Smiths". The piece is most memorable for its opening salvo: "He goes by a single name, Morrissey. He calls himself 'a prophet for the fourth gender', admits he's gay, but adds that he's also celibate." Morrissey, who had always strenuously resisted such classifications, later castigates the journalist for his presumptuousness. "That brought a lot of problems for me," he says of the article. "Of course, I never made such a statement." Full of indignation, he complains, "I just think it's so untrue and so unfair... That person said I was gay and he never asked me; he never approached the subject... I think it was just wishful thinking on his part. Ultimately, people will see what they want to see in the whole aspect of what I do and my motivations. I'm not embarrassed about the word 'gay', but it's not in the least bit relevant. I'm beyond that frankly."

Within the *Rolling Stone* piece, there is indeed no "admission" of gayness and the singer is given leave to trot out his familiar lines about the errors of sexual classification: "I don't know anybody who is absolutely, exclusively heterosexual. It limits people's potential in so many areas. I think we should slap down these barriers."

The Smiths perform 'Heaven Knows I'm Miserable Now' on *Earsay*. Morrissey stresses his lack of interest in touring internationally, a reaction which may have been prompted by the unfortunate Finland trip. He also hints at new ventures, which will remain unrealized. "I'm very interested in this particular screenplay that I'm blustering through at the moment," he notes. "But to talk about these things seems incredibly pompous and ostentatious. It almost sounds entirely careerist."

BEFORE AND AFTER: The Smiths at Glastonbury, June 1984.

10 JUNE
The Smiths appear at the GLC "Jobs For A Change" Festival on a bill that includes Mari Wilson, Misty In Roots, Hank Wangford, Billy Bragg and The Redskins. After arriving at the Jubilee Gardens on London's South Bank, tour manager Stuart James encounters trouble back stage. "Mike and Andy were throwing flowers out of the window, which landed on a car," he recalls. "Twenty screaming fans climbed all over it, leaving a large dent." James is aggrieved to discover that the owner is a member of the catering staff for the forthcoming Glastonbury Festival. Meanwhile, the group complete their 14-song set, despite Morrissey's aversion to "festivals".

Set List: 'Nowhere Fast'; 'Girl Afraid'; 'This Charming Man'; 'William, It Was Really Nothing'; 'Heaven Knows I'm Miserable Now'; 'I Don't Owe You Anything'; 'Still Ill'; 'Jeane'; 'Barbarism Begins At Home'; 'Hand In Glove'; 'What Difference Does It Make?'; 'You've Got Everything Now'; 'Pretty Girls Make Graves'; 'Miserable Lie'.

12 JUNE
The Smiths travel north to the Market Hall, Carlisle. Morrissey maintains his distance from the crew, while preparing for the evening's show. "He was always saying that he didn't like to see people on the stage that he didn't know or recognize," Oz McCormick maintains. "He didn't like local crew or security men standing in the shadows. While on stage, he wanted his back to be covered by faces that he knew."

Set List: 'Nowhere Fast'; 'Girl Afraid'; 'Handsome Devil'; 'This Charming Man'; 'William, It Was Really Nothing'; 'Heaven Knows I'm Miserable Now'; 'Still Ill'; 'I Don't Owe You Anything'; 'Jeane'; 'Barbarism Begins At Home'; 'Hand In Glove'; 'What Difference Does It Make?'; 'You've Got Everything Now'; 'Pretty Girls Make Graves'; 'Miserable Lie'; 'These Things Take Time'.

13-17 JUNE
The group undertake a short tour of Scotland. They play identical sets at their first four dates: Barrowlands, Glasgow (13th), Caley Palais, Edinburgh (14th), Caird Hall, Dundee (15th), Capital Theatre, Aberdeen (16th).

Set List: 'Nowhere Fast'; 'Girl Afraid'; 'Handsome Devil'; 'William, It Was Really Nothing'; 'This Charming Man'; 'Heaven Knows I'm Miserable Now'; 'Still Ill'; 'I Don't Owe You Anything'; 'Jeane'; 'Barbarism Begins At Home'; 'Hand In Glove'; 'Pretty Girls Make Graves'; 'Miserable Lie'; 'What Difference Does It Make?'; 'You've Got Everything Now'.

14 JUNE
The Smiths return to *Top Of The Pops* for another airing of 'Heaven Knows I'm Miserable Now'."I find *Top Of The Pops* great fun," Morrissey remarks, "which is something that's very hard for the old lips to say. They always give us a semi-royal reception. I know I should spit on the whole idea of *Top Of The Pops*, but I can't. I think the groups who criticize *Top Of The Pops* are those that probably know they'll never get on there."

17 JUNE
The mini-tour of Scotland ends at Eden Court, Inverness. One of the more amusing aspects of this period is Morrissey's inclusion of riders in his contract demanding "Flowers to the approximate value of £50 sterling. No roses or other flowers with thorns". For Stuart James, it proves an enlightening introduction to Morrissey's eccentricity. "That was the first time I was presented with these riders," the tour manager recalls. "There was always the odd one, and then they started getting odder and odder. It started with flowers and then went on to a tree."

Set List: 'Nowhere Fast'; 'Girl Afraid'; 'Handsome Devil'; 'William, It Was Really Nothing'; 'Heaven Knows I'm Miserable Now'; 'Still Ill'; 'I Don't Owe You Anything'; 'Jeane'; 'Barbarism Begins At Home'; 'Hand In Glove'; 'Pretty Girls Make Graves'; 'Miserable Lie'; 'Handsome Devil'; 'You've Got Everything Now'.

20 JUNE
The Smiths' visit to the Opera House, Blackpool, proves very memorable. Viv Nicholson, the sometimes tragic Sixties pools winner whose face had graced the sleeve of 'Heaven Knows I'm Miserable Now', pays her respects to Morrissey. "He requested to meet her," recalls Stuart James. "They had a walk on the prom, chatted, and got on very well. Afterwards, she was in the hotel sat down with Morrissey, surrounded by the gutter press. Whether she had asked the press, or more likely had a press agent, I don't know. But the paparazzi were there trying to get a story." The tour manager is also presented with a birthday surprise by the crew. "We told him some lies to get him into the dressing room, which was already full of the crew and band," recalls Oz McCormick. "I don't think Morrissey was there because a girl got her tits out. She was a kissogram. Stuart was totally shocked!"

Set List: 'Nowhere Fast'; 'Girl Afraid'; 'Handsome Devil'; 'This Charming Man'; 'William, It Was Really Nothing'; 'Heaven Knows I'm Miserable Now'; 'Still Ill'; 'I Don't Owe You Anything'; 'Jeane'; 'Barbarism Begins At Home'; 'Hand In Glove'; 'Pretty Girls Make Graves'; 'Miserable Lie'; 'What Difference Does It Make?'; 'You've Got Everything Now'.

22 JUNE

The Smiths appear at the Cornish Coliseum, St Austell, Cornwall, a venue that seldom sells out in advance for the group. This was one of the few gigs on the tour from which tapes were not readily available.

23 JUNE

The Smiths play the Glastonbury CND Festival on a bill that includes Weather Report, Black Uhuru, Ian Dury, Joan Baez, The Band, Fela Kuti, General Public, Christy Moore, Dr John, Fairport Convention, Brass Construction, The Staple Singers, Paul Brady, Amazulu, Steve Joliffe and Billy Bragg. The *NME* provides an on-the-spot report. "The arrival of The Smiths at tea-time," they note, "transformed the crowd in front of the stage who were suddenly infiltrated and then usurped by the day-ticket holders. Teenage lust and adoration temporarily replaced love and peace as Morrissey cavorted his fragile form and chaste (or chased, as he is these days) romanticism across the stage... Their set was even shorter than usual because the organizers wanted to squeeze in Amazulu who'd arrived late. And an invasion of the stage by a few brainless day-trippers prevented the encore that The Smiths deserved and the crowd wanted."

Morrissey is far more critical of the gig than his supporters on the *NME*. "It was quite strange," he confessed in a subsequent radio interview. "It's not something that, quite honestly, I'd like to re-live. It wasn't the best of our performances and there was animosity from certain sections of the crowd... I didn't think The Smiths really worked at Glastonbury. I'm not exactly sure why... perhaps because we built our following in smaller clubs and now we've advanced to larger halls. We're very much a live group and it was always very intimate and personal, which is something we couldn't capture at Glastonbury."

Further problems beset tour manager, Stuart James, who spends much of the day dealing with the repercussions of the previous GLC Festival. "At Glastonbury, we had hassles with the backstage crew because of what had happened at the GLC with one of the caterer's cars," he explains. "We didn't feel it was our responsibility to pay for it. Certainly, the group didn't feel it was their responsibility... As for the stage invasion – about three or four people managed to climb up the side of the pyramid which at that time was made of corrugated iron. You could get very badly cut if you were clinging to the top of this corrugated iron, but a few people managed to get up there."

As a result of The Smiths' appearance at Glastonbury, Morrissey is later questioned about his views on nuclear disarmament and declares that the world must be rid of nuclear weapons. "I would say that violence on behalf of CND is absolutely necessary," he stresses. "I don't think that it is terrorism, it's more a self-defence." Despite his proselytizing tone, it is noticeable that Morrissey takes pains to steer clear of festivals after the Glastonbury reception.

Set List: 'Nowhere Fast'; 'Girl Afraid'; 'Handsome Devil'; 'This Charming Man'; 'William, It Was Really Nothing'; 'Heaven Knows I'm Miserable Now'; 'Still Ill'; 'Jeane'; 'Barbarism Begins At Home'; 'Hand In Glove'.

JULY

Morrissey inspects the accounts for the tour. "He was very suspicious about the use of a video camera," Stuart James recalls with a wry smile. Other less notable extravagances buried in the fulsome accounts book are "Audio cassettes for records: £2.48" and "Sponge for the car to wash it down: 60 pence". A reel-to-reel film of the Glastonbury Festival for £7 is also accepted by the vigilant Morrissey as a legitimate expense. Having displayed his credentials as a prospective tax inspector, Morrissey returns to the recording studio where the group are finishing work on their next single.

AUGUST

One of the relatives of the murdered John Kilbride hears 'Suffer Little Children' on a pub juke-box. Assuming that The Smiths are exploiting the murders, he voices his complaints to other members of the family and the press are alerted. Although the story is primarily of local interest, its impact on Morrissey will soon be felt.

IN AN INTERVIEW WITH THE MAGAZINE *DÉBUT*, Morrissey denies the likelihood of ever feeling fulfilled. "It is almost impossible to be content," he regrets. "It's absolutely humanly impossible. You spend your entire life with this driving force for contentment, and you never actually arrive. You're putting everything off for a day in your life that never happens... It's like whether you decide to marry or stay single – no matter which path you take, a certain amount of guilt creeps up on you. You realize that your life is passing, and you think, 'What exactly have I done, and have I lived?'

Marr, meanwhile, pre-empts Morrissey's famous "pop is dead" quote by five years with the following prognosis: "I think it's sad that teenagers seem to be getting too sophisticated to be teenagers any more. I think that very soon we're going to reach the age where the very idea of being in a group is uncool. The very idea that someone plays an instrument and tries to say something serious to their contemporaries is very soon going to be deemed uncool. The pop group industry certainly is soon going to be dead."

4 AUGUST

With time on his hands, Morrissey is invited to review this week's singles in *Melody Maker*. His apparent distaste for the work of Diana Ross emerges in the stinging dismissal, "One can only pray loudly for its final deletion," while the ephemerally popular Howard Jones receives a classic back-handed compliment: "Howard is a sweet man. But a steady diet of sweets sickens."

9 AUGUST

Radio 1 broadcast the latest Peel sessions, produced by John Porter on 1 August, featuring 'William It Was Really Nothing', 'Nowhere Fast', 'Rusholme Ruffians' and 'How Soon Is Now?'

24 AUGUST

'William, It Was Really Nothing' is released and soon climbs to number 17. The theme of settling down in a humdrum town has strong echoes of *Billy Liar*, but some commentators detect gay connotations in this tale of small town life. When questioned about this, Marr instinctively supports Morrissey's love of ambiguity. "I haven't managed to work out his exact angle on that one yet," he admits.

"Usually his lyrics are very much black and white to me, but this one is taking a little bit longer. 'William' is quite a whimsical song really. I don't think it's broken all the rules in pop music, but to start with a short verse and then follow it with three choruses is quite good... It wouldn't upset me if tomorrow Morrissey wrote a boy meets girl type song, but it's good to have songs that cater for no gender specifically. One of the reasons our records are timeless is because the lyrics are so good, and whatever gay overtones are there I endorse 100 per cent."

24 AUGUST

Amazingly, the 12-inch version of 'William, It Was Really Nothing' features an extra track

that many regard as one of their more famous: 'How Soon Is Now?'. "I thought, 'This is it!'," recalls producer John Porter. "I got on to the record company and said, 'We've got one here'. But I don't think the record company liked it. The Smiths liked it, but the record company put it out originally as a B-side. They later released it as an A-side. They totally threw it away, wasted it. Everybody knew The Smiths' fans had it. The record company blew it with that track."

30 AUGUST

The Smiths return to *Top Of The Pops* to promote 'William, It Was Really Nothing'. Mid-way through the song, Morrissey strips off his shirt to reveal the message "Marry Me" engraved on his torso.

THE MANY MOVES of Morrissey's stage craft in evidence in Paris, December 1984.

31 AUGUST

Morrissey answers phone-in questions from listeners on London's LBC radio. During the show he has to fend off several marriage proposals from his more ardent admirers.

SEPTEMBER

Morrissey's lease on his Kensington flat expires and he completes the move back to Manchester by purchasing a house in Halebarns. "What a great joy it is," he announces, "to finally have somewhere decent to live. It's this nice, neat little house. It's just a pleasure." Having settled at the abode named "Venlo", Morrissey casts a critical eye on his home city. In one of his more fanciful moments, he even posits the unlikely notion of entering local politics. "Seriously," he protests, "I feel strongly about politics. I would like to have some kind of involvement with local politics here in Manchester. I feel so strongly about the way the city is being completely defaced and made uninhabitable. It's so ugly now, vastly ugly. And it reflects itself in the attitudes of the people. I wonder why somebody like me cannot get involved in local politics?" The rhetorical question remains unanswered.

8 SEPTEMBER

Proof of The Smiths' enduring self-confidence is to be found in *Record Mirror*, in which the normally retiring Rourke asserts: "We are the best band in the world, there's nobody better. We have potentially vast amounts of status and we're getting better all the time." Marr is also in arrogant mood when explaining his songwriting skills. "Sometimes I wake up," he says, "and I say to myself – today I have to write a song, because I might not have written one for two or three days. It's good to do that as a discipline, to prove to myself that I can still write great pop songs. Sometimes it only takes me four minutes to write a song."

15 SEPTEMBER

Following local rumour and speculation in the Manchester media, a headline in the *Melody Maker* belatedly breaks the story nationally: "The Smiths In 'Moors' Row". The complaint about the lyrical content of 'Suffer Little Children' on a pub juke-box now switches to high street shops, culminating in the banning of 'Heaven Knows I'm Miserable Now' and *The Smiths* from branches of Boots and Woolworths.

Fearing a nationwide blanket ban on The Smiths' recordings, Scott Piering immediately releases a statement defending Morrissey's controversial lyric. "The Smiths stand behind 100 per cent of the lyrics to all of their songs and 'Suffer Little Children' is no exception," he begins. "The song was written out of a profound emotion by Morrissey, a Mancunian, who feels that the particularly horrendous crime it describes must be borne by the conscience of Manchester and that it must never happen again. It was written out of deep respect for the victims and their kin and The Smiths felt it was an important enough song to put on their last single even though it had already been released on their LP. In a word, it is a memorial to the children and all like them, who have suffered such a fate. The Smiths are acknowledged as writing with sensitivity, depth and intelligence and the suggestion that they are cashing in on a tragedy at the expense of causing grief to the relatives of its victims is absolutely untrue. Morrissey has had a lengthy conversation with the mother of Lesley Ann Downey, Mrs West, and she understands that the intentions of the song are completely honourable. Furthermore, he's willing to speak to any of the families involved so there will be no

SMITHS HIT BACK AFTER 'CHILD-MOLESTING' SLUR

MANCHESTER band the Smiths have this week hit bac[illegible] furiously at press reports linking their music to paedophilia, claiming that a recent BBC session had be[illegible] censored as a result.

Their lawyers have been in contact with the newspapers involved and are threatening legal action i[illegible] apologies and retractions are not provided. The controversy centres on a song called "Handsome Devil". Smiths singer Morrissey said this week: "I can't understand why anybody should write such a thing about us. We must stress that 'Handsome Devil' is aim[illegible] entirely towards adults and has nothing to do with child[illegible] children, and certainly nothing to do with child molesting. It's an adult understanding of quite intimate matters.

"On our David Jensen session, one song, 'Reel Arou[illegible] The Fountain' was chopped simply because the word 'child' was mentioned and they were frightened people might put the wrong interpretation on it. But at the end [of] the day, the BBC turned out to be allies."

At the group's record company, Rough Trade, a spokesman said: "We're horrified by the whole thing. There's no truth in any of the allegations about the songs."

The band's lawyers commented: "The allegations are absolutely and wholly denied by the band."

VARIOUS SCENES of the 1984 tour, including the soundcheck and waiting backstage in Paris, December 1984, (OPPOSITE PAGE MAIN PICTURE AND TOP INSET).

misunderstanding." One more controversy dogging the single is the photograph of the bouffant Viv Nicholson on the sleeve, which some mistakenly credit as Myra Hindley. Piering adds, "The photo was taken in 1961 and was first published in the *News Of The World* years before the tragic event occurred. The decision to put 'Suffer Little Children' on the B-side was made well after the choice of Ms Nicholson's photo had been made and although it is a chilling coincidence, there is no further connection."

22 SEPTEMBER

The Moors controversy is further diffused now that Piering has persuaded Morrissey to correspond with Ann West. "I had a long conversation with her," Piering recalls, "and I assured her and sold her on the case. I sent her the records, I sent photos and asked Morrissey if he'd write... I made sure these people really understood and went to the buyers. It ended up with Mrs West sending us a letter saying that she truly believed Morrissey was a good boy and was serious about the way he wrote the song, and she loved the song and thought it was very touching. She was strongly on our side and really helped us. Eventually, The Smiths brought her and her husband down and we put them up in an hotel and met them." Members of the Kilbride family are also assuaged after some money from the song is donated to charity as a sign of goodwill. Morrissey subsequently pours vitriol on the press for blowing up the issue. "This is the world we live in," he laments. "It's not a reflection on me, it really reflects the absolute and barbaric attitudes of the daily press. I don't feel that I was in the dock; I feel they were really. Some of the reports were so full of hate, it was like I was one of the Moors Murderers, that I'd gone out and murdered these children. It was incredible."

24 SEPTEMBER

The Smiths play a low-key show at the Leisure Centre, Gloucester. "There's absolute harmony within the group," claims Morrissey, "and as each day passes it becomes stronger, which is more important to me than anything else. I have no interest in solo success or individual spotlights."

Set List: 'William, It Was Really Nothing'; 'Handsome Devil'; 'Nowhere Fast'; 'How Soon Is Now?'; 'Barbarism Begins At Home'; 'Rusholme Ruffians'; 'This Charming Man'; 'Reel Around The Fountain'; 'Jeane'; 'You've Got Everything Now'; 'Girl Afraid'; 'Heaven Knows I'm Miserable Now'; 'Still Ill'; 'These Things Take Time'; 'Please Please Please Let Me Get What I Want'; 'Hand In Glove'; 'Miserable Lie'.

25 SEPTEMBER

The group commence a lightning tour of Wales at the University of Cardiff. "That was the start of the tree!" Stuart James explains, recalling the increasingly eccentric riders attached to the group's contracts. "It got to the point where I was walking about with a saw in my case with all the accounts. I had a tour manager briefcase and a saw in it because we'd get to the gig and the promoter would say: 'Would you like to come round and look at the tree?' Quite often, if it was a dodgy promoter you could tell he'd got the tree from somebody's backyard. If it was a good promoter it'd arrive in a parcel and I'd have to saw it down to Morrissey's specifications, and trim some branches. It'd be about seven foot, so that he could wield it around the audience. Not all promoters took the tree seriously, but they soon learned that it had to be taken seriously."

Set List: 'William, It Was Really Nothing'; 'Handsome Devil'; 'Nowhere Fast'; 'How Soon Is Now?'; 'Barbarism Begins At Home'; 'Rusholme Ruffians'; 'This Charming Man'; 'Reel Around The Fountain'; 'Jeane'; 'You've Got Everything Now'; 'Girl Afraid'; 'Heaven Knows I'm Miserable Now'; 'Still Ill'; 'These Things Take Time'; 'Please Please Please Let Me Get What I Want'; 'Hand In Glove'; 'Miserable Lie'.

26 SEPTEMBER

The tour moves on to the Mayfair, Swansea. The Woodentops are the regular support and there is still a feeling of camaraderie among The Smiths' retinue. "It wasn't a case of gross excess on the hotel bills," Stuart James confirms. "Everything was fairly reasonable. Even though they'd suddenly got a lot of success and were starting to sell records, they weren't squandering all of it – that'd come later!"

Set List: 'William, It Was Really Nothing'; 'Handsome Devil'; 'Nowhere Fast'; 'How Soon Is Now?'; 'Barbarism Begins At Home'; 'Rusholme Ruffians'; 'This Charming Man'; 'Reel Around The Fountain'; 'Jeane'; 'You've Got Everything Now'; 'Girl Afraid'; 'Heaven Knows I'm Miserable Now'; 'Still Ill'; 'These Things Take Time'; 'Please Please Please Let Me Get What I Want'; 'Hand In Glove'; 'Miserable Lie'.

OCTOBER

Morrissey makes a rare appearance at Manchester's Haçienda and is besieged by well-wishers. "For the entire night I was simply sandwiched between all these Smiths' apostles telling me about their problems and what they should do to cleanse themselves of improprieties," he recalled. "When I meet people like this I start to stumble with words and certainly in a night club situation it's almost impossible to say the most basic things clearly. Lots of people march away thinking I'm a totally empty-headed sieve because I haven't said, 'Go forth and multiply!' or something."

12 OCTOBER

An IRA bomb intended to assassinate Margaret Thatcher and most of the British Cabinet devastates the Grand Hotel, Brighton. Three people lose their lives and 30 more are badly injured. "Today we were unlucky," the IRA claim, "but, remember, we only need to be lucky once." Morrissey later

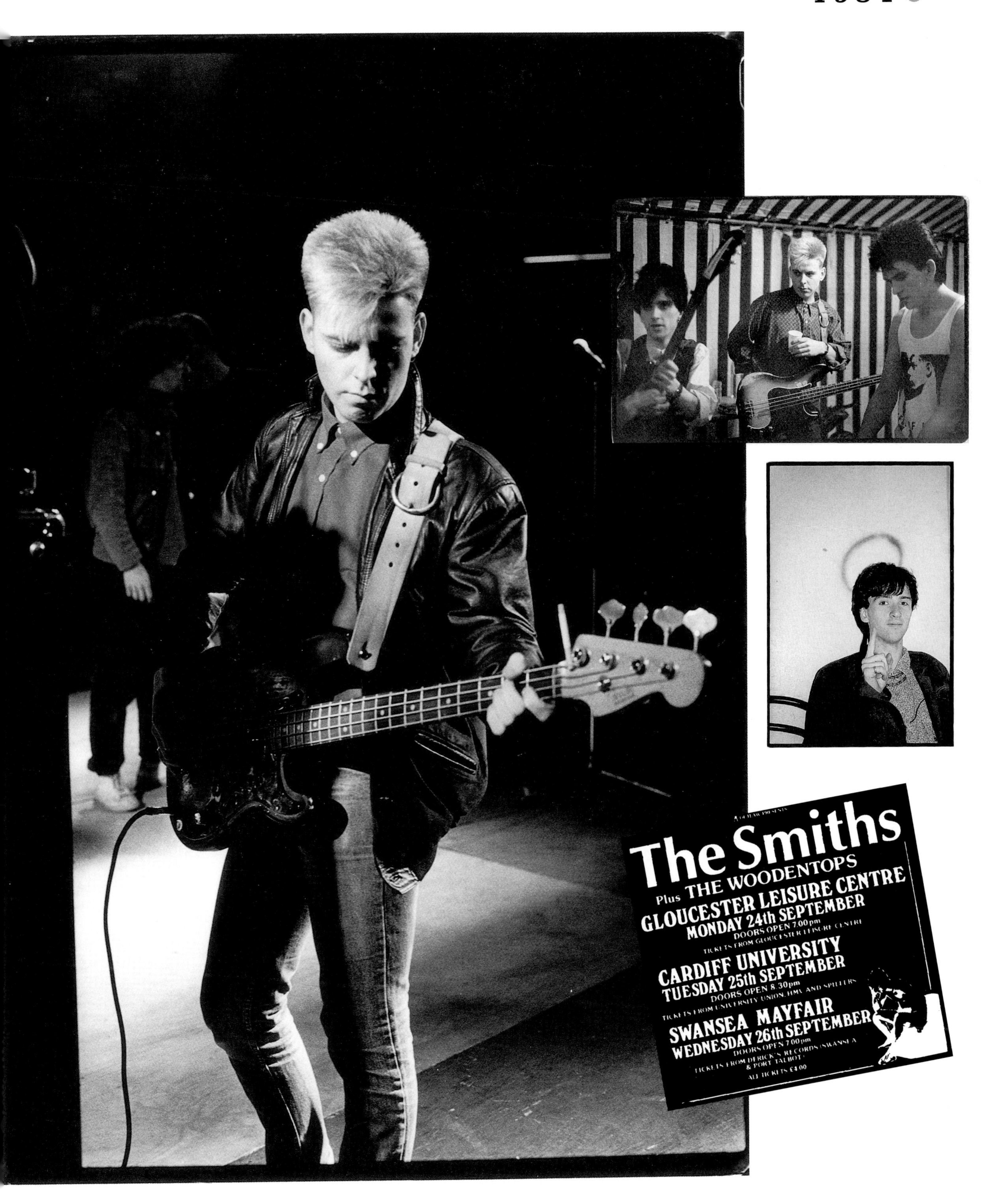
The Smiths
Plus THE WOODENTOPS
GLOUCESTER LEISURE CENTRE
MONDAY 24th SEPTEMBER
DOORS OPEN 7.00pm
TICKETS FROM GLOUCESTER LEISURE CENTRE
CARDIFF UNIVERSITY
TUESDAY 25th SEPTEMBER
DOORS OPEN 8.30pm
TICKETS FROM UNIVERSITY UNION, HMV AND SPILLERS
SWANSEA MAYFAIR
WEDNESDAY 26th SEPTEMBER
DOORS OPEN 7.00pm
TICKETS FROM DERICK'S RECORDS (SWANSEA & PORT TALBOT)
ALL TICKETS £4.00

ON THE Smiths' tour bus in Paris, with the future Angie Marr next to the guitarist.

adds his views on the terrorism in an equally chilling aside: "The sorrow of the Brighton bombing is that Thatcher escaped unscathed. The sorrow is that she's still alive. But I feel relatively happy about it. I think that for once the IRA were accurate in selecting their targets." One person who was taken aback by Morrissey's comments was his father. "When he spoke about Thatcher and the Brighton bombing I was shocked," he remembers. "Absolutely. I couldn't believe it. For him to walk out there and not be afraid. I thought, 'This man is tougher than I thought he was; he's either brave or daft'. He says things I wouldn't dare say – even about you (being killed in a motorway pile-up). I wouldn't say that to my worst enemy, but he just rattles these things off."

21 OCTOBER

Concert promoters are presented with The Smiths' latest rider clauses, which provide an amusing insight into the basic needs of the group and crew. The document reads:
"In addition to the terms of the contract, the promoter will provide the following at no charge to the artiste:

A solid stage of minimum dimensions, 25 feet wide, 20 feet deep and 4 feet high. Stage floor to stage ceiling, clearance must be a minimum 15 feet.

On the arrival of the PA/crew at the venue the promoter shall provide: tea, coffee, milk, sugar and biscuits, an electric kettle, five litres of whole milk, 12 large cans of Pilsner lager (cold). The PA crew onstage times – 12 large cans of Pilsner lager.

On arrival of the band at the venue, the promoter will provide: an electric kettle, tea, coffee, sugar and a selection of biscuits, 12 large cans of German Pilsner lager (cold), two large bottles of Lucozade and six small bottles, 3x75cl bottles of Beaujolais and Valpollicelli. 3x75cl bottles of Soave (cold). A selection of fresh fruit. A packet of variety cereal with a bowl, spoon and milk. A bowl of salted, good quality cashew nuts, 40 Silk Cut cigarettes.

One hour before onstage time, the promoter will provide good quality hot meals for up to 12 people (two vegetarian). A selection of hot food to be agreed with the tour manager 15 days before the performance."

3 NOVEMBER

Melody Maker publish one of the more perceptive Morrissey interviews of the period, rigorously conducted by Ian Pye. The journalist is struck by Morrissey's latest sartorial image. "Gone are the old Levis and sloppy smock," he observes. "In their place he's wearing smart black trousers, a baggy black and white check jacket, and a green and white striped shirt from his favourite shop, D.H. Evans... There's not a bead in sight, the hat he's holding is, one suspects, more of a prop for the photographer than for wearing, his quiff having reached worrying proportions. Now the look is more James Dean than Jean Marais." The singer provides some interesting insights into his childhood, home life, school days, fascination for The New York Dolls, attitudes to Margaret Thatcher, politics, celibacy, America, pop star rivalries, attitudes to drugs and sexually ambiguous lyrics. In damning videos ("We'll never make a video as long as we live!"), he pays a passing compliment to Dead Or Alive's 'That's The Way I Like It' and expresses an ambition to one day meet their vocalist Pete Burns, who is described as "stunning". In summing up the

POSING on the streets of Paris, December 1984.

present state of The Smiths, Morrissey is clearly at his most optimistic. "There's absolute perfect harmony within the group," he enthuses, "and as each day passes it becomes stronger, which is more important to me than anything else. I have no interest in solo success or individual spotlights."

10 NOVEMBER

The Smiths' trusty white Mercedes breaks down, just as they are about to commence a tour of Ireland. Stuart James is forced to hire a mini-bus, much to the group's consternation. Further drama occurs on the ferry from Holyhead to Dun Laoghaire. "Almost everybody was sick," Stuart James recalls, "particularly Johnny, who had heavy flu and sea-sickness. Morrissey was actually OK on the water." Seasick yet still docked, Marr gets worse during the crossing, prompting one member of the crew to phone ahead for an ambulance. "The ambulance arrived and we rushed straight off the ferry to this horrible Dublin hotel and Dublin hospital," James remembers. "We sat there waiting to be seen while family feuds and casualties were being stretchered in, blood pouring out of them... It did help seeing those people as Johnny realized that he was feeling a bit better and he wasn't as bad as other people."

12 NOVEMBER

Hatful Of Hollow, an aesthetically pleasing and economically gratifying album, is issued at a bargain £3.99. Morrissey explains the rationale behind its release: "A good portion of our mail contains imploring demands that we release versions of our songs that we recorded for Radio 1 sessions, and the band and I suddenly realized that we hadn't even proper-sounding tapes of them ourselves, except for a few dire bootlegs, that we bought at our concerts. As far as we're concerned, those were the sessions that got us excited in the first place, and apparently it was how a lot of other people discovered us also. We decided to include the extra tracks from our 12-inch singles for people who didn't have all of those and to make it completely affordable." The album features one track previously unavailable in any form on vinyl: 'This Night Has Opened My Eyes'. Several lines from the song are borrowed from Shelagh Delaney's play *A Taste Of Honey*, a debt which Morrissey freely admits to. "I've never made any secret of the fact that at least 50 per cent of my writing can be blamed on Shelagh Delaney," he exclaims, with his modest and characteristic disregard for percentages.

Reviews of *Hatful Of Hollow* are mixed and, looking back, it is interesting to see how the three big music weeklies reacted to the "interim" release. *Melody Maker*'s Adam Sweeting took a very jaundiced view of the proceedings, and admitted that he had still to be won over by The Smiths' alleged charm. "The things which go on in Morrissey's head from dawn to dusk and beyond are a damn sight more interesting than Smiths' records," he complains. "I keep waiting for the exception, but so far all I've come up with is 'Back To The Old House', an affecting little piece where The Smiths' formulaic modal melodies match neatly with a lyric where, for once, Morrissey isn't trying to be Dorian Gray." In mitigation, Sweeting concedes that, "For £3.99 it's a generously-filled package, always assuming, of course, you want more Smiths in the first place. I can't for the life of me see why anybody would want to own a copy of

STAGE angst in evidence.

cascading mandolins that close 'Please Please Please...' and it will be clear just how much he has come on. His role in the band is now worthy of at least equal billing with Morrissey... "

Although not the longest of the three reviews, *Sounds'* summation by early Smiths' champion Bill Black arguably proves the most enthusiastic, offering an impressive four star award. Having bravely criticized the group's début at the time of its release, Black takes the opportunity to applaud the demos which spiked his interest in the first place. With Morrissey and Marr under dissection in the previous two reviews, it is gratifying to see Black commending Rourke and Joyce, whom he describes as "maligned but magnificent... those drums and bass just keep turning; prodding and pricking the gossamer sheen of Marr's guitar and the lacy skin of Morrissey's vocal". The acquisitive reviewer ends his piece with a fan's plea for the imminent release of the Troy Tate sessions.

'William, It Was Really Nothing' under any circumstances, especially if they already had a copy of the almost identical 'What Difference Does It Make?'" While commending, in part, the sinister quality of 'How Soon Is Now?' and 'Reel Around The Fountain', Sweeting remains unconverted to the cause and finally dismisses the group as too clever for their own good. "Perhaps Morrissey should be read and not heard," he ends the piece wryly.

The *NME* follows The Smiths' fan line more closely, perceiving that the album "is a patchy, erratic affair and often all the better for it". For Adrian Thrills, the hero of the hour is not Morrissey but Marr, whose virtues are catalogued at length. "The most staggering changes are not in Morrissey's beguiling, ambivalent obsessions, which have remained similar throughout," he claims, "but in the flowering of Johnny 'Guitar' Marr, that chiming man, into one of the era's truly great instrumentalists. Compare the monosyllabic flatness of his early picking with the

THE IRISH TOUR BEGINS AT THE SAVOY, Waterford. James are the support act and, for this date only, there is a third act on the bill – The Village. Lead singer Paddy Jacobs, an executive on the co-operative Music Moves, secures Morrissey a 'young sapling' from the local florist. The surprise addition of The Village to the evening's performance came about as a result of the co-operative's policy. "We could afford to run things on a non-profit basis,".explained the group's manager Bruno. "Most other promoters couldn't. We were a co-operative so any money we got went into getting other bands into town. There were a lot of good Irish bands around who were worth £4-a-night. We charged £2. We could therefore afford to pay those kinds of bands. Denis Desmond of MCD felt he owed us one, so he gave us The Smiths. It was 50:50, with us and The Smiths. On all the gigs we ran we always worked on the basis that we lost a tenner. So we ran The Smiths at 50:50 with a guarantee of several thousand pounds. It was a 660 seater at £6-a-head. We got 660 in and lost a tenner on the gig." The evening certainly goes spectacularly well with some good old-fashioned fan mania to enliven proceedings. "Two radiators were broken," recalls The Village's drummer. "Two rows of chairs were taken out of the floor. People were standing on the radiators. We got an insurance fee." In retrospect, Paddy Jacobs reckons that The Smiths' magical touch may have backfired on The Village. "They had a full crew, two trucks, the whole business," he reminisces. "It was big for us. They were our idols. We were only together about three months as a band. That was our first big break. Their crew gave us a wonderful sound. It was the ruination of us!"

Set List: 'Please Please Please Let Me Get What I Want'; 'William, It Was Really Nothing'; 'What She Said'; 'Nowhere Fast'; 'Pretty Girls Make Graves'; 'Reel Around The Fountain'; 'Heaven Knows I'm Miserable Now'; 'This Night Has Opened My Eyes'; 'How Soon Is Now?'; 'Still Ill'; 'I Want The One I Can't Have'; 'Miserable Lie'; 'This Charming Man'; 'Hand In Glove'; 'Jeane'; 'These Things Take Time'; 'What Difference Does It Make?'

JOYCE in nicotine repose.

SINGLE SLEEVES (1983-87)

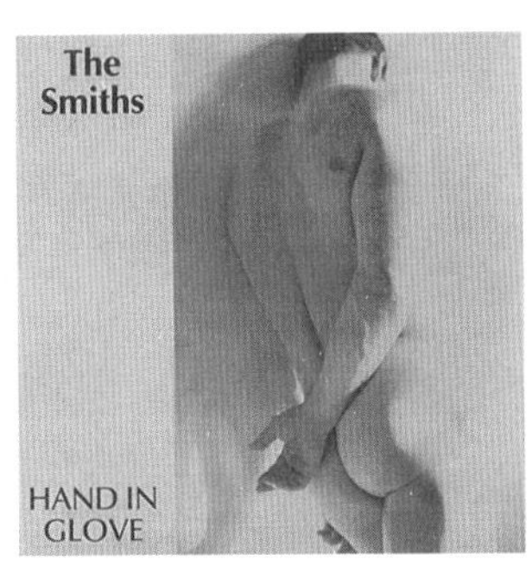

Hand In Glove

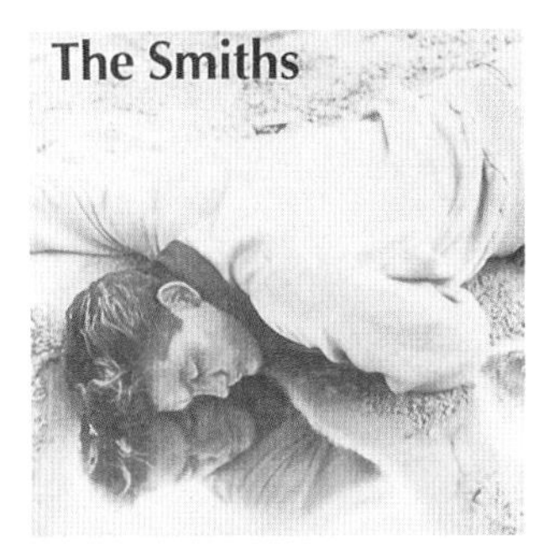

This Charming Man

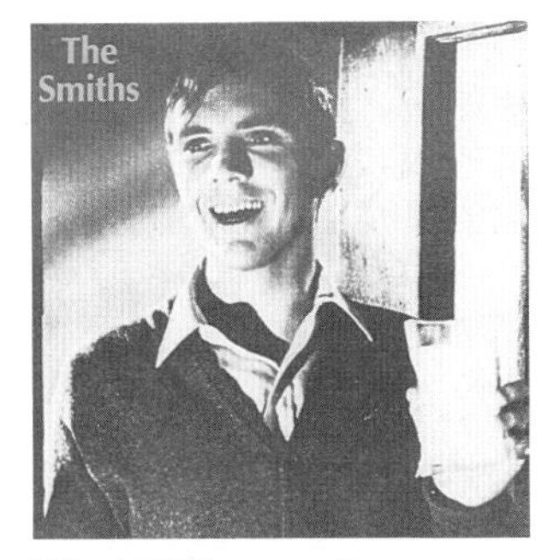

What Difference Does It Make?

Heaven Knows I'm Miserable Now

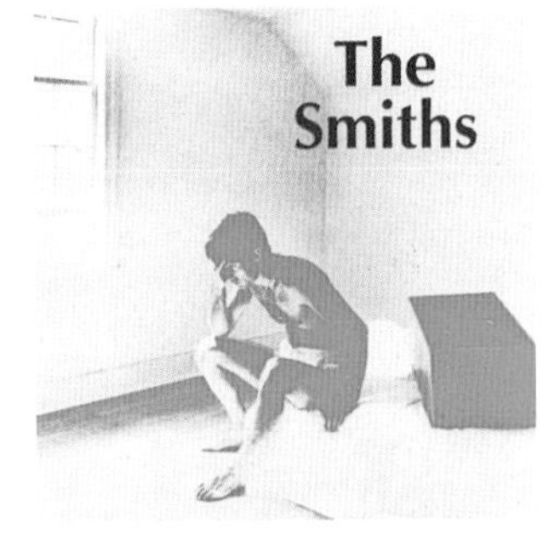

William, It Was Really Nothing

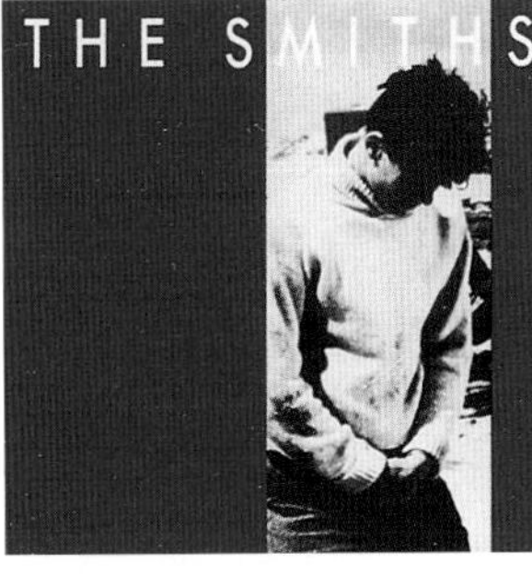

How Soon Is Now?

Shakespeare's Sister

That Joke Isn't Funny Anymore

The Boy With The Thorn In His Side

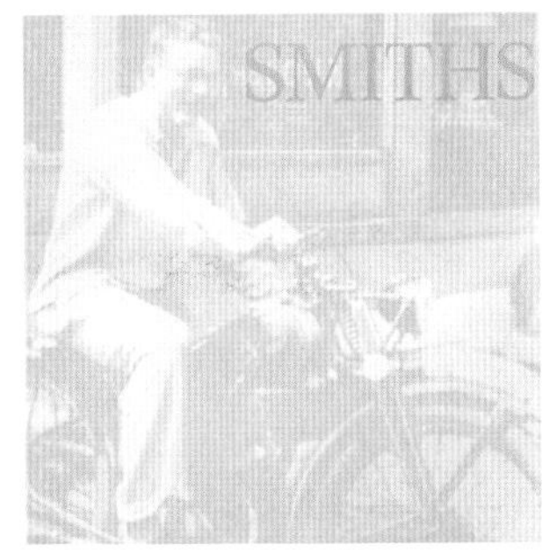

Bigmouth Strikes Again

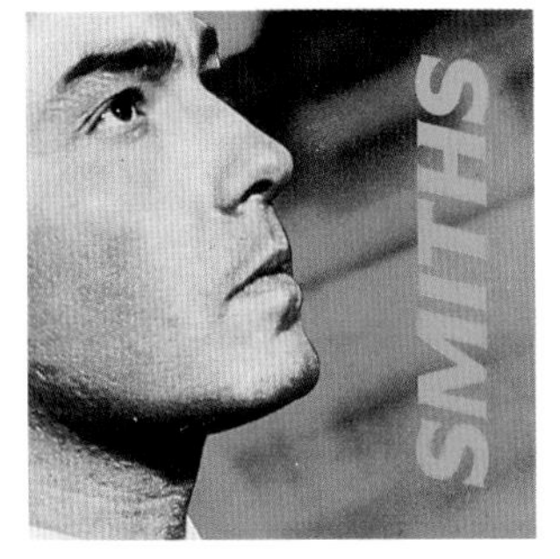

Panic

Ask

Shoplifters Of The World Unite

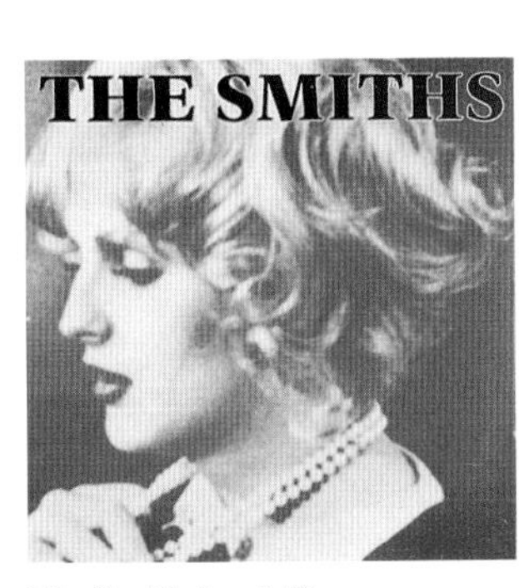

Sheila Take A Bow

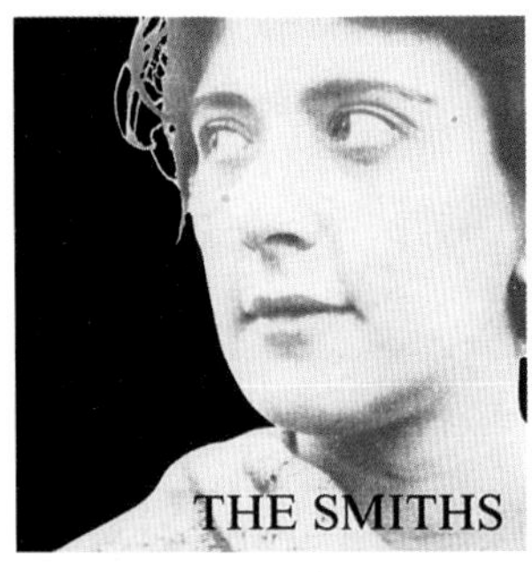

Girlfriend In A Coma

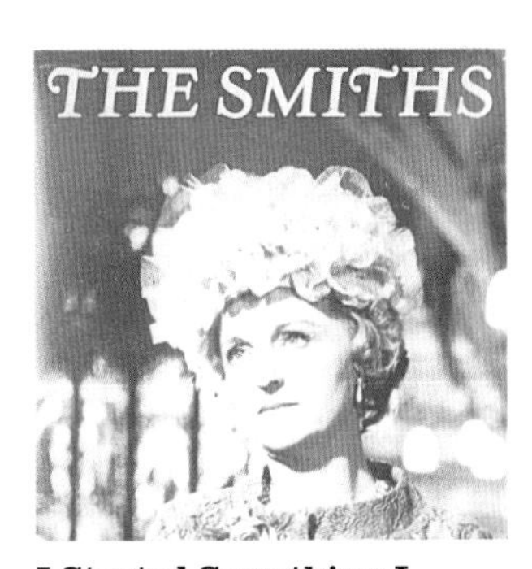

I Started Something I Couldn't Finish

Last Night I Dreamt That Somebody Loved Me

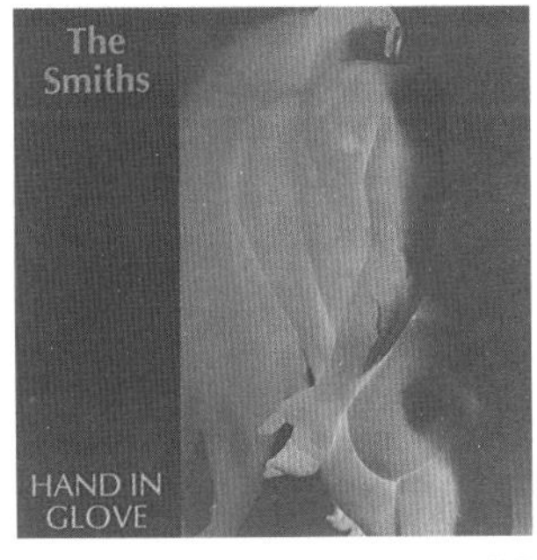

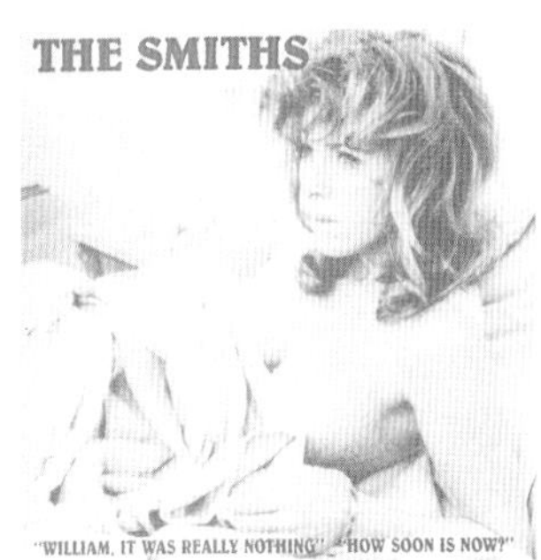

ALTERNATIVE SLEEVES

JOHNNY MARR 1985.

MORRISSEY in America, summer 1976, and below as a Smith.

MIKE JOYCE 1984.

ANDY ROURKE 1984.

ABOVE AND RIGHT: Rourke, Marr and Joyce in rehearsal, 1984.

BELOW: On 'The Oxford Road Show', 1984.

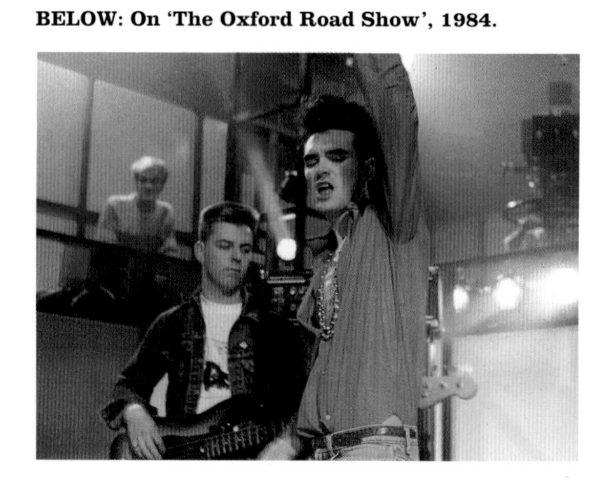

BELOW: Group shot, 1985.

SOUNDS
Debbie Harry
Aztec Camera
Girlschool
Einsturzende Neubauten
Dio
Care
CHARMED and ready
THE SMITH[S] page eight

'Sounds', 19 November 1983

MORRISSEY surrounded by his Oscar Wilde collection.

'Melody Maker', 28 November 1983

MORRISSEY and Sandie Shaw, 1984.

MORRISSEY and Pete Burns, 1985.

'NME', 4 February 1984

'Record Mirror', 8 September 1984

'Smash Hits', 9 October 1985

Tour Brochure, 1985

RED WEDGE TOUR: **Andy Rourke, Billy Bragg and Johnny Marr.**

CRAIG GANNON joins the group in early 1986.

Craig Gannon, Andy Rourke, Mike Joyce and Johnny Marr soundcheck on the UK 'The Queen Is Dead' tour.

Grant Showbiz and dedicated Japanese fan 'Oska' in Ireland - she flew from Japan for each tour.

Andy and Mike at Pier 84, New York, 6 August 1986.

Phil Powell and Andy Rourke on the US tour bus.

Backstage in the US: Marr, guitar roadie Phil Powell, Angie Marr, lighting person John Featherstone.

Grant Showbiz relaxing in the pool in Miami at the end of the last Smiths US tour.

Morrissey wears his manifesto on his chest during 'The Queen Is Dead' tour.

CLOCKWISE: The many hands of Morrissey, 1983-86.

'Time Out', 7 March 1985

'Record Mirror', 3 August 1985

One of the last Smiths photo sessions, the Albert Finney shop, 1987.

Johnny Marr, 1986.

'Record Mirror', 14 June 1986

Andy Rourke and Mike Joyce, 1993.

Morrissey all wrapped up, 1985.

Last Of The English Roses

Before Love

Before Love Live In Oxford

Devil's Charm

The Smiths

James Dean Is Dead

Eldorado

Misery Loves Company

Never Had No One Ever

A Nice Piece Of Meat

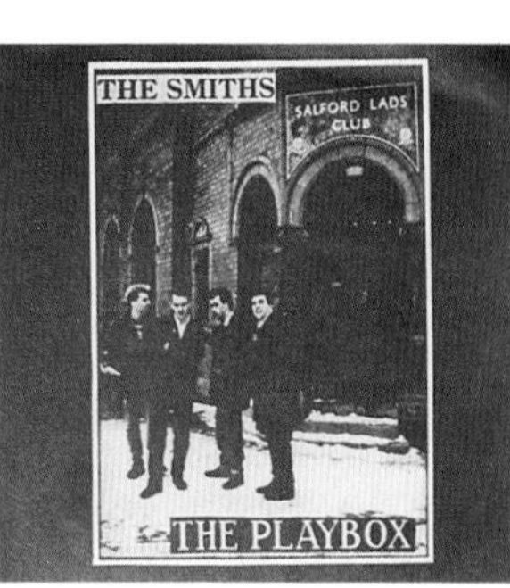
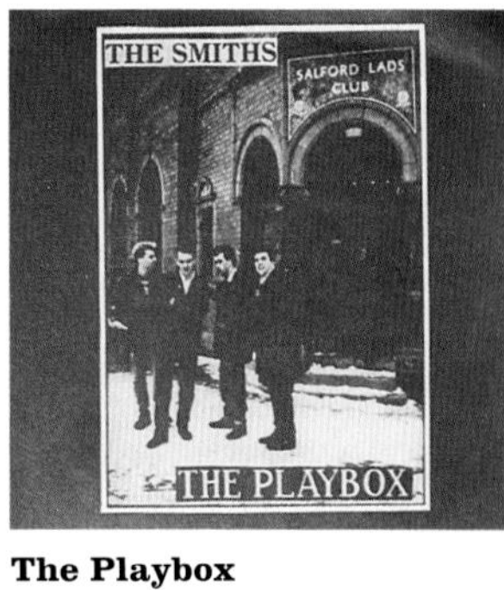

The Playbox

Royal Command Performance

Same Day Again

The Smiths

The Handsome Devils

Stealers

The Final Gig

THE SMITHS in peak performance, 1984.

13 NOVEMBER

The Smiths journey northwards to the SFX Dublin where promoter Denis Desmond presents them with their own security officer, James Connolly. "He worked as a security person at Dublin SFX," Stuart James recalls. "He was suggested to the group as someone who could travel around with them, and he had a lot of contacts." Morrissey is so impressed by his presence that he will retain his services long after the Irish tour.

Set List: 'Please Please Please Let Me Get What I Want'; 'William, It Was Really Nothing'; 'What She Said'; 'Nowhere Fast'; 'Reel Around The Fountain'; 'Heaven Knows I'm Miserable Now'; 'Rusholme Ruffians'; 'This Charming Man'; 'How Soon Is Now?' 'Still Ill'; 'Barbarism Begins At Home'; 'I Want The One I Can't Have'; 'Miserable Lie'; 'Hand In Glove'; 'What Difference Does It Make?'; 'Jeane'; 'These Things Take Time'.

14 NOVEMBER

A second night at the SFX coincides with Peter Morrissey's appearance backstage. Hours later, it will be the 47th birthday of Steven's mother, and probably the only occasion that he has spent that anniversary in the company of his father.

Set List: 'Please Please Please Let Me Get What I Want'; 'William, It Was Really Nothing'; 'What She Said'; 'Nowhere Fast'; 'Reel Around The Fountain'; 'Heaven Knows I'm Miserable Now'; 'Rusholme Ruffians'; 'This Charming Man'; 'How Soon Is Now?'; 'Still Ill'; 'Barbarism Begins At Home'; 'I Want The One I Can't Have'; 'Miserable Lie'; 'Hand In Glove'; 'What Difference Does It Make?'; 'Jeane'; 'These Things Take Time'.

16 NOVEMBER

The entourage drives to the Savoy, Limerick, with support group James following in happy pursuit. "They were travelling around in their own van," Stuart James remembers. "They had their own organically grown food with them. They were in a heavy veggie stage at that time. That's possibly why there was a bit of empathy between the groups. James were travelling in this old van and living on next to nothing. The crew liked James and there was never a sense of 'We're doing the sound for you. We want £20 each'."

Set List: 'William, It Was Really Nothing'; 'What She Said'; 'Nowhere Fast'; 'Reel Around The Fountain'; 'Rusholme Ruffians'; 'This Charming Man'; 'How Soon Is Now?'; 'Still Ill'; 'Barbarism Begins At Home'; 'I Want The One I Can't Have'; 'Miserable Lie'; 'Hand In Glove'; 'What Difference Does It Make?'; 'Jeane'; 'These Things Take Time'; 'Handsome Devil'.

17 NOVEMBER

Next stop, the Leisureland, Galway. The tour diary reveals a fan's name, 'Oska'. "She was from Japan," Stuart James recalls. "A big Morrissey fan. She started appearing at gigs. She'd always be there. She was incredibly shy. I think she worked in Tokyo, and would save some money (or maybe she had rich parents), then fly over for the tour. It got to the point later on where she'd ring me up before a tour and I'd give her the hotel details and she'd book herself in. Sometimes I was booking her in because I had to book everybody else in anyway! The band were quite happy about it. She used to bring them gifts."

Set List: 'Please Please Please Let Me Get What I Want'; 'William, It Was Really Nothing'; 'What She Said'; 'Nowhere Fast'; 'Pretty Girls Make Graves'; 'Reel Around The Fountain'; 'Heaven Knows I'm Miserable Now'; 'This Night Has Opened My Eyes'; 'How Soon Is Now?'; 'Still Ill'; 'I Want The One I Can't Have'; 'Miserable Lie'; 'This Charming Man'; 'Hand In Glove'; 'These Things Take Time'; 'What Difference Does It Make?'

18 NOVEMBER

Having already played at a former cinema turned bingo hall in Waterford, The Smiths appear at another Savoy in Cork. Again, they receive a tumultous welcome from enthusiastic fans.

Set List: 'Please Please Please Let Me Get What I

CLASSIC guitar pose, December 1984.

was paranoia or not, I think we all built it up in our minds. But travelling across borders you'd see heads moving in the bushes or a gun sticking out."

22 NOVEMBER

On the anniversary of John F. Kennedy's assassination, The Smiths return to Belfast's Ulster Hall. There is still a degree of tension in the air following the hotel switches and concern with security. Memories of Morrissey's comments on the IRA go through Stuart James's mind as they arrive in Belfast. "Morrissey had made some sweeping comments in the press and offended a lot of people," he reminds me. "When they went to Ireland, with the Troubles, they were worried about more extreme attitudes because they had affiliated themselves with the IRA. Well, not 'affiliated', but Morrissey had made some comments." Fortunately, the gig passes without incident and the group enjoy a stupendous response.

Want'; 'William, It Was Really Nothing'; 'What She Said'; 'Nowhere Fast'; 'Reel Around The Fountain'; 'Heaven Knows I'm Miserable Now'; 'Rusholme Ruffians'; 'How Soon Is Now?'; 'Still Ill'; 'I Want The One I Can't Have'; 'Miserable Lie'; 'Hand In Glove'; 'What Difference Does It Make?'

20 NOVEMBER

Prior to their arrival at the Leisure Centre in Letterkenny, Donegal, there is a minor drama when a doctor is called for Morrissey. "I can't remember that," says Stuart James, musing over the tour diary. "On the first dates after that terrible crossing Johnny was still pretty ill. I think Morrissey came out in sympathy at that particular point. It passed pretty quickly. I remember thinking, 'Oh, now Morrissey needs a doctor!' We were just getting Johnny better. It seemed like Morrissey came out in sympathy, but maybe that's just cynicism!"

Set List: 'How Soon Is Now?'; 'Still Ill'; 'This Charming Man'; 'I Want The One I Can't Have'; 'Handsome Devil'; 'Hand In Glove'; 'What Difference Does It Make?'; 'Jeane'; 'You've Got Everything Now'.

21 NOVEMBER

After a tremendously successful series of gigs in Eire, The Smiths cross the border for a gig at the University of Coleraine. A sense of melodrama accompanies them. "I know on that Irish tour we changed hotels a couple of times because of this threat of extreme... whatever," Stuart James muses. "Whether it

ENGINEER/producer Stephen Street.

NOVEMBER/DECEMBER

Work is in progress on the next Smiths' album with Stephen Street at the console. "They asked me to come along and record and engineer with them," he explains. "So we disappeared off to Liverpool on some godforsaken industrial estate where Amazon Studios used to be, and we drove every day from Manchester. It was amazing. We worked in Liverpool, but stayed in Manchester... Things were really happening for the band and it was a pleasant session. We'd got the bass and drums done pretty quickly and then it was a case of sitting down with Johnny most of the time and letting the tapes roll." The sessions progress more smoothly than anyone could have expected and the recordings are completed in less than two months. "The album came together quickly in about five to six weeks," Street confirms. "I was still learning a lot myself then, so I don't think the mixes were by any means the best we did on that album, but I think it's a lot more sprightly than the first LP... I think Morrissey's voice is livelier and not so down or deep. He really found the style that we now know as Morrissey on that album. I always tried to put a bit more work and emphasis on the vocal sound than John Porter might have done."

1 DECEMBER

A mini-European gig is set up for December, commencing at the Versailles, Paris. "It always felt as though it didn't really matter what happened in other countries because the *NME* didn't come along," Stuart James observes. "They were always a bit reluctant to go to Europe." By the time they take the stage in Paris, hopes of a European jaunt have already evaporated, and a performance in Copenhagen is cancelled at short notice. "It was a case of we don't want to go there," remarks the tour manager. "I can't even remember the reason."

Set List: 'William, It Was Really Nothing'; 'Shakespeare's Sister'; 'Nowhere Fast'; 'Reel Around The Fountain'; 'Heaven Knows I'm Miserable Now'; 'How Soon Is Now?'; 'Still Ill'; 'Rusholme Ruffians'; 'This Charming Man'; 'Barbarism Begins At Home'; 'I Want The One I Can't Have'; 'Hand In Glove'; 'What Difference Does It Make?'; 'Handsome Devil'; 'Miserable Lie'.

DECEMBER

While The Smiths are busily recording their new album, Bob Geldof has herded a smidgen of the pop élite together for a charity single in aid of the starving in Ethiopia. Band Aid's catchy 'Do They Know It's Christmas?' instantly tops the charts, selling a staggering three million copies along the way. The scale of the tragedy in Ethiopia has a profound effect on public opinion, so it is hardly surprising that Morrissey's tastelessly flippant comments on the disaster are universally vilified. As the criticism increases even Morrissey curbs his tongue. "Band Aid is the great undiscussable, I'm afraid," he wearily announces shortly afterwards.

22/29 DECEMBER

The year ends with a lengthy Morrissey interview in the seasonal double issue of *NME*. The bard discusses CND, politics and the forthcoming album. Marr chips in briefly to defend The Smiths from accusations of Sixties revivalism. "We've always had that thrown back at us," he complains. "If it weren't for Roger McGuinn's Rickenbacker or the Sandie Shaw collaboration... it was just lazy journalism. The idea of taking that spirit of optimism and of possible change and trying to use it in 1984 I don't see anything wrong with at all. But more important than that are the images we grew up with: smoky chimneys, back streets, the impressions I get from Morrissey's lyrics. It isn't just nostalgia, it's a Northern spirit, a working man's spirit – and here I'm trying not to sound like Gary Kemp doing the working class bit. But we're more about the working class values in the Sixties than Rickenbackers and Brian Jones haircuts... What I'm saying is we do not confuse roots with formula."

DECEMBER

The *NME* interview is superseded by a far more penetrating piece in *Jamming!* in which Morrissey pours forth on a range of subjects. The fact that this small magazine has effectively scooped the weeklies in terms of classic interview material is both gratifying and fitting, given The Smiths' adherence to the indie ideals of the period. During the interview, Morrissey bemoans the dangers of media overexposure. "All the interviews were becoming completely predictable, because everybody was asking me the same questions," he reflects. "When it appeared in print, it seemed as though I was very boring and that I could only talk about a limited number of things. That wasn't true; it was just that I was answering the same questions. I needed to step back..." With deadpan assurance, Morrissey goes on to produce some of his most humorous anecdotes in true George Formby/Ken Dodd fashion. "The other night, I went out for the first time in ages," he confides, "and somebody came up to me and said, 'Do that funny dance you do!' I felt completely repellent – as if I was some character off a situation comedy; some stand-up comic with a woolly hat and a tickling stick. It seems, at times like that, as though everything has got completely out of hand." The subject of Morrissey's "backside bush" elicits a similarly comic interlude. "People stop me in the street and say, 'Where's your bush?', he complains very indignantly, "which is an embarrassing question at any time of the day. I mean what do you say to people? 'I've left it behind on the mantelpiece'. I don't even mind if people remember me for my bush or my hearing aid – as long as it's for artistic reasons. It was all done to bring life to *Top Of The Pops* and other programmes. I don't do anything just to surprise people. I'm not thinking, 'Now, what will fox them next?' I'm not some trapeze artiste."

'Jamming!', December 1984

With one of the most memorable years in his life virtually over, Morrissey provides a neat and canny summation of a fascinating 12 months. "We've done a lot of work this year," he observes. "and achieved a great deal, much more than we've been given credit for. It's been a most thrilling year and as four individuals, we are closer than ever. Although everything written in the press has been strong, it has become quite difficult to live with. I've been quite aware for a few months that many journalists were trying to prise Johnny and I apart in some way. We've weathered that and we've weathered the most difficult backlash, which occurred in the beginning of the summer. I feel we're quite impenetrable."

THE GHOST of Keith Richard, Paris, 1984.

'Roll Over Bob Dylan And Tell Madonna The News – The Smiths' Morrissey Is Pop's Latest Messiah!'

'PEOPLE' MAGAZINE HEADLINE

CHAPTER FOUR

The Lifeblood Of Pop

MOST MORRISSEY AFICIONADOS will probably have their favourite phase in the history of the group. For some, it is those early gigs, long before they reached fame, or that period around the time of the release of the first album when they were the new darlings of the indie scene. For others their greatest achievement lay in their last couple of years when they threatened to become a major stadium group, only to break up before that dream – or nightmare – was realized. For this writer, however, it is The Smiths' mid-period that is recalled with greatest fondness. The Meat Is Murder *tour introduced a group that appeared to have greatness at its fingertips and, a decade on, the vision of Morrissey and Marr in unison, allied to the powerful rhythm section of Rourke and Joyce, is a reassuring memory. Despite what their contracts said or the complexity of the group dynamics, when they were onstage The Smiths were truly a four-man unit. Few who witnessed their concerts will forget that ineffable magic that characterized the group at their peak. The appeal lay partly in the contrasting personalities of the individual members and the strange way in which Marr's melodies merged with Morrissey's lyrics to create music that was at once familiar yet marvellously original.*

Who can forget The Smiths cascading across the UK, playing small theatres and dazzling audiences with some of the greatest live performances of the era? They also toured Eire, then made significant forays into the American market with a short but memorable tour. The release of Meat Is Murder*, the group's sole chart topping album, was an event in itself. Morrissey ensured that by his ubiquitous presence in the pages of the music press. His proselytizing tone could be glimpsed in countless captioned quotes as he effortlessly adopted the role of pop's most audacious orator. Wildean witticisms and political asides reinforced the lyrical thrust of The Smiths' latest album and, for once, the product was worthy of the press attention.* Meat Is Murder *brilliantly embraced funk, pop, folk, psychedelia and even touches of heavy metal to maximize its appeal. The clarity of production and noticeable improvement in Morrissey's vocal style immediately impressed. As a package, the work was much more focused than its predecessor with a loose but consistent thematic framework, highlighting personal and political violence from the schoolyard to the grave. Morrissey's self-righteous lyrics were both passionate and compassionate, a fusion that was seldom seen in his subsequent solo work. The real key to the album's success, however, lay in the combined contributions of all four members. Rourke's lengthy funk interlude on 'Barbarism Begins At Home' brought an unexpected musical influence to the familiar Smiths' sound, while Joyce was given a freedom of expression all too frequently denied on the first album. Marr's timely development as a producer and arranger coincided with an even keener appreciation of pop melody that was always startling. The guitar work on 'The Headmaster Ritual' saw Johnny in search of the perfect rock riff, set against*

JOHNNY Marr, the Palace, Manchester, 1985.

'MEAT IS MURDER' press advertisement.

Morrissey's petulant tragi-comic lyrics and pained vocals. On paper, the combination seemed unworkable, but the track was a classic. The same effect could be seen on 'That Joke Isn't Funny Anymore' in which Morrissey's pained observations appeared both melancholic and celebratory thanks to Marr's wonderful waltz-time arrangement. The essence of a great partnership could be heard in these songs and was reinforced by the overall consistency of the material.

Meat Is Murder *may not have won as many critics' polls as its successor, but it is arguably the group's most abrasive and satisfying work. In retrospect, though, it seems unfair to glorify any particular Smiths album from this fruitful period. The quality of their mid-Eighties output was so strong that almost every release deserved special attention. Even the frequently maligned 'Shakespeare's Sister' was defended vigorously by both Morrissey and Marr, who seemed genuinely surprised by its lacklustre reception. Marr is right when he says, "Don't forget our singles". In analysing almost any post-Sixties group, albums usually dominate the conversation, but The Smiths never forgot that the single was the lifeblood of pop. Frustratingly, that love could not be translated into record sales. The Smiths never achieved a number one single to stand alongside* Meat Is Murder, *but they respected the form sufficiently to ensure that a large proportion of their recordings appeared exclusively on 45.*

BELOW: The 'Meat Is Murder' 1985 tour itinerary.

Phil McIntyre and Outlaw presents
THE SMITHS
New Album 'Meat is Murder' - Out Soon
New Single 'How Soon is Now - Out Now

CHIPPENHAM GOLDIGGERS Wednesday 27th February SOLD OUT
GUILDFORD CIVIC HALL Thursday 28th February SOLD OUT
BRIXTON ACADEMY Friday 1st March SOLD OUT
PORTSMOUTH GUILDHALL Sunday 3rd March SOLD OUT
READING HEXAGON Monday 4th March SOLD OUT
POOLE ARTS CENTRE Wednesday 6th March
BRIGHTON DOME Thursday 7th March
MARGATE WINTER GARDENS Friday 8th March
SOUTHEND CLIFFS PAVILION Sunday 10th March
IPSWICH GAUMONT Monday 11th March SOLD OUT
NOTTINGHAM ROYAL CENTRE Tuesday 12th March SOLD OUT
HANLEY VICTORIA HALL Saturday 16th March SOLD OUT
BIRMINGHAM HIPPODROME Sunday 17th March SOLD OUT
OXFORD APOLLO THEATRE Monday 18th March SOLD OUT
SHEFFIELD CITY HALL Friday 22nd March
MIDDLESBOROUGH TOWN HALL Saturday 23rd March SOLD OUT
NEWCASTLE CITY HALL Sunday 24th March SOLD OUT
LIVERPOOL ROYA COURT THEATRE Wednesday 27th Mar
BRADFORD St. GEORGES HAL Thursday 28th March
NORTHAMPTON DERNGATE Friday 29th March SOLD O
MANCHESTER PALACE THEATRE Sunday 31st March SOLD OUT
LEICESTER DE MONTFORT HA Monday 1st April
BRISTOL HIPPODROME Thursday 4th April
ROYAL ALBERT HALL Saturday 6th April SOLD O

MEAT IS MURDER

Tickets £5.00 from the Box Offices Poole (685222) Margate (292795) Southend (351135) Liverpool (051 709 4321) Tickets £5.00 £4.50 from the Box Offices Brighton (682127) Sheffield (735295/6) Bradford (752368) Leicester (544444) Bristol (299444)

This, then, was The Smiths at their peak. On reflection, it is worth considering how much the nature of their appeal owed to their own sense of history in the making. For this was a period when they had acquired that almost palpable touch of greatness, by which you knew that virtually everything they recorded displayed distinction. The aesthetic appreciation lay not merely in present time, but in the sure-fire knowledge that what was forthcoming would still sound fresh a decade on. For myself, great pop is captured in that feeling of temporal dislocation – an intense absorption in the moment, reinforced by the feeling that the instant is of such significance that it will later be recalled with similar and possibly greater intensity in the future. In The Smiths' case there was the added attraction and drama of knowing that this was a group in mid-flight. The power of Meat Is Murder *could not distract from the conclusion that this might not necessarily be their creative summit. You knew instinctively that the next album would certainly rival* Meat Is Murder *and, God knows, might even surpass it in critical and commercial acclaim. That dynamic always creates a dramatic and pleasing sense of witnessing history in the present and that is the story of The Smiths in 1985.*

JAMES, support act on the first leg of the 1985 tour.

JANUARY
A 12-inch version of 'Barbarism Begins At Home' is issued as a promotional disc in a limited edition of 500 copies. With its funky bass work, the track has already proven a perennial live favourite. "It was just that the crowd went mad and we enjoyed playing it," Rourke recalls, "so we carried on and on till Johnny gave us the nod. Sometimes, as you say, it would last 15 minutes."

5 JANUARY
The *NME* publishes its annual chart points survey, looking back at 1984. Frankie Goes To Hollywood dominate proceedings, emerging as overall champions, while The Smiths languish in 28th place. In the singles section, Frankie's 'Relax' scores a staggering 619 points, while 'Two Tribes' logs second place with an impressive 396 points. The Smiths have to be content with a lowly 89th position for 'What Difference Does It Make?' Lionel Richie's *Can't Slow Down* tops the album listing, while The Smiths' début creeps in at number 20.

31 JANUARY
Smash Hits conduct an interview with Morrissey in which sarcasm is rife. Interviewer Tom Hibbert grills the vocalist about his militant vegetarianism and, after commenting on his unhealthy pallor, cheekily suggests, "A good McDonald's quarter pounder would put you back on your feet in no time." Morrissey retorts, "I sincerely doubt it," after which the conversation trickles to a halt.

2 FEBRUARY
Melody Maker vote 'How Soon Is Now?' single of the week: "Morrissey and Co have again delved into their Sixties treasure trove and produced visceral power capable of blowing the dust off Eighties inertia. The majestic ease of Morrissey's melancholic vocals are tinted with vitriol, as they move through vistas of misery with plaintive spirals around the pulse of Johnny Marr's vibrato guitar... Each repeated phrase intensifies the hypnotic waves, with results that outflank anything since 'This Charming Man'. Catharsis has rarely been tinged with so much regret, and shared with so much crystalline purity." Despite this pleasing reception, there is already a fear that the track, previously available both as a flip side and on *Hatful Of Hollow*, has been heard once too often. Rough Trade's unconvincing excuse for its sudden release is that fans are paying an extortionate price for Dutch import copies of the record.

12 FEBRUARY
The Smiths appear on BBC's *Whistle Test* performing extracts from their forthcoming album, including a fine version of 'Nowhere Fast'. The song is most notable for its aggressive attitude to the royal family, summed up in the line: "I'd like to drop my trousers to the Queen." In interviews, Morrissey is keen and willing to castigate royalty at any given opportunity. "I despise royalty," he sneers. "It's fairy tale nonsense. The very idea of their existence in these days when people are dying daily... to me, it's immoral." When pushed on his objections to the Royals, Morrissey frequently turns the conversation towards the plight of the elderly. "What I dislike is that they don't really care," he accuses. "There's a lot of people in this country who are living under serious and dangerous conditions. Old people die every single day and we accept that fact. And there's nobody fighting for old people in this country... Certain members of the royal family are of considerably advanced years, but they don't seem to care about people of their own time."

14 FEBRUARY
The Smiths' *Meat Is Murder* is released and, that same day, Morrissey invites a battalion of fanzine writers to the offices of Rough Trade, where he undergoes what amounts to an indie press conference. The meeting is chaired by *Melody Maker*'s Allan Jones and features representatives from such august journals as *Eat Yourself Fitter, Debris, Running Order, Bucketful Of Brains, Abstract* and *Inside Out.* From the outset, it is clear that Morrissey respects the fanzine tradition, and still regards The Smiths as idealistic outsiders working in the music industry. "Now that we have a big audience it's really important to me that people realize that we haven't become sloppy and we haven't become cushioned and we haven't become fat and lazy," he stresses. "We didn't want to go into the big league, as it were, and adhere to all the rules. That's pointless. It makes the history of The Smiths totally pointless. There has to be something that separates us. And, to be quite honest, we are very angry... We're very angry about pop music, and I think it's time somebody said something and somebody did something that is of value." Playing the angry young man for the assembled company, Morrissey makes plain his feelings about war, nuclear weapons, vegetarianism, Myra Hindley, songwriting, adolescence and human relationships.

> **'I can't understand why "How Soon Is Now?" wasn't a Top 10 single, but perhaps I'm being naïve.'**
>
> GEOFF TRAVIS

'Melody Maker', 14 February 1984

THE SMITHS UNLEASH THEIR NEW SINGLE 'How Soon Is Now?' on *Top Of The Pops.* Although regarded as one of their finest songs, its previous appearance as a 12-inch B-side and as part of *Hatful Of Hollow* is reflected in the relatively low chart position of 25. Even in America, where the track is even more highly regarded, the sales prove disappointing. "That was one of our real problems with the Warner Brothers' promotional department," Geoff Travis laments. "I can't understand why 'How Soon Is Now?' wasn't a Top 10 single, but perhaps I'm being naïve. If only their singles had been played on the radio. 'How Soon Is Now?' is a rock record, it's one of their few ones, it's a lot of people's favourite Smiths track. It's one of those that contains more traditional rock elements and is much more palatable. That's the one I thought was going to break them in America and that would have been the difference."

16 FEBRUARY
The music press sinks its collective teeth into The Smiths' second album proper, *Meat Is Murder. Sounds* former Smiths champion Bill Black awards the album four-and-a-half stars out of five and gives due credit to Johnny Marr: "Bold enough to summon the ghost of Scotty Moore for 'Nowhere Fast' or his bastard grandson Gary for the sub HM filling of 'What She Said', the magician

LEFT: Morrissey in coy mood. BELOW: The group relaxing.

Marr is equally happy hugging Morrissey's voluminous skirts with just a hand free to brush a mellow acoustic."

The *NME* seems a little more restrained than usual but concludes its understated review with an ambiguous tribute to the personality of Morrissey. "We afford him the sort of licence that's normally only extended to children or idiots, sensing the presence of an innocence and simplicity that's been civilized out of the rest of us, and a kind of insight also. The deaf-aids, the flowers, the NHS specs, they're all the trappings of an artful vulnerability."

By far the most perceptive review comes from *Melody Maker*'s Ian Pye, who opens on a suitably dramatic note: "The Smiths' second album is a brooding missive from a blackness that's quite sickening to contemplate..." After dissecting the work's musical strengths and weaknesses, the reviewer turns his attention to the singer's artistic development, noting: "Morrissey hasn't quite steered clear of his own clichés – that particular style of overtly romantic phrasing which has swooned its way through many a Smiths' song – but he has broadened his approach. His falsetto flights are especially arresting: I never realized he could yodel, and sometimes the timbre of his voice is so tender he might be crying. The Smiths have been misguidedly elevated to the level of gods by their followers but their music is well beyond the trivial novelty we've come to know as pop. *Meat Is Murder* is not for the squeamish, but the real torture of this record has little to do with the righteous accusations behind the banner sloganeering." For Pye, the work is ultimately personal rather than political and his concluding line ironically anticipates the lyrics of 'Piccadilly Palare': " Raw. bloody and naked, the meat on the rack is Morrissey's."

18 FEBRUARY

Morrissey offers his whimsical views on celibacy, sex and groupies on Belfast's Downtown Radio.

23 FEBRUARY

The Smiths secure their first and only number 1 record when *Meat Is Murder* supplants Bruce Springsteen's *Born In The USA* at the top of the British album charts. That same week, the quartet is voted Best Group in the annual *NME* readers' poll, with only Frankie Goes To Hollywood as realistic challengers. However, the Frankies completely outmanoeuvre their rivals in the Best Single stakes where 'Relax' and 'Two Tribes' prove dominant. Morrissey himself dutifully fills in his poll entry for the *NME* and the results make interesting casual reading (not least his comments on reggae!).

THE GROUP taking some time out for tea and snooker.

MORRISSEY'S 1984 'NME' POLL

Best Group: James
Male Singer: Pete Burns
Best New Act: Shock Headed Peters
Best Single: 'Nu Au Soleil' (Ludus)
Best LP: *Fried* (Julian Cope)
Best Songwriter: Don't Be Silly
Best Dressed Sleeve: *Jeans Not Happening* (Pale Fountains)
Creep Of The Year: Sade
Most Wonderful Human Being: John Walters
TV Show: *Victoria Wood As Seen On TV*
Radio Show: Richard Skinner
Film: *The Dresser*
Soul Act: Nico
Reggae Act: Reggae Is Vile
Instrumentalist: Johnny Marr
Best Dressed: Linder (Ludus)
Promo Video: All Videos Are Vile

27 FEBRUARY

The opening show of the 1985 tour takes place at a low key venue: Golddiggers, Chippenham, Wiltshire. Reviewers dutifully comment on the proselytizing nature of Morrissey's latest live extravaganza. "The Smiths are rarely bombastic," notes *Sounds*, "but these days they seem to be vigorously preaching the importance of ecological consciousness. 'Meat Is Murder' is probably the strongest call yet within pop of the virtues of vegetarianism and a new song, 'Stretch Out And Wait', insisted that 'Nature must still find a way'. All of this, and the flurry of peace signs from the audience during 'William, It Was Really Nothing' seem to suggest that The Smiths reflect a latent desire within the populace to bring on the advent of New Hippiedom."

Set List: 'William, It Was Really Nothing'; 'I Want The One I Can't Have'; 'What She Said'; 'Handsome Devil'; How Soon Is Now?'; 'Shakespeare's Sister'; 'Heaven Knows I'm Miserable Now'; 'That Joke Isn't Funny Anymore'; 'Reel Around The Fountain'; 'Rusholme Ruffians'; 'Hand In Glove'; 'The Headmaster Ritual'; 'Nowhere Fast'; 'Still Ill'; 'Meat Is Murder'; 'Miserable Lie'.

28 FEBRUARY

The sound of Buzzcocks can be heard backstage at the Civic Hall, Guildford, Surrey. "There was a request for a pre-show cassette of The Buzzcocks 'Going Steady'," recalls tour manager Stuart James. "That was to play before the songs."

Set List: 'William, It Was Really Nothing'; 'I Want The One I Can't Have'; 'What She Said'; 'Handsome Devil'; How Soon Is Now?'; 'Shakespeare's Sister'; 'Heaven Knows I'm Miserable Now'; 'That Joke Isn't Funny Anymore'; 'Rusholme Ruffians'; 'Hand In Glove'; 'The Headmaster Ritual'; 'Nowhere Fast'; 'Stretch Out And Wait'; 'Miserable Lie'; 'Still Ill'; 'Meat Is Murder'; 'Barbarism Begins At Home'.

1 MARCH

A memorable return to London at the Brixton Academy encourages journalist Eleanor Levy to wax euphoric in *Record Mirror*. "With The Smiths now on their way to being the greatest group that ever set foot on God's earth..." she opens breathlessly, before providing a more prosaic account of the evening's entertainment. " Marr, Rourke and Joyce arrive on stage. Andy Rourke studies his bass and his belly button while Johnny Marr stares into space, head bobbing like one of those nodding dogs you find in the back of Ford Cortinas. Morrissey strolls on last in an obvious piece of pop star management (tut, tut), but looking anything but, in a hat too big for him, glasses, and an old man's Marks and Spencer cardi. An intended visual paradox? Perhaps, but he looks dead sweet." Summing up their moment in Brixton, Levy concludes: "It sends shivers down the spine to think how good The Smiths are... You just have to hope they won't burn themselves out but, tonight at least, they showed no signs that that was any possibility at all."

Morrissey's immemorial critic Steve Sutherland begs to disagree. The *Melody Maker* journalist is left cold by The Smiths' charm and clearly regards Morrissey as a complete charlatan. After bemoaning the sheepishness of The Smiths' audience, he turns on Morrissey and sneers: "Elevating idiot dancing to an art form, the man with the mouth still couldn't disguise his paucity of inspiration and the sheer moaning monotony of the material. 'Heaven Knows I'm Miserable Now' reached, punch drunk, into the new single, 'Shakespeare's Sister', which sounded more like a clumsy homage to The Buzzcocks than anything else, while another new song was alarmingly reminiscent of Al Stewart.

"Has Morrissey gone soft? Maybe... Over prolific or just plain pompous, The Smiths weren't the tease or the catalyst or the sparkle they should be. There was a hollowness to them as if the notion of The Smiths should be enough for us and sod the actual show... Maybe The Smiths should ease up or give up or maybe the cynics are right and Morrissey should be seen and read but seldom heard. Whatever, tonight the spirit was undoubtedly willing but the flesh was, sadly, too weak."

Set List: 'William, It Was Really Nothing'; 'I Want The One I Can't Have'; 'What She Said'; 'Handsome Devil'; How Soon Is Now?'; 'Shakespeare's Sister'; 'Heaven Knows I'm Miserable Now'; 'That Joke Isn't Funny Anymore'; 'Reel Around The Fountain'; 'Rusholme Ruffians'; 'Hand In Glove'; 'The Headmaster Ritual';

'Nowhere Fast'; 'Still Ill'; 'Meat Is Murder'; 'Miserable Lie'; 'Barbarism Begins At Home'; 'You've Got Everything Now'; 'These Things Take Time'.

CLOCKWISE: Morrissey runs the gamut of stage emotion at the Hexagon, Reading, 4 March 1984.

3 MARCH

The tour continues at the Guildhall, Portsmouth. Already, there is a feeling that the group are hitting new peaks in their live performances, which seem both tighter and better rehearsed. Mike Joyce remembers these dates as some of The Smiths' finest. "With *Meat Is Murder* I realized the power behind us," he stresses. "We were becoming harder, which fitted more into my field of playing. 'The Headmaster Ritual' and 'What She Said' and others were all in your face. It was a lot harder and Morrissey was writing some of his best stuff."

Set List: 'William, It Was Really Nothing'; 'I Want The One I Can't Have'; 'What She Said'; 'Handsome Devil'; How Soon Is Now?'; 'Shakespeare's Sister'; 'Heaven Knows I'm Miserable Now'; 'That Joke Isn't Funny Anymore'; 'Reel Around The Fountain'; 'Rusholme Ruffians'; 'Hand In Glove'; 'The Headmaster Ritual'; 'Nowhere Fast'; 'Still Ill'; 'Meat Is Murder'; 'Miserable Lie'; 'Barbarism Begins At Home'; 'You've Got Everything Now'.

4 MARCH
At the Hexagon, Reading, Morrissey decides to encore with one of Rourke's least favourite Smiths' songs, 'Miserable Lie'. The bassist has trouble adapting to the frantic pace of the song, which does not suit his style of playing. It is interesting to observe how the song has altered subtly over the years, along with Morrissey's eccentric yodelling technique.

Set List: 'William, It Was Really Nothing'; 'I Want The One I Can't Have'; 'What She Said'; 'Handsome Devil'; How Soon Is Now?'; 'Shakespeare's Sister'; 'Heaven Knows I'm Miserable Now'; 'That Joke Isn't Funny Anymore'; 'Reel Around The Fountain'; 'Rusholme Ruffians'; 'Hand In Glove'; 'The Headmaster Ritual'; 'Nowhere Fast'; 'Still Ill'; 'Meat Is Murder'; 'Barbarism Begins At Home'; 'Miserable Lie'.

6 MARCH
The Arts Centre in Poole, Dorset, gains a certain notoriety as the only venue on the tour that fails to sell out in advance. Ticket sales throughout the tour have been excellent as would be expected given the group's well publicized chart topping album.

Set List: 'William, It Was Really Nothing'; 'I Want The One I Can't Have'; 'What She Said'; 'Handsome Devil'; How Soon Is Now?'; 'Shakespeare's Sister'; 'Heaven Knows I'm Miserable Now'; 'That Joke Isn't Funny Anymore'; 'Reel Around The Fountain'; 'Rusholme Ruffians'; 'Hand In Glove'; 'The Headmaster Ritual'; 'Nowhere Fast'; 'Still Ill'; 'Meat Is Murder'; 'Miserable Lie'.

7 MARCH
The Smiths bypass London en route to the Dome, Brighton, where they have a small gay following. Morrissey is also the object of female desire and testifies to a regular mailbag of fulsome fan letters. "I get these letters and I read them and we appear on stage and girls scream and they want to touch me," he notes. "I look at them, I read these letters and I say, 'This is very interesting', but I do feel slightly detached from it... This sexual... this desirable person is not really me."

Set List: 'William, It Was Really Nothing'; 'I Want The One I Can't Have'; 'What She Said'; 'Handsome Devil'; How Soon Is Now?'; 'Shakespeare's Sister'; 'Heaven Knows I'm Miserable Now'; 'That Joke Isn't Funny Anymore'; 'Reel Around The Fountain'; 'Rusholme Ruffians'; 'Hand In Glove'; 'The Headmaster Ritual'; 'Nowhere Fast'; 'Meat Is Murder'; 'Still Ill'; 'Miserable Lie'.

7-13 MARCH
Morrissey is interviewed in *Time Out* under the rather clichéd title "This Charming Man". Despite his recent retreat from London to Cheshire, the singer sounds anything but content. Railing against imaginary foes, he complains about media intrusion and portrays himself as a subersive force in the music industry: "I'm not a rock'n'roll character. I despise cigarettes, I'm celibate and I live a very serene lifestyle. But I'm also making very strong statements lyrically, and this is very worrying to authoritarian figures." Even his fellow workers in the music business are cast as bitter and twisted individuals. "The industry is just rife with jealousy and hatred," he announces. "Everybody in it is a failed bassist. Everybody wants to be on stage – it doesn't matter what they do, they all want to be you." On a brighter note, Morrissey looks back at his failed attempts to achieve any inroads into journalism and vows to put the matter right by interviewing several of his favourite icons. Having recently spoken to Pat Phoenix, he hopes for a similar *tête à tête* with Sixties' pools winner Viv Nicholson. Although there is fanciful talk of an entire book collating the "Morrissey interviews", the project immediately founders under the weight of Steven's premature ambition. Journalist Simon Garfield concludes a spiky interview by attempting to tease an epitaph from his host. "I don't mind how I'm remembered," Morrissey muses, "so long as they're precious recollections. I don't want to be remembered for being a silly, prancing, nonsensical village idiot. But I really do want to be remembered. I want some grain of immortality. I think it's been deserved. It's been earned."

MARR, 1985.

8 MARCH
At the Winter Gardens, Margate, the group introduce subtle changes in the set, bringing forward 'Barbarism Begins At Home' for dramatic effect. Mike Joyce is greatly impressed by Andy Rourke's contribution to the song. "The bass line was a killer," he gleefully asserts. "It was interesting how Andy got his head around it... when we'd stop he'd continue with a Stanley Clarke bass line. It was incredible the way he could shift into that."

Set List: 'Nowhere Fast'; 'Barbarism Begins At Home'; 'Still Ill'; 'How Soon Is Now?'; 'Shakespeare's Sister'; 'Handsome Devil'; 'The Headmaster Ritual'; 'Reel Around The Fountain'; 'That Joke Isn't Funny Anymore'; 'Hand In Glove'; 'Rusholme Ruffians'; 'I Want The One I Can't Have'; 'What She Said'; 'William, It Was Really Nothing'; 'Meat Is Murder'; 'Miserable Lie'.

10 MARCH

The Smiths' appearance at the Southend Cliffs Pavilion is cancelled. "It was something to do with the stage lighting," recalls Stuart James. "It was blown out for a technical reason."

11 MARCH

At the Gaumont, Ipswich, Dead Or Alive's Pete Burns is added to the guest list. "He started hanging out," Stuart James recalls. "It culminated in an appearance at the Royal Albert Hall towards the end of the tour." Morrissey is already touting Burns as a subversive talent with whom he feels a strong kinship. "If a character like Pete Burns existed within classical music, it would be a world revelation," Morrissey exclaims. "But because he doesn't, he's just there and he's very silly and he's very funny and he's very entertaining and ultimately he doesn't mean anything... I think he's a wonderful person. He's one of the few people I can feel a great affinity with. Namely because he says exactly what he wants to which, of course, is a national sin within music, especially considering the things he wants to say".

Set List: 'William, It Was Really Nothing'; 'Nowhere Fast'; 'I Want The One I Can't Have'; 'What She Said'; 'How Soon Is Now?'; 'Stretch Out And Wait'; 'Heaven Knows I'm Miserable Now'; 'That Joke Isn't Funny Anymore'; 'Handsome Devil'; 'The Headmaster Ritual'; 'Shakespeare's Sister'; 'Rusholme Ruffians'; 'Hand In Glove'; 'Still Ill'; 'Meat Is Murder'; 'Barbarism Begins At Home'; 'Miserable Lie'.

12 MARCH

At the Royal Centre, Nottingham, a rider note from Marr is left lying around with the message, "Tuna sandwiches, no butter or margarine, Lucozade, white wine etc." Suitably stuffed, despite a tendency to throw up before performing, the guitarist is on top form throughout the tour.

Set List: 'William, It Was Really Nothing'; 'Nowhere Fast'; 'I Want The One I Can't Have'; 'What She Said'; 'How Soon Is Now?'; 'Shakespeare's Sister'; 'Heaven Knows I'm Miserable Now'; 'Stretch Out And Wait'; 'That Joke Isn't Funny Anymore'; 'Rusholme Ruffians'; 'Hand In Glove'; 'The Headmaster Ritual'; 'Still Ill'; 'Meat Is Murder'; 'Barbarism Begins At Home'.

16 MARCH

Dave Haslam, Manchester journalist and editor of the magazine *Debris*, is added to the tour guest list for the performance at the Victoria Hall, Hanley, Stoke-on-Trent. That same day, his contribution to the Morrissey "Trial By Jury" fanzine interrogation is published in *Melody Maker*.

Set List: 'William, It Was Really Nothing'; 'Nowhere Fast'; 'I Want The One I Can't Have'; 'Handsome Devil'; 'What She Said'; 'How Soon Is Now?'; 'Heaven Knows I'm Miserable Now'; 'Stretch Out And Wait'; 'That Joke Isn't Funny Anymore'; 'Shakespeare's Sister'; 'Rusholme Ruffians'; 'The Headmaster Ritual'; 'Still Ill'; 'Hand In Glove'; 'Meat Is Murder'; 'Miserable Lie'; 'Barbarism Begins At Home'.

17 MARCH

The Smiths celebrate St Patrick's Day at the Hippodrome, Birmingham. The festivities obviously interrupt the normal recording of gigs as no tape of this show is readily available for analysis. Back at the Holiday Inn, Andy is entertaining his mother, who has flown in from Spain to visit the family and attend the show. Nick Kent spots her in the hotel lounge reading her pop star son extracts from a Spanish newspaper. "Los Smiths... now here it is, 'basso gee-tarro', " she trills. "That's you Andy!" As Kent recalled: "Rourke seemed to be sinking further and further into the couch in an attempt to feign invisibility." The bassist laughs at the memory and recalls his amusement upon seeing his glamorous mother, looking like Joan Collins and dancing among fans near the front of the stage.

18 MARCH

'Shakespeare's Sister' is released, complete with a cover photograph of *Coronation Street* star Pat Phoenix. Marr is particularly enthusiastic about the track. "As a seven-inch single for the group at that point in time, it was quite inventive," he argues. "There was something about that riff that I really wanted to do. I just flipped all the way while we were recording it." That evening the group appear at the Apollo, Oxford, for one of the best shows on the tour. The concert is recorded and subsequently broadcast on BBC Radio 1.

Set List: 'William, It Was Really Nothing'; 'Nowhere Fast'; 'What She Said'; 'Hand In Glove'; 'How Soon Is Now?'; 'Stretch Out And Wait'; 'That Joke Isn't Funny Anymore'; 'Shakespeare's Sister'; 'The Headmaster Ritual'; 'Still Ill'; 'Meat Is Murder'; 'Miserable Lie'; 'Barbarism Begins At Home' ; 'You've Got Everything Now'.

22 MARCH

The Smiths appear on the *Oxford Road Show* performing their new single,'Shakespeare's Sister', and 'The Headmaster Ritual'. The latter briefly causes a minor furore in Morrissey's home city and it is widely reported that his former headmaster has appeared on local radio to provide a more flattering appraisal of St Mary's. In fact, the subject of the song, Vin "Jet" Morgan, had retired the same year that Morrissey left school and remains silent. The new headmaster who appears on radio is actually Mr Thomas, who had once taught Morrissey History, a subject that the singer failed at O-Level.

The Smiths are regularly hitting the big cities and the next stop is the City Hall, Sheffield. "All these gigs from hereon, the group would leave immediately because there'd be more fans," Stuart James recalls. "They'd come off, get their towels, do the encore, then I'd get a plastic bag for their butties. That's what it was like. 'Have I got Johnny's tuna sandwiches?' It got to be ridiculous. All that took away from the main aspect of the job. They became actually more important. I'd be saying: 'I've picked up the money, now what about the tuna sandwiches and Smarties'."

Set List: 'William, It Was Really Nothing'; 'Nowhere Fast'; 'I Want The One I Can't Have'; 'What She Said'; 'Hand In Glove'; 'How Soon Is Now?'; 'Stretch Out And Wait'; 'That Joke Isn't Funny Anymore'; 'Shakespeare's Sister'; 'Rusholme Ruffians'; 'The Headmaster Ritual'; 'Still Ill'; 'Meat Is Murder'; 'Miserable Lie'; 'Barbarism Begins At Home'; 'You've Got Everything Now'; 'Handsome Devil'.

23 MARCH

At the Town Hall, Middlesbrough, The Smiths impress the audience with a sprightly version of 'Rusholme Ruffians'. Morrissey remembers the origins of the song, with an air of uneasy nostalgia. "As a child I was educated at fairs," he recalls. "It was the big event. It was the reason why everybody was alive... It was a period of tremendous violence and hate and distress and high romance, and all the truly vital things in life. It was really the patch of ground where you learned about everything instantaneously whether you wanted to or not."

Set List: 'William, It Was Really Nothing'; 'Nowhere Fast'; 'I Want The One I Can't Have'; 'What She Said'; 'Hand In Glove'; 'How Soon Is Now?'; 'Stretch Out And Wait'; 'That Joke Isn't Funny Anymore'; 'Shakespeare's Sister'; 'Rusholme Ruffians'; 'The Headmaster Ritual'; 'Still Ill'; 'Meat Is Murder'; 'Miserable Lie'; 'Barbarism Begins At Home'; 'You've Got Everything Now'.

24 MARCH

The English tour reaches its northern limits at the City Hall, Newcastle-upon-Tyne. Morrissey is impressed with the fanatical response he is receiving and praises his faithful followers. "Touring's interesting because it's fascinating to me to meet the people who buy our records, which is strange. You can have a hit record, or whatever, and loads of people can buy your records, but you don't actually meet them... I never meet Smiths apostles ever, so it's only by touring that I can actually come face to face with these people."

Set List: 'William, It Was Really Nothing'; 'Nowhere Fast'; 'I Want The One I Can't Have'; 'What She Said'; 'Hand In Glove'; 'How Soon Is Now?'; 'Stretch Out And Wait'; 'That Joke Isn't Funny Anymore'; 'Shakespeare's Sister'; 'Rusholme Ruffians'; 'The Headmaster Ritual'; 'Still Ill'; 'Handsome Devil'; 'Meat Is Murder'; 'Miserable Lie'; 'Heaven Knows I'm Miserable Now'; 'Barbarism Begins At Home'.

THE SMITHS' second appearance on the 'Oxford Road Show', promoting 'Shakespeare's Sister', 22 March 1985.

MORRISSEY and Marr during a pause between takes for the 'Oxford Road Show'.

27 MARCH

Having previously played college venues in Liverpool, The Smiths go upmarket with an appearance at the Royal Court. A strident version of 'The Headmaster Ritual' is one of several highlights that evening. The distinctive opening track on *Meat Is Murder* remains one of Marr's favourite Smiths' tracks. "I'm really pleased with the guitars on it and the strange tuning," he reminisces. "For my part, 'The Headmaster Ritual' came together over the longest period of time I've ever spent over a song. I first played the riff to Morrissey when we were working on the demos for our first album with Troy Tate. And then I nailed the rest of it in Earl's Court when I moved there. That was around the time when we were being fabulous."

Set List: 'William, It Was Really Nothing'; 'Nowhere Fast'; 'I Want The One I Can't Have'; 'What She Said'; 'Hand In Glove'; 'How Soon Is Now?'; 'Stretch Out And Wait'; 'That Joke Isn't Funny Anymore'; 'Shakespeare's Sister'; 'Rusholme Ruffians'; 'The Headmaster Ritual'; 'Still Ill'; 'Meat Is Murder'; 'Heaven Knows I'm Miserable Now'; 'Barbarism Begins At Home'; 'Miserable Lie'.

28 MARCH

By the time the tour reaches the St George's Hall, Bradford, Morrissey's propagandist pronouncements have become all too familiar. "There has to be a brave message in the Top 30," he insists. "I find people are still being very otherworldly and very whimsical... 'Meat Is Murder' is obviously a title that shouldn't be there and is obviously a title that will cause great discomfort and has done. I know it has done which, of course, can give maximum pleasure."

Set List: 'William, It Was Really Nothing'; 'Nowhere Fast'; 'I Want The One I Can't Have'; 'What She Said'; 'Hand In Glove'; 'How Soon Is Now?'; 'Stretch Out And Wait'; 'That Joke Isn't Funny Anymore'; 'Shakespeare's Sister'; 'Rusholme Ruffians'; 'The Headmaster Ritual'; 'Still Ill'; 'Heaven Knows I'm Miserable Now'; 'Meat Is Murder'; 'Handsome Devil'; 'Barbarism Begins At Home'; 'Miserable Lie'.

29 MARCH

Initial sales of 'Shakespeare's Sister' are disappointing and will not improve as the single stalls at number 26, their lowest chart placing since 'Hand In Glove'. Morrissey is deflated by the single's chart position. "'Shakespeare's Sister', regardless of what many people feel, was the song of my life," he protests. "I put everything into that song and I wanted it more than anything else to be a huge success and, as it happens, it wasn't." Cursory radio promotion and a lack of confidence from the record company are seen as crucial factors in its failure. "I really loved doing it, but we didn't get much support from Rough Trade on that one," Marr concludes. "They didn't like it very much." Characteristically, Morrissey later goes further by fancifully suggesting that the BBC blacklisted the record as a result of his comments on the BPI Awards. As news of the single's failure reaches the group, the foursome content themselves with a staunch performance at the Derngate Centre, Nottingham.

Set List: 'William, It Was Really Nothing'; 'Nowhere Fast'; 'I Want The One I Can't Have'; 'What She Said'; 'Hand In Glove'; 'How Soon Is Now?'; 'Stretch Out And Wait'; 'That Joke Isn't Funny Anymore'; 'Shakespeare's Sister'; 'Rusholme Ruffians'; 'The Headmaster Ritual'; 'Still Ill'; 'Meat Is Murder'; 'Heaven Knows I'm Miserable Now'; 'Miserable Lie'; 'This Charming Man'; 'Handsome Devil'.

30 MARCH

Following the Morrissey interview ("Trial By Jury") featured in *Melody Maker* on 16 March, there is a strong reaction against the singer in the letters column. "Will *MM* give us a break from Mr Righteous God Almighty Morrissey?" cries one harried correspondent. "It's becoming more like a Smiths' annual." Among the topics that rile the *MM* readership are Band Aid ("He's a hypocritical bastard too. How can he say that the Band Aid single is tuneless when his stuff sounds like a spy being tortured"), Animal Liberation violence ("Morrissey, you ain't seen anything if the Lunatic Animal Libbers kill any of my kids...") and vegetarianism ("*MM* could solve most of Morrissey's problems by arranging a confrontation with a full-grown lion, a Bengal tiger, an alligator, or some other carnivore to see if his platitudes can influence their diet!").

> **'Me and Mike gave up meat at that time... I stuck with it for about two years and used to sneak out for a burger and stuff.'**
>
> ANDY ROURKE

31 MARCH

Fittingly, the group's latest Manchester homecoming sees them at the Palace, a plush venue known for housing several West End musicals. Morrissey is clearly affected by the heat generated by a mass of writhing bodies and introduces the sublime 'That Joke Isn't Funny Anymore' with the quip: "This is a song off our LP 'Breathing Is Murder'." In defiantly acerbic mood, Morrissey lightly criticizes the audience for its solemnity and pours scorn on radio producers for not playing 'Shakespeare's Sister'. "We hope you're just shy not bored," he tells his local followers, which at least prompts a singalong 'Heaven Knows I'm Miserable Now'. The concert concludes with an encore featuring 'You've Got Everything Now', Morrissey's acerbic message to those who once considered themselves his betters. For the onlooking Tony Wilson, however, Morrissey's song of social superiority has an unintended ironic resonance. "I remember a feeling of absolute revulsion," Wilson begins, "standing at the side of the stage at the Palace watching Stuart James, who's a brilliant engineer, a good producer and a fine young man, scurrying across the stage with eight freshly cleaned towels for Morrissey. That's the part of Steven I can't deal with – the way people are used." Stuart James still argues that Wilson over-emphasized his little humiliation at the Palace. "What Tony Wilson saw wasn't very important," he counters. "I didn't feel particularly used and abused. If anything, it was something I took on myself. It wasn't as if Morrissey was saying, 'I *must* have this!' Looking back, I regret doing that [with the towels], but it's something you get caught up in. I only resented it when I realized they'd come to expect it."

Set List: 'William, It Was Really Nothing'; 'Nowhere Fast'; 'I Want The One I Can't Have'; 'What She Said'; 'Hand In Glove'; 'How Soon Is Now?'; 'Stretch Out And Wait'; 'That Joke Isn't Funny Anymore';

ROURKE reconsiders vegetarianism.

'Shakespeare's Sister'; 'Rusholme Ruffians'; 'The Headmaster Ritual'; 'Still Ill'; 'Meat Is Murder'; 'Heaven Knows I'm Miserable Now'; 'Handsome Devil'; 'Barbarism Begins At Home'; 'Miserable Lie'; 'You've Got Everything Now'.

1 APRIL

As the group head for the De Montfort Hall, Leicester, in preparation for their evening's performance, the rhythm section is still coming to terms with vegetarianism. Joyce is a willing convert and credits the song 'Meat Is Murder' with changing his viewpoint. "Making that track is better than doing benefits for animal rights because it's there forever," he claims. "It made me think about eating meat, and I became a vegetarian because of it." For Andy Rourke, however, the lack of meat protein proves more difficult to accept. "We all became vegetarian," he remembers. "Morrissey already was, and Johnny was, virtually. Me and Mike gave up meat at that time. Obviously, we couldn't tour and be seen eating meat with an album called *Meat Is Murder*. I stuck with it for about two years and used to sneak out for a burger and stuff. At that time there wasn't the variety of food, unless you liked egg and chips..."

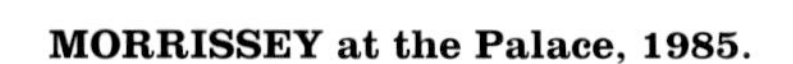

MORRISSEY at the Palace, 1985.

Set List: 'William, It Was Really Nothing'; 'Nowhere Fast'; 'I Want The One I Can't Have'; 'What She Said'; 'Hand In Glove'; 'How Soon Is Now?'; 'Stretch Out And Wait'; 'That Joke Isn't Funny Anymore'; 'Shakespeare's Sister'; 'Rusholme Ruffians'; 'The Headmaster Ritual'; 'Still Ill'; 'Meat Is Murder'; 'Heaven Knows I'm Miserable Now'; 'Handsome Devil'; 'Barbarism Begins At Home'; 'Miserable Lie'; 'Barbarism Begins At Home'.

4 APRIL

The UK tour nears its climax with a memorable gig at the Hippodrome, Bristol. "The *Meat Is Murder* tour had run very smoothly," Stuart James concludes. "It was like a rock'n'roll tour without the rock'n'roll trappings. Europe (which followed) was a different deal. We didn't have our own equipment and were relying upon Italian or Spanish promoters to get their act together which, invariably, they didn't."

Set List: 'William, It Was Really Nothing'; 'Nowhere Fast'; 'I Want The One I Can't Have'; 'What She Said'; 'Hand In Glove'; 'How Soon Is Now?'; 'Stretch Out And Wait'; 'That Joke Isn't Funny Anymore'; 'Shakespeare's Sister'; 'Rusholme Ruffians'; 'The Headmaster Ritual'; 'Still Ill'; 'Meat Is Murder'; 'Heaven Knows I'm Miserable Now'; 'Handsome Devil'; 'Miserable Lie'.

6 APRIL

The grand finale to the UK tour is an important appearance at London's Royal Albert Hall which, nevertheless, produces contrasting reviews, each analysing The Smiths' contribution to Eighties music. *Sounds'* Hugh Fielder throws down the critical gauntlet with some sharp criticisms. He reminds us of Morrissey's words at the close of the gig: "We probably picked the wrong venue. Never mind." For Fielder, this admission casts a worrying shadow over the group's long term prospects. "The fact remains that the Royal Albert Hall is a prestige gig for any group and The Smiths bottled it," he claims. "At least they acknowledged the fact before it was over. What made it more curious was that they'd set themselves up for it. As the

houselights went down, searchlights roamed the plush interior of the hall as Prokofiev's *Romeo And Juliet* blared pompously forth. Not surprisingly, the band's entrance was little short of gladiatorial... But it didn't last. Maybe they got self-conscious about their own charisma. At any event, they wasted the build-up and sank into a constricted parody of themselves that reached its nadir with 'Shakespeare's Sister'. Morrissey briefly stirred himself once more during the encore when he brought Pete Burns onstage to duet with him on 'Barbarism Begins At Home', but he relapsed immediately afterwards and walked off half-way through 'Miserable Lie'. The gig left a question mark over The Smiths' future, namely, where do they go from here? Their natural charm has carried them this far with disarming ease, but the next obvious stage forward requires a ruthless dedication and purpose that they can't quite summon up. Not all of them, anyway. But if they don't sort it out, then it may all end in tears."

The opposite case is put forward by the *NME*'s Danny Kelly, who comes out fighting like the archetypal Smiths' apostle. "Those believing that The Smiths will burn out or fade away must banish such thoughts," he commands, "not because they may not be right (six months is forever in pop) but because faced with such a performance like this, such a notion seems churlish, pathetic. England is theirs at the very least." With the hyperbole in full flow, Kelly explodes into paragraphs of breathless adulation before summing up the gig with the unlikely tease, "I'm glad when it ends." Why? It seems he fears a cardiac arrest. "How much more excitement could one body – ours, Morrissey's – take?" he gushes melodramatically. "When they set out on this tour a month ago, The Smiths were attempting to prove themselves the best band on these islands. As it turns out, the planet may currently provide scant opposition. "

Set List: 'How Soon Is Now?'; 'Nowhere Fast'; 'I Want The One I Can't Have'; 'What She Said'; 'Hand In Glove'; 'Stretch Out And Wait'; 'That Joke Isn't Funny Anymore'; 'Shakespeare's Sister'; 'Rusholme Ruffians'; 'The Headmaster Ritual'; 'You've Got Everything Now'; 'Handsome Devil'; 'Still Ill'; 'Meat Is Murder'; 'William, It Was Really Nothing'; 'Heaven Knows I'm Miserable Now'; 'Barbarism Begins At Home'; 'Miserable Lie'.

20 APRIL

Morrissey is interviewed in *Sounds* by Antonella Black, a young ex-*NME* contributor, who has already libelled Cliff Richard in one of the most appalling, offensive and disgraceful live reviews ever published in a music paper. Not surprisingly, her interview takes the form of sexual banter, in which Morrissey plays the camp comedian. Amid the innuendo, the singer unexpectedly hints at the inspiration behind some key lines in 'That Joke Isn't Funny Anymore'. "I do find many things erotic," he observes. "As a child in the Sixties, when the seats of cars were made of leather, to me there was something highly erotic about actually being in a car ... there was just something about the old leather seats..." Although the interview is abruptly terminated shortly after this, Black manages a brief introduction in which she pinpoints some of Morrissey's many contradictions: " Steven is celibate, yet Steven has a double bed. Steven isn't paranoid, yet he now has all interviews doubly recorded. Steven shrills long and loud about castrated cows and lambasted lambs, yet he confesses to finding leather seats highly erotic. Steven is a funny little kettle of fish."

MAY

The Face publishes the most informative and provocative article on The Smiths to date, courtesy of Nick Kent. The investigative piece is intercepted by Morrissey prior to publication, and he is deeply concerned about Kent's fascination for his pre-Smiths history. The real revelations, however, emerge from some unusually frank comments by Marr, who is sufficiently enamoured of Kent to drop his guard. Thus we learn for the first time about Marr's brief foray into criminality and

JOHNNY MARR dropped his guard in a revealing interview in 'The Face' in May 1985. FAR RIGHT: Morrissey's favourite fedora of 1985.

Rourke's teenage flirtation with barbiturates. The article even touches on Morrissey's sexuality, with Marr sympathetically analysing his musical partner's problems: "But try and imagine the hang-ups most people have in bed. All that 'Is she enjoying it? Is there something more than this?' Confusion. Now, magnify that a hundred times and you've got the beginnings of Morrissey's dilemma."

Less characteristically for a Smith in 1985, Marr closes the article with a flippant riposte, "But I must say that when he gets really upset, frankly, I think it's just because he needs a good humping." According to Kent, the piece resulted in his exile from The Smiths' camp for the best part of two years.

Marr subsequently makes some negative comments about the article in another paper, but refuses to dwell on its shortcomings. Perhaps this is because he realizes Kent has come closer than anybody yet to telling the truth about the group. Marr's colleagues still smile at the memory of the encounter, suggesting that the guitarist naïvely gave too much away. And as Kent rightly reminds us: "The more truthful the stuff you write, the more people seem to get upset."

13 MAY

A delegation from Rough Trade descends upon Heathrow Airport in an attempt to persuade The Smiths to appear on Italian television. Such occurrences are becoming increasingly common as Morrissey's caprice reaches new heights. According to Scott Piering, even getting Morrissey out of bed was a Herculean task. "I went over to his flat to collect him," Piering notes. "Morrissey wouldn't answer. He was hiding in the bedroom. After 10 minutes of banging and pleading I had to climb over the ledge from another flat and get at him. I thought he might be dead. If he decides he's not into something you have serious problems."

14 MAY

Following their arrival in Rome, The Smiths indulge in a spot of hotel hopping as preparations are underway for their television appearance and evening concert in Tendetrise. "We had a hotel booked," Stuart James recalls. "We checked into one hotel, then another one that was more stylish, then one that was nearer to the television studio. We'd already done three hotels, which was beginning to wind me up. Then we did the television rehearsals... Just prior to recording the playback, Morrissey decided that was it, and didn't want to do it. They were in the dressing room and had been there all day.

'How Soon Is Now?'; 'Stretch Out And Wait'; 'That Joke Isn't Funny Anymore'; 'Shakespeare's Sister'; 'Rusholme Ruffians'; 'The Headmaster Ritual'; 'Hand In Glove'; 'Still Ill'; 'Meat Is Murder'; 'Heaven Knows I'm Miserable Now'; 'Handsome Devil'; 'This Charming Man'; 'Miserable Lie'; 'You've Got Everything Now'.

17 MAY

As they fly into Madrid, The Smiths learn that they have lost face with their record company. "We hadn't done the television show and Rough Trade were really pissed off with this because they'd already met us at Heathrow and the group had said they'd do it," Stuart James remembers. "They'd gone through all the preliminaries and didn't end up doing it. Then we flew to Madrid and changed hotels to avoid Rough Trade people, and also to hide from Scott Piering."

> **'Drag queens would come on with a ghetto blaster and mime. Most of them got canned off stage. That wasn't popular with promoters...'**
>
> STUART JAMES

Someone said, 'OK – let's do it!', and the answer was 'No!' I got annoyed. Even at that point I didn't have their confidence. I'd have felt a lot more excited about it if I'd been part of that and could feel, 'Now we're going to do it!' All the time I was trying to liaise with Virgin Italy. They said, 'We'll never get an English group on Italian television again'. Fortunately, the gig at Tendetrise went OK."

Set List: 'William, It Was Really Nothing'; 'Nowhere Fast'; 'I Want The One I Can't Have'; 'What She Said';

18 MAY

More drama as Scott Piering arrives in search of his reluctant charges. "He didn't even have a room or money," Stuart James claims. "He was sleeping in the lobby." Scott corrects this mistaken impression. "I didn't stay at the hotel because it was full up," he explains. "I stayed at another hotel. I was snubbed and warned not to go by Mike Hinck. It was all about the American tour. At this point, I think they said the American tour was off after we'd spent all this time doing it. By God, I figured this was my last shot. If the worst was to happen I'd at least find out. So I went. I was advised to stay away. I knew they were hiding from me. I hung out and didn't pressurize them. I let them know I was there, made myself available and had a few words with them, but they just didn't deal with it... They thought I was pursuing them, and I was. I was their conscience and they had to deal with it."

Although Piering is losing the confidence of the group and has all but surrendered his frustrating role as caretaker-manager, he at least manages to enjoy their performance at Paseo De Camoens, which is filmed and later broadcast on the Spanish programme *Edad de Oro*. "I treated myself to a week in Madrid and saw the festival," Piering concludes. "The *Meat Is Murder* tour was my peak period."

Set List: 'William, It Was Really Nothing'; 'Nowhere Fast'; 'I Want The One I Can't Have'; 'What She Said'; 'How Soon Is Now?'; 'Stretch Out And Wait'; 'That Joke Isn't Funny Anymore'; 'Shakespeare's Sister'; 'Rusholme Ruffians'; 'The Headmaster Ritual'; 'Hand In Glove'; 'Still Ill'; 'Meat Is Murder'; 'Heaven Knows I'm Miserable Now'; 'Miserable Lie'; 'Barbarism Begins At Home'; 'This Charming Man'; 'You've Got Everything Now'.

24 MAY

The Smiths appear on *Studio One* performing 'Still Ill', 'Meat Is Murder' and 'Barbarism Begins At Home'.

5 JUNE

The Smiths fly to America where they are booked for a short summer tour, accompanied by Billy Bragg. They now have a new manager, Matthew Sztumph, who also oversees Morrissey's favourites Madness. "I wasn't a huge Smiths fan," Sztumph recalls. "I didn't fall into the category of love them or hate them. I went and met Morrissey and seemed to get on with him. Then I didn't hear anything for months... I then got a phone call from Mike Hinck saying Morrissey wanted me involved... I'd toured America a few times and had a lot of contacts and fancied the challenge of putting together an American tour in 10 days. They had the dates booked but nothing else."

ROURKE, 1985.

7 JUNE

The US tour opens at the Aragon Ballroom, Chicago. Morrissey, perhaps recalling James Maker's appearances during the early days of The Smiths, decides that something exotic is required to trumpet their arrival. "We got to the first gig in Chicago and Morrissey wanted drag queens," Stuart James remembers with a smile. "That wasn't popular with promoters at all. Drag queens would come on with a ghetto blaster and mime. Most of them got canned off stage."

"If you have great sympathy with Gay Culture, you are immediately transsexual," Morrissey complains to *The Face* shortly afterwards. "I did one interview where the gay issue was skirted over in three seconds and when the interview emerged in print, there I was emblazoned across the headlines as this great voice of the gay movement, as if I couldn't possibly talk about anything else. I find that extremely harmful and simply don't trust anyone anymore."

Set List: 'William, It Was Really Nothing'; 'Nowhere Fast'; 'I Want The One I Can't Have'; 'What She Said'; 'How Soon Is Now?'; 'That Joke Isn't Funny Anymore'; 'Stretch Out And Wait'; 'Shakespeare's Sister'; 'Rusholme Ruffians'; 'The Headmaster Ritual'; 'Hand In Glove'; 'Still Ill'; 'Meat Is Murder'; 'Please Please Please Let Me Get What I Want'; 'Heaven Knows I'm Miserable Now'; 'This Charming Man'; 'Miserable Lie'.

8 JUNE

A more restrained welcome is evident at the Royal Oak Theater, Detroit. Nevertheless, the group continues to attract a solid fan base, much to the appreciation of US promoters. "They amazed us with the power of their live show and the reaction they were getting from audiences," Matthew Sztumph reflects. The manager also found his dietary habits changing after travelling with the group. "They even converted me to being a vegetarian," he remembers. "Nobody was eating meat so unless I snuck off to McDonald's there was no way I was going to get any meat. Having spent that much time not eating meat, the next time I did I felt really uncomfortable... physically uncomfortable."

Set List: 'William, It Was Really Nothing'; 'Nowhere Fast'; 'I Want The One I Can't Have'; 'What She Said'; 'How Soon Is Now?'; 'That Joke Isn't Funny Anymore'; 'Stretch Out And Wait'; 'Shakespeare's Sister'; 'Rusholme Ruffians'; 'The Headmaster Ritual'; 'Hand In Glove'; 'Still Ill'; 'Meat Is Murder'; 'Please Please Please Let Me Get What I Want'; 'Heaven Knows I'm Miserable Now'; 'This Charming Man'; 'Miserable Lie'.

Back in England, *NME* print a surprisingly uncontroversial interview with Morrissey titled "The Further Thoughts Of Chairman Mo". Interviewer Danny Kelly seems, on this occasion, smitten to the point of sycophancy, but a few passing comments from Morrissey sound some warning bells. Record company gripes ("Rough Trade have done their job and no more. They're bored with The Smiths now. I've seen maximum evidence of this") and the Marr connection ("I feel very defensive about our relationship. Some things have to be shielded, but the dedication I feel to him is quite solid and impregnable") are particularly worth noting at this point.

'NME', 8 June 1985

9 JUNE

The Smiths' first appearance in Canada takes place in Toronto. "They played the Kingswood Theatre," recalls Matthew Sztumph, "only it wasn't a theatre but an open air affair. They put 12,000 people in there that night and they'd only ever sold 10,000 albums in Canada." Among the spectators at Kingswood is Sire president Seymour Stein, who shows off his rock'n'roll credibility by mixing with the masses. "Seymour was right down the front squashed against a crash barrier for the entire show," Sztumph laughs. "He was really into it. That's the great thing about Seymour. He always has been a music fan and always will be. What MD of a record company would spend an entire evening squashed up against a crash barrier at the front of a gig?"

Set List: 'William, It Was Really Nothing'; 'Nowhere Fast'; 'I Want The One I Can't Have'; 'What She Said'; 'How Soon Is Now?'; 'That Joke Isn't Funny Anymore'; 'Stretch Out And Wait'; 'Shakespeare's Sister'; 'Rusholme Ruffians'; 'The Headmaster Ritual'; 'Hand In Glove'; 'Still Ill'; 'Meat Is Murder'; 'Heaven Knows I'm Miserable Now'; 'This Charming Man'; 'Please Please Please Let Me Get What I Want'; 'Miserable Lie'.

11/12 JUNE

The Smiths move steadily from the Warner Theater, Washington to the Tower Theater, Philadelphia. The set lists on both these nights are identical and the group sound fresh and well-rehearsed. Morrissey is overwhelmed with the reception that the group receives. "When you play concerts in America which are highly successful, it really colours your vision of the entire country," he explains. "You're quite reluctant to think of the bad points because suddenly it seems like the most perfect patch of land on this planet. I've been there many times and had many unshakeable criticisms which have now, of course, been shaken."

Set List: 'William, It Was Really Nothing'; 'Nowhere Fast'; 'I Want The One I Can't Have'; 'What She Said'; 'How Soon Is Now?'; 'That Joke Isn't Funny Anymore'; 'Stretch Out And Wait'; 'Shakespeare's Sister'; 'Rusholme Ruffians'; 'The Headmaster Ritual'; 'Hand In Glove'; 'Still Ill'; 'Meat Is Murder'.

14 JUNE

Melody Maker's Dave Thomas turns up at the Opera House, Boston, to offer a view from abroad. His appreciation is decidedly lukewarm. "To the British observer, The Smiths tonight offer up little in the way of surprises," he concludes. "True, there is a little more emphasis on provincial eccentricity, Morrissey playing up his sensitivities out of deference to an audience who've probably only ever seen him on LP sleeves prior to this, but The Smiths' formula is already so sharply defined that they could never truly deviate even if they wanted to."

The American based reviewers prove more enthusiastic, and it is interesting to see Marr taking many of the accolades. "From the opening strains of 'I Want The One I Can't Have', this is Johnny's show," reviewer Charles Dodson proclaims. "The band rips off two more rockers, 'What She Said' and 'How Soon Is Now?', before Morrissey warms to the task and rips his shirt open. Now the crowd is eating it up, no crumbs left. Johnny coaxes Morrissey from one song to the next, then retreats to his harplike guitar ripple, leaving the lead singer to mumble barely audible thanks in between. Seven songs later, the band shuffles off stage... and then the show begins in earnest. By the second encore, the stage is awash with hundreds of 14-year-old dancing girls who, strangely, keep a respectful distance from Morrissey. Then up

THE SMITHS in buoyant mood.

MORRISSEY and inspirational icon Billy Fury, later to grace the cover of 'Last Night I Dreamt That Somebody Loved Me'.

rushes a man who slaps a dollar bill squarely upon Morrissey's sticky-with-sweat forehead and 'Miserable Lie' takes on a whole new life."

Set List: 'William, It Was Really Nothing'; 'Nowhere Fast'; 'I Want The One I Can't Have'; 'What She Said'; 'How Soon Is Now?'; 'That Joke Isn't Funny Anymore'; 'Stretch Out And Wait'; 'Shakespeare's Sister'; 'Rusholme Ruffians'; 'The Headmaster Ritual'; 'Hand In Glove'; 'Still Ill'; 'Meat Is Murder'; 'Heaven Knows I'm Miserable Now'; 'This Charming Man'; 'Please Please Please Let Me Get What I Want'; 'Miserable Lie'; 'Jeane'; 'Barbarism Begins At Home'.

17 JUNE

A dramatic day for Stuart James who is compiling a guest list for The Smiths' gig that evening at the Beacon Theater, New York. One of his more arduous tasks is informing Seymour Stein, the president of Sire Records, that he should not attend the gig. "Morrissey wanted him off the guest list," James recalls. "I rang Seymour at home from a New York hotel and said, 'I'm sorry Seymour, Morrissey says he doesn't want you on the guest list...' Half an hour later, he's ringing me back and saying: 'Ah, Stuart, you must put me on the guest list at that particular gig'."

Set List: 'William, It Was Really Nothing'; 'Nowhere Fast'; 'I Want The One I Can't Have'; 'What She Said'; 'How Soon Is Now?'; 'That Joke Isn't Funny Anymore'; 'Stretch Out And Wait'; 'Shakespeare's Sister'; 'Rusholme Ruffians'; 'The Headmaster Ritual'; 'Hand In Glove'; 'Still Ill'; 'Meat Is Murder'; 'Heaven Knows I'm Miserable Now'; 'This Charming Man'; 'Please Please Please Let Me Get What I Want'; 'Miserable Lie'; 'Jeane'; 'Barbarism Begins At Home'.

18 JUNE

On their second performance at the Beacon Theater, The Smiths show off their versatility by completely restructuring their set. A seven minute version of 'Meat Is Murder' is brought forward to set the evening off in spectacular fashion. According to Morrissey, last night's show was all about Tom Boys, whereas tonight it's dedicated to "the poetic librarians". Marr is in particularly playful mood throughout the show, incorporating a snatch of Jimmy Justice's 'When My Little Girl Is Smiling' into 'I Want The One I Can't Have', and The Beatles' 'Day Tripper' riff into 'Jeane'. Ticket sales for both New York concerts are exceptionally high and testify to The Smiths' popularity in the bigger American cities.'

Set List: 'Meat Is Murder'; 'The Headmaster Ritual'; 'Reel Around The Fountain'; 'Shakespeare's Sister'; 'Nowhere Fast'; 'I Want The One I Can't Have'; 'This Charming Man'; 'That Joke Isn't Funny Anymore'; 'Stretch Out And Wait'; 'Heaven Knows I'm Miserable Now'; 'What She Said'; 'Still Ill'; 'How Soon Is Now?'; 'William, It Was Really Nothing'; 'Hand In Glove'; 'Please Please Please Let Me Get What I Want'; 'Rusholme Ruffians'; 'Miserable Lie'; 'Jeane'; 'Barbarism Begins At Home'.

MORRISSEY with feline friend.

19 JUNE

Having completed the East Coast leg of the tour, The Smiths are due to fly West, but all is not well with their singer. "Morrissey's fear of flying was at its height then," Stuart James remembers. "We were doing a lot of flying at the time. We'd broken the New York/East Coast part of the tour, which went relatively smoothly. Then there was the flight to San Francisco and the West Coast... I remember the difficulty getting the group on the plane. Morrissey wasn't too keen on even going to the West Coast. At that time, I thought, 'Oh, we're going to fly home tomorrow!' He was really not into flying at that time. We were on the tarmac. We were taxi-ing down the runway and he wanted to get off even then. How he got on the plane in the first place, I'll never know. I thought, 'I can't handle this. I'm going back to my seat'."

20 JUNE

A momentous day for Johnny Marr, who marries his long-time girlfriend Angela Brown in San Francisco. The wedding is a very quiet affair with a minimum of fuss and seemingly undertaken in a moment of spontaneity. "We stayed at this Japanese hotel that had these big Japanese tubs in the bathroom," Andy Rourke recalls. "They got married in some evangelist church. It was pretty bizarre. There were about 10 of us there, including the crew. The ceremony only lasted about 15 minutes. I was a witness. Afterwards, they hired a function room in the hotel and we had champagne and a buffet. It was a nice day, but it was just weird. It didn't seem real. You know what it's like in America – everything's plastic and phoney. It just didn't seem like a proper wedding. No relatives were there."

JOHNNY AND ANGIE MARR on their wedding day, 20 June 1985.

21 JUNE
Johnny Marr celebrates his first day of married life with a performance at the Kaiser Auditorium, Oakland. As The Smiths move further away from the epicentre of the US record industry, their reception is less fanatical. Nevertheless, Morrissey is greatly impressed with the response of his devoted followers and even finds himself warming to record company officials. "Meeting the people there was an extraordinary eye opener," he reflects, "because one is fed all these fixed impressions of the American music buying public and they didn't turn out to be that way. They turned out to be rational, incredibly sensitive poetic human beings."

Set List: 'William, It Was Really Nothing'; 'Nowhere Fast'; 'I Want The One I Can't Have'; 'How Soon Is Now?'; 'Stretch Out And Wait'; 'That Joke Isn't Funny Anymore'; 'Shakespeare's Sister'; ' Please Please Please Let Me Get What I Want'; 'Miserable Lie'; 'The Headmaster Ritual'.

24 JUNE
Morrissey finds fame throughout mid-America by making the pages of *People* magazine. In typically hyperbolic style, they trumpet his arrival with the headline: "Roll Over Bob Dylan And Tell Madonna The News – The Smiths' Morrissey Is Pop's Latest Messiah".

25 JUNE
By the time the group reaches the State University Open Air Theater, San Diego, Stuart James is reflecting on how well the tour has progressed. "It was a bit easier," he recalls. "There weren't problems with food. That was a big help – not having to find them something to eat. As a veggie, I now appreciate the difficulties more than I did."

Set List: 'Meat Is Murder'; 'The Headmaster Ritual'; 'Shakespeare's Sister'; 'Hand In Glove'; 'Nowhere Fast'; 'I Want The One I Can't Have'; 'This Charming Man'; 'That Joke Isn't Funny Anymore'; 'Stretch Out And Wait'; 'Heaven Knows I'm Miserable Now'; 'What She Said'; 'Still Ill'; 'How Soon Is Now?'; 'William, It Was Really Nothing'; 'Jeane'; 'Please Please Please Let Me Get What I Want'; 'Rusholme Ruffians'; 'Miserable Lie'; 'Barbarism Begins At Home'.

27 JUNE
The Smiths arrive at the Palladium Theater, Los Angeles, in some style. "We were into limos at that point," Stuart James explains. "It was the whole American thing. I got back into it at that point. For some reason, because it got bigger, it got more organized and everything went more efficiently... I rose to the challenge and the group seemed a lot easier to deal with. I enjoyed the travelling and the US success. I was paid more too."

Set List: 'Meat Is Murder'; ' Hand In Glove'; 'Shakespeare's Sister'; 'The Headmaster Ritual'; 'Nowhere Fast'; 'I Want The One I Can't Have'; 'This Charming Man'; 'That Joke Isn't Funny Anymore'; 'Stretch Out And Wait'; 'Heaven Knows I'm Miserable Now'; 'How Soon Is Now?'; 'William, It Was Really Nothing'; 'Jeane'; 'Barbarism Begins At Home'.

28 JUNE
The second gig at the Palladium Theater is enormously well received. "I was proud of the fact that there weren't problems," Sztumph remembers. "Potentially, the whole thing could have been a complete disaster. It was really only by having the contacts I had that we were able to pull it off. It went very smoothly."

Set List: 'Meat Is Murder'; ' Hand In Glove'; 'I Want The One I Can't Have'; 'Nowhere Fast'; 'Shakespeare's Sister'; 'That Joke Isn't Funny Anymore'; 'Stretch Out And Wait'; 'Heaven Knows I'm Miserable Now'; 'What She Said'; 'Still Ill'; 'How Soon Is Now?'; 'Jeane'; 'The Headmaster Ritual'; 'Reel Around The Fountain'; 'William, It Was Really Nothing'; 'This Charming Man'; 'Miserable Lie'.

29 JUNE.
The US tour concludes with a stage invasion at the Irvine Meadows Amphitheater, Laguna Hills. The guest list reveals the presence of Andy Somers, who may not have been aware of Morrissey and Marr's uncomplimentary comments on The Police earlier in their career. The Los Angeles sojourn provides some memorable anecdotes, not least Morrissey's appearance in the plush restaurant, The Ivy. "We went for dinner a few times and Seymour Stein sang all these songs because that's what Seymour likes to do at dinner," Sztumph remembers. "Morrissey would know them all, and they got on fine. There was one night at a restaurant in Los Angeles when Seymour sang away and he pulled Paul Simon over from another table. I think that thrilled Morrissey meeting Paul Simon, who was having dinner with Whoopi Goldberg." Everyone agrees that the Irvine Meadows show is a suitably exciting note on which to end the tour.

Set List: 'Meat Is Murder'; ' Hand In Glove'; 'I Want The One I Can't Have'; 'Nowhere Fast'; 'Shakespeare's Sister'; 'That Joke Isn't Funny Anymore'; 'Stretch Out And Wait'; 'Heaven Knows I'm Miserable Now'; 'What She Said'; 'Still Ill'; 'How Soon Is Now?'; 'Jeane'; 'The Headmaster Ritual'; 'Reel Around The Fountain'; 'William, It Was Really Nothing'; 'This Charming Man'; 'Miserable Lie'; 'Barbarism Begins At Home'.

MORRISSEY contemplates the final solution.

1 JULY
The entourage returns to England and, at Heathrow, Matthew Sztumph has a brief conversation with Morrissey about his future as manager. I said, 'Give me a call in a couple of days and we'll take it from there'," Sztumph remembers. "I never heard from him. That was the end of that."

5 JULY
'That Joke Isn't Funny Anymore' is released as a single. The 12-inch version features four live tracks recorded at the Oxford Apollo (18 March): 'Shakespeare's Sister', 'Meat Is Murder', 'Nowhere Fast' and 'Stretch Out And Wait'. Despite its quality, the single barely scrapes into the Top 50, peaking at number 49. Marr still speaks of the song as if it was worthy of reaching number one. "My favourite song on *Meat Is Murder* now is 'That Joke Isn't Funny Anymore'," he confides. "That's the way the melody came out, in waltz time." For Morrissey, the song served as a riposte to his more forceful media interrogators. "When I wrote 'That Joke Isn't Funny Anymore'," he notes, "I was just so completely tired of all the same old journalistic questions and people trying to drag me down and prove that I was a complete fake."

13 JULY
The celebrated Live Aid concert in London and Philadelphia makes world headlines, but wins scant approval from the acerbic tongue of Morrissey. In one of his less aggressive broadsides, he sneeringly dismisses the event with the cursory quip, "It was Hollywood." The charity record industry clearly offends Morrissey's sensibilities and he remains unimpressed by the results. "I feel that situations like Ethiopia could quite easily be solved," he adds, "and they're not solved for specific reasons, and I find concerts and benefit records and so forth quite pointless."

19 JULY

The Smiths are scheduled to appear on the chat show *Wogan*, but in a classic prima donna display Morrissey disappears. "That was the low point of my career," laments Matthew Sztumph. "Sitting at Wogan at 3.30 in the afternoon when they're supposed to be there at 3.00 and there's no Morrissey. He'd gone back to Manchester. He hadn't called anybody to let them know. He'd just gone back to Manchester. I think, ultimately, Morrissey decided that The Smiths should not be on *Wogan*, but unfortunately he decided it the night before the show and hadn't told either myself or the members of the band, and we were all sat there. The show was due on air at 7pm and I was not a popular person. I obviously made up some excuse that he was ill. It could have caused all sorts of repercussions... The embarrassment was having the members of the band and myself sitting in the studio waiting for him, and the lack of consideration Morrissey had for us. The least he could have done was tell his own band!... I don't recall it causing a lot of friction at Rough Trade. Maybe they were more used to it than I was." Mike Joyce certainly seemed stoical. "Some people feel as though they have to make an impression," he casually remarked of the latest Morrissey fiasco.

MIKE JOYCE was stoical about Morrissey's non-appearance on 'Wogan'.

27 JULY

Rumours intensify that The Smiths are about to leave Rough Trade due to the poor progress of their recent singles. A tight-lipped Geoff Travis insists that The Smiths' future recordings will continue to appear on his label and points out that they are still under contract. A few days later, a spokesperson from Rough Trade attempts to soothe the troubled waters with some philosophical public relations spiel: "Every band has a feeling of dissatisfaction with their record label from time to time, a sort of hate the label week. But invariably it's only a passing phase. We feel that our relationship with The Smiths is, generally speaking, very good and we believe Morrissey realizes they are far better off with us than with any of the majors." Meanwhile, the singer is characteristically maintaining the suspense by refusing to comment on the issue.

28 JULY

Work is underway on the next Smiths' single, 'The Boy With The Thorn In His Side'. "They decided to go to a little 8-track studio in Manchester," producer Stephen Street recalls. "I think they were meant to do a demo. Sometimes, Morrissey would say, 'That sounds brilliant, we can't do any better'. That's what happened. So they decided to release the demo as a single."

3 AUGUST

Melody Maker win an exclusive interview with Johnny Marr in which he talks about his relationship with Morrissey, confirms that The Smiths will be staying at Rough Trade and reminisces about his youth. Intriguingly, he unveils plans for the yet to be recorded third Smiths' album, suggesting that it will be a radical departure from the group's previous work. "There will be a move away from the old jingly-jangly guitars," he stresses. "Everybody knows I can do that... That doesn't mean that there will be less guitar playing on the album. By no means! It just means that I will be playing different kinds of stuff, very much in the R&B groove of, say, 'Shakespeare's Sister'... I like to think that it will horrify a lot of people. I am fairly obsessed at the moment with Elmore James and John Lee Hooker and early Elvis and it's going to be very rootsy. I've still got my pop sensibilities and the melodies will still be there but it will certainly be much less of a radio sounding album than the other two."

Marr goes on to court controversy by attacking Bryan Ferry, whom he accuses of gross expediency in plugging his new material at Live Aid. His fiercest barbs, however, are reserved for former hero Keith Richard, whom he insists cannot play the guitar anymore. "He was my biggest influence in the early days," Marr laments, "and now I have no respect for him at all." Two years hence, Marr will be collaborating with both Ferry and Richard, which just goes to show how capricious some musicians can be. In retrospect, Marr's biting put-downs partly reflect his impatience with the popular image of The Smiths as a predominantly Sixties-influenced group. "I loathe most of the stuff from the late Sixties," he sneers unexpectedly. "If The Smiths had walked onto the stage at Monterey, they would have blown away every single one of those bands. We are an Eighties band. There is a lot of worth in the Eighties. This generation is very honourable and valorous and quite a brave generation, certainly compared to the decadence of the late Sixties."

FRESH FROM AMERICA, MORRISSEY APPEARS ON the front cover of *Record Mirror* in one of his better interviews of 1985. Amazingly, he has the audacity to plead penury at a time when The Smiths are reaping the substantial rewards provided by their lucrative profit-sharing agreement with Rough Trade, "I'm still too much acquainted with the whole aspect of poverty," Morrissey moans very unconvincingly. "I'm tired of being broke, very tired of that, and it's especially hurtful when you meet so many in the industry who

> **'Everybody was pissed up or smoking draw. Grant Showbiz, the sound man, was drinking the worm out of a bottle of mescaline.'**
>
> GARY ROSTOCK

don't quite have your status but are laughably rich."

Ironically, while Morrissey is complaining about his supposed lack of money, Joyce and Rourke are feeling even more out of pocket and require some detailed accounts of the recent US tour. Upon asking their fellow Smiths, however, they are greeted with the reply: "Don't you trust us?" As Joyce remembers: "I just wanted to see for myself what was happening. Of course, the accounts never came about, so I started to get worried, really." The messy financial arrangements that hark back to the formation of The Smiths will continue to dog the group long after their break up.

NOT TO BE OUTDONE BY THE SENIOR MEMBERS OF The Smiths, Mike Joyce makes a rare appearance in print, talking to the magazine *No. 1*. Intriguingly, he speculates on the break-up of the group and, in doing so, unwittingly prophesies his own feelings many years later. "There's a story going round that The Smiths will never make another album," he complains. "I just don't take any notice of them. I know The Smiths will go on for a good long while yet – I'm going to sound like Mick Jagger, but who knows how long it'll last? I don't know what I'd do if it ended – be heartbroken for three years probably."

AUGUST

The Smiths move down to London and enter RAK studios for preliminary work on their next album. 'Bigmouth Strikes Again' is attempted along with 'Asleep' and 'Rubber Ring'. "That was a great session," Stephen Street remembers. "At that point I was putting in a lot of ideas. When you're the only person working with the band, you start to become, by the nature of the work, co-producer. I remember that night the session went really well and I asked Johnny and Morrissey whether they'd consider giving me a production point, just one per cent of the sessions that I'd do. They thought about it and said, 'Fine'. So that's how I stepped up from engineer to co-producer."

SEPTEMBER

Tour manager Stuart James unveils the latest Smiths' riders for a forthcoming tour of Scotland. It reads:

"The Promoter shall provide onstage at no charge to the artiste a live tree with a minimum height of 3 feet and a maximum height of 5 feet, species and type to be agreed by the tour manager at least 15 days before the performance."

16 SEPTEMBER

'The Boy With The Thorn In His Side' is released but despite its commercial lilt only reaches number 23. Remarkably, this will prove the group's best chart position of the year. Critical response to the single is also surprisingly lukewarm. "Seems like Morrissey himself gives up the song halfway through when he stops the words and uses up the rest of the needle-time with yodelling," complains one review. "If it's too much to expect a revision of world music with every record, we could at least ask for something a little less enervating." Enervating was a word that more aptly described the maudlin B-side, 'Asleep'. Arguably Morrissey's most despairing song, the track reflected the singer's ambiguous feelings about suicide.

EASTERHOUSE supported The Smiths on a mini-tour of Scotland.

22 SEPTEMBER

The Smiths embark on a mini-tour of Scotland, supported by Morrissey favourites and fellow Rough Trade signings Easterhouse. Following a route marked out by Echo And The Bunnymen on a previous tour, The Smiths determine to play several venues in obscure places. The tour opens at the Magnum Leisure Centre, Irvine, a venue touted as the largest sports centre in Europe. The performance is encouraging, especially given the unusual venue. "The Smiths conquered what could have been a gruesome situation convincingly," reviewer Tom Morton notices. "A large young, very sober audience went predictably mental at the first proper gig their town has seen in three years, rejoicing in scaling the low stage and touching the Morrissey torso... the Morrissey human windmill syndrome was still much in evidence, counterpointed by the newly-shorn Johnny Marr, devoid of shades and looking frighteningly like a young Keith Richards in white shirt and black jacket." Easterhouse manager John Barratt is equally impressed. "Everyone was blown away," he notes. "As it turned out, it wasn't that great a night for them. But they were so rock'n'roll – a powerhouse." The set concludes with 'Meat Is Murder', before which Morrissey reminds his followers: "Just remember one thing, dear friends, next time you bite into that big fat sausage, you're eating somebody else's mother."

Set List: 'Shakespeare's Sister'; 'I Want The One I Can't Have'; 'What She Said'; 'What's The World?'; 'Nowhere Fast'; 'The Boy With The Thorn In His Side'; 'Frankly Mr Shankly'; 'Bigmouth Strikes Again'; 'That Joke Isn't Funny Anymore'; 'Stretch Out And Wait'; 'Still Ill'; 'Rusholme Ruffians/(Marie's The Name) His Latest Flame (Medley)'; 'How Soon Is Now?'; 'The Headmaster Ritual'; 'Meat Is Murder'; 'Heaven Knows I'm Miserable Now'; 'Hand In Glove'; 'William, It Was Really Nothing'; 'Miserable Lie'.

24 SEPTEMBER

After the sports centre, the next venue is the contrasting Victorian-styled Playhouse, Edinburgh. "They were a lot better suited to the Playhouse," recalls John Barratt. "The Scottish tour was the first time they played 'Bigmouth Strikes Again' and 'Frankly Mr Shankly'. I remember 'Frankly Mr Shankly' really suited the place. Morrissey has always reminded me of Tommy Trinder and it sounded very music hall. Morrissey seemed much more at home in the velour surroundings, with the balcony and ornate setting. It was a good gig. They were getting better with each gig and were inspiring Easterhouse too."

Set List: 'Shakespeare's Sister'; 'I Want The One I Can't Have'; 'What She Said'; 'What's The World?'; 'Nowhere Fast'; 'The Boy With The Thorn In His Side'; 'Frankly Mr Shankly'; 'Bigmouth Strikes Again'; 'That Joke Isn't Funny Anymore'; 'Stretch Out And Wait'; 'Still Ill'; 'Rusholme Ruffians/(Marie's The Name) His Latest Flame (Medley)'; 'How Soon Is Now?'; 'The Headmaster Ritual'; 'Meat Is Murder'; 'Heaven Knows I'm Miserable Now'; 'Hand In Glove'; 'William, It Was Really Nothing'; 'Miserable Lie'.

25 SEPTEMBER

With *The Tube* cameras present, Morrissey is interviewed by Margi Clarke at the Barrowlands, Glasgow. For the entourage that attended the gig, this was undoubtedly the highlight of the tour. "At Glasgow people were fainting," recalls Easterhouse drummer Gary Rostock. "It was the best gig I ever played. We went down a storm. Then they came on and people were dropping like flies. St John's Ambulance people were taking them out. It was pretty wild. Everyone rushed to the front and got crushed." Among the revellers are Easterhouse's Ivor Perry and manager John Barratt. "It was really buzzing," Barratt remembers. "Ivor wanted to get nearer and we got to the side and couldn't see anything. Eventually, we got locked between the exit doors and the inside and it was like a sauna. Condensation was dripping from the walls. The crowd was going mad. Onstage, Andy and Mike were really important. They kept it all together and gave Johnny the freedom to do what he wanted. They'd always be with him onstage, they were so tight. When Mike walked off the stage his legs buckled because he'd been playing that hard and had given it everything. They were all covered in towels. Then, as soon as Johnny came off, the roadie Phil Powell just stuck a spliff in his mouth about the size of a coconut tree. That was Ivor's biggest thing. He said to me: 'That's what I want, a spliff roadie!' They were brilliant. A great rock'n'roll band. This whole thing about Morrissey being fey, no way. You looked at him and thought, 'He's up there with Jagger and the rest'. I was really stunned. I was a big U2 fan and it was then that I realized how weedy they were beside The Smiths." Afterwards, Barratt confronts Geoff Travis who, in the post gig euphoria, claims that this is the best gig he has ever seen The Smiths play. With the evening's performance still reverberating in their heads, Easterhouse retire to their hotel which, appropriately enough, is called "Smiths".

Set List: 'Shakespeare's Sister'; 'I Want The One I Can't Have'; 'What She Said'; 'What's The World?'; 'Nowhere Fast'; 'The Boy With The Thorn In His Side'; 'Frankly Mr Shankly'; 'Bigmouth Strikes Again'; 'That Joke Isn't Funny Anymore'; 'Stretch Out And Wait'; 'Still Ill'; 'Rusholme Ruffians/(Marie's The Name) His Latest Flame (Medley)'; 'Heaven Knows I'm Miserable Now'; 'Meat Is Murder'; 'This Charming Man'; 'Hand In Glove'; 'William, It Was Really Nothing'; 'Miserable Lie'.

THE SMITHS at the far end of Coronation Street, December 1985.

26 SEPTEMBER

After the triumph of Glasgow, there is a great sense of anti-climax when playing the Caird Hall, Dundee. "It wasn't sold out," Barratt recalls. "Glasgow had been dynamite, but this was a weird place. You felt there should have been an orchestra there. It was a real comedown." After the gig, various members of the touring party attempt to gain admittance to a local nightclub, but the bouncers refuse to allow them entry.

Set List: 'Shakespeare's Sister'; 'I Want The One I Can't Have'; 'What She Said'; 'What's The World?'; 'The Boy With The Thorn In His Side'; 'Nowhere Fast'; 'That Joke Isn't Funny Anymore'; 'Stretch Out And Wait'; 'Frankly Mr Shankly'; 'Bigmouth Strikes Again'; 'Still Ill'; 'Heaven Knows I'm Miserable Now'; 'Meat Is Murder'; 'This Charming Man'; 'Hand In Glove'; 'William, It Was Really Nothing'; 'Miserable Lie'.

27 SEPTEMBER

The Scottish tour reaches its outer limits as the touring party set sail for the Shetland Isles. A long boat trip is inflicted upon the crew and support group, while The Smiths are allowed the relative luxury of a chartered flight. All is far from well, however, and a touch of turbulent weather causes a few missed heart beats. "Their plane flipped on the way over," recalls Easterhouse's Gary Rostock. "They were all quite freaked out by it. Morrissey's nerves were all over the place." The rest of the crew are granted an easier passage. "We went over on the ferry," John Barratt explains. "It was a sleep-over. We got there at about seven in the morning. There was only one hotel there. The irony was that the hotel was near the place where the sheep were brought to be taken off to be slaughtered."

28 SEPTEMBER

Having settled in, The Smiths appear at the Clickerman Centre, Lerwick, for one of the strangest performances of their career. Amazingly, there is a reviewer on hand to provide a brief summation. "The crowd of 700 were bereft of pretence and prejudice," writes Tim Barry. "The Smiths were just four guys. And as Morrissey sagely noted, 'This is our new single and you can buy it in Aberdeen, if you know how to swim.' Three new Smiths' songs badly in need of fine tuning got an airing, and what better place than

MORRISSEY and Pete Burns, soul mates for much of 1985.

out of earshot of London, which is farther away than the Arctic Circle."

For Easterhouse's Ivor Perry, the Shetlands sojourn proved particularly memorable. "It was a good laugh," he recalls. "It was such an out of the way place that there were dead unusual people. Some were quite old and there were families with kids, and even a few sheep, if I remember. We went on first and they didn't really know how to react to bands. So, when we played, we went down really well. When The Smiths came on, Morrissey had a lot of aggravation with the audience slagging him off and vice versa. He didn't look too happy with it." Gary Rostock confirms this account of The Smiths' unexpected fall. "We went down better than them," he boasts. "They hated it because they went down pretty badly which I hadn't seen on the whole tour. But it was a strange place. It was like playing a gig with 'The Wicker Man'."

"Easterhouse were playing grungy rock'n'roll like Deep Purple," John Barratt laughs. "The audience could relate to that!" After the gig, the entourage enjoy a few drinks and The Smiths present birthday boy drummer Gary Rostock with two bottles of champagne. "We all stayed up afterwards in the bar at the hotel," remembers John Barratt, who was still recovering from the shock of having to deal with the venue's no alcohol policy. "That was the first night we'd seen them close up. Morrissey was one of the lads that night. Ivor chatted to him and he was friendly. But it was all a bit like the Queen Mother being there. Even the crew were a bit reticent and didn't let themselves go. I think Morrissey was aware of that, loved it, and played up to it. Then he went to bed and everyone got pissed and raved it up."

Set List: 'Shakespeare's Sister'; 'I Want The One I Can't Have'; 'What She Said'; 'Nowhere Fast'; 'What's The World?'; 'The Boy With The Thorn In His Side'; 'That Joke Isn't Funny Anymore'; 'Stretch Out And Wait'; 'Frankly Mr Shankly'; 'Bigmouth Strikes Again'; 'Still Ill'; 'Rusholme Ruffians/(Marie's The Name) His Latest Flame (Medley)'; 'Heaven Knows I'm Miserable Now'; 'Meat Is Murder'; 'This Charming Man'; 'Hand In Glove'; 'Miserable Lie'.

30 SEPTEMBER

The performance at the Capital Theatre, Aberdeen, is solid enough, but Easterhouse are clearly still recovering from the excesses of the previous night. "We were really knackered after the Shetlands," Gary Rostock confesses. Nevertheless, the camaraderie among the crew and musicians remains intact and everyone speaks well of The Smiths. "They were pretty nice to us," Rostock remembers. "I'd played in support bands before and you often get treated like shit, but we got treated quite well. They were all right. You could see that they were making that transition to being a big band, playing in front of a bigger audience. They were moving up a gear, and Morrissey was becoming a better performer. It was a good tour. If I was a fan watching both bands I'd feel I'd got my money's worth."

Set List: 'Shakespeare's Sister'; 'I Want The One I Can't Have'; 'What She Said'; 'What's The World?'; 'Nowhere Fast'; 'The Boy With The Thorn In His Side'; 'That Joke Isn't Funny Anymore'; 'Stretch Out And Wait'; 'Frankly Mr Shankly'; 'Bigmouth Strikes Again'; 'How Soon Is Now?'; 'Still Ill'; 'Rusholme Ruffians/(Marie's The Name) His Latest Flame (Medley)'; 'Heaven Knows I'm Miserable Now'; 'Jeane'; 'Meat Is Murder'; 'This Charming Man'; 'Hand In Glove'; 'William, It Was Really Nothing'; 'Miserable Lie'.

1 OCTOBER

The tour concludes at the Eden Court, Inverness. "It was a beautiful place," Rostock remembers. "The hall was really nice. It wasn't a particularly brilliant gig for The Smiths, but they were good." In order to show their appreciation for The Smiths, the Easterhouse contingent decide to buy them a present. "After deliberating for God knows how long, they ended up buying them a pair of tartan socks," laughs John Barratt. "They were expensive though. Gary made a real point of saying how he thought it was a really good present. I remember going into the dressing room and giving them this present. I think Morrissey was quite touched, actually." Later, Easterhouse are invited to The Smiths' post-gig party back at the hotel. "We had quite a wild time," Rostock remembers. "The hotel management were quite upset with us and The Smiths and the crew. Everyone was pissed up or smoking draw. Grant Showbiz, the sound man, was drinking the worm out of a bottle of mescaline. He did all the rock'n'roll stuff that you were supposed to do. He was well into that. We were wide-eyed boys really doing our first major tour."

With all the inebriation it is perhaps not surprising that there should be some minor misunderstanding among the revellers, which finally spills over when the rival guitarists from the two groups get together. It is generally acknowledged that, throughout the tour, Johnny has been polite, cordial and helpful beyond the call of duty. At the party, he is still in a good mood but when humour turns into mild impertinence, he betrays the indignant air of a man who is not about to suffer fools gladly. "It was all a little adventure and had gone pretty well," Barratt reflects. "They invited us to their drinks party and I was with Ivor and some of the fans. We got into a conversation and were having a beer. Johnny was like, 'I want to be one of the

MORRISSEY with New York Dolls T-Shirt, 1985.

MORRISSEY as scribe for 'Melody Maker'.

lads, but you're not allowed to take the piss or step over the mark'. He said, 'We think you're great and you can support us for as long as you want'. We were going to be their toy support band. He even said we could come to America. It was great. But Ivor was getting steadily pissed and he's the sort of guy that if he felt he was having to toady he'd hate it. There was this feeling that even though Johnny had been great, The Smiths would let us know somewhere along the way that we were the peasants and they were the main live act. They hadn't been like that really or bad in any way at all. But when you're a support band with a chip on your shoulder that's the way you can be. Ivor mentioned the Shetlands and started taking the piss and saying, 'We blew you off the stage'. He wasn't bad, but Johnny was obviously thinking: 'Look at you. We've given you this really big break and you're abusing us'. It was light banter... but it ended a bit sour. It wasn't a big deal, but Johnny took the hump and, I felt, without good reason." Such minor drunken banter was probably forgotten by the participants in the cold light of morning and certainly did not spoil the occasion. "We enjoyed the tour," Perry confirms, laughing off the cheeky conversation with Marr at Inverness. "It didn't cause any problems."

Set List: 'Meat Is Murder'; 'Shakespeare's Sister'; 'I Want The One I Can't Have'; 'What She Said'; 'What's The World?'; 'Nowhere Fast'; 'The Boy With The Thorn In His Side'; 'That Joke Isn't Funny Anymore'; 'Stretch Out And Wait'; 'Heaven Knows I'm Miserable Now'; 'Frankly Mr Shankly'; 'Bigmouth Strikes Again'; 'Asleep'; 'Hand In Glove'; 'This Charming Man'; 'William, It Was Really Nothing'; 'Miserable Lie'.

8 OCTOBER

Top Of The Pops features The Smiths performing 'The Boy With The Thorn In His Side'. The group look more accomplished than ever, with Morrissey perplexing viewers by having the word "BAD" stencilled on his neck. By now, it is public knowledge that the group have agreed to sanction the limited use of videos, albeit with reluctance. "It was record company pressure," Morrissey insists in the face of an apparent *volte face*."The fact that we didn't want to make videos has always irked Rough Trade. They want videos, *Smash Hits* covers and to be heard on daytime radio. These are the things they live for..."

9 OCTOBER

Smash Hits feature Morrissey and Pete Burns on its cover, accompanied by the headline: "The Very Odd Couple". The interview is riddled with camp innuendo, as each artiste pours fawning praise on the other. Morrissey calls Dead Or Alive's 'You Spin Me Round' "a hallmark in British music that will never date". Burns buries his flatterer with gifts of flowers ("Nothing brings him out like a bunch of flowers. Send him a bunch of daffodils and he's anybody's"). Although this mutual appreciation society gains considerable autumnal press, the friendship, like so many of Morrissey's pop star fixations, ultimately proves ephemeral. Morrissey even looks back on the interview with vexation. "It was completely laced with camp symbolism," he complains. "They made us look like a couple of dippy queens."

27 OCTOBER

'The Boy With The Thorn In His Side' is featured on the US show, *The Cutting Edge.*

WINTER

The Smiths enter Jacobs Studios to work on their next album, tentatively called 'Margaret On A Guillotine' in a pointed reference to Morrissey's provocative comments on Margaret Thatcher. However, a song of that title fails to emerge at this time and instead the album will be called *The Queen Is Dead.* Stephen Street recalls the euphoric feeling upon completing the title track. "It came out really great," he stresses. "It was really steady and constant. Then Johnny went in and did this wild wah wah and it was one take. As he was changing the pedal it kept changing tone. He played blindingly on that track. It was fantastic. In fact, we recorded eight to nine minutes worth. I had to edit it down. There was more on the 24-track than there is on the mix but we decided that it was a little bit too long so we cut it down. At the beginning there was the harmonized voice."

"I just traced it back," Marr reflects. "It was Morrissey's idea to include 'Take Me Back To Dear Old Blighty', and he said, 'I want this on the track'. But he wasn't to know that I was going to lead into the feedback and drum rolls. It was just a piece of magic. I got the drum riff going and Andy got the bass line, which was one of his best ever and one that bass players still haven't matched. I went in there with all the lads watching and did the take and they just went, 'Wow!' I came out and I was shaking. When I suggested doing it again, they just said, 'No way! No way!' What happened with the feedback was I was setting my guitar up for the track and I put it onto the stand and it was really loud. Where it hit the stand, it made that note of feedback. I did the guitar track, putting the guitar on the stand, and while we were talking, it was like, 'Wow! That sounded good'. So I said, 'Right, record that!' It was through a wah-wah from the previous take, so I just started moving the wah wah and it was getting all these different intervals, and it definitely added a real tension. I loved Morrissey's singing on that, and the words. But it was very MC5. Morrissey has a real love for that music as well. I remember him playing The Ramones as much as he played Sandie Shaw."

During the recording of the album, group morale is good, although Andy Rourke's on/off drug abuse is becoming more noticeable. "At that time Andy was having his problems with drugs and he was a little remote sometimes," recalls Street. "He was literally doing his bass track, then he would disappear. Most of the time it would be Johnny and myself in the studio. We were building up the arrangements and orchestrations."

Although Marr rises to the challenge of producing the album, he feels the administrative strain that the group has brought on itself through lack of effective management. "It was really tough," he confesses. "I knew we were working on something really good. There was a feeling, both in the songs and in the studio, that we were at an important point in our career... It was so difficult, I knew it was going to be good. It polarized my life at the time. Andy was in the studio in the live room trying to play a bass part and I was coaxing him into doing what I wanted and needed. The phone rang and it was this guy Jay from Rough Trade saying that Salford Van Hire had been on to him and they were going to press charges because one of the roadies had not brought the van back from a previous session and it was scratched. I was dealing with Andy on the other side of the glass and, meanwhile, I was trying to come up with the middle eight for the song that we were working on. I just thought, 'This is really getting too much because I was taking care of that side of the group far too much'." As the year ends, Marr and Morrissey return to their respective homes while the album they have completed remains locked in the vaults awaiting the outcome of their cold war with Rough Trade.

MARR jointly produced the new LP with Stephen Street.

'The Queen is dead. England in ruins, but here, in the marrow of this extraordinary music, something precious and innately honourable flourishes.'

NICK KENT 'MELODY MAKER' JUNE 1986

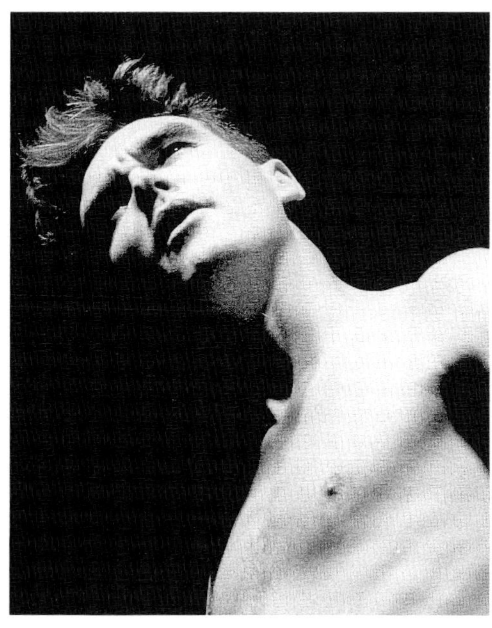

CHAPTER FIVE

The Great Debate

1986 WAS A YEAR OF GREAT transition for The Smiths. Once a promising pop group, they were now threatening to become an international rock band. Music press polls underlined their increasing popularity in the student heartland, but The Smiths seemed determined to extend their following and eagerly embraced the idea of conquering America. Along the way, they fell victim to the problems that plague many successful groups and revealed themselves as terribly human in the process.

Rourke's heroin addiction and dismissal from the group tarnished The Smiths' image, not merely because it contradicted Morrissey's anti-drugs broadcasts, but because it destroyed the treasured myth of friendly unity. It was, perhaps, the first public admission that The Smiths were Morrissey and Marr and not "four young lads against the world". When Morrissey coldly placed a note on Rourke's car window saying, "Andy , you have left The Smiths. Goodbye..." the group's non-democracy was finally exposed. The recruitment of Gannon underlined this point, suggesting that the concept of The Smiths could just as easily be a quintet as a quartet. Many older fans found these sudden changes awkward, and there were more to follow.

ANDY ROURKE was briefly dismissed from The Smiths in 1986.

Looking back, it is fascinating to note the division among The Smiths' following: many fans who perceived the group as the bastion of the indie ethic felt that their heroes were in danger of losing their way. What was actually occurring was a shift in values as old dogmas were no longer deemed workable. Suddenly, The Smiths became more ambitious, careerist and mutable. The concession towards making videos and the defection from Rough Trade to EMI were symptomatic of the group's new realism and caused more ripples among idealistic die-hard indie pop fans. This was a time for growing up.

THE SMITHS on 'The Old Grey Whistle Test' with Craig Gannon on rhythm guitar, 20 May 1986.

While the changes were underway, The Smiths found themselves back in commercial favour. During 1985, their singles sales had dipped alarmingly, but mid-way through 1986, the exuberant 'Panic' revitalized their chart profile and simultaneously increased their audience, whose constituency now embraced students, townies and even hard rock fans. Followers reared on Morrissey's parochial charm and detestation of the rock mainstream were forced to readjust their prejudices and priorities. Suddenly The Smiths had a bigger audience, filled with a less discerning, more brutal membership. Spitting, jostling and riotous behaviour were now more representative of Smiths concerts than gladioli, national health spectacles or touching embraces. Much had changed. The lengthy stadium tour of the USA confirmed that the group were on the brink of becoming international rock stars, should they choose. They returned from the States more rockier than ever, trampling underfoot all the clichés about their supposed feyness and sensitivity.

By this point, the cries of heresy were heard not only from a quorum of disillusioned fans, but a sizeable number of journalists and concert reviewers. Marr bore the brunt of the attack from those critics offended by the group's shift in musical direction. It was a strange paradox. On the one hand, the guitarist was acclaimed for his studio work, while his contributions in concert were frequently derided as clumsy hard rock. Marr was deemed the Keith Richard of 1986 and caricatured as a would-be stadium rocker who might ultimately lead The Smiths the way of lesser mortals like Simple Minds.

Morrissey fared little better than his colleague in the letters columns of the music press. Once seen as some sort of pop deity, he was now deigned to have feet of clay and found himself roundly castigated for his crass comments on black music. A minor debate about the racially divisive lyrics of 'Panic' festered into bitter antagonism following an incisive interview in Melody Maker *in which the singer amplified his antipathy towards disco and reggae in a particularly clumsy and inflammatory manner. The "Is Morrissey A Racist?" debate continued for the remainder of the year, petering out in December when The Smiths appeared at an Anti-Apartheid concert and reminded the world of their liberal credentials.*

It would be an understatement to say confusion reigned in Smithdom during 1986. On one level, we seemed to be witnessing the familiar story of an idealistic group growing up, embracing fame and leaving the provinces to conquer the world. Of course, The Smiths were never as simple as that. Nothing was certain. Morrissey's attitude towards fame remained frustratingly ambivalent, veering from a greedy acceptance of rock godhead to an abrupt retreat to the seclusion of his bedroom. Marr, for all the naïve castigation he received, was never simply rock's latest aspiring guitar star but a more complex figure, uncertain of his direction. Ironically, by the end of the year, he also betrayed symptoms of Morrissey's infectious ambivalence. The excesses of the US tour weakened Marr's resolve, both physically and mentally, while a much publicized car crash provided a grim reminder of his mortality. Add to that the weight of music press derision and the ongoing business hassles and you have the picture of an ambitious musician who, in private, must have been wondering whether it was all worthwhile after all.

For all the problems they faced in 1986, any fears about the Smiths' place in modern popular music should have been made redundant following the release of The Queen Is Dead. *Delayed by several months, the album received universal acclaim at a time when the group seemed in imminent danger of dethronement. Cohesive and challenging, the new work almost rivalled* Meat Is Murder *in terms of consistency and quality, and surpassed it in terms of variety. The arrestingly intense title track set the scene for a rich panorama of sound and colour, embracing the maudlin despair of 'I Know It's Over', the romantic melodrama of 'There Is A Light That Never Goes Out', the playful plagiarism of 'Cemetry Gates', the mock self-aggrandisement of 'Bigmouth Strikes Again', the music hall frivolity of 'Frankly Mr Shankly' and the irreverent* Carry On *humour of 'Some Girls Are Bigger Than Others'. The work was a potent mixture of social commentary, personal neuroses, bawdy comedy and carefully plotted theatricalism. No wonder it was to figure so prominently in all-time great album polls. Those ignoramuses who still regarded Morrissey as the embodiment of misery were forced to concede that he did indeed possess an engaging streak of humour.*

The Smiths ended 1986 with many questions unanswered. Would they increase the pressure and push towards international stardom with a new album and world tour? Their gigging schedule, record sales and eagerly-anticipated tie-in with EMI all suggested that this would be the case. America looked increasingly attractive and those of us not weighed down by misplaced ideals about The Smiths' value system looked forward to more albums and extensive tours. Who among their audience at the Brixton Academy in December could have correctly predicted that they were witnessing the group's final UK concert? What had seemed a new beginning was to prove the beginning of the end.

MORRISSEY at the G-Mex, 19 July 1986.

ALAIN DELON, 'The Queen Is Dead' cover star and tour backdrop, 1986.

4 JANUARY

NME publishes its annual chart points table. It makes salutary reading to see that no Smiths' recording has managed to reach the Top 100 of either the singles or albums sections. In the list of top singles artistes Madonna reigns supreme, while The Smiths languish in 83rd spot. Even at this midpoint in their careers, the group are far removed from the chart mainstream in terms of consistency. Further proof of this trend is highlighted in *Melody Maker*'s listing of the best-selling records in the UK during 1985. While Bruce Springsteen's *Born In The USA* secures pole position, The Smiths' chart-topping *Meat Is Murder* languishes at number 30. Significantly, the group do not even figure in the Top 50 singles section.

18 JANUARY

James Maker, interviewed in *Melody Maker* about the prospects of his new group Raymonde, issues a challenge to an old friend: "I know a certain someone isn't going to like this but I'm entitled to defend the group, just as he would his. I think we're better and far more exciting than The Smiths and what's more we'll prove it in the next year."

31 JANUARY

The Smiths appear at the City Hall, Newcastle-upon-Tyne on the Red Wedge tour. Marr and Rourke had previously played alongside Billy Bragg at earlier dates and the full line-up convenes for a four-song set. Despite his recent political pronouncements, Morrissey shies away from any strong

RAYMONDE: support act.

engagement with the cause. "I didn't really understand what was going on onstage," he observes. "It all seemed a little limp to me, even though there were people involved that I admire." The singer also betrays a jaundiced view of the Labour Party leader. "I can't really see anything especially useful in Neil Kinnock," he yawns. "I don't feel any alliance with him but if one must vote, this is where I feel the black X should go."

Set List: 'Shakespeare's Sister'; 'I Want The One I Can't Have'; 'The Boy With The Thorn In His Side'; 'Bigmouth Strikes Again'.

8 FEBRUARY

The Smiths join New Order and The Fall in a benefit concert for 49 Liverpool councillors, who are being taken to court by the government for refusing to set a legal rate. The show titled "From Manchester With Love" takes place at the Royal Court Theatre, Liverpool. *NME*'s John McCready is on hand with a cutting summation: "The Smiths saved the worst for last. 'Shakespeare's Sister' gives Morrissey the chance to do all the things you've read he does. The worker Smiths keep a perfect beat. Johnny dreams of a little guitar shop in the country while the tall one revolves on one leg, tugs at his clothes, raises an arm in the air, feigns a fall and sings very, very badly. As I had feared, The Smiths lean towards their live predeliction for fast and perishable rock songs with only occasional relief in the dwindling ways they manage to juggle the cliché... All recorded subtleties are trampled underfoot. A foolish waste. And there is an end to it all. The trucks, their drums and wires, the jolly pop groups and their happy, modern sounds will soon be grumbling back up the A580. Thank you Manchester. But, Steven, it was really nothing."

Set List: 'Shakespeare's Sister'; 'I Want The One I Can't Have'; 'Vicar In A Tutu'; 'Frankly Mr Shankly'; 'Rusholme Ruffians'; 'The Boy With The Thorn In His Side'; Cemetry Gates'; 'Nowhere Fast'; 'What She Said'; 'There Is A Light That Never Goes Out'; 'Bigmouth Strikes Again'; 'William, It Was Really Nothing'; Meat Is Murder'; 'Stretch Out And Wait'.

ABOVE & LEFT: Contrasting scenes at Liverpool Royal Court, 8 February 1986.

10 FEBRUARY

The Smiths' short tour of Ireland begins at the National Stadium, Dublin. It is at this point that Rourke's heroin use is threatening his future in the group. "Andy had lost it," notes Grant Showbiz. "Out of 10 notes, he was playing three. He was completely gone and just stopped playing numbers..." Rourke concedes that this was the case, but recalls other factors which made him sound even worse. "It was partly my fault," he reflects. "I used to be in quite a state before I went onstage because of the tablets I was taking. But, also, the guitar roadie I had didn't always know what he was doing. I had two basses, one tuned to E and one tuned to F-sharp for different songs, and we had to swap them about. On a couple of occasions he handed me the wrong bass. We'd go into a song and I'd be playing in a totally different key to everybody else and it sounded absolutely ridiculous. I then had to stop, put another bass on and start again. I used to get the blame for that... but I was in a state, looking back."

Amid the drama, Grant Showbiz recalls Peter Morrissey making one of his rare appearances backstage, having been on holiday in Dublin at the time of the tour. "Morrissey's father turned up and we tried to avoid him the whole time we were there," Grant smiles. "He was a nice guy and very chuffed that it was happening for the group."

Set List: 'Shakespeare's Sister'; 'I Want The One I Can't Have'; 'Vicar In A Tutu'; 'Rusholme Ruffians/(Marie's The Name) His Latest Flame (Medley)'; 'Cemetry Gates'; 'Still Ill'; 'Stretch Out And Wait'; 'That Joke Isn't Funny Anymore'; 'Nowhere Fast'; 'What She Said'; 'The Boy With The Thorn In His Side'; 'There Is A Light That Never Goes Out'; 'Bigmouth Strikes Again'; 'Meat Is Murder'; 'William, It Was Really Nothing'; 'Heaven Knows I'm Miserable Now'; 'Miserable Lie'.

11 FEBRUARY

Rourke's performance improves at the next gig in the Fairways Hotel, Dundalk. Nevertheless, it is still a difficult time. One of the ironies, to which both Rourke and Marr testify, is that the bassist's condition worsens when trying to stay off heroin. "He just wasn't in a state to play," Johnny notes, matter of factly. "It was more so when he was trying to come off heroin, and that's what happened on that Irish tour. He finally took too much methadone and wasn't fun to be around."

Set List: 'Shakespeare's Sister'; 'I Want The One I Can't Have'; 'Vicar In A Tutu'; 'Rusholme Ruffians/(Marie's The Name) His Latest Flame (Medley)'; 'Cemetry Gates'; 'Still Ill'; 'Stretch Out And Wait'; 'That Joke Isn't Funny Anymore'; 'Nowhere Fast'; 'What She Said'; 'The Boy With The Thorn In His Side'; 'Bigmouth Strikes Again'; 'Hand In Glove'.

RIGHT: The Smiths in early 1986.

12 FEBRUARY

The group travels to Northern Ireland for an appearance at the Whitla Hall, Queen's University, Belfast. Despite gradual improvement, Rourke remains distant from the others, including his pal Mike Joyce. "It reached the point where it got a bit sour," the drummer notes. "I spoke to Andy on a few occasions about it but he took a weird attitude. I felt as though he was saying, 'You don't understand'. Now, I didn't understand, because I've never been in that situation myself. It's easy to say, 'You shouldn't be doing this, Andy, because it's wrong, and not only is it wrong, but it's bad for you, and not only is it bad for you, but it's costing you a lot of money, and you're messing up your relationship with the group, and your playing'... but once you're ensnared in the spider's web, it's difficult... I thought it was best left to Johnny because he went back a lot further. I felt the only person that could change Andy was Johnny... I was involved in discussions in the same way that if I fell by the wayside Andy would be involved. It was getting a bit embarrassing. What you do in your personal life is what you do in your personal life as long as it doesn't affect the rest of the band... Around the time of the Irish tour, however, Andy was well out of it. It not only affected the playing but when we were together. It was a bit difficult to get through to him."

Set List: 'Shakespeare's Sister'; 'I Want The One I Can't Have'; 'Vicar In A Tutu'; 'Rusholme Ruffians/(Marie's The Name) His Latest Flame (Medley)'; 'Cemetry Gates'; 'Still Ill'; 'Stretch Out And Wait'; 'That Joke Isn't Funny Anymore'; 'Nowhere Fast'; 'What She Said'; 'The Boy With The Thorn In His Side'; 'There Is A Light That Never Goes Out'; 'Bigmouth Strikes Again'; 'Meat Is Murder'; 'William, It Was Really Nothing'; 'Heaven Knows I'm Miserable Now'; 'Hand In Glove'.

FEBRUARY

In the wake of the Irish tour, Rourke is fired from The Smiths. Always wary of personal confrontations, Morrissey simply leaves a note on the bassist's car window informing him that his Smiths' days have ended. Distraught, Rourke subsequently contacts Marr who confides that there may be a way back if Morrissey can be convinced that he can stay straight. In the meantime, a new Smiths bassist is recruited in the form of guitarist Craig Gannon, a former member of Aztec Camera, The Colourfield, and The Bluebells. Having been recommended by Simon Wolstencroft, Gannon is driven to Marr's house for a social evening and jamming session.

"He played me the new single 'Bigmouth Strikes Again' and also the B-side 'Money Changes Everything'," Gannon remembers. "We went downstairs and I was then introduced to Mike Joyce. We had something to eat and drink, then me and Johnny started playing guitar together. He showed me the song 'Some Girls Are Bigger Than Others'. We then played a couple of Stones songs. Johnny then told me about Andy's drug problem and that it was getting out of hand. He said, 'If you want to play bass in The Smiths the job is yours now, but I know you're a guitar player, so we could find another bass player and you could play guitar'." Although Gannon has not played bass professionally, Marr feels that he will function as an excellent utility player in The Smiths. After several weeks' rehearsal at Marr's house in Hale, Johnny expresses his confidence in the 19-year old whizz kid. It is anticipated that, should Rourke successfully return, Gannon can be retained as second

guitarist, thereby allowing Marr a greater freedom in live performance.

In the weeks that follow further drama occurs when Rourke is arrested for possession of heroin, then reinstated as bassist. As Morrissey drily observes: "His leaving seemed more wrong than his staying." Elaborating on that point, he explains, "When he left he became even more depressed than when he was with the group... It was getting quite serious. So he really had to come back. And on coming back it really has been his salvation, and it's worked so well, strangely, for the other group members... It seemed very unnatural and ridiculous to even consider such things as session musicians and people from other parts of the country."

Nevertheless, the decision to recruit Gannon is ratified at a meeting between Marr and Morrissey in London. "At this point, I still didn't know the situation with Andy," Gannon remembers, "but I got the feeling that they were having second thoughts about sacking him. After a while, Morrissey and Johnny went into another room for a private chat which was obviously about me. James Maker from Raymonde was also at Morrissey's flat. When they finished talking it was time to go. Everyone said 'Goodbye' and got in the car. Johnny turned around to me and said, 'Well that's it then. Morrissey likes you. We like you. That's it – you're in The Smiths playing guitar'."

> **'Andy wasn't in a state to play. It was when he was trying to come off heroin. He finally took too much methadone and wasn't fun to be around.'**
>
> JOHNNY MARR

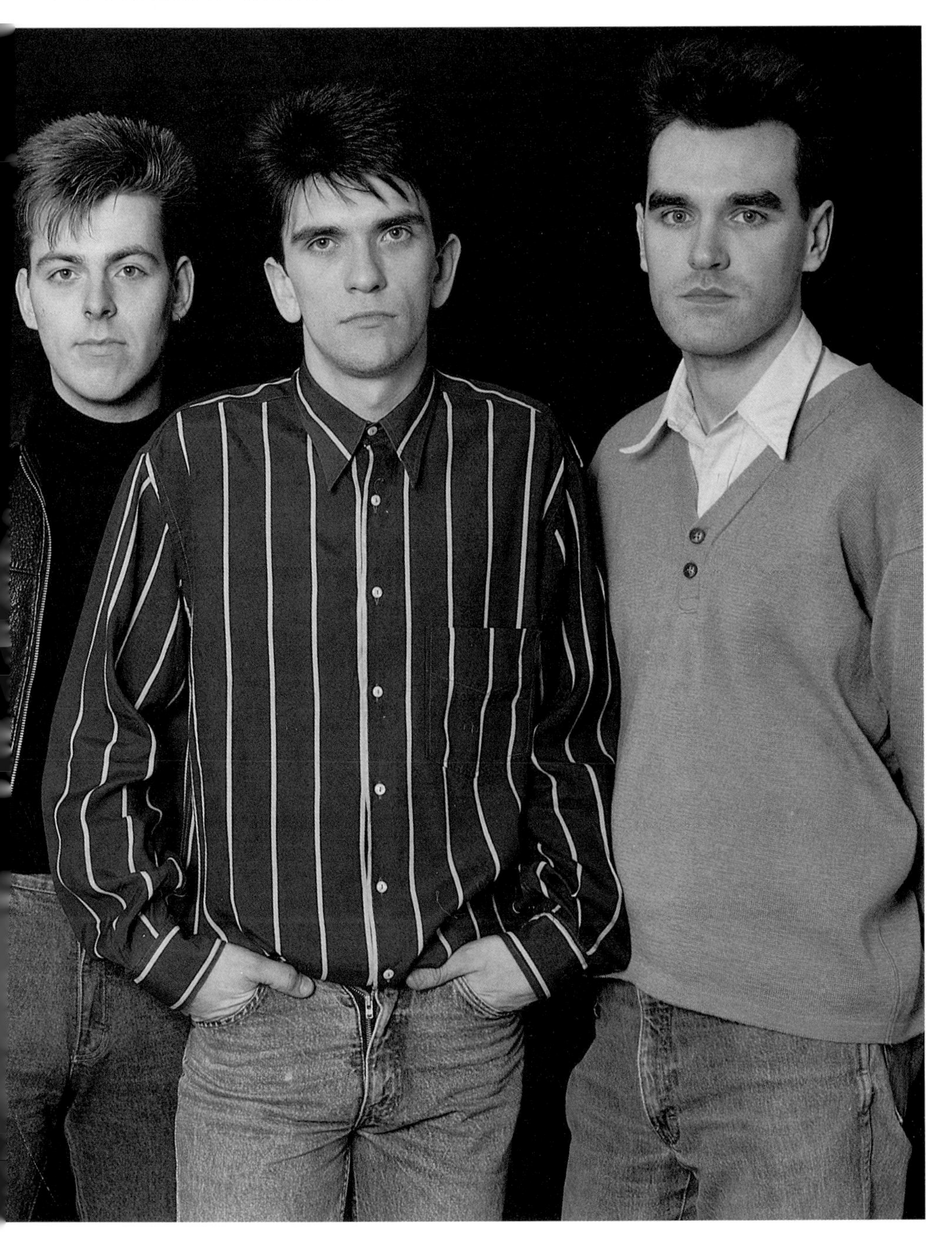

WHILE THE ROURKE DRAMA IS UNFOLDING, Marr conducts a short interview with *Record Mirror*'s Eleanor Levy. However, the speed of events leaves the interviewer with many questions unanswered and the continued delay in the release of the new album ensures that the piece is left half-finished. "Johnny seemed subdued and tired, " Levy recalls, "and as the release date for the records slipped backwards and changes in the line-up occurred, that interview got less and less relevant." Eventually, Levy decides to wait until the Rough Trade dispute is resolved before requesting another interview with the troubled guitarist.

MARCH

Matthew Sztumph is reinstated as Smiths' manager as Morrissey and Marr begin negotiations with Rough Trade over their contract. Geoff Travis holds firm to the conditions of the original contract but agrees to reduce the group's remaining commitments from two albums to one (excluding compilations and live recordings). Sztumph subsequently accompanies Morrissey and Marr to New York for a similarly successful meeting with Sire's Seymour Stein. The songwriting duo briefly consider relocating to America to record their next album, but after looking at several apartments, the notion is abandoned.

Meanwhile, the financial arrangements with new recruit Gannon remain vague and unrecorded in any written agreement. "I was told that there would be wages as soon as their PAYE system was sorted out," he explains. "I was handed a cheque for £500 by Johnny which was signed by him and Morrissey. I received nothing in writing from them at all. Obviously, having just joined the band I hadn't really earned any money from them and I wasn't about to ask any further questions regarding money. I thought, 'Well, it will all be sorted out eventually'. Also, money was not in the forefront of my mind at that moment. I wanted to fit in with the band and play the best I could."

1 MARCH

Morrissey fills in his poll form for the *NME*. His answers make interesting reading:

MORRISSEY'S 1985 'NME' POLL
Best Group: June Brides.
Best Male Singer: George Formby.
Female Singer: Linder.
New Act: Barry McGuigan.
Single: 'All Day Long' (Shop Assistants).
LP: *This Nation's Saving Grace* (Fall).
Best Dressed Sleeve: *Unkiss The Kiss* (Stephen "Rust Rust" Duffy).
Creep Of The Year: Paula Yates.
Most Wonderful Human Being: Victoria Wood.
TV Show: Cagney And Lacey.
Best Dressed: "It's All In The Mind!"
Worst Dressed: "Jim Kerr by a furlong."

ROURKE, Gannon and Morrissey on 'The Old Grey Whistle Test'.

8 MARCH
NME 's poll results confirm The Smiths as best group, ahead of The Jesus And Mary Chain. *Meat Is Murder* is voted best LP, edging out the JMC's *Psychocandy* and New Order's *Low Life*, respectively. The Reid brothers gain some revenge with a victory in the best singles section, where 'Never Understand' pips 'How Soon Is Now?' Perhaps the most surprising result, however, is in the Live Group category. Despite some great performances on their current tour, and at the very time concert goers are filling in their poll forms, The Smiths still lag behind The Pogues and U2. Moreover, those regarding The Smiths' artwork as exceptional are also in the minority if the "best dressed sleeve" category is to be given credence. *Meat Is Murder* finishes a disappointing fifth, beaten by the big four: *Rum Sodomy And The Lash* (Pogues), *Low Life* (New Order), *Little Creatures* (Talking Heads) and *Our Favourite Shop* (Style Council). The Morrissey/Weller rivalry dominates the remainder of the poll, with the Mancunian marginally showing the upper hand. Morrissey/Marr are voted best songwriters ahead of the former Jam vocalist, who also finishes second to Morrissey in the best dressed and best haircut categories.

While Morrissey also wins best male singer (beating Bono), the gratifying title of "Most Wonderful Human Being" is reserved for Bob Geldof. The Live Aid organizer is also voted "Biggest Mouth", a category in which the oft-quoted Morrissey finishes a surprising fifth, well below Derek Hatton, Mark E Smith and Jeffrey Archer. All things considered , the 1986 readers' poll proves the best performance yet by The Smiths and suggests that despite recent chart positions all may yet be well.

22 MARCH
Melody Maker offer some information about the forthcoming Smiths' album in their gossip column "Talk Talk". Apart from the humorous mistitle 'Vicar In A Ton Ton', their sources prove surprisingly accurate, with a full and correct track listing. They also reveal an ongoing drama about the choice of the next Smiths' single. "There has been a great debate over whether the single should be Morrissey's autobiographical 'Frankly Mr Shankly' or Marr's choice,'Bigmouth Strikes Again' (lots of wild guitar with Mazz warbling on about Joan Of Arc). Finally, they've decided on 'There's A Light'... Travis insists 'There's A Light' will provide the elusive crossover."

12 APRIL
According to *Melody Maker*, The Smiths are to headline a four-day festival in Portsmouth from 23-26 May at Southsea Castlefield. The booking is never confirmed.

26 APRIL
Morrissey and Marr tune in to Radio 1's lunch-time slot and are shocked to hear an

CRAIG GANNON: The fifth Smith.

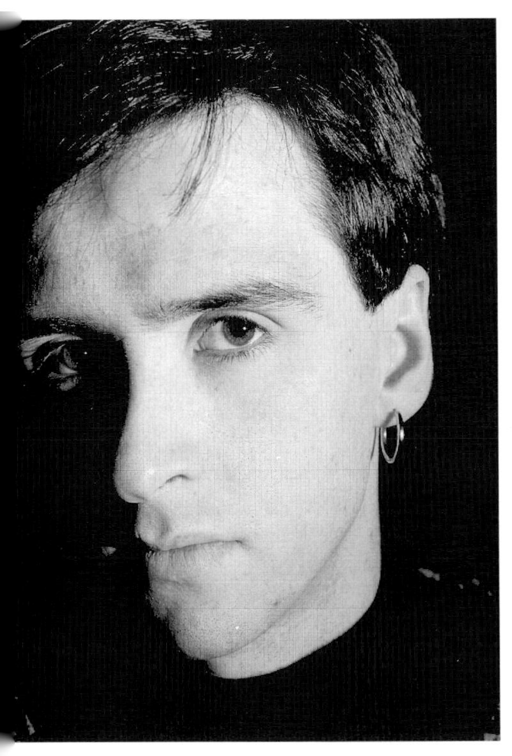

MARR: Voted 'premier instrumentalist'.

account of the Chernobyl disaster, followed by a playing of Wham's upbeat and vacuous 'I'm Your Man'. Immediately, they begin work on a protest song castigating the quality of daytime radio programming, from which Morrissey insists they have been deliberately excluded. The song will later emerge as 'Panic'.

Bigmouth Strikes Again

2 MAY

Mick Middles, then in litigious combat with Morrissey over an article in the Manchester magazine *Muze*, receives a missive from the singer addressed to "The Fried Egg Of Rock 'n' Roll". Inside is the enigmatic message: "Halebarns 6, Hyde 0".

3 MAY

The Smiths find themselves in the bridesmaid's slot in *Melody Maker*'s Readers' Poll, finishing second to U2 as best band and best live act. *Meat Is Murder* continues the trend, pipped by The Cure's *Head On The Door*. Indications that The Smiths' singles status is slipping is confirmed by the appearance of 'The Boy With The Thorn In His Side' at a disappointing sixth, beaten by 'She Sells Sanctuary' (Cult), 'Bring On The Dancing Horses' (Echo And The Bunnymen), 'Between The Wars EP' (Billy Bragg), 'Inbetween Days' (Cure) and 'Running Up That Hill' (Kate Bush). Morrissey's sole victory as best dressed pop star (implausibly above David Bowie) is tainted somewhat by fourth position in the worst dressed category. The coveted male singer award goes to Bono, while the scruffily attired Bob Geldof walks away with the Chap Of The Year accolade, with Morrissey second in both categories. Despite the imminent release of 'Bigmouth Strikes Again', both Geldof and Mark E Smith are elected bigger Lips Of The Year. Even in terms of sheer eccentricity, Morrissey is considered engagingly normal when placed sixth "Fruitcake", beneath Prince, Margaret Thatcher, Ronald Reagan, Kevin Rowland and Robert Smith. The most gratifying result in the poll, however, is Johnny Marr's emergence as premier instrumentalist, above Mark Knopfler. Even that triumph is brought earthwards later that week when Marr bumps into Rob Allman and his wife in Manchester. "I think they should have had a recount," Allman suggests, in disbelief at his old colleague's placing above the accomplished Knopfler. "Nah, I'm better than him!" Marr retorts unamused. "He's too old!"

16 MAY

The long-awaited new Smiths' single 'Bigmouth Strikes Again' is issued. Marr describes the song as his 'Jumpin' Jack Flash' and it certainly sounds one of the most convincing and strident singles they have ever recorded. Despite this, and the dramatically long gap since 'The Boy With The Thorn In His Side', the track only reaches number 26 in the UK charts. The relative chart failure of the song comes as a considerable shock, clearly indicating a lull in The Smiths' popularity and testifying to their greater acceptance as albums artistes. Morrissey, at least, considers the poor sales of the single as indicative of the public's false image of the group. "I often wonder if we shouldn't explain ourselves more," he notes, "especially as an astonishing number of people completely misunderstand The Smiths' humour. Take 'Bigmouth'. I would call it a parody if that sounded less like self-celebration, which it definitely wasn't. It was just a funny little song." Part of the humour of the song lay in the accompanying esoteric word play. The reference to the additional vocalist "Ann Coates", for example, was a play on the Manchester district, Ancoats. The mystery second vocalist was, in fact, Morrissey himself, recorded at a faster speed. His warbling references to "Joan Of Arc" also inspired Rough Trade publicist and occasional photographer Pat Bellis to adopt the punning pseudonym Jo Novark. Marr may also have felt a touch of sardonic humour in titling the instrumental flip side 'Money Changes Everything'. At a time when the group were heavily involved with solicitors, renegotiations, internal disarray and sorting out outstanding debts, it seemed an apt comment on the times. Marr would have smiled to have been reminded of a Morrissey comment from earlier in The Smiths' career: "Money doesn't change anything".

20 MAY

The new five-piece Smiths make their début on the *Whistle Test* performing the newly released 'Bigmouth Strikes Again' and 'Vicar In A Tutu'.

24 MAY

Sounds proclaim 'Bigmouth Strikes Again' "single of the week". However, the accolade is undermined by some sniping at Johnny Marr who is increasingly being portrayed as a devil with a guitar. "Popular critical opinion would have it that Morrissey has lost all his endearing young charm and that only Johnny 'Brian' Marr still cuts it in this camp," reviewer Roger Holland notes. "And, as usual, popular critical opinion can't tell its arse from its elbow. Morrissey's vocal whimsies are as enhancing as ever, they paint a loving smile wide across these customarily sneering lips... Meanwhile, Johnny Marr should never have been allowed to believe his own hype. For I am getting well fed-up of B-sides chocker with plodding instrumental dross when I could be marvelling at Morrissey. Popular critical opinion, in its preening self-righteousness, has convinced both itself and Johnny Marr that he is today's precious guitar guru. But in truth it is his lauded guitar patterns which are increasingly restricted and blinkered. And if there is any threat at all to the future well-being of my favourite Mancunian act, then it lies in his inability to deal with his position in the frame of things. Someone will have to take young 'Brian' in hand."

7 JUNE

'NME', 7 June 1986

The most enlightening Morrissey interview in aeons appears in *NME* courtesy of Ian Pye. Under the title "Some Mothers Do 'Ave 'Em", the interviewer relates how he was invited to Morrissey's Chelsea home and discovered the singer dancing maniacally in a room, clad in a ballerina's tutu. The Morrissey abode contains the same old books and icons described in previous interviews. When Pye, not unreasonably, suggests a few worthwhile authors not featured on Steven's bookshelf, he is greeted with indignation. Despite the singer's much touted absorption in literature and film, it is clear that, as with his general education, there are massive gaps. Pye passes on the subject of Morrissey's philistinism, but offers some convincing asides on the state of his psyche. "What Morrissey does appear to suffer from is a state of permanent adolescence," Pye remarks with assurance. "The lyrics of the new LP, littered as they are with notions of leaving home put you in no doubt as to who Morrissey's real hero or heroine is... his mother". The singer more or less concedes the point in observing: "Mentally, I don't believe I've ever left home".

Warming to his inquisitor, Morrissey spews forth on a range of topics and directs his bile against such easy targets as Madonna, Prince, Bob Geldof, Band Aid, Red Wedge and Mick Middles. The singer also provides what amounts to a track-by-track commentary on *The Queen Is Dead* unequalled in any other publication. On a more serious note, we learn that over the previous two years, six people who were "alarmingly dedicated to The Smiths" have committed suicide. Morrissey discusses the issue sympathetically, yet strangely matter of factly. "Their friends and parents wrote to me after they'd died," he notes, "it's something that shouldn't really be as hard to speak about as it is because if people are basically unhappy and people basically want to die then they will." The illuminating interview ends on a contrastingly comic note with Morrissey reviewing his genitalia, which are described as "a cruel practical joke".

12 JUNE

A brief interview with Morrissey in *City Limits* serves as promotion for the new album. A discussion of the Moors Murders prompts the singer to spout reactionary sentiments worthy of a tabloid leader writer. "I think she should have hung" he says of the still imprisoned Myra Hindley. Retributive violence remains a key characteristic of the supposedly pacifist vegetarian.

14 JUNE

A bumper bundle package of Smiths' interviews/reviews hits the news stands. *Sounds* print a short but inconsequential interview with Morrissey in which he is given leave to reflect indulgently on various neuroses ("I'm thin, but I stoop. I stoop... I hate most people. And I don't want to. It's an awful way to be. But the human race gives me no comfort"). The rival *Record Mirror* provides a far more insightful piece courtesy of Eleanor Levy, who concludes her interview with Johnny Marr, having abandoned a first draft four months earlier. In contrast to the mournful creature she met at the height of the group's problems, Marr now seems completely revitalized, energetic and boyishly enthusiastic. Relocated to London, where he is working on 'The Draize Train', the guitarist appears merry but philosophic. "We've come through a lot," he notes wistfully, "but everything's really good now, really positive. It's all happiness in Smithstown — for once." The qualification emphasizes the problems that the group have encountered over recent months when the stalemate over the release of *The Queen Is Dead* seriously troubled Marr . His new-found exuberance is reflected in his consumption of potent Red Stripe lager. "My love of booze has come back as well, which is great," he notes. "It went after we started doing tours, because you'd be on stage every night for five weeks going 'glug glug glug' and your adrenaline keeps you going, but when you get off stage, you're really pissed, so I stopped." The guitarist comments briefly on Rourke's departure, Gannon's recruitment, the new album, and ends the interview with some jokes about his credentials as a sex symbol.

The interviews are complemented by a spree of album reviews as the music press pays tribute to *The Queen Is Dead*. *Sounds'* Roger Holland proffers five stars and clawing the wall for suitable adjectives, concludes: "*The Queen Is Dead* flows over with charm. With self-pity. With mother love, with endless introspection. With poetry, with favouritism, and with despair at the fools who cannot see that to base a song around a line from a film is a tribute not a cheat. 'The Boy With The Thorn In His Side' was the most pleasantly relaxed and beautifully soul searching pop single of its time. Six of the other songs here match up to that marvellous moment. This makes *The Queen Is Dead* the album of the *month*. A year is a long time in pop music."

The *NME* proves more analytical and devotes an entire page to the album, a clear indication of how seriously The Smiths are now taken. Although contemptuous of recent Smiths offerings, reviewer Adrian Thrills soberly concludes: "*The Queen Is Dead* is an excellent record, let down only by one spot of neo-psychedelic posturing and a couple of mediocre singles. Sure, the age-old concerns are well to the fore, but they have never been so powerfully or eloquently expressed... The band's loyal legions will love *The Queen Is Dead,* but even the doubters should find something in the uncanny catchiness of seven of these ten tracks – a good ratio by anyone's standards these days. Maybe the next LP should be the quantum shift in musical emphasis that some expected from this set. But, for now, Britain's best band are sticking very agreeably to what they do best, simply being The Smiths."

The trilogy of music press reviews is completed by *Melody Maker* which offers the definitive statement from *NME's* former star journalist Nick Kent. He has no carping doubts about the quality of the recording and characteristically scents a classic. His opening paragraph serves as a convincing call to arms: "This is neither the time nor the place to indulge in trivial banter; suffice to say that The Smiths' peculiar career manoeuvres, which have caused their audience much exasperation of late, are rendered utterly obsolete by the splendour of *The Queen Is Dead,* the album which history will in due course denote as being the key work in forcing the group's philistine opposition to down chisels and embrace the concept of The Smiths as the one truly vital voice of the Eighties." Kent concludes on a similarly high note, exclaiming: "There's so much that I could write about this record, about The Smiths and why I still fervently believe they stand head and shoulders above the rest. Unfortunately, this context is way too limiting to properly express said feelings. Suffice to say, this group is the one crucial hope left in evoking a radical restructuring of what pop could – nay, should – essentially be moving towards. *The Queen Is Dead* will help bury the one-dimensional misery-guts attitude so beloved of the group's denigrators, while further displaying to all and sundry the simple fact that this is essentially music brimming with valorous intent. The Queen is dead. England in ruins, but here, in the marrow of this extraordinary music, something precious and innately honourable flourishes. The thrill is here, right enough."

16 JUNE

After reading in the *Manchester Evening News* that he should be given an Oscar, Morrissey duly puts pen to paper and despatches another sarcastic message to Mick Middles. Addressed to The Irish Wheelchair League, the letter complains, "Yes, but who actually wins the Oscar? Don't tell me, let me guess... Meryl Streep."

21 JUNE

Rough Trade officially confirm that auxiliary Smith Craig Gannon is now a full-time member of the group.

28 JUNE

A brief Morrissey feature appears in the pop

'The Queen Is Dead'

DEATH had a morbid fascination for Morrissey, symbolized in 1986 on the new LP's 'Cemetry Gates'.

MARR: Another image change.

magazine, *No.1.* Here we learn that Marr will be working with both Keith Richard and Bryan Ferry, the very artistes he slagged off in *Melody Maker* the previous year. Not surprisingly, Morrissey speaks euphemistically about Andy's "personal problem", describing the bassist as "ill" but making no reference to drugs. When speaking of his own neuroses, the singer is considerably more forthcoming. "I'm still embedded in a fascination for suicide and intensified depression," he exclaims in a moment of near self-parody. "I feel a great deal inside me that must be tapped. I have to sing about what is ensnared in me."

5 JULY

The Smiths line up alongside The Eurythmics, The Pet Shop Boys, Simply Red and Simple Minds on a special edition of *The Tube.* Two Morrissey/Marr compositions are featured: 'There Is A Light That Never Goes Out' and 'Panic'.

16 JULY

The UK tour commences at the Barrowlands, Glasgow, scene of The Smiths' triumphant show in October 1985. Support group The Stockholm Monsters deserve a passing mention, for they were a contributory factor in Factory Records' failure to sign The Smiths. Tony Wilson recalls seeing The Smiths, recognizing their talent, but feeling handcuffed by his label's low commercial aspirations. "I had a group called Stockholm Monsters who put out a record or two," he reminisces. "I believed deeply in Stockholm Monsters, and still do to this day. I think they could and should have been a great group... So, I was thinking, 'Hey another great Manchester group but, wait a minute, something's wrong with Factory'. It was only years later that I realized we'd become a dinosaur. All I knew was that I was depressed that I couldn't sell any Stockholm Monsters' records, so why take on Steven and his group if I can't take on any of my records... I just felt, 'No point. I can't do anything for these people. I can't sell Stockholm Monsters'. So I was down. That's my story."

Set List: 'Bigmouth Strikes Again'; 'Panic'; 'Vicar In A Tutu'; 'Frankly Mr Shankly'; 'There Is A Light That Never Goes Out'; 'Ask'; 'I Want The One I Can't Have'; 'Never Had No One Ever'; 'Cemetry Gates'; 'The Boy With The Thorn In His Side'; 'Is It Really So Strange?'; 'Shakespeare's Sister'; 'What She Said'; 'That Joke Isn't Funny Anymore'; 'The Queen Is Dead'; 'I Know It's Over'; 'Rusholme Ruffians/(Marie's The Name) His Latest Flame (Medley)'; 'William, It Was Really Nothing'.

17 JULY

The Smiths' provoke mixed reactions at the Mayfair, Newcastle-upon-Tyne, a venue known to attract a large proportion of heavy metal followers. A local fan recalls the crude way in which Morrissey was egged off the stage: "The trouble was started by a group of *Sun* readers gobbing at him. During 'Hand In Glove' one of them hit home, right in his eye. He stopped mid-sentence, stood and looked at the crowd expressionless and then walked off. The band continued not knowing what to do until Marr pulled them up, gently leant forward and through that mop of his blurted out, 'And if the people spit, the people spit!', and off they went after their leader."

'I'm still embedded in a fascination for suicide and intensified depression. I feel a great deal inside me that must be tapped.'

MORRISSEY

ALTHOUGH ONE MIGHT HAVE ANTICIPATED SOME sympathy for the group in the wake of the Newcastle débâcle, further criticism is looming. Already, many dyed-in-the-wool fans are complaining about the group's new, heavier sound which, they argue, makes The Smiths appear like a crude rock group. One disgruntled customer makes his disillusionment felt with a stinging missive which the music press pick up on. He complains: "After 45 minutes onstage the band walked off in the middle of 'Hand In Glove' and refused to come back due to some dickheads down the front gobbing on them. Sounds fair enough? Don't you bloody believe it. The Smiths' attitude all night sucked – the fact that they were charging £6 (or £6.30 on the door) to get into the Mayfair was a disgrace to begin with, but their whole outlook seemed to be geared towards getting off as quickly as possible. Not only that, but they now look like the new Rolling Stones and sound like Led Zeppelin. Johnny is actively pushing his rock star image as far as he can – it was bloody horrendous to see him pandering to the 'Johnny clones' in the audience and 'rock, rock rockin' his axe'. If I want to see The Rolling Stones I'll go and pay £20 to see the Stones, not £6 to see a second rate impersonation."

Set List: 'Bigmouth Strikes Again'; 'Panic'; 'Vicar In A Tutu'; 'Frankly Mr Shankly'; 'There Is A Light That Never Goes Out'; 'Ask'; 'I Want The One I Can't Have'; 'Never Had No One Ever'; 'Cemetry Gates'; 'The Boy With The Thorn In His Side'; 'Is It Really So Strange?'; 'Shakespeare's Sister'; 'Stretch Out And Wait'; 'That Joke Isn't Funny Anymore'; 'The Queen Is Dead'; 'I Know It's Over'; 'Rusholme Ruffians/(Marie's The Name) His Latest Flame (Medley)'; 'Hand In Glove'.

19 JULY

The Smiths are second on the bill, beneath New Order, at Manchester's G-Mex "Festival Of The Tenth Summer". Among the luminaries celebrating Manchester's contribution to pop are The Fall, John Cooper Clarke, The Worst, The Virgin Prunes, Wayne Fontana And The Mindbenders, OMD, Sandie Shaw, Pete Shelley, Howard Devoto and John Cale. Ever on the case, *NME* captures the moment with a succinct appraisal of The Smiths' contribution: "This was sublime pop, veering between swirling frivolity and a deeper sense of loss... Their peak was finally reached during the closing 'The Queen Is Dead', with Morrissey alternating between removing his shirt and brandishing a banner emblazoned with the song title before leaving the stage as Johnny Marr entered the realms of psychedelia. And then they were back with a mournful 'I Know It's Over' and their still brilliant 'Hand In Glove' jewel, which sounded as stunning as ever."

Sounds' James Brown was equally enthusiastic: "Morrissey, that creamy clot of sexuality in an eggshell-white cardigan with a chest to match, twists his tongue and bod into every different song, subtly easing his way into the kitchens of Albion, Steven has amassed the love of the nation and then ripped it into sharp confetti-sized pieces. His politics are personal and punchy, but politics all the same... 'Meat Is Murder', 'The Queen Is Dead'... As he waved that sign, as he sang those lines, as Marr played those chords, into the open ears and hearts of a Ray-Ban-ed audience, as the whole of G-Mex rang with 'The Queen Is Dead', they were preparing a coffin at Windsor Castle. Such is the power of pop, that image of Morrissey with his banner and his band won't leave me."

Despite the favourable reception, Morrissey felt strangely out of place among the cream of Manchester's rock élite. He later explained his misgivings to the local listings magazine *City Life*. "I hoped that the atmosphere backstage wouldn't be as I imagined, which was the typical Manchester iciness," he lamented. "Nobody really speaks to each other and when they do it's on a really superficial digging nature. I found it very abstract. I think it was probably a little too much for the people backstage to deal with. It just seemed so unreal... I'm not really sure whether it happened. I didn't really feel any sense of unity or celebration. Certainly not backstage. Maybe it's just me, I don't know, maybe it's just the way people behaved towards me... Nobody put their arms around me and said, 'Isn't this wonderful?'"

Johnny Marr recalls one reason why those backstage might have been a little reluctant to embrace The Smiths prior to their appearance onstage: copious vomiting. "It's quite funny," Marr remembers. "Derek Jarman came backstage to meet us before we went on at G-Mex. He walked in the dressing room and I was in the corner heaving away. He'd been introduced to the band, 'This is Morrissey', and you could see him looking over to the corner and thinking, 'Is anybody going to help that person?'... 'This is Andy and Mike, and Johnny's over there'. He said, 'Is he OK?' and they said, 'Oh yeah, he does this all the time'. I was like 'Arrrgh!' I didn't eat very much. I was quite a worrier at the time..."

Set List: 'Bigmouth Strikes Again'; 'Panic'; 'Vicar In A Tutu'; 'Frankly Mr Shankly'; 'There Is A Light That Never Goes Out'; 'Ask'; 'I Want The One I Can't Have'; 'Cemetry Gates'; 'The Boy With The Thorn In His Side'; 'Is It Really So Strange?'; 'Shakespeare's Sister'; 'Stretch Out And Wait'; 'That Joke Isn't Funny Anymore'; 'The Queen Is Dead'; 'I Know It's Over'; 'Rusholme Ruffians/(Marie's The Name) His Latest Flame (Medley)'; 'Hand In Glove'.

20 JULY

The group remain in their hometown for an appearance at the University of Salford. Easterhouse's drummer Gary Rostock turns up hoping to see a classic and is not disappointed. "The only time I ever saw The Smiths play better than they did at Barrowlands in 1985 was at Salford University," he reminisces. "The PA stack nearly came off the stage and they had to do structural repairs after the gig downstairs.

THE SMITHS, with Craig Gannon in residence, on 'The Tube' with (ABOVE) tuneful schoolboy on guest vocals.

Craig got me in!" After the gig, the Maher family meet Craig's parents and John Maher Snr expresses Johnny's great enthusiasm for Gannon's playing ability.

Set List: 'Panic'; 'Shakespeare's Sister'; 'Frankly Mr Shankly'; 'Vicar In A Tutu'; 'Ask'; 'I Want The One I Can't Have'; 'Cemetry Gates'; 'Never Had No One Ever'; 'Is It Really So Strange?'; 'The Boy With The Thorn In His Side'; 'There Is A Light That Never Goes Out'; 'That Joke Isn't Funny Anymore'; 'What She Said/Rubber Ring (Medley)'; 'The Queen Is Dead'; 'Money Changes Everything'; 'I Know It's Over'; 'Bigmouth Strikes Again'; 'Rusholme Ruffians/(Marie's The Name) His Latest Flame (Medley)'; 'Hand In Glove'.

21 JULY

With their US tour imminent, The Smiths issue their second single of the year, 'Panic'. With a riff based on T Rex's 'Metal Guru', the track proves teasingly infectious, while the controversial lyric "burn down the disco/ Hang the blessed DJ" represents a double-pronged attack on inane dance music and bland radio pop. *Melody Maker* congratulates

MORRISSEY at the G-Mex Festival Of The Tenth Summer.

the boys on a return to form, seemingly forgetting the excellent 'Bigmouth Strikes Again' in their enthusiasm: "Just when you thought it was safe to write off The Smiths as the ultimate albums band, here comes 'Panic' to re-establish Morrissey and Marr as undisputed champions of pop's most vital art form... The very thought of Morrissey ever getting involved in anything more dangerous than a nosebleed is funny enough, but when he brings the young lad in at the end for the "hang the deejay" chant, it's impossible not to join in and echo the sentiments of anyone who has ever once attended a youth club disco." It will not be long, however, before the debate over the single's lyrical content spreads far beyond youth club discos and reaches the murkier areas of underlying racism.

JULY

It is feared that Rourke's arrest for possession of heroin may prevent him from accompanying The Smiths on their forthcoming US tour. As a result, session musician Guy Pratt is recruited as substitute bassist and Rourke magnanimously takes him through the group's set. Although Pratt cuts his hair in preparation for the trip, his chances of becoming an auxiliary Smith are dashed when Rourke is granted a visa.

30 JULY

The Smiths begin their tour of Canada with an appearance at the Centennial Hall, London, Ontario. Morrissey enjoys playing the narcissist, stretching himself across the stage apron, while grateful members of the audience caress his chest and stroke his hair. Eventually, a security officer adopts the paternal role, takes Morrissey gently by the wrist and deposits him in a safer position. Marr watches the proceedings with an air of aloofness, while sucking on a fag that never leaves his lips. "The Canadian gigs were more or less warm-ups for the tour proper," Mike Joyce recalls. "We did those because we didn't know what was going to be happening in Canada, reaction-wise... It was really a build-up for us to hit the States."

Set List: 'Panic'; 'Still Ill'; 'I Want The One I Can't Have'; 'Vicar In A Tutu'; 'Frankly Mr Shankly'; 'Is It Really So Strange?'; 'Cemetry Gates'; 'What She Said/Rubber Ring (Medley)'; 'There Is A Light That Never Goes Out'; 'The Boy With The Thorn In His Side'; 'That Joke Isn't Funny Anymore'; 'Ask'; 'Shakespeare's Sister'; 'William, It Was Really Nothing'; 'How Soon Is Now?'; 'Heaven Knows I'm Miserable Now'; 'The Queen Is Dead'; 'Money Changes Everything'; 'Please Please Please Let Me Get What I Want'; 'Bigmouth Strikes Again'; 'Hand In Glove'.

31 JULY

After a year's absence, The Smiths return to Toronto's answer to Wonderland, the Kingswood Music Theatre. Upmarket ticket touts are selling backstage passes embossed with the words "God Save The Queen" for a hefty $50. 00. For fans completely deluded by the prospect of meeting their heroes, it seems a reasonable alternative to the standard $5.00 ticket price. Lesbian singer Phranc opens the show and so impresses Morrissey that several years later he will offer her the support slot on his UK tour. The Toronto appearance ends with a stage invasion, after which Morrissey is interviewed on the local radio station CFNY. Even at this distance from England, he still cannot resist commenting on Radio 1's seeming reluctance to treat the group fairly. "We still cannot get on to the daytime radio A-list," he complains bitterly. "It's an absolute political slice of fascism to gag The Smiths."

Back at the hotel, Craig Gannon is celebrating his 20th birthday with the other Smiths. "Almost every night me, Mike and Andy ended up back at the hotel bar drinking cocktails," Craig recalls. "But it wasn't everyone having parties all the time. The only time we went down to the hotel's club was on my birthday and everyone except Morrissey was there. Of everyone I hung around with, it was probably Mike and Andy most of the time."

Set List: 'Panic'; 'Still Ill'; 'I Want The One I Can't Have'; 'Vicar In A Tutu'; 'Frankly Mr Shankly'; 'Is It Really So Strange?'; 'Cemetry Gates'; 'What She Said/Rubber Ring (Medley)'; 'There Is A Light That Never Goes Out'; 'The Boy With The Thorn In His Side'; 'That Joke Isn't Funny Anymore'; 'Ask'; 'Shakespeare's Sister'; 'William, It Was Really Nothing'; 'How Soon Is Now?'; 'The Queen Is Dead'; 'Money Changes Everything'; 'Please Please Please Let Me Get What I Want'; 'Bigmouth Strikes Again'; 'Hand In Glove'.

2 AUGUST

At the Capital Congress Centre, Ottawa, the group are filmed performing 'Panic'. Later they complete a memorable concert, during which several fans successfully invade the stage. While The Smiths continue their Canadian tour, the debate about their "rockist" tendencies continues in the music press. In the wake of recent accusatory letters, it is not surprising to see apologists emerging to remind us why The Smiths are special in the first place. Journalist Len Brown eloquently rises to the defence with a passionate appraisal of The Smiths' importance, and some flattering words about Morrissey's stage persona. "His presence alone makes The Smiths a unique live force," Brown insists. "Joyce is buried beneath drums, Rourke's like a zombie, new recruit Gannon's as stiff as the juvenile Ed Collins, while Marr – the brilliant budgie – calmly controls our changing moods. The new Rolling Stones? Don't talk crap. Jagger never *really* meant it."

The Morrissey tribute continues unabashed. "His open-hearted poetry is gilded with a passionate humour which only the insensitive, the deaf and the emotionally deformed choose to reject. Live, there's a marvellous bond between us. Perhaps this music is less infectiously danceable, less call-and-response community-orientated than, say, Trouble Funk, but the latter says little to me about *my* life... The music of Joy Division and The Smiths is 'a catharsis for the artist and works as a catharsis for the listener'... For here we are releasing our fascination with death ('Cemetry Gates'), remembrance for lost loved ones ('I Want The One I Can't Have') and unnatural emotions. Perhaps I'm taking all this too seriously..."

3 AUGUST

At the Center Sportif, Université de Montreal, The Smiths encounter a more traditional rock audience, but a small contingent of hard core fans makes its presence felt. Julie Lawler, who dutifully attended the first leg of the tour, recalls the Montreal visit: "During 'How Soon Is Now?' three huge men clamber over me and pile into the singer. He hits the stage floor hard and curls into himself as they fall upon him, making no effort to escape or fight back. His bodyguard ultimately comes on stage and hauls them off, but Morrissey remains prone for awhile, quietly gathering himself up. He slides back to the drum riser and climbs it slowly until he is standing. Then, pale but perfectly calm, he picks up the mike and resumes performing. There is one last encore, consisting of a seemingly quite heartfelt 'Heaven Knows I'm Miserable Now' and a hurried 'Hand In Glove'. During the latter, a girl approaches Morrissey and, rather than attacking him, simply stands beside him with a kind arm round his waist and strokes him as he sings. The concert ends, she lets go, he heads silently offstage."

5 AUGUST

The US segment of the tour opens at the Great Woods Performing Arts Center, Mansfield, Massachusetts. A healthy student population ensures that The Smiths receive a rousing reception. Unusually, the set opens with 'How Soon Is Now?', the most famous Smiths' song to American ears thanks to Sire's release of an unauthorized promotional video of old concert footage.

Set List: 'How Soon Is Now?'; 'Hand In Glove'; 'I Want The One I Can't Have'; 'Still Ill'; 'Frankly Mr Shankly'; 'Panic'; 'Never Had No One Ever'; 'Stretch Out And Wait'; 'The Boy With The Thorn In His Side'; 'Cemetry Gates'; 'What She Said/Rubber Ring (Medley)'; 'Is It Really So Strange?'; 'There Is A Light That Never Goes Out'; 'That Joke Isn't Funny Anymore'; 'The Queen Is Dead'; 'Money Changes Everything'; ' I Know It's Over'; 'Heaven Knows I'm Miserable Now'; 'Bigmouth Strikes Again'.

6 AUGUST

The Smiths return to New York for a much publicized appearance at Pier 84. "It was incredible," Joyce enthuses. "That was where Mick Jagger turned up. He was at the side of the stage bopping away with Anita Pallenberg. There were a few other heads there – it was very New York, and very hip to be there." A more jaundiced view was offered by New York scribe Valerie Rosner, who wrote: "And the crowd poured in. From every college fraternity and dingy slit in the pavement. How they got there remains a twisted mystery. How did they come upon *this* pop? What could it mean to them? The Smiths played to a New York crowd who demand no surprises, no special treatment, no side curves. And they were justly rewarded... The Smiths wrapped themselves safely in hollow gesticulations hurled from mindless hooligans and CD patrons alike. The almighty bratty beasts took on the band's meagre charm singlehandedly and, with one thoughtless grunt, wiped away everything sacred. They slaughtered the notion of individuality, ignored enchantment, steered clear of subtlety and missed the point. It was here that the ugly called the shots, came to 'party' and went home drunk. Drunk on the same stupidity they arrived with. Drunk on their empty gestures and offensive grins. The porcelain Smiths bowed down in defeat, followed the leader and walked the plank. We heard the hits and misses. The singles, the cracks, the LP tracks. Immaculately delivered

THE FIRST Smiths fanzine appeared in August 1986.

professionalism was the order of the day. Morrissey whined and grimaced and gawked and pranced. He twisted in his own improvisational anguish and raised three fists. The very silly record company smiled and ate hotdogs and said: 'I knew we could break this band'. I ate vegetable lasagne from Morrissey's trailer and said: 'Bring on The Jasmine Minks'."

Set List: 'How Soon Is Now?'; 'I Want The One I Can't Have'; 'Still Ill'; 'Frankly Mr Shankly'; 'Panic'; 'Never Had No One Ever'; 'Stretch Out And Wait'; 'The Boy With The Thorn In His Side'; 'Cemetry Gates'; 'What She Said/Rubber Ring (Medley)'; 'Hand In Glove'; 'Is It Really So Strange?'; 'There Is A Light That Never Goes Out'; 'That Joke Isn't Funny Anymore'; 'The Queen Is Dead'; 'Money Changes Everything'; 'I Know It's Over'; 'Heaven Knows I'm Miserable Now'; 'Bigmouth Strikes Again'.

7 AUGUST

Derek Jarman's promotional video for 'Panic' is featured on *Top Of The Pops*. Despite the group's absence, the single has surprised many by climbing as high as number 11, their highest chart placing since 'Heaven Knows I'm Miserable Now'.

8 AUGUST

The group play the appropriately named Smith Center in Washington. Recent recruit Gannon feels reasonably comfortable with the intense gigging schedule. "Playing the 1986 American tour, I enjoyed it for the most part," he stresses. "I had played there twice before with Aztec Camera, and many of the gigs and stadiums we played, I'd already played in 1983. We'd rehearsed for about two weeks before the tour. Although no one did that much rehearsing, I thought we all played pretty well together and did sound well rehearsed."

11-12 AUGUST

The Smiths play relatively low key gigs at the Music Hall, Cleveland (11th) and Fulton Theater, Pittsburgh (12th). Mike Joyce remembers these shows as two of the most unusual on the tour. "When we got to the gig and came on and started playing 'Still Ill' everybody was still sitting down after the first number," he remembers. "We'd finish and they'd politely applaud and wait... Johnny just turned round to me and said, 'Just treat it like a rehearsal, Mike. Have a good time. Pressure's off'. Because every gig

GANNON, Morrissey and Joyce.

ROURKE on the US tour

we played it was like, 'This has got to be the most important gig ever', which is a great way of thinking instead of sitting back on your laurels and saying, 'Look how good we are!' It kept the band pretty fiery tempered during the whole tour, but I remember Cleveland and Pittsburgh especially because the places were so depressing. There was absolutely nothing there and everybody was skint. A lot of the places we were hanging out... it was predominantly like black ghetto areas, and it was very depressing. Some of those gigs – the Pittsburgh/Cleveland route – were strange."

VIDEO DIRECTOR Derek Jarman.

One of the stranger aspects of the Cleveland sojourn is Morrissey's meeting with journalist Frank Owen (formerly Gavin Owen of Manicured Noise). While reminiscing over their dark days in Manchester, Owen grills the singer about his views on the state of black music. The provocative answers, printed six weeks later in *Melody Maker*, will spark a debate about racism which, on and off, continues to this day.

14-15 AUGUST

The Smiths play the Fox Theater, St Louis (14th) and the Aragon Ballroom, Chicago (15th). "That has one of the biggest free-standing balconies in the world," Mike Joyce enthuses. "It's an incredible place, and Chicago's always a fantastic tour, always a great gig to play."

Set List: 'Still Ill': 'I Want The One I Can't Have'; 'There Is A Light That Never Goes Out'; 'How Soon Is Now?'; 'Frankly Mr Shankly'; 'Panic'; 'Stretch Out And Wait'; 'The Boy With The Thorn In His Side'; 'Is It Really So Strange?'; 'Cemetry Gates'; 'Never Had No One Ever'; 'What She Said'/'Rubber Ring (Medley)'; 'That Joke Isn't Funny Anymore'; 'Meat Is Murder'; 'The Queen Is Dead'; 'Money Changes Everything'; 'I Know It's Over'; 'Hand In Glove'; 'Bigmouth Strikes Again'.

16 AUGUST

While The Smiths take the stage at the Performing Arts Center, Milwaukee, Morrissey is the subject of minor controversy back home. Journalist Paolo Hewitt has denounced the singer as a "dickhead" due to his negative views on black music and, predictably, *NME* is bombarded with letters rushing to Steven's defence. The big question of the day concerns the phrase "burn down the disco" in 'Panic'. Is it enough to excuse the line as merely a comment on the infantile pop propagated by daytime Radio 1? Hewitt persuasively argues that it is not: "If Morrissey wants to have a go at Radio 1 and Steve Wright, then fine. He should then write 'Burn Down Radio 1, hang Steve Wright'. When he starts using words like disco and DJ, with all the attendant imagery that brings up for what is a predominantly white audience, he is being imprecise and offensive. I am not in the job of setting up The Smiths versus The History Of Black Music. That would be ridiculous. The odds are so far against them. But I am in the way (and remember this is the man who wrote in *NME* two years ago that reggae is vile) of picking up on stupidity."

Set List: 'Still Ill': 'I Want The One I Can't Have'; 'There Is A Light That Never Goes Out'; 'How Soon Is Now?'; 'Frankly Mr Shankly'; 'Panic'; 'Stretch Out And Wait'; 'The Boy With The Thorn In His Side'; 'Is It Really So Strange?'; 'Cemetry Gates'; 'Never Had No One Ever'; 'What She Said'/ 'Rubber Ring (Medley)'; 'That Joke Isn't Funny Anymore'; 'Meat Is Murder'; 'The Queen Is Dead'; 'Hand In Glove'; 'Bigmouth Strikes Again'.

19 AUGUST

Derek Jarman's *The Queen Is Dead* video is previewed at the Edinburgh Film Festival. The highlight of the specially commissioned 15-minute movie is Jarman's interpretation of 'Panic', in which he uses fast cuts to suggest disorientation and visually enlivens Morrissey's lyrics of playful urban terror.

22 AUGUST

The West Coast Smiths' extravaganza continues at the Arlington Theatre, Santa Barbara. Living it up in California suits the hedonistic Andy Rourke, who is content to enjoy the party. "I used to be in my element on the road," Rourke recalls, "whereas I don't think it suited Morrissey very much. Me and Mike always used to take advantage and have a good time whereas Morrissey just locked himself in his hotel room. Angie was on the tour most of the time, so she and Johnny stuck together, while Mike and I went out to paint the town red. We always had a good time. We used to be in some state in the morning and a few times we had to leave early on the coach if we had a long drive. We'd be late getting on the coach and all bug-eyed and Morrissey wouldn't speak to us all that day because we'd been drinking the night before. I don't think he really approved of us going out till all hours of the morning. But I enjoyed it. I loved it."

Set List: 'Still Ill': 'I Want The One I Can't Have'; 'There Is A Light That Never Goes Out'; 'How Soon Is Now?'; 'Frankly Mr Shankly'; 'Panic'; 'Stretch Out And Wait'; 'The Boy With The Thorn In His Side'; 'Is It Really So Strange?'; 'Cemetry Gates'; 'Never Had No One Ever'; 'What She Said'/ 'Rubber Ring (Medley)'; 'That Joke Isn't Funny Anymore'; 'Meat Is Murder'; 'The Queen Is Dead'; 'Money Changes Everything'; 'I Know It's Over'; 'Hand In Glove'.

23 AUGUST

The student population of Berkeley's Greek Theatre, UCB, assemble for the arrival of The

JOYCE enjoyed the hedonism of the US tour.

Smiths. "They were great those gigs because all the college kids were just totally out there," Mike Joyce recalls. "A lot of kids that were there were the naughty boys and girls into The Smiths because we were considered a bit rebellious... A lot of the kids that were the waifs and misfits got into us, which was good and made it dead exciting."

Set List: 'Still Ill': 'I Want The One I Can't Have'; 'There Is A Light That Never Goes Out'; 'How Soon Is Now?'; 'Frankly Mr Shankly'; 'Panic'; 'Stretch Out And Wait'; 'The Boy With The Thorn In His Side'; 'Is It Really So Strange?'; 'Cemetry Gates'; 'Never Had No One Ever'; 'What She Said'/'Rubber Ring (Medley)'; 'That Joke Isn't Funny Anymore'; 'Meat Is Murder'; 'Shakespeare's Sister'; 'The Queen Is Dead'; 'Money Changes Everything'; 'I Know It's Over'; 'Hand In Glove'; 'Bigmouth Stikes Again'.

25 AUGUST

The Smiths appear at Studio City's Universal Amphitheatre, one of the more prestigious gigs of the tour. American stringer Jane Garcia is suitably starstruck by the group's performance. "Whoever said that misery loves company wasn't kidding," she reflects. "Almost 12,000 people turned out for The Smiths' two-night stand in Los Angeles. What they heard were 24 perfect pop sparklers, exquisitely executed by maestro Johnny Marr, while the Most Miserable Man in Manchester camped around the stage occasionally stopping to pose languidly across the monitors, or stand nipples to the wind, to face his adoring public. But this was a wondrous journey through The Smiths' songbook from 'Hand In Glove' to 'Panic', with all those funny and anguished points in between... The man himself was at his most winsome, triggering a minor stage invasion by telling the restless crowd: 'If you get stopped by a security guard, kiss him on the lips!' After being pelted with enough flowers to start his own nursery, the singer acceded to popular demand by divesting himself of his shirt, revealing, appropriately, the hairless, caved-in chest look usually associated with seven stone weaklings. Morrissey was, by turns, foppish, humble, funny, and effete, but never dull".

Set List: 'Still Ill': 'I Want The One I Can't Have'; 'There Is A Light That Never Goes Out'; 'How Soon Is Now?'; 'Frankly Mr Shankly'; 'Panic'; 'Stretch Out And Wait'; 'The Boy With The Thorn In His Side'; 'Is It Really So Strange?'; 'Cemetry Gates'; 'Never Had No One Ever'; 'What She Said'/'Rubber Ring (Medley)'; 'That Joke Isn't Funny Anymore'; 'Meat Is Murder'; 'The Queen Is Dead'; 'Money Changes Everything'; 'I Know It's Over'; 'Hand In Glove'; 'Bigmouth Strikes Again'.

26 AUGUST

For their second performance at the Universal Amphitheatre, The Smiths modify the previous night's set. Thanks to the recruitment of Gannon, Marr is able to improvise, which proves a necessity when playing stadiums. "It wasn't just, 'Oh, we're getting big in America, therefore we have to make more noise and run about a bit more'," Marr stresses. "I felt the sort of group we were wasn't going to translate. I was nervous about it translating in those really big venues and I felt that there were so many guitar parts that were essential to the sound that we were going to sound too small for the venue. It wasn't a question of volume, it was a question of parts. Even playing something with my feet was really difficult. To play to that kind of audience had so much riding on it. We had an outro on 'That Joke Isn't Funny Anymore' and I wanted to get the beauty of that across and there was no way we could do that with one guitar. As you said, it was really difficult to do it with two guitars and it was essential with things like 'Bigmouth Strikes Again' that people heard the whole thing."

Set List: 'Please Please Please Let Me Get What I Want'; 'Still Ill'; 'I Want The One I Can't Have'; 'There Is A Light That Never Goes Out'; 'How Soon Is Now?'; 'Frankly Mr Shankly'; 'Panic'; 'Stretch Out And Wait'; 'The Boy With The Thorn In His Side'; 'Is It Really So Strange?'; 'Cemetry Gates'; 'Never Had No One Ever'; 'What She Said/Rubber Ring (Medley)'; 'That Joke Isn't Funny Anymore'; 'Meat Is Murder'; 'Heaven Knows I'm Miserable Now'; 'Reel Around The Fountain'; 'The Queen Is Dead'; 'Money Changes Everything'; 'I Know It's Over'; 'Hand In Glove'; 'Bigmouth Strikes Again'.

28 AUGUST

The Smiths return to the Irvine Meadows, Amphitheatre, Laguna Hills, where they played on the 1985 US tour. Sound engineer Grant Showbiz remembers this as one of the wildest gigs on the tour. "All the kids were on angel dust and leaping eight foot up on to the stage," he recalls excitedly. "Bouncers were coming up to them, but they were lifting them up and pushing them out of the way because this stuff gives you superhuman strength. I think the stage manager fell off the back of the stage and injured himself. It was getting really crazy."

29 AUGUST

The show rolls on to San Diego's Open Air Theater. "A lot of the times the gig went out to the highest bidder", Joyce explains, "because that's the way the agent is going to be doing it. If he puts tenders out to three or

four areas in California, he's just got to take the highest bidder. Of course, the kids will travel, so it's no problem."

Set List: 'Panic'; 'I Want The One I Can't Have'; 'There Is A Light That Never Goes Out'; 'How Soon Is Now?'; 'Frankly Mr Shankly'; 'Still Ill'; 'Stretch Out And Wait'; 'The Boy With The Thorn In His Side'; 'Is It Really So Strange?'; 'Cemetry Gates'; 'Never Had No One Ever'; 'What She Said/Rubber Ring (Medley)'; 'That Joke Isn't Funny Anymore'; 'Meat Is Murder'; 'Heaven Knows I'm Miserable Now'; 'The Queen Is Dead'.

31 AUGUST

Having completed their West Coast commitments, The Smiths travel to Phoenix, Arizona, for a performance at the MESA Amphitheater. The strain is beginning to take its toll on Johnny Marr who has taken to drinking brandy at an alarming rate. "It was terrible," Marr confesses. "All I remember is really bad times like laying on the end of a bed with Angie saying: 'Someone's got to do something about this'. Sophie (the tour manager) had gone and Mike Hinck had come out and we had to get to another city." Drinking to blot out the pressure later reminded Marr of his partner in Electronic. "It's something I've got in common with Bernard," he notes. "He's been in the same position of being hungover, half-drunk, sick on the airport floor and having to get on a plane and get to another soundcheck. I used to drink more than I could handle. I was never into booze really."

Grant Showbiz remembers the hedonistic high jinx threatening to get out of hand, and occasionally felt Johnny and the others were pushing themselves too hard. "There was a lot of romanticism on that tour," he points out. "It was a raving tour for everybody, even Morrissey. He'd have half a bottle of wine and, to him, that was like going crazy. Both of them were certainly ill. There wasn't any overall boss figure. Sometimes I was coming in and saying, 'Listen, guys, you really ought to lay back a bit and give yourselves a rest'. Angie would express concern to me, but not express it directly or get in the way. She was unobstructive in her support."

3 SEPTEMBER

The Smiths appear at the Events Center in Colorado, near the rocky mountain home of Morrissey's Aunt Mary. At the soundcheck, the group work earnestly on 'The Queen Is

THE reconstituted Smiths enjoy some time off playing football during the summer.

Dead', which features some spacey guitar work and terribly off-key vocals from Morrissey. The actual show opens with 'Still Ill' in which Steven sounds strangely hoarse and out of sorts. During 'I Want The One I Can't Have' he sings vibrato, rolling his "r"s and playing with the words. 'There Is A Light That Never Goes Out' sounds subdued and is swiftly followed by 'How Soon Is Now?' in which Marr and Gannon let loose and provoke some much needed applause from the audience. "Thank you very much, you're very kind," Morrissey announces, prompting grateful screams from fans in the auditorium. An oompah version of 'Frankly Mr Shankly' ends with the singer informing the hordes: "You're very brave". A rough version of 'Panic' is succeeded by 'Stretch Out And Wait', a song of dark eroticism that the audience fails to appreciate. 'Is It Really So Strange?' also has a muted quality, which causes Marr to lose his patience. In an uncharacteristic gesture, he walks up to the microphone and complains: "This is like a library. Doesn't anyone ever make any noise in Denver?" Thereafter, the crowd respond more enthusiastically, coaxing The Smiths into a strong medley of 'What She Said'/'Rubber Ring' and a theatrical 'Meat Is Murder', with Morrissey playing a role closer to Jack The Ripper than the sensitive narrator of the recorded version.

Set List: 'Still Ill'; "I Want The One I Can't Have'; 'There Is A Light That Never Goes Out'; 'How Soon Is Now?'; 'Frankly Mr Shankly'; 'Panic'; 'Stretch Out And Wait'; 'The Boy With The Thorn In His Side'; 'Is It Really So Strange?'; 'Cemetry Gates'; 'Never Had No One Ever'; 'What She Said/Rubber Ring (Medley)'; 'That Joke Isn't Funny Anymore'; 'Meat Is Murder'; 'Rusholme Ruffians/(Marie's The Name) His Latest Flame (Medley)'; 'The Queen Is Dead'.

THE QUEEN IS DEAD banner.

A NOOSE to hang the DJ.

5 SEPTEMBER

The vegetarian quartet come dangerously close to the steak capital of the world when they play the Cullen Auditorium, Houston, Texas. Although they do not have a big following in Texas, there are enough supporters to make their presence a minor event. "I'm sure there were pockets of resistance that are there even now," Joyce stresses. "It's why a lot of Smiths' fans get off on it because, as with the Morrissey fans now, it's 'I'm misunderstood youth and he understands me'. I think a lot of them grooved to that."

Set List: 'The Queen Is Dead'; 'Panic'; 'I Want The One I Can't Have'; 'Rusholme Ruffians/(Marie's The Name) His Latest Flame (Medley)'; 'There Is A Light That Never Goes Out'; 'Still Ill'; 'William, It Was Really Nothing'; 'Cemetry Gates'; 'Stretch Out And Wait'; 'Never Had No One Ever'; 'Is It Really So Strange?'; 'That Joke Isn't Funny Anymore'; 'Meat Is Murder'; 'What She Said/Rubber Ring (Medley)'; 'I Know It's Over'; 'Money Changes Everything'; 'How Soon Is Now?'; 'Hand In Glove'; 'Bigmouth Strikes Again'.

> **'Reading your latest interview with Morrissey, I was deeply disturbed by his rash and ultimately racist statements concerning black music.'**
>
> AN OUTRAGED ASIAN

6-11 SEPTEMBER
The arduous US tour takes in the Bronco Bowl, Dallas, Texas (6th), the McAlister Auditorium, New Orleans (8th) and Bay Front Center, Tampa, Florida (10th). At this point, exhaustion takes its toll and the remaining dates in Miami, Atlanta, Nashville and New York are cancelled. "After the Tampa gig it just got so crazy that we were really burned out," Joyce reflects. "We'd put so much into it every night. It wasn't just like, 'Oh, where are we now?' It was more like 'Every gig is the most important gig we play', which is a great way of looking at it, but it certainly takes the wind out of your sails after doing it for 30 nights or 30 gigs."

Set List: 'The Queen Is Dead'; 'I Want The One I Can't Have'; 'Panic'; 'Rusholme Ruffians/(Marie's The Name) His Latest Flame (Medley)'; 'There Is A Light That Never Goes Out'; 'Still Ill'; 'The Boy With The Thorn In His Side'; 'Cemetry Gates'; 'Stretch Out And Wait'; 'Never Had No One Ever'; 'Is It Really So Strange?'; 'That Joke Isn't Funny Anymore'; 'Meat Is Murder'; 'What She Said/Rubber Ring (Medley)'; 'I Know It's Over'; 'Money Changes Everything'; 'How Soon Is Now?'; 'Hand In Glove'; 'Bigmouth Strikes Again'.

20 SEPTEMBER
The late night music feature *Rock Around The Clock* includes the Derek Jarman videos of 'The Queen Is Dead', 'There Is A Light That Never Goes Out' and 'Panic'.

27 SEPTEMBER
"Smiths Sign To EMI" blaze the music press headlines. Rumours abound that EMI will be buying out the remainder of the group's Rough Trade contract and intend to issue The Smiths' next studio album. The independent label's staff are clearly bemused by this latest turn of events. "We knew they were talking to EMI but no-one has told us that papers have been signed," replies Rough Trade's PR Pat Bellis. "We've booked them into a studio to make another LP before the end of the year and we are also hoping to record a live album from their London Palladium concert next month."

EMI are less reticent about the signing and prematurely crow with victory at the thought of a wealth of Smiths' product. "Naturally, we are thrilled to pieces with the news which could mean we get up to four LPs from the band," they enthuse hopefully. "The contracts have been signed, although there are some short term considerations with Rough Trade which have yet to be finished."

WHILE FANS ARE STILL REELING FROM THE EMI news, *Melody Maker* print Frank Owen's infamous interview with Morrissey, in which black music, gay clubs and racism all come under scrutiny. Morrissey castigates all modern black music, singling out Stevie Wonder, Diana Ross, Janet Jackson and Whitney Houston for special abuse. Reggae is once more vilified as "the most racist music in the entire world" and damned as "an absolute glorification of black supremacy". In a sustained bout of crazy logic, Morrissey even maintains that BBC radio programmers are actively favouring black artistes and effectively boycotting The Smiths. The interviewer's mention of a "black music conspiracy" will soon fuel the letters pages of the music press in a long and heated debate about Morrissey's racial views. The singer later denies that he hates black music *per se* and suggests that his quotes, though not inaccurate, have been taken out of context. A disgruntled Marr is sufficiently irked by the negative publicity to threaten Owen publicly and promise a right royal kick-in the next time they meet.

4 OCTOBER
Although late with the news of The Smiths' EMI signing, *Sounds* rightly point to this moment as a watershed in the history of independent music in the UK: "Even though Rough Trade have been expecting to lose The Smiths for some time it will still come as a body blow on the indie scene, as it would seem to confirm that the indies cannot compete with the major labels once a band passes a certain level of success and wishes to progress further".

11 OCTOBER
Travis strikes back. Although The Smiths' contract is due to expire, he will not sanction their move to EMI until they have fulfilled their remaining contractual obligations and recorded a final studio album. Although it is widely reported that EMI have offered Travis far more money than he could reasonably have expected to recoup from the remaining album, he bravely holds his ground. "It appears that Rough Trade have decided that the contract is more important than the cash," notes the music press with surprise.

While the Rough Trade saga continues, the music press briefly return to The Smiths' music. Ignoring official release dates, *Melody Maker*'s Simon Reynolds reviews the new single 'Ask' a fortnight early. Proclaiming the lilting 45 "unavoidable" single of the week, he notes, "With its chugging beat and Kirsty MacColl harmonies, this is perhaps their closest approach to commercial lusciousness. I prefer their moments of reproachful, avenging misery myself, like 'How Soon Is Now?' – this is a little unfraught, a bit too sunny. But then, as someone who can be brought to tears by 'The Queen Is Dead', I'm beyond impartiality and detachment."

The innocuous breeziness of 'Ask' is not sufficient to distract the music press readership from more serious concerns. That same week "An Outraged Asian" from Birmingham accuses: "Reading your latest interview with Morrissey, I was deeply disturbed by his rash and ultimately racist statements concerning black music, especially as I once credited him with vision and intelligence."

After reminding us of many reggae artistes who do not glorify any kind of black supremacy, the reader concludes: "Morrissey is simply encouraging such stereotyped notions. Of course, a person's ethnic/social background will influence their creative output, but it doesn't mean that if someone has a different colour pigmentation than Herr Morrissey (which I have) the latter will be able to lump them all together under one heading. Morrissey is encouraging a return to pre-Motown music in one corner and white rock in the other and builds a wall between them. Thank God, bands like The Specials and Talking Heads proved Morrissey wrong yonks ago. I for one will no longer purchase any Smiths' product and I will be most disappointed and angry if Morrissey doesn't get the stick he deserves for coming out with such ill-informed and potentially dangerous bullshit."

13 OCTOBER
After a month's rest, The Smiths resume live performances with a UK tour, beginning at the Sands Centre, Carlisle. "When we came back from America with all the histrionics, we then did the North of England, and you're giving off the same kind of vibe," Mike Joyce explains. "We came back and we were like,

JOYCE on the UK leg of the 1986 tour.

'Rock 'n' Roll!!' America was a pretty big tour and we were screwed up by the end of it. Then we came back, had a bit of time off, and it was – 'Yeah, let's go!'" The strong rock element in The Smiths' performance is immediately transformed into critical cliché, with Rolling Stones comparisons bandied about in various reviews. *Record Mirror*'s Dave Sexton is clearly intrigued by this apparent metamorphosis. "The more I see, the more I'm convinced of two things," he notes. "The first is that The Smiths are probably the best band in Britain. The second is that they are, slowly but surely, turning into The Rolling Stones. This is not as daft as it may sound – think not of The Rolling Stones of today, the flabby, flatulent, dried out and dried up Stones. Think rather of old film of them – very old film – and you'll see what I mean. It is the unlikely brooding sexuality and skittish posturing of the Morrissey/Jagger figure and the now unashamed 'axe-hero' stance of Johnny Marr – the new Keith Richard."

Set List: 'The Queen Is Dead'; 'Panic'; 'I Want The One I Can't Have'; 'Vicar In A Tutu'; 'There Is A Light That Never Goes Out'; 'Rusholme Ruffians/(Marie's The Name) His Latest Flame (Medley)'; 'Frankly Mr Shankly'; 'The Boy With The Thorn In His Side'; 'What She Said/Rubber Ring (Medley)'; 'Ask'; 'Is It Really So Strange?'; 'That Joke Isn't Funny Anymore'; 'Never Had No One Ever'; 'Cemetry Gates'; 'London'; 'Meat Is Murder'; 'I Know It's Over'; 'The Draize Train'; 'How Soon Is Now?'; 'Still Ill'; 'Bigmouth Strikes Again'.

14 OCTOBER

The Smiths continue their North East travels, appearing at the Town Hall, Middlesbrough. By this time, 'Ask' has been in the set for several months and pre-release copies of the new single are available. Craig Gannon is a little taken aback to discover that his chord sequence contribution to the single has not won him a co-writing credit. "Up until the release of 'Ask' I still thought I'd be given a writing credit," he recalls. "When I found out that I wasn't given a writing credit, it didn't really bother me, but I thought it was pretty bad that no one even acknowledged that it was my idea in the first place. The thing I hate is that in the past I've been accused of trying to put my name to a song, as if I was trying to grab what I could get when that was not the case at all. In any other situation where it would have been up to me to choose to make a song out of such a basic song idea, I probably wouldn't have expanded on that idea, although I do think the song ended up really good." In the circumstances, Gannon decides to remain silent about his misgivings in the presence of Marr and deliberately avoids any personality clash.

Set List: 'The Queen Is Dead'; 'Panic'; 'I Want The One I Can't Have'; 'Vicar In A Tutu'; 'There Is A Light That Never Goes Out'; 'Ask'; 'Rusholme Ruffians/(Marie's The Name) His Latest Flame (Medley)'; 'Frankly Mr Shankly'; 'The Boy With The Thorn In His Side'; 'What She Said/Rubber Ring (Medley)'; 'Is It Really So Strange?'; 'Never Had No One Ever'; 'Cemetry Gates'; 'London'; 'Meat Is Murder'; 'I Know It's Over'; 'The Draize Train'; 'How Soon Is Now?'; 'Still Ill'; 'Bigmouth Strikes Again'.

15 OCTOBER

Stopping off in the Midlands, The Smiths appear at the Civic Hall, Wolverhampton. Their opening song, 'The Queen Is Dead', continues to attract attention, especially in view of Morrissey's much publicized verbal assaults on the Royal Family. "It doesn't necessarily mean Queen Elizabeth," Morrissey protests to journalist Bruce Dessau. "There's the safety net in the song... that the 'old queen' in the lyrics is actually me. So when they lynch me or nail me to the cross, I have that trapdoor to slide through. But, having said that, the song is certainly a kind of general observation on the state of the nation." The singer's reading of his own lyrics doesn't quite accord with the actual words. It is clear from the song that the narrator is not the "old queen" but rather his "eighteenth pale descendant".

Set List: 'The Queen Is Dead'; 'Panic'; 'I Want The One I Can't Have'; 'Vicar In A Tutu'; 'There Is A Light That Never Goes Out'; 'Ask'; 'Rusholme Ruffians/(Marie's The Name) His Latest Flame (Medley)'; 'Frankly Mr Shankly'; 'The Boy With The Thorn In His Side'; 'What She Said/Rubber Ring (Medley)'; 'Is It Really So Strange?'; 'Never Had No One Ever'; 'Cemetry Gates'; 'London'; 'Meat Is Murder'; 'I Know It's Over'; 'The Draize Train'; 'How Soon Is Now?'; 'Still Ill'; 'Bigmouth Strikes Again'.

17 OCTOBER

At the Coliseum, St Austell, Cornwall, The Smiths are joined onstage by Raymonde's James Maker, making his first appearance with the group since their early gigs in Manchester. Those unable to attend the show can at least watch the promotional video of 'Ask' on *The Chart Show*.

Set List: 'The Queen Is Dead'; 'Panic'; 'I Want The One I Can't Have'; 'Vicar In A Tutu'; 'There Is A Light That Never Goes Out'; 'Ask'; 'Rusholme Ruffians/(Marie's The Name) His Latest Flame (Medley)'; 'Frankly Mr Shankly'; 'The Boy With The Thorn In His Side'; 'What She Said/Rubber Ring (Medley)'; 'Is It Really So Strange?'; 'Never Had No One Ever'; 'Cemetry Gates'; 'London'; 'Meat Is Murder'; 'I Know It's Over'; 'The Draize Train'; 'How Soon Is Now?'; 'Still Ill'; 'Bigmouth Strikes Again'.

18 OCTOBER

"Perhaps The Smiths, dwarfed beneath the enormous Alain Delon projection, are trying a little too hard," remarks reviewer Will Smith of this evening's performance at the Leisure Centre, Gloucester. "The recruitment of Craig Gammon [sic] on additional guitar is a mixed blessing," he notes, "for though he relieves Johnny Marr of his more mundane rhythmic duties, he also allows his superior a freedom to take full advantage and roam somewhat sloppily unchecked through the boisterous vigour of 'The Queen Is Dead', 'I Want The One I Can't Have' and 'What She Said', inadvertently suffocating the songs with the unfortunate compulsion to explode. Morrissey, meanwhile, is equally alive and kicking. Exchanging as few words as possible, he is as mouth-wateringly provocative as ever and seems to have finally abandoned the sensitive, pitiful persona of a man in torment for a new, improved one of strength and precociousness." Summing up, the concert commentator carefully notes, "The Smiths carry 'I Know It's Over' to its glorious finale, and the connection with their recorded supremacy is made but, in general, tonight bore more resemblance to a crude battle for rock establishment..."

Set List: 'The Queen Is Dead'; 'Panic'; 'I Want The One I Can't Have'; 'Vicar In A Tutu'; 'There Is A Light That Never Goes Out'; 'Ask'; 'Rusholme Ruffians/(Marie's The Name) His Latest Flame (Medley)'; 'Frankly Mr Shankly'; 'The Boy With The Thorn In His Side'; 'What She Said/Rubber Ring (Medley)'; 'Is It Really So Strange?'; 'Never Had No One Ever'; 'Cemetry Gates'; 'London'; 'Meat Is Murder'; 'I Know It's Over'; 'The Draize Train'; 'How Soon Is Now?'; 'Still Ill'; 'Bigmouth Strikes Again'.

19 OCTOBER

One of the most eventful and notorious gigs in The Smiths' performing history occurs at the Leisure Centre, Newport, Wales. The Sunday show ends on a dramatic note when Morrissey, dancing perilously close to the edge of the stage, is pulled to the floor. "Somebody grabbed his hand and he lost his balance," explained a spokesperson for Rough Trade. "The crowd parted and he hit the floor headfirst. They were already 40 minutes into the set when it happened so the show was nearly over anyway. Morrissey wanted to carry on but the doctor thought it would be better for him to rest." Morrissey's accident proves less serious than that of the unfortunate Grant Showbiz, who has the unenviable task of informing the disgruntled audience that The Smiths will not be returning. Mid-way through his apologia, he is struck by a bottle, then taken to hospital and treated for cuts and concussion. The evening ends in a mêlée of ripped seats, tribal chanting and six arrests by the local police.

Above: Morrissey and Gannon at Carlisle, 31 October 1986. Right: Marr was demoralized by the outbreaks of violence at Smiths gigs.

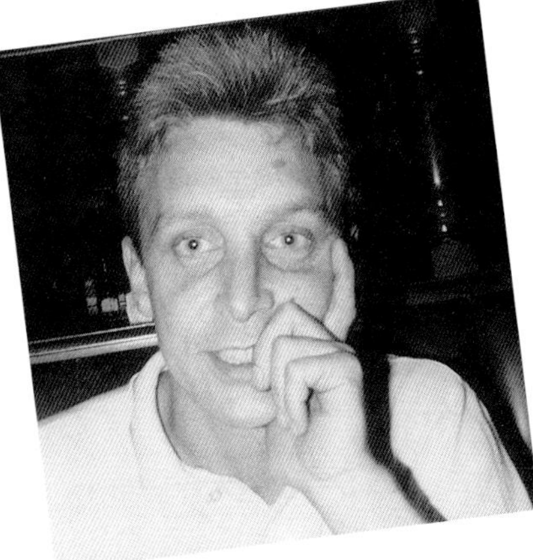

GRANT SHOWBIZ with the scar caused by a stray bottle.

Not surprisingly, the curtailed set prompts several angry letters to the music press in which eye-witnesses recount their own impressions of the eventful evening. One reader recalls: "The band took the stage to a rapturous reception and straight away treated us to some of their most popular songs. After they had played about nine songs, Morrissey started flirting with the audience, touching hands etc. It was a case of now you see him – now you don't, as he over-balanced and toppled into the loving crowd, closely followed by the band's crew, who hauled the singer to safety. Morrissey was led away clutching his head and the band followed soon after. We know the guy isn't exactly famed for his strong constitution and is, in fact, the most celebrated wimp in the country. But one little knock and he was gone. We were then informed that he was getting his breath back and would return to the stage soon. It was with some disbelief we saw the road crew packing up the equipment. Cue much muttering and a little disquiet among the faithful. Before you could say 'Meat Is Murder' half the local constabulary had descended on the place and arrested some of the more aggressive elements. The whole business of offering the prospect of a resumption to the gig was obviously a delaying tactic by the organizers while the cavalry was called in. In other words – The Smiths' credibility went up in smoke. A refund? No chance. Perhaps another gig at a later date? Sorry. Some 2,000 people had travelled from half-way across the country for the honour of being conned by the fey one. Perhaps their much touted move to EMI has dulled their senses."

Set List: 'The Queen Is Dead'; 'Panic'; 'I Want The One I Can't Have'; 'Vicar In A Tutu'; 'There Is A Light That Never Goes Out'; 'Ask'; 'Rusholme Ruffians/(Marie's The Name) His Latest Flame (Medley)'; 'Frankly Mr Shankly'; 'The Boy With The Thorn In His Side'; 'The Draize Train'.

20 OCTOBER

The new single 'Ask' is issued and wastes little time in climbing to number 14 in the charts. Despite its commercial appeal, producer John Porter is disappointed with the end product, which was taken out of his hands and remixed. "It was another one that didn't come off," he notes with regret. "There's some fabulous stuff on the tape. There were a lot of guitars and only I knew how they fitted together. There were too many of them – stuff that shouldn't be there all the time. It was a jigsaw puzzle of guitars and there was this bit in the middle where it all broke down. There was this great breakdown with the big wave splashing. It was the most theatrical effect, with seagull noises done by Johnny on the guitar. It was fantastic but, on record, you don't notice it. It's just gone. I was really pissed off because that was a spectacular track."

Porter found little consolation on the 12-inch B-side, which featured the extra track 'Golden Lights', a cover of Twinkle's minor Top 30 hit from 1965. Once again the track was remixed, much to Porter's chagrin. "It sounds appalling to me," the producer regrets, "but what's on the tape is great. It's beautiful. It has a Mexican feel to it. It has beautiful stuff on the tape and that's not on the mix... I didn't hear it until it came out and I thought, 'Oh, no!'" Remembering this fraught period, Porter feels he became innocently caught up in the interpersonal conflicts within the group, or at least those within Morrissey's head. "I think Morrissey was down on me because of my friendship with Johnny and it was just about the last time I worked with him," he reflects. In fact, Porter would attempt one last single with the group the following year, but despite his consistently productive working relationship with Marr, that too would end on a silent but regrettable note.

21 OCTOBER

The tour continues at the Royal Concert Hall, Nottingham. For Craig Gannon, the pleasure of playing in The Smiths has already been tainted by the cold treatment he is receiving from those already aware of his impending dismissal. "By this point the feelings I was getting, mainly from Johnny, were pretty grim," he remembers. "Bad vibes and stuff. Nothing was said really, just bad feelings. For the majority of the period I was with Johnny, personally and conversationally, it was a disaster. It was obvious before this point that something was going on. Everyone knew there was something going on."

Set List: 'The Queen Is Dead'; 'Panic'; 'I Want The One I Can't Have'; 'Vicar In A Tutu'; 'There Is A Light That Never Goes Out'; 'Ask'; 'Rusholme Ruffians/(Marie's The Name) His Latest Flame (Medley)'; 'Frankly Mr Shankly'; 'The Boy With The Thorn In His Side'; 'What She Said/Rubber Ring (Medley)'; 'Is It Really So Strange?'; 'Never Had No One Ever'; 'Cemetry Gates'; 'London'; 'Meat Is Murder'; 'I Know It's Over'; 'The Draize Train'; 'How Soon Is Now?'; 'Still Ill'; 'Bigmouth Strikes Again'.

23 OCTOBER

The performance at the National Ballroom, Kilburn is recorded in full and 14 of the 22 songs are later featured on the live album, *Rank*. As sound engineer, Grant Showbiz takes on a quasi-producer's role and receives a one per cent royalty from sales of the album. Thanks to the inclusion of 'The Draize Train', Marr stands to make more money from the project than his fiscal minded partner. The set ably captures the group at their rocking zenith, with Marr's spacey guitar work on 'The Queen Is Dead' proving a spectacular highlight of an eventful evening. Morrissey throws in a few witticisms to lighten proceedings, at one point wryly announcing: "Could I please ask the journalists to stop throwing things." At this date only, the support slot is given to an obscure Manchester outfit called Soil. Interestingly, their drummer is none other than Gary Farrell, the kid that turned down an opportunity to join The Smiths before they recruited Joyce. "The lead singer met Morrissey on a train coming back from London and gave him a tape," Farrell remembers. "He liked it, so we got the gig. It was really good. That was the only time I saw The Smiths." Later that evening Granada Television feature a pre-recorded film of Morrissey reviewing Norman Tebbitt's autobiography on Tony Wilson's arts programme *The Other Side Of Midnight*.

NATIONAL BALLROOM
KILBURN
THURSDAY
23rd OCTOBER. 1986
at 7-30 p.m.
Phil McIntyre presents
THE SMITHS
Plus Support
£6-50
(£4-50 UB40 Card Holders)
R.O.A.R.
No 001669
Exchanged or Money Refunded
To be retained

Set List: 'The Queen Is Dead'; 'Panic'; 'I Want The One I Can't Have'; 'Vicar In A Tutu'; 'There Is A Light That Never Goes Out'; 'Ask'; 'Rusholme Ruffians/(Marie's The Name) His Latest Flame (Medley)'; 'Shakespeare's Sister'; 'Frankly Mr Shankly'; 'The Boy With The Thorn In His Side'; 'What She Said/Rubber Ring (Medley)'; 'Ask'; 'Is It Really So Strange?'; 'Never Had No One Ever'; 'Cemetry Gates'; 'London'; 'Meat Is Murder'; 'I Know It's Over'; 'The Draize Train'; 'How Soon Is Now?'; 'Still Ill'; 'Bigmouth Strikes Again'.

MORRISSEY by the poster advertising the autumn UK tour and (RIGHT) taking a break.

THE SMITHS, minus Gannon, take time out for a record company photo session.

24 OCTOBER

With The Railway Children as support, The Smiths play London's Brixton Academy. This gig proves one of the more unusual on the tour thanks to the recruitment of a second drummer, The Impossible Dreamers' Fred Hood. In a parody of The Glitter Band, Hood takes the stage during Marr's instrumental 'The Draize Train' and stays on for a powerful rendition of 'How Soon Is Now?' As Hood remarked of his onstage cameo with The Smiths: "It was like scoring a goal at Wembley!"

Set List: 'The Queen Is Dead'; 'Panic'; 'I Want The One I Can't Have'; 'Vicar In A Tutu'; 'There Is A Light That Never Goes Out'; 'Ask'; 'Rusholme Ruffians/(Marie's The Name) His Latest Flame (Medley)'; 'Shakespeare's Sister'; 'Frankly Mr Shankly'; 'The Boy With The Thorn In His Side'; 'What She Said/Rubber Ring (Medley)'; 'Is It Really So Strange?'; 'Cemetry Gates'; 'London'; 'Meat Is Murder'; 'I Know It's Over'; 'The Draize Train'; 'How Soon Is Now?'; 'Still Ill'; 'Bigmouth Strikes Again'.

26 OCTOBER

The plush décor of the London Palladium is invaded by Smiths' aficionados old and new. Support group Raymonde are suffering from bad press, having been cursed by Smiths comparisons throughout their brief career. "We couldn't move for it," singer James Maker attests. "It was very difficult to establish our own identity." Having declined a full tour support, Maker finds little joy at the Palladium, a show he damns as "the nadir of my career".

The Smiths' performance, by contrast, receives a rapturous response by a partisan audience. Among them is reviewer Karen Swayne, taking particular notice of the changing public face of Steven Morrissey. "In dark glasses, blazer and white trousers, the singer looked more like a refugee from The Style Council than singer with the country's most popular indie group," she notes. "In fact, members of the audience, with hearing aids and NHS specs looked more like him than he did." After noting the structuring of the evening's set, with its intermingling of fast and slow numbers, Swayne next trains her eye on the lead guitarist. "On the subject of Mr Marr," she pencils, "he's swopped the loveable mop top, shades and jeans for a baggy suited Yuppie style (Yamamoto, natch) which is far less appealing. And he looks like he's become a 60-a-day man, spending half his time enveloped in smoke from an ever present cigarette hanging out of his mouth". After applauding the encores, the reviewer describes how "Morrissey punched his fist proudly in the air, Johnny Marr did a final bit of his drunk student still on the dance floor at the end of the disco gimpy dancing, and then they were off."

For *NME*'s Mat Snow, the quality of the music on offer is a far weightier consideration. While he clearly appreciates the power of The Smiths' five piece assault, he feels a sense of loss at the absence of former subtleties such as understated emotion. "Morrissey's campy rock literate self-mockery shouldn't double bluff you from the fact that tonight Johnny Marr calls the shots, cheerfully vandalising The Smiths' most distinctive and precious qualities..." he reports. "On stage, music that at one time made no apologies for ringing melancholy – though its terseness always kept sentimentality at bay – has hardened with the rigours of the road and pressures of career into something slightly coarse, mannered and untrue to itself. I, for one, regret this 'progress'."

While the debate about The Smiths' performance rages in the foyer, journalists are not privy to the happenings backstage, where Morrissey's father waits outside the dressing room door. "He had a bodyguard there and he stood against me," Peter Morrissey recalls.

"I said, 'Oh, I'm Morrissey's dad', and he said, 'Wait there!' Then he went in. I was expecting him to say, 'It's OK, go on in!', but he said 'Yes, he'll be out to see you when he's ready'. I was embarrassed. I couldn't believe this. Johnny Marr, Mike Joyce and Andy Rourke came out of the dressing room, and the three of them grabbed hold of me and were squeezing me. I know Steven's a bit shy, but he came out and shook my hand as if he'd just met me. I thought, 'I can't believe what's going on here!'"

Set List: 'The Queen Is Dead'; 'Panic'; 'I Want The One I Can't Have'; 'Vicar In A Tutu'; 'There Is A Light That Never Goes Out'; 'Ask'; 'Rusholme Ruffians/(Marie's The Name) His Latest Flame (Medley)'; 'Shakespeare's Sister'; 'Frankly Mr Shankly'; 'The Boy With The Thorn In His Side'; 'What She Said/Rubber Ring (Medley)'; 'Is It Really So Strange?'; 'Never Had No One Ever'; 'Cemetry Gates'; 'London'; 'Meat Is Murder'; 'I Know It's Over'; 'The Draize Train'; 'How Soon Is Now?'; 'Still Ill'; 'Bigmouth Strikes Again'.

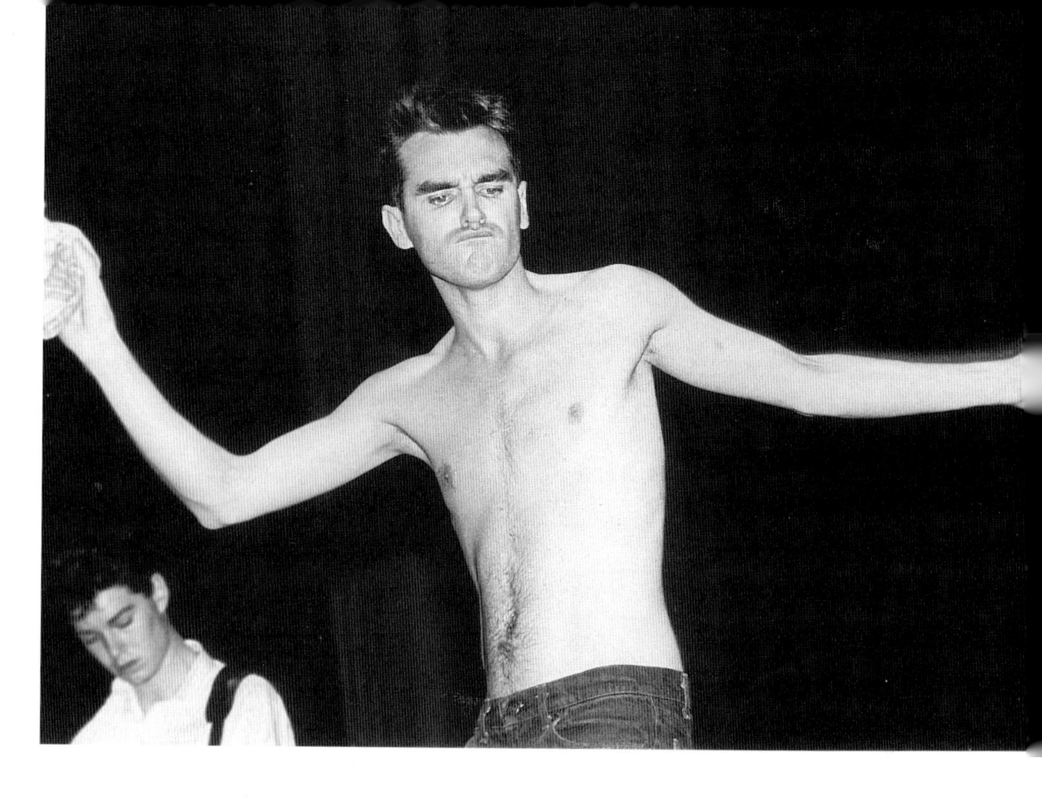

27 OCTOBER

The shortest live set in Smiths' history takes place at the Guildhall, Preston, when the evening ends after the opening number, 'The Queen Is Dead'. The singer is apparently rushed to hospital suffering from a minor head injury. According to one observer: "Morrissey was hit above the forehead with an object which had been thrown from the crowd. He didn't know what it was, but his head was bleeding and he left the stage. The tour manager said it was a coin." According to other members of the audience, Morrissey was hit by a drumstick, from an irate punter impatient at the long delay before The Smiths deigned to take the stage. Escaping from the venue unscathed apparently proved quite a challenge. "Loads of people were waiting outside for us," Craig Gannon recalls. "I heard they were going to hijack the van! I can't understand why a drumstick was thrown, but I think it *was* a drumstick. What was a drumstick doing onstage before we went on? Mike Joyce wouldn't have thrown his drumsticks out before we went on. I can't understand that."

As usual, the ever vigilant Smiths' fans had an answer to Craig's question. One waggish music press correspondent exposed the PR explanation with a flourish worthy of Sherlock Holmes: "Disappointed to see you taken in by Rough Trade! Morrissey hit by a sharpened penny stories will not wash with anyone at the Preston gig. It was a drumstick – one that Johnny had thrown back into the crowd two minutes into the set. As for the blood and guts, I rang casualty and spoke to the nurse on admissions who told me a Mr Morrissey had been in, had no visible wound or bleeding and left a few minutes later."

An alternative explanation belatedly came from Marr, who insisted that tabloid reports branding The Smiths anti-royalists had encouraged some hotheads to attend the gig and vent their spleen. "Believe me, I was pretty scared," he noted. "I finished the song and got off. The whole incident was created by the gutter press but the fact that a Smiths gig could be so *ugly* left me incredibly depressed."

28 OCTOBER

The Smiths gig at the Astra Theatre, Llandudno, is cancelled as Morrissey returns to Manchester to lick his wounds. Interestingly, the Astra was one of only two gigs on the tour that did not sell out in advance.

30 OCTOBER

On the eve of Johnny Marr's 23rd birthday, The Smiths return home for a performance at the Free Trade Hall. Craig Gannon is no longer in a position to take part in any birthday celebrations. "The Manchester Free Trade Hall gig was the last gig I played with them," he reflects. "After the gig, when everyone had gone home, I felt quite a relief just being away from it. I didn't hear from anyone after that gig. It wasn't as if I'd fallen out with Johnny, so there was no reason why they couldn't tell me what was happening."

Set List: 'Ask'; 'The Queen Is Dead'; 'Panic'; 'How Soon Is Now?'; 'Vicar In A Tutu'; 'Rusholme Ruffians/(Marie's The Name) His Latest Flame (Medley)'; 'Frankly Mr Shankly'; 'The Boy With The Thorn In His Side'; 'There Is A Light That Never Goes Out'; 'Cemetry Gates'; 'Is It Really So Strange?'; 'What She Said/Rubber Ring (Medley)'; 'That Joke Isn't Funny Anymore'; 'London'; 'Meat Is Murder'; 'Still Ill'; 'The Draize Train'; 'I Know It's Over'; 'Bigmouth Strikes Again'.

NOVEMBER

Although it remains unannounced in the music press, The Smiths have decided to dispense with the services of Craig Gannon. "Craig wasn't terribly interested, in a nutshell," Morrissey muses. "We had to force him to turn up to studio work. We had to force him to come to rehearsals." Marr reiterates that contentious criticism. "Craig was lazy," he spitefully complains. "We could have picked a thousand people from our audience who would have made us feel that they were pleased to be in the group. Trying to have a conversation with Craig was impossible after five minutes. He had nothing to say and nothing to contribute. When he did come up with his own parts, others said it was like something I'd played on the last single. It wasn't exactly his own style. Musically, he fitted in in that respect, but he was a lazy bastard and that's all there is to it."

Others in The Smiths' camp argue that Gannon was merely diffident and that the songwriting duo unjustly misinterpreted his humility as apathy. "I've been accused by The Smiths of being too quiet in the studio and not coming up with ideas," Gannon reflects, "but, believe me, the atmosphere and the vibes going round were not very pleasurable. I'd sometimes walk into a room and everything would go silent. I may not have given much input after I put a couple of guitar tracks down but they never made me feel that I was in the situation where I could start taking control myself... I started to feel this was how The Smiths worked, so they can't slag me off for forcing me into that situation."

Whatever reservations Morrissey and Marr may have had about Gannon, the circumstances of his leaving were cruel, unfair and regrettable. He discovered his fate not from

Top: The new rockist audience attracted to Smiths gigs in 1986.

any of The Smiths, but through Gary Rostock, the drummer in Easterhouse. The news had already been passed on through Geoff Travis and Ivor Perry, who was stunned by the announcement. "To be told your own mate has been kicked out of The Smiths," Perry pauses, "and he doesn't even know. That was shocking. It was pretty callous."

Gannon had mixed feelings about his dismissal. "I received no notification from The Smiths or anyone connected with them," he points out. "When I first heard the news that I wasn't with them any more I did feel a big relief and glad in a way that it was all over, although I don't think I would have left them at that point. I felt relieved not to be with them but, at the same time, disappointed that it never did work out because I still had enormous respect for their music... They were all great musicians."

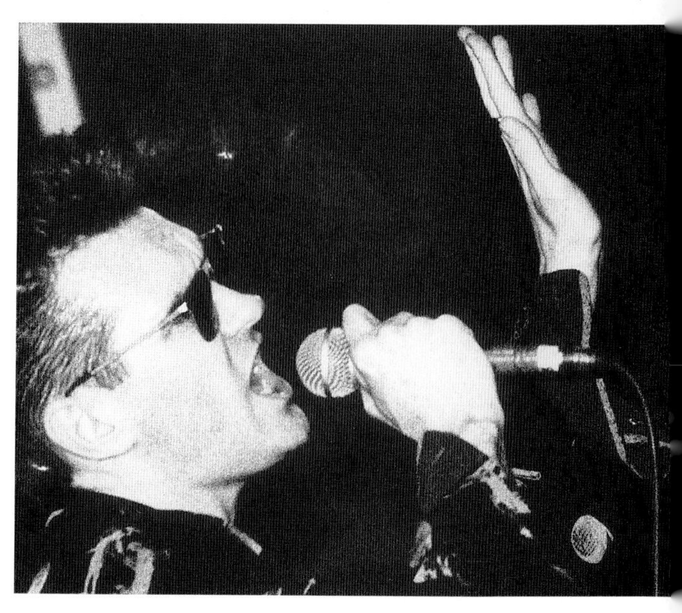

GANNON felt he was shoddily treated.

11-12 NOVEMBER

Marr is temporarily hospitalized after a near escape from death in a car crash. "I'd been out with Mike and his girlfriend," Marr recalls. "We'd had a lot of tequila and wine. He didn't live too far away, so I dropped him off. Then I got to literally 150 yards from my house. There's some lights stopping you from getting to the road and the road forks off one way. There was a cassette in the machine and it had gone round to the other side and, just as I was at the lights, the other side of the tape had started up, so I put my foot down and thought, 'Right, I'll take a two minute diversion around the block'. But I just put my foot right down and drove at this bend in the pouring rain at full speed as fast as the car would go. It went completely out of control and ended up bouncing off a couple of walls and into the middle of the road. I jumped out and saw that the car was completely crushed. I just couldn't believe I was still there." Marr literally ran home, falling over several times along the way. He was put to bed, but the following day awoke with shooting pains in his arms, fingers and neck. Part of his body had stiffened, so he was admitted to hospital and fitted with a neck brace and splints. Joyce later saw the car wreckage and was shocked. "It was like a concertina up to the windscreen," he exclaims. "One corner of the car had completely disappeared. I'm surprised the engine hadn't come through the front and removed his legs. Johnny was very lucky to keep his legs really."

> **'For the majority of the period I was with Johnnny, personally and conversationally, it was a disaster.'**
>
> CRAIG GANNON

13 NOVEMBER

Nick Kent receives a call from Rough Trade's Pat Bellis informing him of Marr's condition and adding that he wants to be interviewed. Pleased that his ostracism from Smithdom is over, Kent subsequently phones the guitarist at his home and catches up on the latest gossip. According to Johnny "The Smiths have really grown up" since their last confrontation with Kent and, having weathered the storm of Rourke's heroin battle, a lengthy US tour and a move to EMI, are now set for far greater heights. Kent is anxious to hear more and sets a tentative date for a formal interview. Alas, Marr has a change of heart and thwarts Kent's attempts to reach him by changing his phone number.

14 NOVEMBER

The Smiths' appearance in support of the Anti-Apartheid movement at the Royal Albert Hall alongside The Fall is cancelled due to Marr's injuries. Although the news is relayed on certain radio music programmes, many ticket holders, including myself, gather outside the venue in blissful ignorance. The shock news that Marr has been involved in a car crash is greeted with a mixture of sympathy and suspicion as the details have yet to appear in the press.

15 NOVEMBER

The Morrissey racial debate continues in the letters columns of the music press. Disgust at some of his asides has now worsened to a state of encroaching disenchantment among many "Hell hath no fury" Smiths' apostles. "A Disillusioned Ex-Smiths Fan" writes: "Before anyone says it, you cannot justify what he says just because he likes The Tams! (well, one of their records). Why has Johnny Marr, who listened to Motown and blues from an early age, allowed him to get away with it? Are the rest of The Smiths without a

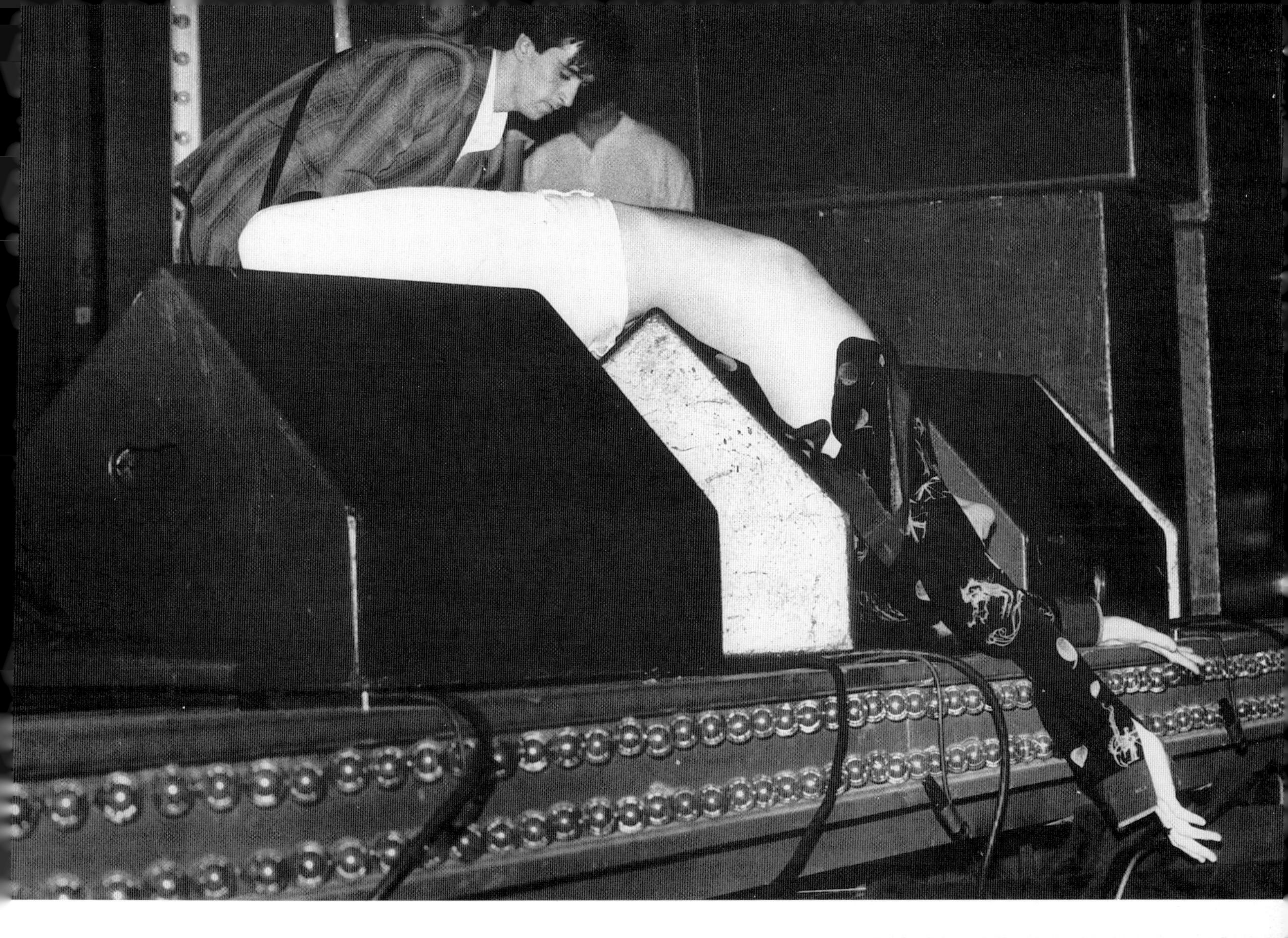

voice of their own? Smiths' fans think that Morrissey is OK because he gets off scot free and flaunts the powers that be. We've all heard of anarchy, but when they influence so many young people, isn't it time they started behaving more responsibly? Isn't it time Morrissey grew up and stopped being me me me all the time?... I used to trust them but because of their sheer greed (what makes you think they will sound any different on EMI?) they now have succeeded in wiping out their good names. They blamed Rough Trade for their mistakes, but they will never be able to pay them back enough. Think how Geoff Travis feels! He's been a bloody saint to them. Old fans are now treated with contempt because we've served our purpose and they now welcome the new generation of under twenties to pander to their egos."

22 NOVEMBER

Marr's car smash is reported in the music press. According to *NME*, Marr had been driving with his wife when the car hit a brick wall. This, however, is a red herring, deliberately put out to disguise the fact that Marr was driving alone, without a licence. The official line from Rough Trade in the aftermath of the accident is cautious optimism: "At this point, we don't really know how long Johnny will have to wear the brace. His injuries aren't terrible but they are painful. We don't want fans to get unduly worried about his condition, the doctors are very optimistic that his recovery will be speedy and complete." As a contingency plan, the postponed gig is rescheduled for December at the Brixton Academy.

MORRISSEY and Marr showing off at the London Palladium, 26 October 1986.

30 NOVEMBER

Morrissey appears on Manchester's Piccadilly Radio, where he is asked the pertinent question: "Could you see yourself writing songs with anyone other than Johnny Marr?" The singer's reply suggests that he has no sense of any impending rift in The Smiths' ranks. "Not really – I really don't think about that, it does not really seem necessary," he claims. "No, I'm perfectly happy; very, very happy... lots of groups go on for a very long time and

MARR at the Brixton Academy, 12 December 1986.

they can be quite useful and productive – and I think The Smiths will really. And that's not just ostentatious and blabbering – I really think they will."

6 DECEMBER

Hints that the racist inquisition may now be ending is indicated in a weary letter to *Melody Maker:* "I'm sick to death of reading about Morrissey's alleged racism. None of The Smiths are racist and I wish these ill-informed idiots would stop trying to smear them. It's so counter-productive."

12 DECEMBER

The rescheduled Anti-Apartheid Movement concert takes place at the Brixton Academy, London. Few who attended the concert would have guessed that this was to be the final Smiths' concert on UK soil. They will close their British concert career as a four-piece following the dramatic departure of Gannon. The venue is packed solid and, for those fans who feel they've seen it all before, there is the welcome attraction of two songs fresh to live performance, 'Shoplifters Of The World Unite' and 'Some Girls Are Bigger Than Others'. Morrissey's vocal inflexions are more eccentric than ever, never more so than on the medley 'London' / 'Miserable Lie'. 'This Night Has Opened My Eyes', played for the first time since November 1984, proves one of the surprise highlights. Perhaps it is mere nostalgia to see significance in the ordering of their set, but it is noticeable that they reach back to 'William, It Was Really Nothing' during the encore and then end the evening with 'Hand In Glove', the song that began their recording career on Rough Trade back in 1983.

ARTISTS AGAINST APARTHEID
AAA & LMS
Present THE SMITHS
And THE FALL
Live IN CONCERT
FOR THE ANTI-APARTHEID MOVEMENT
ROYAL ALBERT HALL
FRIDAY 14th NOVEMBER 8.30pm
Tickets: £8, £7, £6 and £5
Box office: Royal Albert Hall, Kensington Gore, SW7
Telephone 01 589 8212. Credit Card: 01 589 9465
And from usual agents

The music press regards this as merely another gig in the group's extensive itinerary, although the fact that it occurs near the end of the year and has a political link attracts additional attention. After all the racial debate in the letters columns of the music press, it is refreshing to see The Smiths actively supporting an Anti-Apartheid cause, indicating that actions can speak louder than flippant remarks in an interview. *Melody Maker*'s Simon Reynolds is pleased to see the group in a more positive light after all the recent bitterness. "Perhaps this Anti-Apartheid benefit will *finally* knock on the bonce the interminable 'Is Morrissey A

A FOUR-PIECE again, early December 1986.

Racist?' debate", he suggests. "Not that it isn't pertinent to talk about the gulf, the antipathy even, between indiepop and black pop. But the irony is that it's precisely the indie fans most estranged from black culture who are most likely to be anti-racist and politically committed. This was an anti-apartheid concert with a near-total absence of black faces in the audience... Smiths' music is about as albino you can get this side of The Fall – an amalgam of rockabilly, 'Jeepster'-ish chords and folk rock, low on sensuality, high on yearning. R&B is a remote, fourth-hand trance". Having observed the conflict between The Smiths' inherent traditionalism and potent radicalism, Reynolds concludes perceptively: "Perhaps for things to really change we'd have to allow a woman to be an equivalent seer figure. For now, The Smiths are still the greatest *rock* group on the planet."

New musical genres are also on the mind of the *NME*, which vaguely attempts to place The Smiths in the vanguard of an Eighties-styled folk movement. "Despite the almost excessive claustrophobia of these Smiths Events, Morrissey and his flock's concerns are still sufficiently broad and communicative for this music to deserve a freshly relevant 'folk' tag," suggests Donald McRae. "The Smiths' celebratory angst might seem to ignore the existence of any life outside white England but from such insularity comes a heightened bond of shared feeling. Even to the outsider, the Academy's massed refrain of line after line of 'England is mine and it owes me a living' type lyricism emerges with the resonance that can only swell out of some emotively communal experience... The Smiths will always retain a purity and pertinence which prevents them from being just another common pop phenomenon."

Set List: 'Ask'; 'Bigmouth Strikes Again'; 'London'; 'Miserable Lie'; 'Some Girls Are Bigger Than Others'; 'The Boy With The Thorn In His Side'; 'Shoplifters Of The World Unite'; 'There Is A Light That Never Goes Out'; 'Is It Really So Strange?'; 'Cemetry Gates'; 'This Night Has Opened My Eyes'; 'Still Ill'; 'Panic'; 'The Queen Is Dead'; 'William, It Was Really Nothing'; 'Hand In Glove'.

17 DECEMBER

Radio 1 broadcasts the final John Peel session, produced by John Porter , featuring 'Is It Really So Strange?', 'London', 'Half A Person' and 'Sweet And Tender Hooligan'.

20 DECEMBER

In the wake of the Brixton gig, the music press belatedly learn that Craig Gannon, at 20, is now an ex-member of four major groups. Although he tries to underplay his sacking by insisting that he has left to form a new group, Rough Trade confirm that he has been fired. Pat Bellis provides the party line: "He hasn't really been doing much with the group, like rehearsing or recording. His involvement, recording wise, has hardly been anything at all. He just didn't seem very interested and there were times when he didn't turn up for rehearsals". Responding to this at the time, Gannon concedes that it was his lifestyle that may have contributed to his fall. "I knew they weren't happy over the past four months with me, personally," he states. "I just got that impression and that's one of the reasons I left. I think they thought I was a bit too wild as well, drinking. They all do it, but I just do it more."

MORRISSEY makes sure of his post-gig order at the bar.

27 DECEMBER

The *Melody Maker*'s Writers' Poll underlines The Smiths' fall from grace among the hacks of the day. 'Panic' is voted eighth best single, while the supposedly classic *The Queen Is Dead*, barely beats The The's *Infected* for sixth position. The Top Five makes interesting retrospective reading: *Licensed To Ill* (Beastie Boys), *Parade* (Prince), *Blood And Chocolate* (Elvis Costello), *Throwing Muses* (Throwing Muses) and *King Of America* (The Costello Show).

That same week *NME* publishes its Vinyl Finals, a list that reflects the staff's interest in dance music. Intriguingly, The Smiths fare even worse here than in the *MM*'s Writers' Poll. 'Panic' is voted 22nd best single (one place below The The's 'Sweet Bird Of Truth'), while 'Ask' crawls in at number 29. *The Queen Is Dead* barely scrapes into the Top 10 albums of the year. Those works considered superior comprise: 1. *Rapture* (Anita Baker), 2. *Control* (Janet Jackson), 3. *Evol* (Sonic Youth), 4. *Word Up* (Cameo), 5. *Graceland* (Paul Simon), 6. *Bend Sinister* (Fall) and 7. *Raisin' Hell* (Run DMC). The startling disparity between the writers' preferences and their readers' tastes will not be revealed until the readers' poll in the New Year.

NME's editor Ian Pye attempts an overview on The Smiths, looking back at the events of the previous 12 months. "Morrissey's dislike of modern music virtually led to him being branded a racist," he notes, "something of which I am sure he is not guilty. It was all reminiscent of Lennon's 'The Beatles are bigger than God' – at least Morrissey could claim divine right. For me, it was something else that let The Smiths fall from grace. Something almost indefinable but there nevertheless, looming nastily in the background. Nostalgia clung like a worry blanket, the fervent Sixties orthodoxy, the tangible fear of the future. It culminated with the addition of a Smiths drug habit, an extra guitarist, and Johnny Marr coming on like Keith Richard. God forbid. The Smiths were mutating into The Rolling Stones."

In their annual round-up, *Melody Maker* adopt the guise of fortune tellers and present the Mancunians with a New Year's message: "The Smiths are bigger than ever. 1987 should see whether they can manage to combine their stature with being a mischievous and volatile pop presence."

Nobody even considers the possibility that The Smiths may no longer exist one year hence.

'Whenever anyone got close to Johnny they had to leave. I think maybe that all got to Johnny and he had enough.'

ANDY ROURKE

CHAPTER SIX

I Won't Share You

AFTER THE RIGOURS OF THE previous year, The Smiths began 1987 seemingly intent on consolidating their reputation as the UK's most important group. Instead, the attempt at reconstruction became the act of falling apart. The demise of the group was a sad tale, full of disillusionment, poor communication and comic confusion. At the heart of the drama was Johnny Marr, increasingly frustrated with his role in the group and weary of Morrissey's selfishness, musical insularity and possessiveness.

Nevertheless, the prospects seemed promising when the group entered the studios in February to record their new album. The old camaraderie was rekindled during the sessions, which progressed relatively smoothly. Outside the studio, however, familiar problems reasserted themselves. Legal disputes, which should have been promptly and effortlessly resolved, dragged on. The latest litigant was Craig Gannon, claiming monies from the US tour and disputing the authorship of the group's hit 'Ask'. Morrissey and Marr resisted the claim, but they were hardly a unified team in their business dealings. New manager Ken Friedman fared little better than his many predecessors in winning their complete trust. While Marr was more than happy to trust his advisor with his career, Morrissey declined to surrender the management reins. Anyone who came between him and Marr was ultimately perceived as a threat rather than an ally. The other Smiths listened to the playback of a new song, 'I Won't Share You' and pondered its implications. "I always felt that was obviously about Johnny," Rourke recalls. "But who he wouldn't share him with, I don't know... Whenever anyone got close to Johnny they had to leave. I think maybe all that got to Johnny and he had enough." Certainly, Marr was annoyed by the never-ending business hassles and suffocated by his partner's intensity, particularly regarding the Smiths. "I think Morrissey was very *fascinated with Johnny," Rourke says of the hero-worshipping singer. At one time, Marr remembers "counting his blessings" at having found such a close friend and musical ally, but after five years of plotting and scheming The Smiths' career, the adventure was no longer enjoyable. As Marr later admitted: "Ultimately, I was giving every single second of my life to somebody else. I started to feel very unnatural and very abnormal". An additional worry was the degree of scrutiny that The Smiths suffered and the pressures placed upon them to submit to a pre-packaged set of values and musical influences. In interviews Marr sounded almost apologetic about his "rock 'n' roll lifestyle" and later suggested that he felt himself stuck in a musical cul-de-sac. At least the successful recording of the new album,* Strangeways, Here We Come, *suggested that the musical links were still intact, but as the months passed, they too would diminish.*

Marr's eagerness to tour and promote The Smiths in a professional manner was a logical ambition after more than half a decade in the music business. The group had never previously failed to exploit a major new release and it was anticipated that they would take to the road after the autumn release of Strangeways. *Morrissey, however, was no longer merely vacillating, but seemed venomously resistant to any major tour. In various*

MARR QUITS

SMITHS SPLIT – A SECOND EXCLUSIVE...

MARR SPEAKS

TOP: A flurry of press coverage followed Marr's departure.

ABOVE: John Porter, long term Smiths producer.

interviews, he insisted that he did not want The Smiths to become world renowned superstars. "I don't want The Smiths to become a huge untouchable mega-group," he insisted. "I don't want that to happen. And it could happen. I'd rather just make the records and go home." On other occasions he suggested that The Smiths might never tour again. I believe Morrissey was sincere in these objections, although more cynical commentators might argue that these were further mind games, possibly directed against Marr's tour-minded manager. At least Morrissey was pinning his faith in The Smiths' recorded output and although he hinted at changes ahead, there was no doubting his continued belief in the group's importance.

The release of the compilation The World Won't Listen *was a timely reminder of what made The Smiths special. Although they appeared to the public like a big time rock group heading for major label success and Stateside stadia tours, they were still at heart The Smiths. Their love of true pop and continued belief in the power of the single was manifested in the new collection and its US cousin* Louder Than Bombs. *In both, The Smiths stood as guardians of the old tradition, and invited listeners to remember the hits and sample a secret world of flip sides, whose quality frequently surprised, and often astonished.*

A STRAINED final year for The Smiths saw Marr at the end of his patience.

By May, the rift between Morrissey and Marr had grown to a chasm. The threads of musical companionship remaining on Strangeways *were now cruelly exposed as chimerical. Marr had grown weary of the element of Sixties whimsy associated with the group and the musical straitjacket in which they had bound themselves. His renewed interest in dance music and the burgeoning club scene in Manchester seemed increasingly at odds with Morrissey's embarrassingly kitsch icons. As Marr told Manchester DJ Dave Haslam, "Towards the end of The Smiths, I realized that the records I was listening to with my friends were more exciting than the records I was listening to with the group. Sometimes it came down to Sly Stone versus Herman's Hermits. And I know which side I was on."*

The silent conflict between the parties reached an unexpected head at the final Streatham sessions, just days before Morrissey's 28th birthday. The last straw for Marr was finding himself working on a remake of Cilla Black's 'Work Is A Four Letter Word'. "I didn't form a group to perform Cilla Black records," he curtly informed me. Indeed, Marr did not even wish to attend the session, feeling that the group deserved a break after already recording an entire album.

The culmination of all of the above, combined with the belief that The Smiths were in danger of becoming a hoary old rock institution, convinced Marr that enough was enough. He called a group meeting at a Kensington fish restaurant and informed Rourke and Joyce that he was considering leaving The Smiths. Morrissey was also informed of Marr's discontent but nothing more was said. The guitarist took off for a holiday in Los Angeles and, coincidentally, Morrissey followed soon afterwards, but the two never met.

IVOR PERRY and Craig Gannon.

Back in England, rumours of dissension in The Smiths' camp were spreading throughout Manchester. It was not until late July that they reached the London music press and were translated into gossipy speculation about the nature of the split. At that point nothing had yet been officially confirmed, despite the obvious rift. Marr then returned from holiday to be confronted with a "Smiths Split" story in the NME. *He jumped to the rash conclusion that the tale bore the Machiavellian mark of Morrissey. Convinced that he was being "blackmailed" into denying the split and thereby forced back into the fold, he characteristically rebelled and confirmed his departure. Up until I spoke to him in 1991, Marr still maintained that Morrissey had planted the split story through some labyrinthine means. On this occasion, however, the singer seemed genuinely innocent of any mind games and was totally bemused by the rapid series of events.*

There followed the rather pathetic spectacle of the remaining Smiths clinging to the wreckage and attempting to continue without their musical director. By late August, Morrissey realized the futility of maintaining The Smiths without Marr and, after receiving some tapes from Stephen Street, elected to draw a veil over the proceedings and embark on a solo career. After weeks of drama and uncertainty, The Smiths' story had reached its final page.

'It was utter misery...The group were falling to pieces...It was total madness... Everybody was losing it...'

THE SMITHS recall their final recording session

In the wake of The Smiths break-up, Strangeways, Here We Come *received rapturous reviews, as did the live set* Rank, *released the following year. The live album featured the group that had been criticized for "rocking out" at the time of recording the Kilburn concert... now, people wished they were still rocking. Instead, they became something of a legal phenomenon along the lines of Jarndyce v. Jarndyce. Gannon, Joyce and Rourke were each suing The Smiths' partnership, an inevitable fall out given the group's abysmal business affairs. Morrissey's novel answer to litigation was to round up all his adversaries for a grand farewell at the Wolverhampton Civic Hall, a short concert that also served as his first post-Smiths performing venture.*

The aggrieved litigants met with mixed fortunes. Rourke gave up after two years' struggle during which he had been reduced to claiming income support. He took what was on offer, got married and attempted to forget the financial arguments. Gannon, with much less to gain and lose, persevered and secured a late but welcome settlement of £44,000. Throughout all this, Morrissey and Marr were still estranged and out of contact. The guitarist conceded that the friendship had ended with the dissolution of the group and added: "There's nothing uniting us now except memories of the old days. We don't want to work together." Morrissey, by contrast, prayed for a reunion and reconciliation before finally accepting that it was over for ever. Admitting he was still bitter, he slumped into a kind of maudlin fatalism, insisting: "I know we will never see each other again".

Five years passed before Morrissey and Marr did see each other again, and with good reason. The indomitable Joyce had continued to pursue his action with vigour and as each month passed the Holy Grail of the High Court drew closer. A backlog of royalties, swelled by compound interest, awaited the victors. With The Smiths' catalogue increasing in value following the reissue agreement with WEA, Joyce's 25 per cent claim was something that Morrissey/Marr could no longer afford to ignore. Communication lines were reopened. The drama was heightened when Andy Rourke returned to the fray. In the aftermath of The Severed Alliance, *he decided to reopen the case, arguing that he had signed away his original claim under duress. "More and more I've grown up and thought about it and it's out of order," Rourke insists. "I can't live with it. It needs sorting out. It's just something that as I get older I can't live with... Maybe it was Morrissey's idea, but Johnny went along with it... It's all right blaming it on Moz, but Johnny's made fortunes from it. Me and Mike never begrudged them the publishing... We at least deserved a quarter of the performing royalties." With the influx of income that will emerge from The Smiths' back catalogue, the songwriting duo seemed poised to become more financially secure than ever. "They'll be laughing!" Rourke quips. "But, hopefully, when this court case comes up it'll wipe the smile off their faces a bit." Morrissey and Marr, meanwhile, grew closer and the guitarist privately revealed to friends that they were working together. The details of the alleged reunion were not published or confirmed by either Morrissey or Marr. It still seems unlikely that the pair will ever be reunited as of old, but in the High Court the old partnership could well enjoy one final turn.*

PORTRAIT of the artist as a glam-rock ghoul.

MORRISSEY poses beside the poster for 'Shoplifters Of The World Unite.'

JANUARY
The Smiths begin the year with a new manager, Ken Friedman. The American has previously represented Simple Minds and UB40 and quickly establishes himself as a plausible character capable of overseeing the group in the next phase of their career. "Ken was younger and hipper than anyone else who tried to manage them," recalls Grant Showbiz. "You could hang out with him. He'd been around and was pretty cool." Friedman's personable character also captures the loyalty of Marr, but Morrissey appears more ambivalent in his response. Although he initially favours Friedman, the relationship between the two becomes increasingly distant during the next couple of months.

3 JANUARY
The Gannon departure continues to pick up belated press coverage with the official line now suggesting that it was a "mutual decision". That euphemism is immediately exploded by Rough Trade's simultaneous comment on the guitarist's final days in the group: "They basically felt that he wasn't particularly interested and towards the end he was not even turning up for rehearsals. One week they were meant to be on *Top Of The Pops* and he just wasn't around, he disappeared. That was the final straw." Characteristically, Gannon declines to respond to this latest accusation. Six years on, he reflects: "I was at every rehearsal that The Smiths did while I was with them and to say I missed any is rubbish... One report stated that the final straw for my future in The Smiths was when they were supposed to do a *Top Of The Pops* and they couldn't find me. There was no way they *couldn't* find me, if anyone had tried to get in touch with me. They would have done the gig anyway, even if they couldn't find me."

26 JANUARY
The new single, 'Shoplifters Of The World Unite', is dedicated to Ruth Polsky, the group's American booking agent, "48-hour" manager, and recent fatal victim of a bizarre road accident in New York. *NME* greets the release with a discernible lack of enthusiasm: "This record might be the stuff of tragicomedy, but the funereal tone with cumbersome guitars and world-weary singing kills any irony that may be hidden in the lyrics." Morrissey seems equally world weary, and when asked about the meaning of the song responds: "Every time we slap anything on to vinyl, one way or another, I have to give this great Biblical sermon about 'Shoplifters Of The World Unite' and how it's immediately connected with a Colombian cocaine ring, or something."

27 JANUARY
The Smiths perform 'Shoplifters Of The World Unite' on *Top Of The Pops* in one of their best television appearances. Morrissey sports an Elvis Presley T-shirt, while Marr resembles a rock god of the Fifties. Although the single is less catchy than most of its predecessors, it still manages to reach number 12, a sure sign of the group's high commercial standing.

7 FEBRUARY
Hundreds of "faulty" copies of 'Shoplifters Of The World Unite' have been shipped out to record shops as a result of "a mistake at the pressing plant". In place of the A-side, listeners are greeted with the still unreleased 'You Just Haven't Earned It Yet, Baby', a previous contender as the new single. According to Rough Trade a clerical error resulted in the wrong stamper being used on several batches of pressings. "The mistake has nothing to do with the record company", Rough Trade insist. "Without apportioning blame, there was a mistake at the pressing plant and we

only knew about it when a couple of shops rang us." Morrissey, who has already insisted that the track be included on The Smiths' forthcoming compilation, is naturally sceptical about Rough Trade's explanation. "I'm very intrigued," he smiles. "I do smell a rat somewhere because suddenly these mispressings are available in massive quantities. I did hear someone in the hallway of Rough Trade talking about, 'Anything to get the single up the charts'. But I find it depressing and if it was a mistake I feel surely the records can be grasped and destroyed." Travis's staff duly insist that they are carrying out their resident star's wishes. "We're now checking every copy as it leaves the factory. Anyone with a faulty copy can either go back to the shop or contact Rough Trade," they say. Whether anyone was foolish enough to surrender this collector's item remains undisclosed.

WHILE THE 'SHOPLIFTERS' STORM IN A TEACUP continues, The Smiths undertake what is to be their final performance at the San Remo Festival in Italy. Playing before a massive television audience, the group find themselves in the company of a veritable *Who's Who* of UK pop, including Spandau Ballet, The Pet Shop Boys, Paul Young and The Style Council. Despite a dispute about appearing on a revolving stage, The Smiths finally bow to the dictates of Continental television. Although Morrissey betrays some shyness in the company of the pop élite, he manages to strike up a friendly conversation with Patsy Kensit. Marr, meanwhile, is much more sociable, a trait encouraged by new manager Ken Friedman. "The Smiths would go and do television shows and there'd be six other groups there," Friedman points out. "In the past, they'd go into the dressing room with the door locked and nobody would wander in and say hello or have a beer. I've been in the business for a long time and I'm very sociable and I know a lot of people." While the ligging continues around them, it is left to the roguish Rourke to play the Joker in the pack, by making fun of a fellow pop star. "We went out to a disco one night and Spandau Ballet were there," he recalls. "I was really drunk and I went up to Steve Norman and I was calling him 'Plonker'. That was his nickname in the *NME*. I was calling him Plonker Norman and he got pretty upset. That was when we were all drinking a lot and doing a lot of other things to excess."

Set List: 'Shoplifters Of The World Unite'; 'There Is A Light That Never Goes Out'; 'The Boy With The Thorn In His Side'; 'Panic'; 'Ask'.

11 FEBRUARY

Morrissey and Marr are in Dublin, where they undertake some promotion. Morrissey makes a surprise appearance on Dave Fanning's show on RTE and speaks confidently about the future of the group: "The last stretch has been the best time in every way recording wise, and we do feel a great sense of power, which is good." Looking back over last year's battle with Rough Trade, Morrissey expresses relief that The Smiths have survived and thrived. "It was personally so damaging and awful in every way," he laments, "that it would have crushed a less resilient group. But the fact that we came through it quite proudly and then had a good stretch towards the end of the year was a great triumph."

13 FEBRUARY

The Smiths appear on RTE's *Megamix* performing 'Shoplifters Of The World Unite', which has recently jumped to number 7 in the Irish charts.

14 FEBRUARY

A Valentine's Day bonanza for *NME* readers who tuck into Danny Kelly's revealing interview with Johnny Marr. Topics covered include the gruelling 1986 American tour ("I was doing a bottle of Remy Martin each evening"), Smiths fans' anguish over the EMI signing ("I'd have thought they'd be more concerned with a record's grooves than its label"), crowd violence, the rise and fall of Gannon, and Rourke's rehabilitation ("Andy's fine now. I guess something positive has come out of it... We found we really missed him and he discovered how important he is").

In addition to the Kelly interview, the paper prints the results of the annual readers' poll. What is most noticeable is the stark contrast between its contents and that of the recent *NME* writers' poll. The latter was dominated by dance records and black artistes, but this latest reader response shows an overwhelming preference for white indie pop. The Smiths are at last in a position where all effective opposition has been vanquished. After years of fighting it out with such major rivals as Echo And The Bunnymen, Frankie Goes To Hollywood, The Jesus And Mary Chain and Paul Weller, the Mancunians at last find themselves ruling the roost.

The Smiths effortlessly win the best group section from The Housemartins, while *The Queen Is Dead* triumphs over *London 0, Hull 4*. Marr is confident enough to laugh off the twin threat posed by the modestly unambitious runners-up. "I couldn't acknowledge The Housemartins without a smile on my face," he crows. "And if they really are our closest rivals, it's no wonder I'm so confident about The Smiths". The remainder of the poll testifies to his confidence. 'Panic' not only secures the best single award but even flies in the face of hip hop hypocrisy by appearing as sixth best dance single. Morrissey predictably emerges as top male singer and Most Wonderful Human Being and finishes third favourite sex symbol behind Joanne Whalley and Madonna.

28 FEBRUARY

The *NME* writers choose their all-time Top 150 singles. The last time such a poll was conducted the award went to Bob Dylan's 'Like A Rolling Stone', with The Beatles' 'Penny Lane'/'Strawberry Fields Forever' in second place. In the present climate of black music revisionism, however, such pop/rock classics are replaced by the less ambitious anthem 'I Say A Little Prayer' (Aretha Franklin) and 'Tired Of Being Alone' (Al Green). In the circumstances, The Smiths can expect no better than two entries: 'This Charming Man' (22nd) and 'How Soon Is Now?' (66th).

On the same day, the paper reviews the new Smiths compilation, *The World Won't Listen*. Manchester based Dave Haslam pens a sensitive and perceptive appreciation in which he concludes: "In their finest moments, The Smiths make music that tugs on your memory and gives you great hope; the last Romantics, they provoke a more direct emotional response than any other band in the world." By contrast *Melody Maker* print an even longer review in which The Smiths' arch enemy Steve Sutherland is given leave to condemn Morrissey as a complete charlatan: "From the Moors Murders scandal early in their career, to the statements supporting the Brighton bombers, to the brief flirtation with the sensual, to the recent reclusive, bemused intellectual, it's apparent that Morrissey will stop at nothing to manufacture confrontations with the norm in order that The Smiths remain special." After dismissing the contents of this extremely good, value for money, compilation, Sutherland cynically reduces the entire exercise to a calculated marketing ploy. "All the classic Morrissey manoeuvres are brought into play here," he claims. "The rumours (denied) that this LP is a way of hastening out of the Rough Trade contract (scandal!), the title with its implications of reaching a wider audience (Messianic!), the cover, a dated paean to teenage delinquency (self-parody!) – yet pull all that away and it's you, the Smiths' fan, who Morrissey's mocking. A career in outrage is a fine place to be but some jokes just aren't funny anymore."

MARCH

Work is already underway on The Smiths' next album. The sessions take place at the Wool Hall, Bath, and among those in attendance at the studio is manager Ken Friedman.

SALFORD Lads Club revisited, 1987.

"You could tell that Morrissey didn't want him around," Stephen Street recalls, "but Johnny was insisting that Ken stayed and started sorting out some of the business affairs." Although Friedman attempts to ingratiate himself with Morrissey and encourages him to act more responsibly, the results prove comically ineffective. "I didn't like Johnny bringing strangers into the studio," Morrissey complains. "He allowed anybody in, he was very free with people which I didn't agree with. I wished to preserve our intimacy... The fact that I rejected his friends implied that I was boring and hated the human race." Marr maintains that Morrissey's rejection of Friedman was not an insurmountable obstacle, but adamantly refuses to return to the chaos that had surrounded The Smiths during previous years. "It just seemed that it was never ending," he laments.

Some of the tensions, both financial and musical, are manifested during the first evening's rehearsal from which Morrissey is conspicuously absent. Marr, already weary of the group's reputation as an indie jingle jangle outfit, seems anxious to break new musical ground. His feelings of frustration reveal themselves in an amusing drunken diatribe. "The first night in the studio they all got a bit drunk," Street explains. "I can remember bashing away at a DX7 synth keyboard and the drums and bass were playing at the same time. Johnny was really out of it. As he admitted during the US tour, he'd taken a little liking for brandy and was getting a bit out of order. I can remember him shouting, 'Here, Streety, you don't like this, do you? You want us to sound jingle-jangly, like the good old Smiths days'. You could tell there was tension there. It was definitely, 'You don't like it do you? We're going to do this!' There was no holding it together. It was like a dirge. You really felt Johnny was pent-up. At this point, he fell on his back and the keyboard went crashing to the ground. I was sitting there trying to keep cool and telling myself: 'It's going to be OK. It's the first night in the studio and they've got to leave a bit of tension out. When Morrissey gets in tomorrow, we'll start doing it'. But it was a bit strange."

Following Morrissey's arrival, the recordings proceed relatively smoothly and throughout the spring, The Smiths rediscover some of their old camaraderie while working together in the studio. "There was no musical tension," Street is quick to point out. "Johnny and Morrissey were fine in that respect. *Strangeways* was a great session. We had a really happy time and it was party night most nights."

"The sessions were positive," Mike Joyce reiterates. "We were all getting out of it with the ales. Things were getting quite crazy at times, but that was the beauty of The Smiths – the craziness. A lot of people didn't realize how barmy it got." Despite the excesses, there is none of the drama that featured earlier in the group's career, for Rourke is now a reformed character. "Andy was fine on that session," Street notes. "He seemed to be a little more sprightly. They were happy and having a great laugh. It wasn't bad at all. They got on fine. It was only the Ken Friedman factor in the background and the fact that Morrissey didn't want him to be manager and Johnny did. Johnny said, 'I'm not going to stand down' because up until then he always had. I think Johnny felt a slight regret at what they'd done to people who'd tried to manage them. He felt a loyalty to Ken, which was understandable."

On reflection, Street could only recall one instance when the underlying conflict between the songwriting partners produced a moment of unease. "It was when we recorded 'I Started Something I Couldn't Finish'," he remembers. "Johnny and I had been working on a guitar line all afternoon and got something that we felt had a strong glam rock feel like T. Rex. Morrissey came over to listen to it and said, 'I don't like it'. Johnny wasn't in the room, so I had to go back over to him in the cottage. I said to him, 'Morrissey doesn't like it'. So Johnny said, 'Well, let Morrissey fuckin' think of something'. I thought, 'Hold on a minute! This is the first time!' Normally, Johnny would say, 'OK, I'll have a chat with him and sort it out, but instead it was 'Let Morrissey think of something'. Johnny was fed-up always being relied upon to come up with something all the time and no-one actually telling him what they wanted. Morrissey would just say 'yes' or 'no'. He couldn't say, 'I'd like to do *this* because he doesn't have a musical background. He knows what he likes – that's the main thing with Morrissey."

Although the sessions are briefly interrupted when Morrissey returns to Manchester in search of inspiration, the album is completed fairly quickly and the quartet feel both confident and positive about the work they have produced. As Marr concludes: "We had a good time recording, and I was unhappy before that and I was unhappy after that." In fact, *Strangeways* represented the group's final act of old style gang unity.

> **'Johnny was pent-up. At this point, he fell on his back and the keyboard went crashing to the ground. I was sitting there trying to keep cool.'**
>
> **STEPHEN STREET**

12 MARCH

One month after Morrissey and Marr's return from Dublin, *Hot Press* print their insightful interview with Johnny Marr. The guitarist discusses his passing criminality as a youth, the Rough Trade defection, the Rourke rehabilitation, fans, finances and fame. The recent Gannon sacking is underplayed, although Marr explains the reasoning behind his induction to the group. "I had hoped that it would take some of the pressure off me onstage and lead me into new areas of writing, which it did to a certain extent but I felt that I began to get very complacent in my guitar-playing and that's why we asked Craig to leave. There was no kind of animosity at all because we're still friends with him but it was just that his presence didn't do anything dramatic for the group creatively so we asked him to go."

LATE MARCH

The Gannon problem refuses to go away.

MARR began to show some of the tension he was feeling on the first night of the 'Strangeways' sessions.

MORRISSEY in 1987, unaware that he will shortly be solo.

Correspondence and legal intervention follow as the guitarist attempts to secure outstanding payments for monies allegedly promised on the US tour. The guitarist is also claiming compensation for his contribution to the song 'Ask', a demand contested by Johnny Marr. "We didn't expect it," Marr admits. "He played on the record and should have been paid. Simple as that. Because he asked for more, everything became a court case. And there was the US tour. Again, if we could have got our heads together, he could have been paid and we wouldn't have felt taken advantage of. The fact that we wanted to pay him what he agreed wasn't at issue. The issue was that he was saying we'd agreed on more. He said that we'd agreed to pay him some ridiculous fee that we'd never pay anybody."

Gannon insists that he is in the right and, backed by Legal Aid, continues his claim. After some initial assistance from John Barratt, Gannon's father takes up the fight and is asked what Craig wants from the case. "What he wants is what he earned," he replies. "Nothing more. Nothing less. He wants what he was promised and what he should have earned." There is a glimmer of hope that the group may settle and Friedman briefly enters negotiations with Gannon's garrulous manager John Barratt. However, the monies on offer are considered derisory by the Gannon camp and the suit continues. It will be almost six years before the former Smiths guitarist finally secures an out of court settlement of £44,000.

APRIL

Nick Kent presents a recent overview of The Smiths in *The Face*. Instinctively, he senses the central conflict between Morrissey and Marr concerning career direction. "To Marr the crusade is simple," he points out. "The Smiths, the great white hope of the Eighties, deserve to be more than a cottage industry." But will Morrissey agree? Kent clearly has his doubts: "Smithdom in many respects is his version of Ambrosia, the fantasy land Billy Liar inhabited. It has given him a place to live out his adolescence, given him the frame he so craved yet which hasn't made him contented. Faced by the pressure of success, he has often buckled and vacillated endlessly in matters of life as it is lived." The scepticism concerning Morrissey is not without foundation. In contemporary interviews, he already seems to be moving away from any dreams of world domination through touring or recording. "I don't want to venture beyond the garden gate," he tells the world.

1-4 APRIL

The Smiths' three-day video shoot in Battersea for their new single is rendered a fiasco when Morrissey goes AWOL. Camera crews, lighting technicians and make-up artists await developments, but all to no avail. The promo, mainly intended for the US market, is unceremoniously cancelled. Morrissey's reasoning, as usual, remains unexplained. His non-appearance may be the result of a bad cold, a personal protest against videos, a sneak attack on new manger Ken Friedman, or simply sheer wilfulness. "Ken had organized that video at great expense," Marr recalls. "That was the great breaking point between those two." Friedman also believes the incident may have represented the beginning of the end for the Morrissey/Marr relationship. Back at London's Portobello Hotel the manager looks at Marr and, seeing his weary resignation, concludes that the group are on the brink of breaking-up.

10 APRIL

The Smiths return to *The Tube* to promote 'Sheila Take A Bow' and 'Shoplifters Of The World Unite'.

13 APRIL

'Sheila Take A Bow' is issued and soon becomes The Smiths' most successful chart hit. Although dismissed by some critics for its simplicity, the track is an engagingly commercial offering, with an enthusiastic oompah glam sound, anticipating Morrissey's work on *Your Arsenal*, years hence. One person who does not appreciate the single is the group's erstwhile producer, John Porter, who is appalled to discover that the track has been remixed without his consent or knowledge. "The first thing I knew it was out and it sounded slightly different," he remembers. "When I saw the record it said 'Produced by Stephen Street'. They had gone in with Stephen Street, done the track again, but sampled guitars off the original and put them on this new one without mentioning it to me, asking me, giving me a credit, paying me, or doing anything. That was the last I ever had to do with The Smiths. I never said anything to anybody, but I thought, 'If that's what it's down to. You didn't even ask me'... The original 'Sheila Take A Bow' was just as good as the one they put out. It was just Morrissey trying to prove a point – that they didn't need me."

While Porter felt ostracized by Morrissey, Street maintained a positive relationship with the singer and regarded the "Sheila episode" as an unfortunate accident. "The guys had done the track and it was felt by everyone that it wasn't quite up to scratch and would I like to have a go at recording it, " he recalls. "We did 'Sheila Take A Bow' and 'Girlfriend In A Coma' in February, and it was a very good session. With 'Sheila Take A Bow', we were running a bit short of time and there was a guitar line that Johnny had on the last session with John and he couldn't quite remember who it was that did it, so he said, 'Let's just sample it and put it in'. I think it was a slide bit. This was the episode that John Porter complained about... someone sampling his production work. At the time, I didn't think much about it. I thought it was one of Johnny's guitar lines and if he wanted to put it on the track, fine. It would save a bit of time."

24 APRIL

'Sheila Take A Bow' enters the charts at number 13. The Smiths duly play *Top Of The Pops,* with Morrissey posing exquisitely, while Marr swans around in a beret looking the cool dude. The following week the single peaks at number 10.

MAY

A torturous month for Johnny Marr, who is clearly at the end of his tether. Eager to take a therapeutic break from The Smiths, he is infuriated by Morrissey's insistence that they return to the studio to record some B-sides for the next single. A session at the Wool Hall is scheduled, then cancelled, so the group decide to complete this commitment at the home studio owned by Grant Showbiz and Fred Hood. With the pressure mounting, Marr visits Morrissey and expresses his doubts about the future of the group. There is a subsequent meeting at Geales Fish Restaurant in Kensington where Marr tells Joyce and Rourke that he is intending to leave the group. "Johnny wanted some time," Joyce reflects. "I remember him saying, 'That's it – I don't really want to do it any more'. We felt, 'Surely not. What do you mean you don't want it any more?' It was more of a shock saying that than if it had happened gradually. If we'd recorded another album and things had slowly ground to a halt then it would have been easier to come to terms with. But he was saying, 'I've had enough. I don't want to carry on'. I thought he really meant it, that's why I wanted to sort it out there and then. I thought, 'As soon as we leave this, that's it really'. I remember saying, 'Maybe we should do another album'. That was the obvious thing to say. I was in a state of shock."

DISPLAYING a New York Dolls T-shirt, 1987.

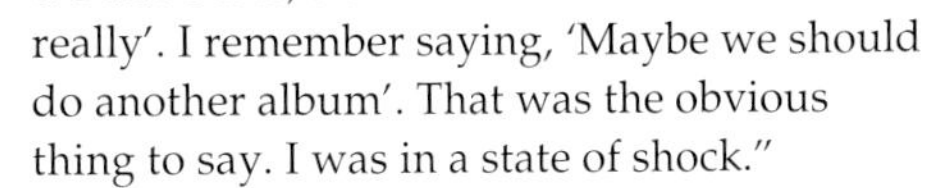

SMITHS in snowy Salford, 1987.

9 MAY

Johnny Marr is featured on Australian television in an interview recorded at Bath during the *Strangeways* sessions. The programme also features various Smiths' promos. During the same period, Morrissey is featured on the American programme *Addicted To Style,* on which he holds forth on the subject of favourite shirts.

19 MAY

Five years after Marr's appearance at 384 King's Road, The Smiths are completing work on the last track they will ever record. 'I Keep Mine Hidden' betrays the influence of George Formby and, despite its lightweight appeal, remains one of Morrissey's favourite Smiths songs. For Marr, the quaint pop that his partner currently favours seems decidedly unexciting and he finds little point or fun in reviving the title track of the Cilla Black movie *Work Is A Four Letter Word.*

"It was utter misery," Marr says of the Streatham recordings. "The group were falling to pieces." Joyce went further and suggested, "It was total madness. Everybody was losing it." Rourke betrayed similarly negative feelings and remembers the session as "a really depressing time". It must have been a particularly poignant and troubling week for the host Grant Showbiz, who could only watch in amazement as the group fragmented in his own garage. "The divergence came at the time we were doing those last tracks," he recalls with some regret. "It was a very odd atmosphere all around... I'd never felt that with The Smiths and didn't really know what was going on. Johnny and Morrissey weren't really talking to each other which was weird. I'd say it was a communication breakdown caused by uncontrollable outside pressures reaching a peak. They were looking to each other for a solution that neither had."

22 MAY

By Morrissey's 28th birthday, The Smiths have broken up in all but name. Marr is heading for Los Angeles to rethink his future, while the remainder of the group uneasily await further developments. Virtually everyone connected with The Smiths still believes that Johnny will return to the fold after he has had a welcome break from all the intensity... but nobody can be sure.

23 MAY

The compilation *Louder Than Bombs* is issued on Sire in the USA. Marr is happy that the Americans will now be able to appreciate the importance of The Smiths' singles catalogue, as well as their official albums. The compilation also appears on import in the UK which prompts Rough Trade to sanction its release later in the year.

28 MAY

Marr appears on Los Angeles' KROQ Radio. With the release of a new album imminent, it still seems unlikely that he will actually go through with his threat and not return to the group.

JUNE-JULY

There is now silence in The Smiths' camp.

'Louder Than Bombs'

ONE of the last group photo sessions, 1987.

MORRISSEY'S 'intellectual' look, which saw out the lifespan of The Smiths.

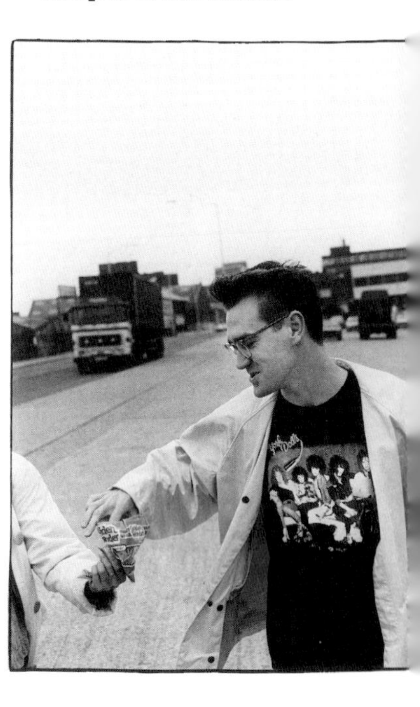

Only the voice of rumour can be heard as musicians' circles in Manchester buzz with the suggestion that The Smiths are having personnel trouble. Marr, meanwhile, confides in David Palmer that he is leaving the group. Back in England, the other Smiths are still uncertain about his ultimate intentions, but secretly suspect the worst. "When he went to America, it was obvious," Joyce suggests. Nevertheless, with no official announcement in the offing, it seems likely that the group will be able to fend off any press speculation with some firm PR denials.

23 JULY

Steven Kingston, a freelance journalist from Manchester, interviews Morrissey in London. Prior to the interview, The Smiths' PR Pat Bellis asks Kingston if he knows anyone in Manchester who has been spreading gossip about the group. Not surprisingly, she emphatically denies that there is any truth in the break-up rumours. Kingston duly takes up the point with Morrissey, who broadcasts a similar denial. "I'm not really sure where they came from," he says of the break-up rumours. "I'd be very interested to hear what the next rumour is... but I don't really have anything to say. Yes, the band's very happy – we all think the next LP is the best record we've made."

That same week, Q magazine prints an interview in which Morrissey claims The Smiths "face the future with more confidence in their ability than at any time previously". Nevertheless, there is no escaping Morrissey's tone of world weariness as he complains about money and expresses his disillusionment with touring. Although there are strong hints that The Smiths will stop playing live for the foreseeable future, the subject of their possible dissolution is not broached.

> **'I didn't want to be Johnny Marr... I didn't even play like him... the other Smiths were there and Morrissey didn't have the guts to break clear.'**
>
> IVOR PERRY

1 AUGUST

The break-up rumours finally reach the national music press as *NME* trumpets "Smiths To Split". Conjecture is rife as the paper attempts to explain the reasons behind the alleged rift in the group. Erroneous tales of Marr interrupting recording sessions and travelling to the USA with Rough Trade money and a suggestion that Morrissey has refused to work with the guitarist again betray the poisonous voice of rumour. Although many of the points are at best fanciful and at worst woefully inaccurate, the piece successfully pinpoints Marr's estrangement from the group. Attempts to confirm the break-up are strenuously resisted by Rough Trade, with Morrissey flippantly adding: "Whoever says The Smiths have split shall be severely spanked by me with a wet plimsoll."

SMITHS TO SPLIT

2 AUGUST

Convinced that Morrissey is somehow behind the split story, Marr decides to break his silence and pre-empt his colleagues by confirming The Smiths' dissolution. He is particularly disappointed that none of his former associates has contacted him in the aftermath of the *NME* story. "What really hurt me was that none of the band phoned me", he explained. "I felt it was blackmail. How could they do that to me?" Ironically, both Rourke and Joyce felt that Marr should have phoned them. "I didn't know what was going on myself," Joyce protests. "I was expecting Johnny or Morrissey to phone me. I didn't have the phone off the hook." Rourke was equally fazed by Marr's "blackmail" accusation and now feels that the participants were victims of a mutual misunderstanding. "The reason we were out of contact was because he wanted more breathing space and wanted to get himself together," he points out. "I don't know why he thought we weren't phoning him. Like you said, it was just a lack of communication."

Morrissey, meanwhile, is in a state of shock. "Nothing would have happened if the *NME* hadn't heard certain rumours about Johnny's intentions," he argues. "They immediately wrote that The Smiths had split up, that Johnny had left, whereas the group still existed... They published a lot of lies about Johnny and me and, suddenly, we were overtaken by events. The rumour became reality. But if everybody had remained quiet, the problems could have been resolved in private." Morrissey's optimistic scenario was based on the belief that Marr might have been won back after rethinking his position. However, the guitarist's decision to confirm the rumours suggests that, in the end he may well have regarded the split announcement as a blessed relief.

8 AUGUST

"Marr Speaks" proclaims the *NME*, advertising one of its best scoops in years. In an emotional phone call to the paper's deputy editor Danny Kelly, Marr attempts to set the record straight. After pointing out various inaccuracies in the previous week's report he concludes: "The major reason for me going was simply that there are things I want to do, musically, that there is just not scope for in The Smiths. I've got absolutely no problem with what The Smiths are doing. The stuff we've just done for the new album is great, the best we've ever done. I'm really proud of it. But there are things I want to do that can only happen outside The Smiths... In the final analysis, the thing that used to make me happy was making me miserable and so I just had to get out."

10 AUGUST

The release of 'Girlfriend In A Coma' is

AND THEN there were two... Morrissey and Rourke, 1987.

largely overshadowed by the dramatic split saga. Nevertheless, the single proves extremely commercial and soon climbs to number 13. Meanwhile, Morrissey has decided to continue using The Smiths' name and the press is full of conjecture about Marr's replacement. Rough Trade supremo Geoff Travis has approached Roddy Frame's manager, but the Aztec Camera mainman expresses no interest in joining The Smiths. A more promising candidate turns out to be Ivor Perry who, unknown to the music press, is already auditioning in London. "Morrissey was trying to keep The Smiths going," Perry remembers. "I told him he was daft. I didn't want to be Johnny Marr, Mark II. I didn't even play like him. It would have been embarrassing trying to live up to somebody. I thought it was a bit weird because the other Smiths were there and Morrissey didn't have enough guts to break clear."

Although a weekend session is booked, the audition founders within 24 hours. "Me and Mike felt uncomfortable", Andy Rourke recalls. "It was the first time we'd played with a new guitarist in about five years." Nevertheless, the group manage to complete rough versions of a couple of songs, including an early version of 'Bengali In Platforms', using Perry's Clash-style arrangement. "They were putting down this slightly chopped-up reggae rock on 'Bengali In Platforms'," Stephen Street recalls. "It was a totally different song. The only similarity with the version on *Viva Hate* was the title. Morrissey often carries around titles. I think the lyrics were different too. We were in the studio and I thought, 'We might as well try and see if it works', although I didn't have much faith in Ivor Perry and Morrissey becoming a songwriting team... Obviously there was a large amount of stress going on in the band at the time. I can remember sitting there with Mike and he said, 'I keep looking up and thinking Johnny is going to come through the door any minute and it'll be all right'.

'I think it is more or less the end of the story. Ultimately, popular music will end... The ashes are already about us...'

MORRISSEY

That summed up the feeling of the session." Joyce, in fact, summed it up more succinctly in his closing comment, "The beauty of The Smiths had gone."

11 AUGUST

Stephen Street is in Paris on his honeymoon. Prior to his departure, he tentatively sends Morrissey some rough tapes with the suggestion that he might consider adding lyrics and engaging in a collaboration.

18 AUGUST

Stephen Street receives a letter from Morrissey which confirms that he is dissolving The Smiths and now intends to record as a solo artiste for EMI. Interestingly, at this stage Morrissey still feels that Mike and Andy may be involved but admits that he has not discussed his plans with them. He is clearly excited about the work Street has despatched and heaps praise on an orchestral piece, which will later emerge as 'Angel Angel, Down We Go Together'. In laying The Smiths to rest, Morrissey cannot resist a final dig at Rough Trade and Radio 1 and sounds appalled at the fact that 'Girlfriend In A Coma' has not cracked the Top 10.

29 AUGUST

Unaware of Morrissey's momentous decision, the *NME* is still speculating about possible replacements for Johnny Marr. They belatedly confirm that Roddy Frame is out of the running, although he declined the offer many weeks before. The latest candidate is apparently another former Easterhouse member Mike Murray. Even the *NME* seem sceptical about this unlikely rumour, noting that Murray never actually wrote anything in Easterhouse.

5 SEPTEMBER

Clearly sick of the rumours, Mike Joyce decides to announce his departure from The Smiths. "I didn't hear from Morrissey for a while," Joyce remembers, "for something like two or three weeks. I was trying to get in touch with him and my calls weren't answered. That's the time when I thought, 'Well, it's hard enough trying to cope without Johnny. It's ridiculous trying to cope when what's left isn't really gelling'. So, rather than go down with the sinking ship I felt, 'I think we should stop here. If Andy and Morrissey want to carry on, they can'." However, Rourke has also been out of contact with Morrissey and it is clear that the singer is now cutting his ties with his fellow Smiths while plotting his solo career.

12 SEPTEMBER

Three weeks after Morrissey's letter to Street, the *NME* finally learn the truth and confirm that "The Smiths are dead". At this stage there is further speculation that Rourke and Joyce may be teaming up with Marr in a separate project but this proves another example of idle rumour.

28 SEPTEMBER

Strangeways, Here We Come is released to critical acclaim, but cannot prevent Paul Simon's *Graceland* reaching number 1. Although many critics later betrayed reservations about The Smiths' final album, its release coincided with a series of eulogies. The *NME* insisted on running its review two weeks before the official release date and allowed Len Brown a full page to overstate its importance. His conclusion summed up the impact that The Smiths had made on the music press over the previous five years: "I don't think there's any point in comparing The Smiths with their pop contemporaries, a couple of dodgy singles aside they remained above and beyond the rest, ploughing their own furrow (digging their own grave?), setting their own standards. I passionately hoped this was not to be their last breath, but nevertheless, in case you haven't guessed by now, *Strangeways, Here We Come* is a masterpiece that surpasses even *The Queen Is Dead* in terms of poetic pop and emotional power."

MORRISSEY and Viv Nicholson on 'The South Bank Show'.

18 OCTOBER

The Smiths are honoured with a posthumous tribute on *The South Bank Show*. With contributions from the group, journalists Nick Kent and Jon Savage, playwright Shaun Duggan, Morrissey icons Sandie Shaw and Viv Nicholson, disc jockey John Peel and friend Linder, the programme attempts to celebrate The Smiths' importance as an Eighties' phenomenon. What is missing is any sense of real conflict. Blink and you miss Joyce and Rourke, while Joe Moss declines to be interviewed and other key figures such as Geoff Travis and Grant Showbiz are conspicuous by their absence. Unfortunately, the interviews took place prior to the split and nobody from The Smiths' camp is available to provide a suitable requiem. However, a snippet of Morrissey's interview is salvaged as a possible coda. Ever the controversialist, he proclaims nothing less than the death of pop itself, with The Smiths cast as pall bearers. "The whole spectrum of popular music is that it is slowly being laid to rest in every conceivable way," he asserts. "I think it is more or less the end of the story. Ultimately, popular music will end. That must be obvious to almost anybody. I think the ashes are already about us if we could but notice them." There are many who would agree with Morrissey and cite The Smiths as pop's last great group, while the debate about the death of pop has flourished in the wake of their demise.

JOYCE and Rourke went on to work briefly together after The Smiths' split.

AS THE SMITHS disintegrated Morrissey turned towards co-producer Stephen Street.

Complete Smiths
UK DISCOGRAPHY

WHITE DICE

Line-up: Johnny Maher (Marr), vocals/guitar; Robin Allman (vocals/guitar); Paul Whittall (keyboards); Bobby Durkin (drums).

Someone Waved Goodbye; American Girl; The Hold; Makes No Sense; On The Beach; It's Over; You Made Me Cry.
F-Beat demos (unreleased) April 1980

FREAK PARTY

Line-up: Johnny Maher (Marr), guitar; Andy Rourke (bass guitar); Simon Wolstencroft (drums).

Crak Therapy
(unreleased) 1981

SMITHS' 7-INCH SINGLES

Hand In Glove/Handsome Devil
RT 131 May 1983

This Charming Man/Jeane
RT 136 November 1983
A limited number of test pressings of the cancelled 'Reel Around The Fountain'/'Jeane' are in existence.

What Difference Does It Make?/Back To The Old House
RT 146 January 1984
During February 1984 a limited number of DJ-only promotional copies of 'Still Ill'/'You've Got Everything Now' (R61 DJ) were circulated in order to plug the group's début album.

Heaven Knows I'm Miserable Now/Suffer Little Children
RT 156 May 1984

William, It Was Really Nothing/Please Please Please Let Me Get What I Want
RT 166 August 1984

How Soon Is Now?/Well I Wonder
RT 176 February 1985

Shakespeare's Sister/What She Said
RT 181 March 1985

That Joke Isn't Funny Anymore/Meat Is Murder (*Live*)
RT 186 July 1985

The Boy With The Thorn In His Side/Asleep
RT 191 September 1985

Bigmouth Strikes Again/Money Changes Everything
RT 192 May 1986

Panic/Vicar In A Tutu
RT 193 July 1986

Ask/Cemetry Gates
RT 194 October 1986

Shoplifters Of The World Unite/Half A Person
RT 195 January 1987

Sheila Take A Bow/Is It Really So Strange?
RT 196 April 1987

Girlfriend In A Coma/Work Is A Four Letter Word
RT 197 July 1987

I Started Something I Couldn't Finish/Pretty Girls Make Graves
RT 198 October 1987

Last Night I Dreamt That Somebody Loved Me/Rusholme Ruffians
RT 200 December 1987

This Charming Man/Jeane
WEA YZ 0001 August 1992

How Soon Is Now?/Hand In Glove
WEA YZ 0002 September 1992

There Is A Light That Never Goes Out/Hand In Glove (*Live*)
WEA YZ 0003 December 1992

SMITHS' 12-INCH & CD SINGLES

This Charming Man (*Manchester*)/This Charming Man (*London*)/Accept Yourself/Wonderful Woman
RTT 136 November 1983

This Charming Man (*New York Mix - Vocal*)/This Charming Man (*New York Mix - Instrumental*)
RT 136 December 1983

What Difference Does It Make?/Back To The Old House/These Things Take Time
RTT 146 February 1984

Heaven Knows I'm Miserable Now/Suffer Little Children/Girl Afraid
RTT 156 May 1984

William, It Was Really Nothing/Please Please Please Let Me Get What I Want/How Soon Is Now?
RTT 166 August 1984

Barbarism Begins At Home/Barbarism Begins At Home
RTT 171 January 1985
(A promotion only release in a limited edition of 500 copies)

How Soon Is Now?/Well I Wonder/Oscillate Wildly
RTT 176 February 1985

Shakespeare's Sister/What She Said/Stretch Out And Wait
RTT 181 March 1985

That Joke Isn't Funny Anymore/Nowhere Fast (*Live*)/Stretch Out And Wait (*Live*)/Shakespeare's Sister (*Live*)/Meat Is Murder (*Live*)
RTT 186 July 1985

The Boy With The Thorn In His Side/Asleep/Rubber Ring
RTT 191 September 1985

Bigmouth Strikes Again/Money Changes Everything/Unloveable
RTT 192 May 1986

Panic/Vicar In A Tutu/The Draize Train
RTT 193 July 1986

Ask/Cemetry Gates/Golden Lights
RTT 194 October 1986

Shoplifters Of The World Unite/Half A Person/London
RTT 195 January 1987
(Initial versions of 'Shoplifters Of The World Unite' were despatched with 'You Just Haven't Earned It Yet, Baby' on the A-side).

Sheila Take A Bow/Is It Really So Strange?/Sweet And Tender Hooligan
RTT 196 April 1987

Girlfriend In A Coma/Work Is A Four Letter Word/I Keep Mine Hidden
RTT 197 July 1987

I Started Something I Couldn't Finish/Pretty Girls Make Graves/Some Girls Are Bigger Than Others
RTT 198 October 1987
(Cassette versions of the single included a cover version of James' 'What's The World?', recorded live in Glasgow).

Last Night I Dreamt That Somebody Loved Me/Rusholme Ruffians/Nowhere Fast
RTT 200 December 1987
(The CD version of this single featured an extra track: 'William, It Was Really Nothing').

Barbarism Begins At Home/Shakespeare's Sister/Stretch Out And Wait
RTT 171 CD November 1988

The Headmaster Ritual/Nowhere Fast (*Live*); Stretch Out And Wait (*Live*)/Meat Is Murder (*Live*)
RTT 215 CD November 1988

This Charming Man (*Manchester Mix*)/Jeane/Wonderful Woman/Accept Yourself
YZ 0001 CD1 August 1992

This Charming Man (*Manchester Mix*)/This Charming Man (*London Mix*)/This Charming Man (*New York Mix*)/This Charming Man (*New York Instrumental*)/This Charming Man (*Peel Session*)/This Charming Man (*Single Remix*)/This Charming Man (*Original Single Version*)
YZ 0001 CD2 August 1992

How Soon Is Now? (*edit*)/The Queen Is Dead/Handsome Devil/I Started Something I Couldn't Finish
YZ 0002 CD1 September 1992

I Know It's Over/Suffer Little Children/Back To The Old House/How Soon Is Now? (*Album Version*)
YZ 0002 CD2 September 1992

There Is A Light That Never Goes Out/Hand In Glove (*Live*)/Some Girls Are Bigger Than Others (*Live*)/Money Changes Everything
YZ 0003 CD1 December 1992

There Is A Light That Never Goes Out/Hand In Glove (*featuring Sandie Shaw*)/I Don't Owe You Anything (*featuring Sandie Shaw*)/Jeane (*featuring Sandie Shaw*)
YZ 0003 CD1 December 1992

In addition to the above, The Smiths have appeared on various samplers, imports and rare special promotion discs and test pressings. Rough Trade retrospectively issued several of The Smiths' 12-inch singles on CD. Strangely, the transference from vinyl to CD single was never completed and the ordering of releases was neither chronological nor logical. Those back catalogue singles that did emerge on Rough Trade CD included 'What Difference Does It Make?', 'William, It Was Really Nothing', 'The Boy With The Thorn In His Side', 'Panic', 'Ask' and 'Last Night I Dreamt That Somebody Loved Me'. Catalogue numbers were the same as the Rough Trade 12-inch releases, with the suffix "CD". Some were manufactured in France, then issued in the UK. Singles were repackaged in various countries, occasionally with edited versions, but the only alternate take of which I am aware is the Italian version of 'How Soon Is Now?' on the flip side of the 12-inch 'William, It Was Really Nothing' (Italy: Virgin VINX 71). On 25 May 1984, the New Musical Express *issued a free EP (GIV 1) featuring 'What She Said'. At one point, a live EP was rumoured for release featuring 'Meat Is Murder', 'Nowhere Fast', 'What She Said', 'Stretch Out And Wait', 'William, It Was Really Nothing' and 'Miserable Lie'. The tracks later appeared on various 7-inch and 12-inch B-sides. A live version of 'Girl Afraid' was also available, by mail order only, on the* NME *Various Artistes compilation* Department Of Enjoyment.

SMITHS ALBUMS

THE SMITHS*
Reel Around The Fountain; You've Got Everything Now; Miserable Lie; Pretty Girls Make Graves; The Hand That Rocks The Cradle; Still Ill; Hand In Glove; What Difference Does It Make?; I Don't Owe You Anything; Suffer Little Children.
Rough 61 February 1984

HATFUL OF HOLLOW
William, It Was Really Nothing; What Difference Does It Make?; These Things Take Time; This Charming Man; How Soon Is Now?; Handsome Devil; Hand In Glove; Still Ill; Heaven Knows I'm Miserable Now; This Night Has Opened My Eyes; You've Got Everything Now; Accept Yourself; Girl Afraid; Back To The Old House; Reel Around The Fountain; Please Please Please Let Me Get What I Want.
Rough 76 November 1984

MEAT IS MURDER*
The Headmaster Ritual; Rusholme Ruffians; I Want The One I Can't Have; What She Said; That Joke Isn't Funny Anymore; Nowhere Fast; Well I Wonder; Barbarism Begins At Home; Meat Is Murder.
Rough 81 February 1985

THE QUEEN IS DEAD
The Queen Is Dead; Frankly, Mr Shankly; I Know It's Over; Never Had No One Ever; Cemetry Gates; Bigmouth Strikes Again; The Boy With The Thorn In His Side; Vicar In A Tutu; There Is A Light That Never Goes Out; Some Girls Are Bigger Than Others.
Rough 96 June 1986

THE WORLD WON'T LISTEN
Panic; Ask; London; Bigmouth Strikes Again; Shakespeare's Sister; There Is A Light That Never Goes Out; Shoplifters Of The World Unite; The Boy With The Thorn In His Side; Asleep; Unloveable; Half A Person; Stretch Out And Wait; That Joke Isn't Funny Anymore; Oscillate Wildly; You Just Haven't Earned It Yet, Baby; Rubber Ring.
(Cassette versions include the instrumental: 'Money Changes Everything').
Rough 101 March 1987

LOUDER THAN BOMBS
Is It Really So Strange?; Sheila Take A Bow; Shoplifters Of The World Unite; Sweet And Tender Hooligan; Half A Person; London; Panic; Girl Afraid; Shakespeare's Sister; William, It Was Really Nothing; You Just Haven't Earned It Yet, Baby; Heaven Knows I'm Miserable Now; Ask; Golden Lights; Oscillate Wildly; These Things Take Time; Rubber Ring; Back To The Old House; Hand In Glove; Stretch Out And Wait; Please Please Please Let Me Get What I Want; This Night Has Opened My Eyes; Unloveable; Asleep.
Rough 255/Sire 9 25569-1 April 1987

STRANGEWAYS, HERE WE COME
A Rush And A Push And The Land Is Ours; I Started Something I Couldn't Finish; Death Of A Disco Dancer; Girlfriend In A Coma; Stop Me If You Think You've Heard This One Before; Last Night I Dreamt That Somebody Loved Me; Unhappy Birthday; Paint A Vulgar Picture; Death At One's Elbow; I Won't Share You.
Rough 106 September 1987

RANK
The Queen Is Dead; Panic; Vicar In A Tutu; Ask; Rusholme Ruffians/(Marie's The Name) His Latest Flame (Medley); The Boy With The Thorn In His Side; What She Said; Is It Really So Strange?; Cemetry Gates; London; I Know It's Over; The Draize Train; Still Ill; Bigmouth Strikes Again.
Rough 126 September 1988

THE PEEL SESSIONS
What Difference Does It Make?; Miserable Lie; Reel Around The Fountain; Handsome Devil.
Strange Fruit SF PS 055 October 1988

BEST... I
This Charming Man; William, It Was Really Nothing; What Difference Does It Make?; Stop Me If You Think You've Heard This One Before; Girlfriend In A Coma; Half A Person; Rubber Ring; How Soon Is Now?; Hand In Glove; Shoplifters Of The World Unite; Sheila Take A Bow; Some Girls Are Bigger Than Others; Panic; Please, Please, Please Let Me Get What I Want.
WEA 4509-90327 August 1992

BEST... II
The Boy With The Thorn In His Side; The Headmaster Ritual; Heaven Knows I'm Miserable Now; Ask; Oscillate Wildly; Nowhere Fast; Still Ill; Bigmouth Strikes Again; That Joke Isn't Funny Anymore; Shakespeare's Sister; Girl Afraid; Reel Around The Fountain; Last Night I Dreamt That Somebody Loved Me; There Is A Light That Never Goes Out.
WEA 4509/90406 December 1992

**US versions of* The Smiths *and* Meat Is Murder *featured the additional 'This Charming Man' and 'How Soon Is Now?', respectively. Smiths' tracks have been packaged differently in various countries and there are a number of examples of edited tracks. Alternate takes are rare, but the Canadian Compilation* Rough Trade *(RTS 1986) features an unavailable live version of 'Miserable Lie', taken from the Apollo Theatre, Oxford, concert of March 18, 1985.*

SMITHS' CD ALBUMS

MEAT IS MURDER
Rough CD 81 March 1985

HATFUL OF HOLLOW
Rough CD 76 December 1985

THE QUEEN IS DEAD
Rough CD 96 June 1986

THE SMITHS
Rough CD 61 October 1986

THE WORLD WON'T LISTEN
Rough CD 101 March 1987

LOUDER THAN BOMBS
Sire 9 25569-2 May 1987

RANK
Rough CD 126 September 1988

THE PEEL SESSIONS
SF PS CD 055 October 1988

BEST...1
WEA 4509-90327 August 1992

BEST...2
WEA 4509-90406 December 1992

See Albums section for track listings.

Warner Brothers reissued The Smiths' CD back catalogue on 15 November 1993. To commemorate their issue, the company also released a series of 10-inch vinyl albums, limited to 5,000 individually numbered copies. The reissued catalogue followed US track listings of The Smiths *and* Meat Is Murder.

SMITHS' BOOTLEGS

LIVE AT THE ELECTRIC BALL-ROOM, 19 DECEMBER 1983
Hand In Glove; Still Ill; Barbarism Begins At Home; This Night Has Opened My Eyes; You've Got Everything Now; What Difference Does It Make?; Miserable Lie; This Charming Man; Back To The Old House; Reel Around The Fountain; Handsome Devil; Accept Yourself; This Charming Man.
TS 24681. Excellent quality recording.

THE SMITHS
Hand In Glove; Heaven Knows I'm Miserable Now; Girl Afraid; This Charming Man; Pretty Girls Make Graves; Still Ill; Barbarism Begins At Home; This Night Has Opened My Eyes; You've Got Everything Now; Handsome Devil; What Difference Does It Make?; These Things Take Time; Barbarism Begins At Home.
This excellent quality bootleg was taken largely from The Smiths' performance at the Markthalle, Hamburg on 4 May 1984, which was filmed for the television show Rockpalast.

MERRY XMAS
I Don't Owe You Anything; Reel Around The Fountain; Hand In Glove; You've Got Everything Now; Handsome Devil; These Things Take Time; This Charming Man; Girl Afraid; Pretty Girls Make Graves; Still Ill; This Night Has Opened My Eyes.
SC 003. Very good quality recording of the Hammersmith Palais gig of 12 March 1984.

WILDE ABOUT MORRISSEY
These Things Take Time; What Difference Does It Make?; The Hand That Rocks The Cradle; Handsome Devil; Jeane; Wonderful Woman; Hand In Glove; Miserable Lie; I Don't Owe You Anything *(featuring Sandie Shaw)*; Reel Around The Fountain; You've Got Everything Now; These Things Take Time; This Charming Man; Still Ill; Pretty Girls Make Graves.
Riot City Records CITY 002. Good quality recording taken from two sources: Haçienda (4 February 1983) and Hammersmith Palais (12 March 1984).

MUSIC IS MAGNIFICENT
The Headmaster Ritual; Rusholme Ruffians; I Want The One I Can't Have; What She Said; That Joke Isn't Funny Anymore; Nowhere Fast; Shakespeare's Sister; Barbarism Begins At Home; Meat Is Murder.
Inferior quality recording of The Smiths at the Ipswich Gaumont (11 March 1985).

LIVE AT THE ELECTRIC BALLROOM
Hand In Glove; Still Ill; Barbarism Begins At Home; This Night Has Opened My Eyes; You've Got Everything Now; What Difference Does It Make?; Miserable Lie; This Charming Man; Back To The Old House; Reel Around The Fountain; Handsome Devil; Accept Yourself; This Charming Man.
A re-release of Live At The Electric Ballroom 19 December 1983.

ROYAL COMMAND PERFORMANCE
Some Girls Are Bigger Than Others; Shoplifters Of The World Unite; Cemetry Gates; This Night Has Opened My Eyes; Still Ill; Panic; The Queen Is Dead; William, It Was Really Nothing; Hand In Glove; Bigmouth Strikes Again; Vicar In A Tutu; Frankly Mr Shankly; There Is A Light That Never Goes Out; Ask; I Want The One I Can't Have; Is It Really So Strange?; Shakespeare's Sister; Stretch Out And Wait; That Joke Isn't Funny Anymore; Jeane *(featuring Sandie Shaw)*; I Know It's Over; Rusholme Ruffians/(Marie's The Name) His Latest Flame (Medley); London; Miserable Lie; The Boy With The Thorn In His Side; Girl Don't Come *(featuring Sandie Shaw)*.
A double album humorously credited to The Vegetarians, this above average quality recording was taken from the G-Mex Festival, Manchester (19 July 1986) and the Brixton Academy, London (12 December 1986).

THE RUSHOLME RUFFIANS
What She Said; Hand In Glove; How Soon Is Now?; Stretch Out And Wait; Shakespeare's Sister; Still Ill; Meat Is Murder; Heaven Knows I'm Miserable Now; Handsome Devil; Miserable Lie; You've Got Everything Now.
Neurotic Records NUT 009. Fair quality recording taken from the Manchester Palace (31 March 1985).

SO THIS IS AMERICA
How Soon Is Now?; Hand In Glove; I Want The One I Can't Have; Still Ill; Frankly Mr Shankly; Panic; Never Had No One Ever; Stretch Out And Wait; The Boy With The Thorn In His Side; Cemetry Gates; What She Said/Rubber Ring (Medley); Is It Really So Strange?;

RARITIES

Stop Me If You Think You've Heard This One Before (Germany).

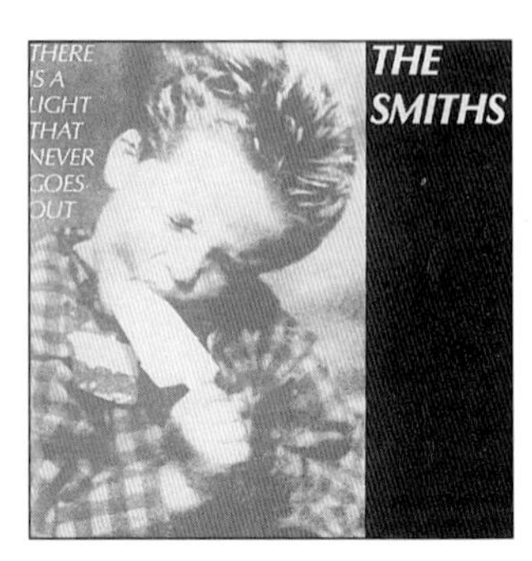

There Is A Light That Never Goes Out (France).

SMITHS picture disc; multi-coloured numbered German promotional album; 'The Headmaster Ritual'.

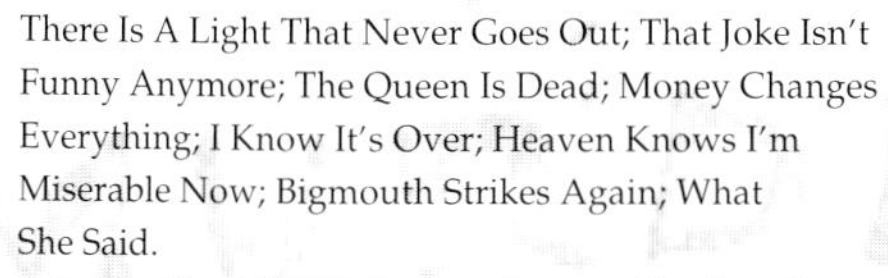

There Is A Light That Never Goes Out; That Joke Isn't Funny Anymore; The Queen Is Dead; Money Changes Everything; I Know It's Over; Heaven Knows I'm Miserable Now; Bigmouth Strikes Again; What She Said.
Indecency Records 102. Good quality recording from Great Woods, Mansfield, Massachusetts (4 August 1986). Strangely, the track listings on the LP are severely erroneous.

NEVER HAD NO ONE EVER

Ask; Bigmouth Strikes Again; London; Miserable Lie; Some Girls Are Bigger Than Others; The Boy With The Thorn In His Side; Shoplifters Of The World Unite; There Is A Light That Never Goes Out; Is It Really So Strange?; Cemetry Gates; This Night Has Opened My Eyes; Still Ill; Panic; The Queen Is Dead; William, It Was Really Nothing; Hand In Glove; Handsome Devil; That Joke Isn't Funny Anymore; Shakespeare's Sister; Rusholme Ruffians; Meat Is Murder; Heaven Knows I'm Miserable Now; This Charming Man; You've Got Everything Now.
An excellent quality double album taken from the Academy Brixton (12 December 1986) and Paseo De Camoens, Madrid (18 May 1985).

A NICE BIT OF MEAT

Panic; Sheila Take A Bow; Purple Haze; How Soon Is Now?; Barbarism Begins At Home; Please Please Please Let Me Get What I Want; Asleep; Unloveable; Wonderful Woman; Reel Around The Fountain; This Night Has Opened My Eyes.
Again credited to The Vegetarians, this wryly titled work, with the famous Marilyn Monroe nude shot on the cover, is an impressive collection. A mish-mash of sources include The Tube *('Panic'; 'Sheila Take A Bow'), the Royal Albert Hall, 6 April 1985 ('Barbarism Begins At Home' featuring guest vocalist Pete Burns) and, most intriguingly, some rare soundcheck material, including Marr's trip through 'Purple Haze'.*

ACID HEAD

Half A Person; Cemetry Gates; I Know It's Over.
This poor quality 7-inch single features the BBC John Peel session recording of 'Half A Person' and two tracks from the National, Kilburn (23 October 1986), which later appeared on Rank.

BRIXTON ACADEMY FRIDAY 20/10/86

The Queen Is Dead; Panic; I Want The One I Can't Have; Vicar In A Tutu; There Is A Light That Never Goes Out; Ask; Rusholme Ruffians/(Marie's The Name) His Latest Flame (Medley); Shakespeare's Sister; Frankly Mr Shankly; The Boy With The Thorn In His Side; What She Said/Rubber Ring (Medley); Is It Really So Strange?; London; Meat Is Murder; I Know It's Over; The Draize Train; How Soon Is Now?; Still Ill; Bigmouth Strikes Again.
A fine quality recording of the Brixton gig from 12 December 1986, which is wrongly dated on the sleeve.

HEAVY HORSES

Bigmouth Strikes Again; Panic; Vicar In A Tutu; Frankly Mr Shankly; There Is A Light That Never Goes Out; Ask; I Want The One I Can't Have; Cemetry Gates; Shakespeare's Sister; Stretch Out And Wait; That Joke Isn't Funny Anymore; The Queen Is Dead; I Know It's Over; Hand In Glove.
TMQ 71103. Inferior quality recording taken from the G-Mex Festival, Manchester (19 July 1986).

ELECTRIC STARS

Hand In Glove; Still Ill; Barbarism Begins At Home; This Night Has Opened My Eyes; Pretty Girls Make Graves; You've Got Everything Now; This Charming Man; Back To The Old House; Reel Around The Fountain; Handsome Devil; Accept Yourself.
TMQ 71109. A re-release of the first Smiths bootleg 'Live At The Electric Ballroom' 19 December 1983.

SORROW'S SON

Handsome Devil; Still Ill; This Charming Man; Pretty Girls Make Graves; Reel Around The Fountain; What Difference Does It Make?; Miserable Lie; This Night Has Opened My Eyes; Hand In Glove; These Things Take Time; You've Got Everything Now.
TMQ 71128. An excellent quality recording from The Old Grey Whistle Test *television broadcast from the Assembly Rooms, Derby (7 December 1983).*

HAÇIENDA

These Things Take Time; What Difference Does It Make?; The Hand That Rocks The Cradle; Handsome Devil; Jeane; Wonderful Woman; Hand In Glove; Miserable Lie.
TMQ 71129. Inferior version of the Haçienda concert, previously available on bootleg vinyl on 'Wilde About Morrissey'.

HAMMERSMITH

Miserable Lie; Heaven Knows I'm Miserable Now; This Charming Man; Girl Afraid; Pretty Girls Make Graves; Still Ill; This Night Has Opened My Eyes; Barbarism Begins At Home; Back To The Old House; What Difference Does It Make?; I Don't Owe You Anything (*featuring Sandie Shaw*); Reel Around The Fountain; Hand In Glove; You've Got Everything Now; Handsome Devil; These Things Take Time.
TMQ 72107. A double album of very good quality, capturing the entire performance from the Hammersmith Palais (12 March 1984).

SMITHSESSIONS

Accept Yourself; I Don't Owe You Anything; Pretty Girls Make Graves; Reel Around The Fountain; This Charming Man; Still Ill; This Night Has Opened My Eyes; Back To The Old House; Handsome Devil; Reel Around The Fountain; Miserable Lie; These Things Take Time; What Difference Does It Make?; You've Got Everything Now; Hand In Glove; Wonderful Woman.
TMQ 72112. Excellent quality recording of the John Peel and Kid Jensen sessions from 1983.

HEADMASTERS

Meat Is Murder; Hand In Glove; I Want The One I Can't Have; Nowhere Fast; Shakespeare's Sister; That Joke Isn't Funny Anymore; Stretch Out And Wait; Heaven Knows I'm Miserable Now; What She Said; Still Ill; How Soon Is Now?; Jeane; The Headmaster Ritual; Reel Around The Fountain; William, It Was Really Nothing; This Charming Man; Miserable Lie; Barbarism Begins At Home.
TMQ 72120. Excellent quality recording, taken from Irvine Meadows Amphitheater (29 June 1985).

LIVE IN ROME 1985

William, It Was Really Nothing; I Want The One I Can't Have; How Soon Is Now?; Stretch Out And Wait; The Headmaster Ritual; Hand In Glove; Still Ill; Heaven Knows I'm Miserable Now; Handsome Devil; This Charming Man.
HS-01. A fair quality recording taken from Tendetrisce, Rome (14 May 1985).

...THE BAD BOY FROM A GOOD FAMILY

The Queen Is Dead; Panic; I Want The One I Can't Have; Vicar In A Tutu; There Is A Light That Never Goes Out; Ask; Rusholme Ruffians/(Marie's The Name) His Latest Flame (Medley); Frankly Mr Shankly; The Boy With The Thorn In His Side; What She Said; Is It Really So Strange?; Never Had No One Ever; Cemetry Gates; London; Meat Is Murder; I Know It's Over; The Draize Train; How Soon Is Now?; Still Ill; Bigmouth Strikes Again.
This recording, taken from the National, Kilburn, London (23 October 1986), features the complete concert from which Rank *was adapted. Although the quality is excellent, the recording speed is disconcertingly awry.*

THE PLAYBOX

Heaven Knows I'm Miserable Now; Jeane; This Charming Man; Hand In Glove.
Allegedly, only 200 copies of this rare bootleg 7-inch EP were pressed. The concert selections are taken from the Capital Theatre, Aberdeen (30 September 1985).

GOODBYE TO ELVIS

Still Ill; Rusholme Ruffians; What She Said; What's The World.
Another 7-inch EP of fine quality, taken from the Capital Theatre, Aberdeen (30 September 1985).

MISERABLE LIES

Girl Afraid; This Charming Man; Barbarism Begins At Home; This Night Has Opened My Eyes; Still Ill; These Things Take Time; Miserable Lie; I Don't Owe You Anything; What Difference Does It Make?; Handsome Devil.

THE FINAL RADIO SESSIONS

Is It Really So Strange?; London; Sweet And Tender Hooligan; Half A Person.
A fair recording of the John Peel session from 17 December 1986.

SPANISH SUN LIVE MADRID 18 MAY 1985

How Soon Is Now?; Handsome Devil; That Joke Isn't Funny Anymore; Shakespeare's Sister; Rusholme Ruffians; Hand In Glove; Meat Is Murder; Heaven Knows I'm Miserable Now; Barbarism Begins At Home.
An Italian bootleg of excellent quality taken from an FM broadcast of the concert.

BETTER LIVE THAN DEAD

William, It Was Really Nothing; Nowhere Fast; What She Said; Hand In Glove; How Soon Is Now?; Stretch Out And Wait; That Joke Isn't Funny Anymore; Shakespeare's Sister; Meat Is Murder; Miserable Lie; Barbarism Begins At Home.
TVO 1D 1038. Excellent quality recording on CD only.

NICE BIT OF MEAT 2

There Is A Light That Never Goes Out; Frankly Mr Shankly; This Charming Man; Jeane; Rusholme Ruffians;

What's The World; Instrumental; How Soon Is Now?; William, It Was Really Nothing; Stop Me If You Think You've Heard This One Before; Disappointed; Interesting Drug; Suedehead; The Last Of The Famous International Playboys; Sister I'm A Poet; Death At One's Elbow; Sweet And Tender Hooligan.
Like its predecessor, 'A Nice Bit Of Meat', this is another mish-mash which includes selections from the National, Kilburn (29 October 1986), a couple of John Peel sessions and, most interestingly, two soundcheck instrumentals, including 'How Soon Is Now?' Side two is a fair quality recording of Morrissey's first solo performance at Wolverhampton (22 December 1988).

THE SMITHS
Wonderful Woman (What Do You See In Him?); Jeane; What's The World?
Released in 1991, this three track single features two songs from the Haçienda concert on 4 February 1983 (erroneously dated as December 1982 on the sleeve) and the James cover 'What's The World?' The track 'What Do You See In Him?' later emerged in slightly different form as 'Wonderful Woman'. The pressing was a limited edition of 1,000.

LIVE AT THE OXFORD APOLLO
William, It Was Really Nothing; Nowhere Fast; What She Said; Hand In Glove; How Soon Is Now?; Stretch Out And Wait; That Joke Isn't Funny Anymore; Shakespeare's Sister; Meat Is Murder; Miserable Lie; Barbarism Begins At Home.
Burning Bush Records An excellent quality recording from the BBC radio broadcast (9 May 1985) of the performance at Oxford Apollo on 18 March 1985.

BEFORE LOVE
Handsome Devil; Reel Around The Fountain; Miserable Lie; These Things Take Time; Hand In Glove; Wonderful Woman; These Things Take Time; Hand In Glove; This Charming Man.
A good quality recording taken from the John Peel and Kid Jensen sessions of 1983, interspersed with interviews on the Jensen show. The last three tracks are live cuts from 1983, recorded out of time.

THE HAND THAT ROCKS THE CRADLE
Reel Around The Fountain; You've Got Everything Now; Miserable Lie; These Things Take Time; Wonderful Woman; Handsome Devil; Hand In Glove; What Difference Does It Make?; I Don't Owe You Anything; Suffer Little Children; Pretty Girls Make Graves.
Trash Records TR7. This was an interesting selection from the unreleased Troy Tate demos. The CD version of this album (New Noize NUN005) included 'Jeane' plus material from The Smiths' BBC radio appearances: 'Miserable Lie', 'I Don't Owe You Anything', 'Reel Around The Fountain', 'Pretty Girls Make Graves', 'Williams, It Was Really Nothing', 'Shakespeare's Sister' and 'Nowhere Fast'.

MISERY LOVES COMPANY
Miserable Lie; Heaven Knows I'm Miserable Now; This Charming Man; Pretty Girls Make Graves; Still Ill; This Night Has Opened My Eyes; Barbarism Begins At Home; Back To the Old House; What Difference Does It Make?; I Don't Owe You Anything (*featuring Sandie Shaw*); Reel Around The Fountain; Hand In Glove; You've Got Everything Now; Handsome Devil; These Things Take Time.
El Topo 003. A good quality album comprising the entire 'Hammersmith' bootleg (bar 'Girl Afraid').

THE CRADLE SNATCHERS
Is It Really So Strange?; London; Sweet And Tender Hooligan; Reel Around The Fountain; You've Got Everything Now; Miserable Lie; These Things Take Time; Wonderful Woman; Handsome Devil; Hand In Glove; What Difference Does It Make?; I Don't Owe You Anything; Suffer Little Children; Pretty Girls Make Graves; How Soon Is Now?; Wonderful Woman; Purple Haze.
EAR 41 CD. This CD bootleg features BBC session appearances, a selection from the Troy Tate sessions, plus live material, including the soundcheck instrumental 'Purple Haze'. The bootleg sleeve mistitles several tracks; the above is the correct listing.

DEVILS CHARM
Handsome Devil; Still Ill; This Charming Man; Pretty Girls Make Graves; Reel Around The Fountain; What Difference Does It Make?; Miserable Lie; This Night Has Opened My Eyes; Hand In Glove; These Things Take Time; You've Got Everything Now; Hand In Glove; Still Ill; Barbarism Begins At Home; This Night Has Opened My Eyes; Pretty Girls Make Graves; What Difference Does It Make?; Miserable Lie; This Charming Man; Back To The Old House; Reel Around The Fountain; Handsome Devil; Accept Yourself.
This very good quality double album includes the BBC broadcast from The Assembly Rooms, Derby (7 December, 1983) and most of The Electric Ballroom (19 December 1983).

THE GLC JOBS FOR A CHANGE FESTIVAL
Nowhere Fast; Girl Afraid; This Charming Man; William, It Was Really Nothing; Heaven Knows I'm Miserable Now; I Don't Owe You Anything; Still Ill; Jeane; Barbarism Begins At Home; Hand In Glove; What Difference Does It Make?; You've Got Everything Now; Pretty Girls Make Graves; Miserable Lie.
A reasonable quality recording of The Smiths' gig at the Jubilee Gardens, London, 10 June 1984.

YOUR FULL OF SMITH
William, It Was Really Nothing; Nowhere Fast; I Want The One I Can't Have; What She Said; Hand In Glove; How Soon Is Now?; Still Ill; Meat Is Murder; Heaven Knows I'm Miserable Now; Barbarism Begins At Home; Miserable Lie.
Another live recording from the spring of 1985. The sleeve wrongly credits several songs; the above is what is actually on the record. The grammatically incorrect "Your" is further evidence of sloppiness.

REST IN PEACE – THE SMITHS LIVE
Sheila Take A Bow; Shoplifters Of The World Unite; This Charming Man; Girl Afraid.
This 7-inch single provides no details of song sources, but they would appear to have been culled from television broadcasts.

A KIND OF LOVING
William, It Was Really Nothing; Nowhere Fast; Hand In Glove; How Soon is Now?; Stretch Out And Wait; That Joke Isn't Funny Anymore; Shakespeare's Sister; The Headmaster Ritual; What She Said; Still Ill; Meat Is Murder; Miserable Lie; Barbarism Begins At Home; You've Got Everything Now.
An excellent quality vinyl bootleg taken from a 1984 concert.

HANDSOME DEVILS
Handsome Devil; Still Ill; This Charming Man; Pretty Girls Make Graves; Reel Around The Fountain; What Difference Does It Make?; Miserable Lie; This Night Has Opened My Eyes; Hand In Glove; These Things Take Time; You've Got Everything Now; Heaven Knows I'm Miserable Now; Barbarism Begins At Home; Miserable Lie; I Don't Owe You Anything; What Difference Does It Make?; Handsome Devil; You've Got Everything Now.
TKCD 1052. This fair quality CD bootleg combines the Derby Assembly Rooms (7 December 1983) with highlights from the Amsterdam Vinyl Party *(21 April, 1984).*

THE SMITHS (MORRISSEY 1959-1986)
These Things Take Time; What Difference Does It Make?; The Hand That Rocks The Cradle; Handsome Devil; Jeane; Wonderful Woman; Hand In Glove; Miserable Lie; There Is A Light That Never Goes Out; Frankly Mr Shankly; London; Half A Person; Sheila Takes A Bow; Shoplifters Of The World Unite.
A fairly good CD bootleg featuring the performance at the Haçienda (4 February 1983), material from Rank, BBC *Sessions and* The Tube.

BEFORE LOVE
William, It Was Really Nothing; Hand In Glove; How Soon Is Now?; That Joke Isn't Funny Anymore; The Headmaster Ritual; What She Said; Still Ill; Miserable Lie; You've Got Everything Now; Nowhere Fast; Stretch Out And Wait; Shakespeare's Sister; Meat Is Murder; Barbarism Begins At Home; Please Please Please Let Me Get What I Want; Asleep; Unloveable; Purple Haze.
A resequenced version of the performance at the Apollo Theatre, Oxford (18 March 1985) taken from the BBC recording of the show. This CD bootleg concludes with live material, including the soundcheck of 'Purple Haze' prior to their performance at Barrowlands, Glasgow (16 July 1986).

RARITIES

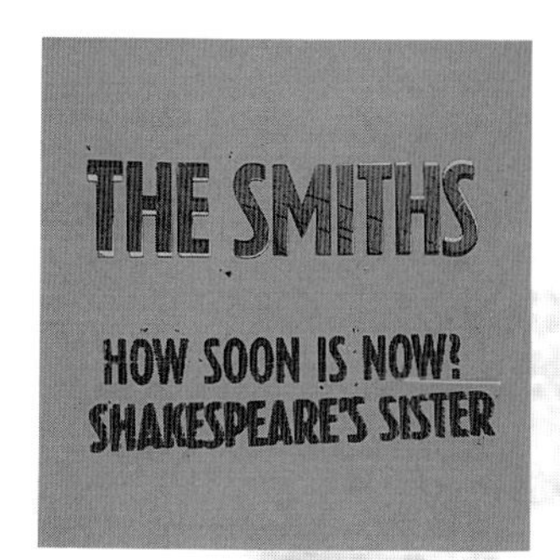

How Soon Is Now?

Shoplifters Of The World Unite (US PROMO)

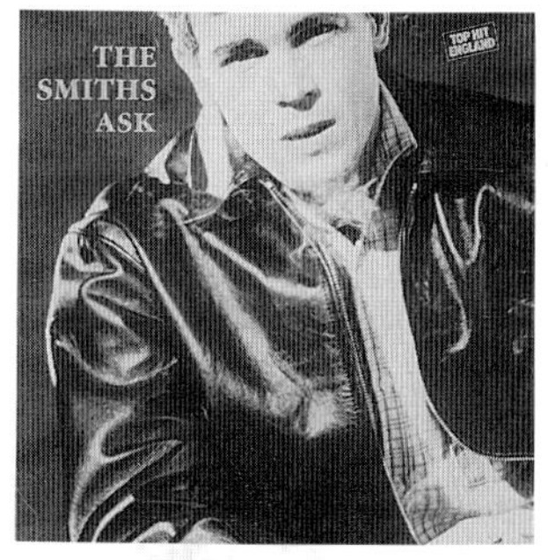

Ask (GERMANY)

What Difference Does It Make?

RUSHOLME RUFFIANS PLAY AT HOME

What She Said; Hand In Glove; How Soon Is Now?; Stretch Out And Wait; That Joke Isn't Funny Anymore; Shakespeare's Sister; Rusholme Ruffians; The Headmaster Ritual; Still Ill; Meat is Murder; Heaven Knows I'm Miserable Now; Handsome Devil; Miserable Lie; You've Got Everything Now.

A CD bootleg featuring the performance at the Manchester Palace (31 March 1985), minus the three opening songs ('William, It Was Really Nothing'; 'Nowhere Fast'; 'I Want The One I Can't Have'). 'Barbarism Begins At Home' is erroneously listed among the tracks.

EL DORADO

Hand In Glove; Heaven Knows I'm Miserable Now; Girl Afraid; This Charming Man; Barbarism Begins At Home; Pretty Girls Make Graves; This Night Has Opened My Eyes; Still Ill; You've Got Everything Now; Handsome Devil; Miserable Lie; These Things Take Time; What Difference Does It Make?; Barbarism Begins At Home.

Tribal 2001. Taken from The Smiths' performance at The Theatre, El Dorado, Paris, this includes all the tracks played except an encore of 'Hand In Glove'.

HOW SOON IS NOW REISSUES

What She Said; Hand In Glove; How Soon Is Now?; Stretch Out And Wait; That Joke Isn't Funny Anymore; Shakespeare's Sister; Rusholme Ruffians; The Headmaster Ritual; Still Ill; Meat is Murder; Heaven Knows I'm Miserable Now.

This CD features highlights from the Palace, Manchester (31 March 1985).

LIVE PANIC

How Soon Is Now?; Nowhere Fast; I Want The One I Can't Have; Bigmouth Strikes Again; Panic; Meat Is Murder; The Queen Is Dead; I Know It's Over; Hand In Glove; The Headmaster Ritual; You've Got Everything Now.

PUNJI 2086. This poor quality CD is a best avoided ragbag of live tracks from 1984 and 1986.

NEVER HAD NO ONE EVER

Take Me Back To Dear Old Blighty; Ask; Bigmouth Strikes Again; London/Miserable Lie (Medley); Some Girls Are Bigger Than Others; The Boy With The Thorn In His Side; Shoplifters Of The World Unite; There Is A Light That Never Goes Out; Is It Really So Strange?; Cemetry Gates; This Night Has Opened My Eyes; Still Ill; Panic; The Queen Is Dead; William, It Was Really Nothing; Hand In Glove; Handsome Devil.

Skeleton Songs SS007. Billed as "Live In Belgium in 1986" but ignoring the fact that The Smiths never played Belgium that year, this is actually a recording from the Brixton Academy, London (12 December 1986), the final British appearance by The Smiths. 'Handsome Devil', not listed on the CD, is taken from the performance in Madrid (18 March 1985).

LIVE IN MADRID

William, It Was Really Nothing; Nowhere Fast; I Want The One I Can't Have; What She Said; How Soon Is Now?; Handsome Devil; That Joke Isn't Funny Anymore; Shakespeare's Sister; Rusholme Ruffians; The Headmaster Ritual; Hand In Glove; Still Ill; Meat Is Murder; Heaven Knows I'm Miserable Now; Miserable Lie; Barbarism Begins At Home; This Charming Man; You've Got Everything Now.

Swinging Pig TSP CD 109. This CD features the complete track listing from Paseo De Camoens, Madrid (18 May 1985).

EURO-MIXX

Two sides named the Blacksmith and the Goldsmith mix, respectively. What we have here is a Smiths' medley featuring songs culled directly from official releases. The compilers fail to provide a track listing, but the medley mix runs as follows: 'Girlfriend In A Coma'; 'Cemetry Gates'; 'Frankly Mr Shankly'; 'Heaven Knows I'm Miserable Now'; 'Pretty Girls Make Graves'; 'The Boy With The Thorn In His Side'; 'Half A Person'; 'Take Me Back To Dear Old Blighty'; 'Panic'; 'I Started Something I Couldn't Finish'; 'There Is A Light That Never Goes Out'; 'Bigmouth Strikes Again'; 'W[illegible] Difference Does It Make?'; 'Some Girls Are Bigger Than Others'; 'Ask'; 'Girl Afraid'.

LAST OF THE ENGLISH ROSES

Big Music BIG 043. This CD bootleg is identical to the TMQ label's 'Hammersmith'. 'Girl Afraid' is erroneously titled, 'I'll Never Make That Mistake Again'.

JAMES DEAN IS DEAD

Exile CD 4004. Wrongly credited as "Live Manchester 1985", this is yet another release of the Burning Bush bootleg 'Live At The Oxford Apollo'.

STEALERS

X Size 38. This is a reissue of 'A Kind Of Loving', again borrowed from the Oxford Apollo concert.

SAME DAY AGAIN

Big Music BIG 061. A complete CD of the Oxford Apollo concert, and the quality is excellent.

LIVE AT AMSTERDAM, MEERVAART 1984

'This Charming Man'; 'Still Ill'; 'Miserable Lie'; 'What Difference Does It Make?'

This three inch CD accompanied the Italian songbook, The Smiths. *The quality is very good and it is noticeable that both 'This Charming Man' and 'Still Ill' were not available on the main Amsterdam bootleg 'Handsome Devils'.*

LIVE IN THE USA

L101. A reissue of 'So This Is America', taken from The Smiths' performance at Great Woods Performing Arts Center, Mansfield, Massachusetts on 5 August 1986.

THE FINAL GIG

Money Maker MR 003. This CD collects the tracks from 'Never Had No One Ever', with the addition of four songs from the final Peel sessions: 'Sweet And Tender Hooligan', 'Half A Person', 'Is It Really So Strange?' and 'London'.

SMITHS' VIDEOS

THE COMPLETE PICTURE

This Charming Man; What Difference Does It Make?; Panic; Heaven Knows I'm Miserable Now; Ask; The Boy With The Thorn In His Side; How Soon Is Now?; Shoplifters Of The World Unite; Girlfriend In A Coma; Sheila Take A Bow; Stop Me If You Think You've Heard This One Before; The Queen Is Dead; There Is A Light That Never Goes Out; Panic.

WEA 4509-91155-3 December 1992

THE ALBUMS (1983-88)

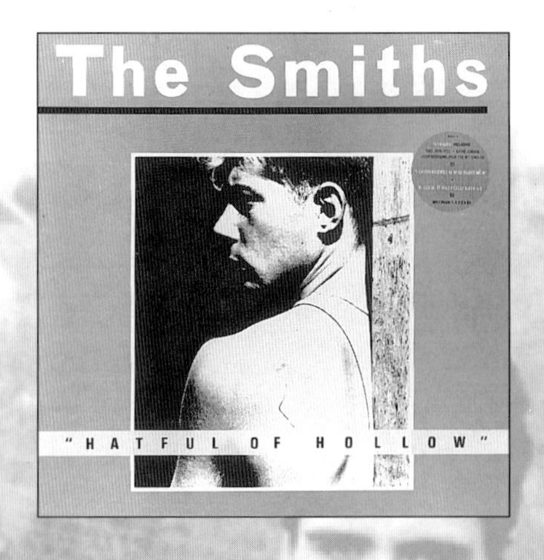

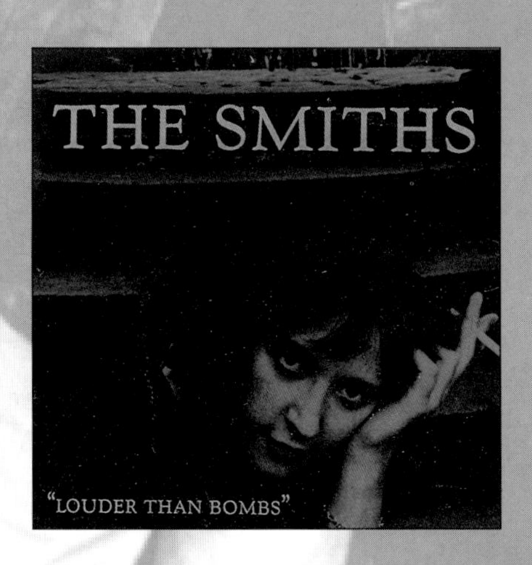

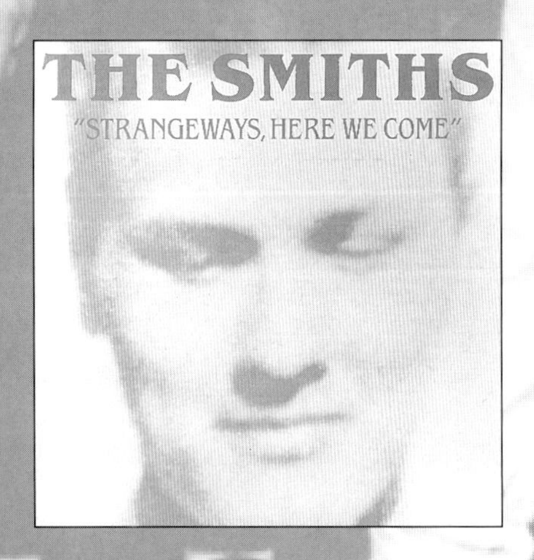

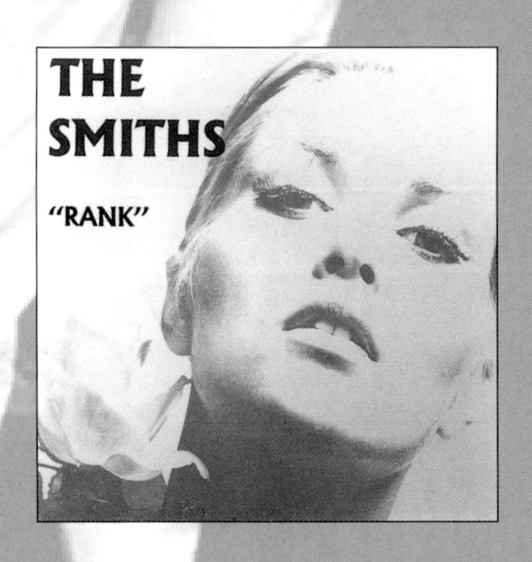